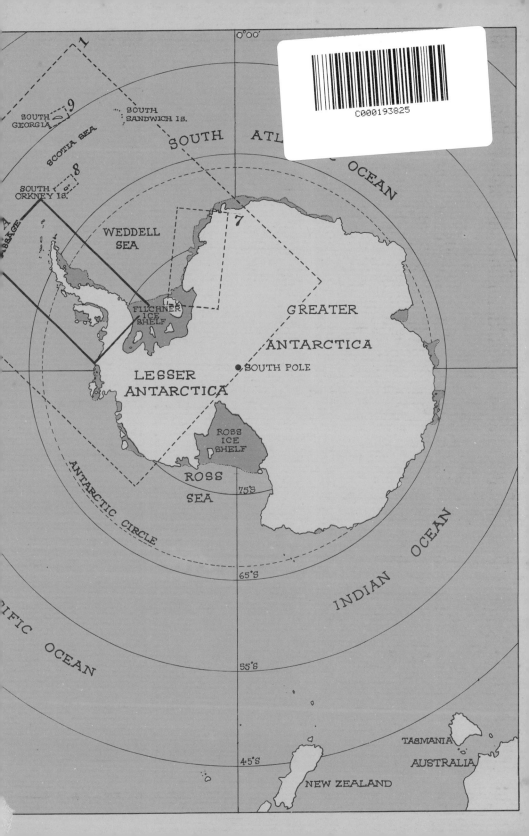

0°00'

1

9
SOUTH
GEORGIA

SOUTH
SANDWICH IS.

SCOTIA SEA

SOUTH ATL

8

SOUTH
ORKNEY IS.

SSAGE

7

WEDDELL
SEA

FILCHNER
ICE
SHELF

GREATER

ANTARCTICA

LESSER
ANTARCTICA

•SOUTH POLE

ROSS
ICE
SHELF

ANTARCTIC CIRCLE

ROSS
SEA

75°S

INDIAN OCEAN

65°S

CIFIC

OCEAN

55°S

45°S

TASMANIA

AUSTRALIA

NEW ZEALAND

The best laid schemes o' mice an' men
  Gang aft a-gley

Robert Burns

V. E. Fuchs
1983

Of Ice and Men

The Story of
the British Antarctic Survey
1943–73
by Sir Vivian Fuchs

Anthony Nelson

First published 1982 by Anthony Nelson
PO Box 9, Oswestry, Shropshire SY11 1BY, England

ISBN 0 904614 06 9

Designed by Alan Bartram

Filmset and printed by BAS Printers Limited
Over Wallop, Hampshire, England

Note:
The British Antarctic Survey,
also known as BAS,
is not connected in any way
with BAS Printers Limited.

Contents

TO THE TAXPAYERS
WHO MADE IT ALL POSSIBLE

In 1956 the Olympic Games were held in Melbourne and I had been invited to inaugurate them on behalf of The Queen. It was while planning to travel out in the Royal Yacht <u>Britannia</u> that I heard about the British Commonwealth Trans-Antarctic Expedition under the leadership of Vivian Fuchs. I conceived the wild idea of paying a visit to the Expedition's base, but after long discussion of all the factors it had to be dropped. However, instead it turned out to be possible to visit a number of the British Antarctic Survey bases in the Graham Land area and so began a continuing interest in the Survey.

I am very glad that Sir Vivian Fuchs has written this account of the little known but most valuable work of a steady stream of adventurous young research workers in these remote bases on the Antarctic continent. Modern conveniences may have made life more tolerable in this rugged area, but the natural conditions remain constant and they continue to demand a high level of courage, endurance and determination.

Antarctica is the least known part of the world and there is every reason to be proud of the British contribution to the international scientific studies, and the knowledge of the resources of the continent and the Southern Ocean. It is also comforting to know that the Antarctic Treaty Powers are very conscious of the need to prevent any harmful exploitation of the wild populations on the land or in the sea.

I notice that the book is dedicated to the Taxpayers. I hope many will read it, enjoy it and reckon that the work of these young men is well worthwhile.

1982

Acknowledgements

The British Antarctic Survey is now a highly regarded orthodox scientific organisation, with a specialised professional staff enjoying graded salaries and pension schemes; but it was never officially established. Rather it emerged from war-time necessity and then, like Topsy, it just grew – sometimes in rather strange ways. I undertook this book because I felt that there ought to be an account of its inception and early struggles for survival and recognition, before the story is lost in the mists of antiquity.

It is also offered as a tribute to the young men who made it all possible, for without their spirit of adventure and willingness to endure it could never have succeeded. I wish that space had allowed me to include all their exploits, but at least the Nominal Roll of Wintering Personnel at the end of the book is there for the record.

I am greatly indebted to Dr R. M. Laws, Director of the Survey, for permission to consult the archives, and very grateful indeed to all members of the staff who have patiently answered my questions, assisted my researches and given me every support. Among many others who helped me I must mention Sir Miles Clifford, Surgeon Captain E. W. Bingham RN, Professor N. B. Marshall FRS, and the late Dr B. B. Roberts who all provided much information about the early days of FIDS.

Personal journals and other writings were made available to me by Dr Ray Adie, Ricky Chinn, Surgeon Captain David Dalgliesh RN, Peter Forster, Peter Gibbs, George Hemmen, David James, Ivan Mackenzie Lamb, John Paisley, Ken Pawson, Derek Searle, Bill Sloman and Andrew Taylor. All provided helpful background to various periods of the story.

Bob Bostleman, John Dudeney, John Green, Dr Stanley Greene, Dr Michael Holmes, Shaun Norman and Dr Bill Sladen kindly sent me anecdotal material and comments or confirmation of uncertain facts.

I acknowledge especially, contributions from Nigel Bonner, Dr Otto Edholm, Dr Roy Piggott and Dr Charles Swithinbank which enabled me to write the Appendix, *The purpose is science*.

It has been possible to include extra colour pictures due to a generous grant from the Directors of Barclay's Bank and to a personal donation from Alan Tritton himself. For this assistance in embellishing the book I am indeed grateful.

'Anne' Todd has taken immense trouble, and given most generously of her time, in seeking out obscure information, checking facts and providing photographs – together with invaluable editorial comment as the work proceeded. Anything I can say is inadequate thanks for all she has done.

Finally, my very special thanks go to Eleanor Honnywill, my personal assistant throughout my directorship, who has typed and retyped many times, criticised, advised and enlivened the story during the years it has taken me to write it.

I would like to place on record how deeply honoured I feel that His Royal Highness Prince Philip, Duke of Edinburgh has been willing to associate himself with our activities by contributing the Foreword.

V.E.F.
1982

'FIDS' and 'Fids'

FIDS is the acronym for 'Falkland Islands Dependencies Survey' which was the original name for the modern 'British Antarctic Survey'. Thus members of the Survey nicknamed themselves *Fids*, referring to retired members as *ex-Fids*, and often to the new recruits on first arrival at a base as *Fidlets*.

The name survived the change of title, and throughout this book FIDS, when shown in capitals, denotes the organisation; but when written in small letters as Fids, it refers to the men themselves.

'Years' and 'Seasons'

In such a complex narrative, covering almost thirty years and many bases, it has been impossible always to record sometimes overlapping events in chronological order. To help a perhaps bemused reader to keep track of time, marginal dates are shown when appropriate.

In the Antarctic ships and aircraft can operate only during late spring, summer, and early autumn – which, in the southern hemisphere, is roughly from October to the end of March. This is the annual 'season', the time of greatest field activity when bases are re-supplied and personnel relieved. As it extends from the end of one year to the beginning of the next, it is referred to by a double date, for instance 1955/6.

Where I speak of a particular season, the dates are always separated by a stroke; but where I refer to events covering more than one calendar year the dates are shown hyphenated, for instance 1955–65.

A glossary is given on page 345 explaining words commonly used to describe polar conditions.

Historical introduction

This book is an account of the first thirty years of an Antarctic expedition which has been continuously at work since 1943, first as a rather impromptu naval operation, then as a politico-scientific exercise, and finally dedicated solely to the interests of science. Yet the men who have served in it have found great adventure. For them it was exploration in its true sense, new lands, wild country and extreme conditions. Whatever part they played, every individual has enjoyed the sense of battle with nature, the wonder and beauty of an unknown world, and the achievement of survival and success. There are few places left today where young men can experience these things and learn the art of self-reliance. But Antarctica is one of them. There both a man's character and his physical strength are tried to the full and, having survived the test, each looks back and remembers with nostalgia only the enjoyable experiences. The awful blizzards, the cold and the crevasses, recalcitrant dog teams or spluttering tractor engines are forgotten. The wonderfully clear days, the sight of new rock beyond the snow rise, the tremendous feeling of freedom among the mountains and glaciers, the close comradeship which develops in isolated groups from shared experience and the growth of mutual confidence: these are the lasting memories.

Antarctica is a cold desert of some five and a quarter million square miles, about twice the size of Australia. Almost circular, only at a few points does its periphery extend north of latitude 67°S. It is masked by an immense ice sheet which covers about ninety-six per cent of the whole area, the depth ranging from a few hundred to some 14,000 feet, its average thickness 6,000 feet. If all this ice suddenly melted, ocean level would rise about 180 feet. Water would lap around the base of the dome of St Paul's Cathedral, and many of the world's cities would be flooded. The annual snowfall which sustains the ice sheet is small, equivalent to only about ten inches of rain – precipitation similar to that expected over many hot deserts. The mean height of about 6,000 feet is greater than that of any other continent. Vast areas of the ice sheet lie above 10,000 feet, while the highest peak, Mount Vinson, rises to 16,860 feet. Consequently, cold air tends to flow downwards and outwards from the centre of this huge 'iced cake', producing violent winds. Even in summer the coastal regions can experience windspeeds of ninety to one hundred knots.

Like all deserts, the Antarctic landmass is largely destitute of plant and animal life, except for a few lichens and mosses which occur sparsely on exposed rock. In a few areas the grass, *Deschampsia*, and a *Colobanthus* are found rarely in the coastal regions. Apart from some microscopic forms and one or two flightless insects there is no land fauna – birds and seals are either migratory or live their lives at sea during winter. This cruel, forbidding continent was the last to be discovered. No man set foot on it until 1820, but another eighty years were to pass before anyone ventured to live there. Virtually all we know about this inhospitable region has been discovered in the last eighty years.

The ancient Greeks first conceived the idea of a frigid southern continent, then spoken of as the 'South Land', to 'balance' the known cold Arctic regions in the north – hence the name Antarctic – but until the eighteenth century maps showed a vast area simply designated *Terra Incognita*. By the end of the fifteenth century sailing ships were being built just large enough to permit long-range voyages, and this led to the famous exploratory ventures of Diaz, Drake, Magellan, Tasman and others. Each reduced the possible size of the 'South Land'. Finally it was a Yorkshireman, Captain James Cook, who between 1772 and 1774 circumnavigated the world further south than anyone had ever sailed, twice crossing the Antarctic Circle. Repeatedly frustrated in his efforts to get further south, he came to believe that the impenetrable ice fields which everywhere barred his way 'extended quite to the Pole'.

Cook's reports of fur seal colonies created great commercial excitement. British and American sealers were soon making annual voyages to South Georgia and the South Shetland Islands, where these unfortunate animals were slaughtered almost to the point of extinction. Such forays led to the first sighting of the Antarctic mainland in January 1820. Today this 700-mile finger of land which beckons towards Cape Horn is known as the Antarctic Peninsula, and it is the main area of FIDS activity.

During the next twenty years James Weddell sailed into the sea which bears his name and John Biscoe circumnavigated the continent and made a number of discoveries including Adelaide Island.

In 1842 Sir James Clark Ross reached the southern coast of the Ross Sea, thereby penetrating further south than anyone. Although sealing expeditions continued until the end of the century, no exploration of the continent itself took place until 1898 when a Belgian expedition, under Lieutenant Adrien de Gerlache de Gomery, made extensive discoveries along the west coast of the Antarctic Peninsula. By misfortune they were the first party to winter when their ship, *Belgica*, was beset. One year later a British expedition led by C. E. Borchgrevink explored Victoria Land on the other side of the continent, where they were the first party to winter on the mainland.

Then began a period which, with good reason, has become known as the 'Heroic Era'. At first the attainment of the South Pole itself constituted the great prize, and this was finally won by the Norwegian Roald Amundsen in 1911, followed only five weeks later by Captain Robert Scott's ill-fated Polar Party. During this time science was coming into its own and geographical discovery ceased to be the sole purpose of polar exploration. To their credit Scott, Ernest Shackleton and the Australian Douglas Mawson all took geologists, biologists, meteorologists and geophysicists on their famous expeditions. They are the stars who shine so brilliantly in the Antarctic galaxy, but apart from Shackleton, whose *Endurance* expedition will be discussed later, they all worked in the New Zealand sector of the continent – 2,000 miles from the Antarctic Peninsula and the Weddell Sea, where our story lies. This brief mention must therefore suffice, as we turn to some account of those expeditions which operated in the region previously known as the Falkland Islands Dependencies, and now as the British Antarctic Territory.

Dr Otto Nordenskjöld's Swedish South Polar Expedition of 1901–4 was a story of courage and endurance outstanding even in the polar context. With a team of nine scientists, he set out in the *Antarctic*, commanded by Captain C. A. Larsen who had already sailed down the east coast of Graham Land to latitude 68°10′S in 1893, discovering the great ice shelf which now bears his name. Having spent weeks re-surveying and correcting previous errors on current charts of the west coast and offshore islands of the Antarctic Peninsula, Nordenskjöld rounded its northern extremity. There he found a strait dividing Joinville Islands from the mainland which was named Antarctic Sound in his vessel's honour. In February the ship anchored off Snow Hill Island, where he landed with five companions and five dogs to establish winter quarters. A scientific programme began which contributed much to the knowledge of Snow Hill and Seymour Islands, and in the following spring the party sledged south over the Larsen Ice Shelf almost as far as the Antarctic Circle.

Returning in February 1903 to meet the relief ship, they found all the approach routes were blocked by ice, and it was clear that they would have to endure a second winter. Penguins and seals were killed to eke out their supplies and the scientific work was extended.

During October Nordenskjöld with one companion, Jonassen, made a sledge journey to Vega Island, which cleared up a number of geographical anomalies. There they were amazed suddenly to encounter two dirty figures dressed in worn skins, with long beards and shaggy hair, and Jonassen suggested that Nordenskjöld should draw his revolver to be prepared.

Two men, black as soot, with black clothes from head to foot, black faces and tall black caps which made Jonassen and myself think of cylinders; the eyes which were covered with strange wooden boxes blended so closely with the black facial colour that the whole seemed like some kind of silken mask with wooden openings for the eyes. Never before had I been confronted with such a mixture of civilisation and the most extreme barbarous appearance. My imagination failed me when I tried to discern what sort of men these might be. At that moment Jonassen suggested that we might be confronted with the appearance of unknown Antarctic aborigines.
Dr Otto Nordenskjöld's Journal

'How do you do, Otto,' said the first savage politely, and the bewildered Nordenskjöld automatically stammered, 'Very well thank you, how are you?' without a glint of recognition.

They turned out to be Dr J. Gunnar Andersson of Uppsala University and Lieutenant Duse, the surveyor. A third man, Seaman Grunden, was some distance behind them. It transpired that having spent the winter of 1902 in sub-Antarctic waters and refitting in South America, Antarctic had sailed south to relieve the expedition in November. It proved to be a bad ice year and they found Antarctic Sound impenetrable. After successive failures to break through, a three-man party under Gunnar Andersson had been landed at Hope Bay to sledge south to Snow Hill Island and bring the main party back to the ship overland. It was agreed that Antarctic would continue trying to penetrate south, but if she still failed, Larsen would return to Hope Bay by 10 March to pick up Andersson's group before winter set in.

Next day Andersson's party had set out for Snow Hill, man-hauling 530 pounds, but after a difficult journey they found themselves facing open water around Vega Island and were forced to return to Hope Bay to await the ship. Antarctic never came back. Very soon it was clear that this little group, with worn clothing, one tiny tent and very few rations, would have to winter where they were. Hastily they found enough flat stones to build four walls over which they placed their sledge, covering the whole with canvas. Inside this primitive shelter (the walls of which still stand) they pitched their tent, and laid in a store of penguins and seals for the larder. When fuel ran out they used seal blubber, and fished with hooks and lines made from brass buckles and seal skin, but for reading matter all they had were the labels on their pitifully few tins. In September 1903 spring came at last, and they sledged across the ice once more, quite by chance coming upon Nordenskjöld on Vega Island. It was a wonderful moment – but where was the ship?

After landing Andersson's party at Hope Bay, Captain Larsen had continued the most strenuous efforts to reach Nordenskjöld and his companions. But on 11 January 1903 *Antarctic* was nipped in the ice, her rudder damaged and a huge hole torn in her side. As ice pressure distorted her it became apparent that she was doomed. On 13 February the order was given to abandon ship. Camping equipment, fuel, food, scientific collections and boats were landed on the ice, then the Swedish flag was hoisted at the gaff, pennants at the main and mizzen, for her gallant company were determined that she would go down in style. Five weeks after besetment *Antarctic* slowly disappeared beneath the pack.

Her crew faced a perilous sixteen-day journey across contorted and moving ice to Paulet Island. There they built a stone house roofed with canvas, killed 4,000 penguins for food and, in their turn, settled down to a very bleak winter. Thus three parties from the same expedition were wintering within a radius of fifty miles, each left to wonder about the fate of the others. The ship's company were always hungry, and most of the time too enervated by cold to manage more than the essential minimum of work.

At the beginning of October the ice began to break up and on the 31st Larsen, with five chosen men, set out by boat to row to Hope Bay through the drifting pack. It was a hard and adventurous undertaking, rowing all day and camping on a floe at night; but when at last they arrived, it was to find a note from Andersson telling them that he had left for Snow Hill a month earlier.

Severe gales pinned them down at Hope Bay for three days, but on 7 November they started out once more, this time to row for twenty hours on end to reach a barrier of ice on which they hauled up at the entrance to Admiralty Sound. The following day they walked the last twelve miles to the wintering station – to find themselves joining in a joyous reunion. More astounding still – that very day an Argentine vessel, *Uruguay*, arrived to rescue them all. They had to believe in miracles.

They learnt that when *Antarctic* had failed to return to South America the previous autumn, the Argentine Government, realising the gravity of the situation, had organised a relief expedition to set out the following season. After so much hardship had been so gallantly endured by all three of Nordenskjöld's parties it was an emotional moment when they saw *Uruguay* coming to their aid, and a truly dramatic ending to their amazing adventures.

On the credit side this expedition had explored the east coast of Graham Land, proving it to be continuous as far as the Antarctic Circle. Many problems about the complicated systems of islands and channels from Joinville Island to the Larsen Ice Shelf had been unravelled. Mount Haddington, first seen by Ross, was found to be on an island (which Nordenskjöld named James Ross Island after him). The Prince Gustav Channel, which separates it from the mainland, had been discovered, mapped and named by the Swedes after their Crown Prince. It had not all been in vain.

From 1902 to 1904 the Scottish National Antarctic Expedition under Dr W. S. Bruce was exploring the northern end of what is now known as the Caird Coast to the east of the Weddell Sea, but they were prevented from landing by continuous high ice cliffs. Bruce therefore decided to winter at Laurie Island in the South Orkney Islands, where they established a meteorological station. On their departure, the Argentine Meteorological Office was persuaded to send staff to continue the observations, and this they still do today.

Two French expeditions under Dr J.-B. Charcot made major contributions to the charts of the west coast of the Antarctic Peninsula, simultaneously carrying out extensive scientific programmes. The first was from 1903 to 1905, and was initiated with the intention of looking for Nordenskjöld's expedition, for by 1903 it was clear that misfortune had befallen them. A special ship, *Français*, was designed and built at St Malo in a remarkably short time and was ready to sail from Brest by 1 August. But when Charcot reached Buenos Aires he found that the Swedish expedition had been rescued. Nevertheless, he decided to continue south to extend the exploration of Graham Land which had been started by de Gerlache de Gomery in *Belgica*.

He made his landfall off Smith Island on 1 February 1904 and passing Hoseason Island, sailed down the Gerlache Strait, to land on Wiencke Island from where he saw and named Mount Français on Anvers Island. The remainder of the season was spent surveying the innumerable islands south of the Bismarck Strait until, on 7 March, *Français* was purposely frozen-in for the winter in a small cove at Booth Island (known at that time as Wandel Island). By Christmas Day the ice had broken up sufficiently for the ship to sail southward towards Adelaide Island and Charcot charted the coast line of the Palmer Archipelago. He mistook Adelaide for a part of the mainland and named it the Loubet Coast, a name which is now applied to the region east of the Biscoe Islands.

Not long afterwards *Français* hit a rock and was holed, the expedition having to retreat northwards to carry out repairs at Port Lockroy. They arrived back in Buenos Aires on 4 March, to discover that there had been growing anxiety as to their whereabouts. Their ship was then sold to Argentina, renamed *Austral*, and unhappily sank when leaving Rio del Plata shortly afterwards.

Charcot's second expedition lasted from 1908 to 1910. This time his ship was of British design and he called her *Pourquoi Pas?*. Manned by a crew of twenty-two and carrying eight scientists, she sailed from Cherbourg on 31 August 1908, reaching Deception Island towards the end of December. She then followed *Français*' track to Port Lockroy and Booth Island. Continuing southwards she went aground and was damaged on a reef off Cape Tuxen, but repairs were finished by 12 January 1909 and she was under way once more for Adelaide Island where Charcot was able to follow the coastline to its southern end. He named the southernmost point Cape Alexandra as a compliment to the English Queen.

Beyond this he discovered and named Marguerite Bay and managed to sail within fifteen miles of Alexander I Land (now Alexander Island) but ice prevented any closer approach. Attempts to reach the Fallières Coast in Marguerite Bay also failed owing to ice conditions, but it was roughly charted from a distance and the party explored the east side of Adelaide Island in a small boat before sailing again for Alexander Island. During the night a violent storm drove the ship through an unknown group of islands and rocks (the Faure Islands) quite out of control. Once she actually grounded, but was swept back into deep water by the wind. To anyone who knows that treacherous group today, it is a miracle that the whole expedition did not founder at this point.

Unable to find a suitable place for the ship to winter in Marguerite Bay, Charcot turned northwards, and on 3 February they took up winter quarters on Petermann Island. Attempts were made to climb up to the Graham Land plateau but these were always frustrated by crevasses and bad weather. When ice conditions allowed they visited Deception and Bridgeman Islands before *Pourquoi Pas?* again headed south to Alexander Island. This time Charcot Land (now Charcot Island) was discovered and later named after his distinguished father, but they were unable to approach nearer than fifty miles. Forced westward by ice they came within one-and-a-half miles of Peter I Island, the first time it had been seen since its discovery by Admiral Bellingshausen in 1821.

So ended Charcot's work. By 11 February 1910 *Pourquoi Pas?* was back in Punta Arenas on her way home. It had been a most fruitful expedition. Earlier charts had been considerably extended and Charcot was always meticulous and painstaking; at no time did he allow himself to plot unconfirmed features. The dotted lines of supposition, so frequent on other maps, are notably absent on his.

In 1910 the German South Polar Expedition under Dr W. Filchner sailed in *Deutschland* to explore the eastern and southern coasts of the Weddell Sea. Luitpold Coast was discovered and part of the south coast charted, but unwittingly the party began building their base on floating ice shelf, which soon calved and drifted away as an iceberg. No sooner had they scrambled back to their ship than she was beset, and for nine months she drifted in the Weddell Sea ice until freed by the summer thaw. Thus their high hopes of inland exploration had to be abandoned, but apart from Captain Vahsel who fell sick and died, all the men survived the hardships of the winter.

Perhaps the most famous expedition of the Heroic Era was Sir Ernest Shackleton's Imperial Trans-Antarctic Expedition, 1914–1916, which culminated in his epic 800-mile open boat journey from Elephant Island to South Georgia. Shackleton's plan had called for a base to be established at the head of the Weddell Sea from which he proposed to cross the continent to McMurdo Sound. But this was never achieved for his ship, *Endurance*, was beset even before she reached the chosen base site. After drifting for a thousand miles while locked in the ice for 281 days, she was finally crushed and disappeared. Her company then took to the floes, on which they existed precariously for a further five-and-a-half months until they at last reached open water. Here they could launch the boats they had so laboriously dragged across the ice and sail to Elephant Island. Leaving twenty-two men with only two upturned boats for shelter, Shackleton himself with five picked companions sailed in the *James Caird* to get help from South Georgia. After sixteen desperate days across the stormiest seas in the world they arrived exhausted, but on the uninhabited side of the island.

Two of the men could go no further, so a third was left to care for them on a stony beach, sheltered by the upturned boat. Shackleton with the remaining two set out on a forced march to pioneer a route through the mountains to Stromness. After thirty-five hours without sleep, and countless frustrations on the way, they arrived at the whaling station where the whole expedition had already been given up for lost. In rags, unkempt and filthy, their hair down to their shoulders, they were not even recognised; but as their story unfolded, the whalers were quick to appreciate the greatness of their achievement and the skill of their seamanship. That same evening a catcher was sent round the island to collect the sick men left on the beach where the little boat had landed them.

Shackleton then made three abortive attempts, in the winter months of May, June and July, to return to Elephant Island and rescue his main party. His fourth try in August, in the Chilean vessel *Yelcho*, succeeded in the nick of time. By now the men, some of them ill, had lived for four months and six days 'packed like sardines in a tin' under their boats, and were down to their last two days' food – boiled seal's backbone, limpets and seaweed. It was deliverance indeed.

Although the expedition itself failed, it is one of the most outstanding and exciting survival stories of all time, and stands as an example of what men *in extremis* can do to save themselves given determination and good leadership.

In 1917 the Colonial Office set up an Inter-departmental Committee on Research and Development in the Falkland Islands Dependencies. This initiated biological studies in the Southern Ocean, with particular reference to whaling. It led to the formation of the Discovery Committee in 1923, and reached fruitation in 1925 when the first Discovery Investigations Expedition established a biological station at King Edward Point, South Georgia. Discovery Investigations continued as a major Antarctic research project until the Second World War. Although most of their work was concerned with the seas of the Falkland Islands Dependencies, more distant studies were also sometimes undertaken, including two circumpolar voyages. The voluminous series *Discovery Investigations Reports* covers all aspects of marine biology, sea ice studies, surveys of harbours and anchorages, and running surveys of various coastlines. In a sense these years of marine investigations were the forerunner of the British Antarctic Survey's complementary terrestrial work, for the whaling dues which paid for them were later applied to the Falkland Islands Dependencies Survey (FIDS), now renamed British Antarctic Survey.

In the period between the two World Wars numerous short-term expeditions also worked in the Dependencies. Most of these were in support of the Norwegian whaling industry, but in the 1928/9 season a German expedition under L. Kohl-Larsen surveyed parts of South Georgia, while Sir Hubert Wilkins led the Wilkins-Hearst Antarctic Expedition which planned to fly from Graham Land across to the Ross Sea. Bad weather precluded the main flight, but shorter sorties led to the erroneous belief that Graham Land was a series of islands separated by ice-filled straits, which Wilkins named respectively the Crane, Casey and Lurabee Channels. These errors remained on the maps for a number of years until the 'channels' were found to be the glaciers which today bear the same names. The following year Wilkins returned for a second attempt to fly to the Ross Sea, but again failed. His local flights appeared to confirm the existence of the channels, but this time he correctly discovered that Charcot Land was in fact an island. His two expeditions demonstrated both the possibilities and limitations of aircraft in Antarctic conditions, but contributed little to knowledge.

The British Graham Land expedition, 1934–7, led by an Australian, John

Rymill, was the first since Nordenskjöld's in 1901–4 to make any significant new contribution to the terrestrial knowledge of the Dependencies. Their first winter was spent at the Argentine Islands, the second at the Debenham Islands in Marguerite Bay. From both bases dog sledge journeys and air flights contributed much both to the geography and geology of the area. Their most notable geographical discoveries were the existence of George VI Sound, which separates Alexander Island from the Antarctic Peninsula, and proof that Wilkins' channels were in reality glaciers.

The United States Antarctic Service Expedition, 1939–41, under Rear Admiral Richard E. Byrd consisted of two groups which wintered respectively at Little America III on the Ross Ice Shelf, and on Stonington Island in Marguerite Bay. The latter party, under Captain Richard Black USN, extended the British Graham Land Expedition's discoveries by demonstrating that the southern end of George VI Sound extends westward to the open sea, making Alexander Land in fact an island.

Politically Britain's claim to this sector of the Antarctic continent was originally based on early exploration – South Georgia, the South Sandwich, South Shetland and South Orkney Islands, and Graham Land, were all discovered by British expeditions – and in particular on the fact that Captain Foster, in command of HMS *Chanticleer* in 1829, had landed on Hoseason Island and Cape Possession, where he formally took possession of the surrounding lands in the name of King George IV. Similarly in 1843 the great Sir James Clark Ross had landed on Cockburn Island to take formal possession of the adjacent regions. The formal acquisition of these lands was promulgated by Letters Patent published in 1908 (amended in 1917) declaring the Antarctic sector between longitudes 20°W and 80°W to be Dependencies of the Colony of the Falkland Islands.

At that time no other nation challenged or even commented on the British claim. It was not until 1925 that Argentina suddenly and surprisingly formulated claims to the South Orkney Islands. More audaciously, in 1927 she extended such claims to include South Georgia and by 1937 had claimed the right to all the Dependencies. When war broke out the early course of hostilities no doubt encouraged her to hope that if Britain was defeated the Dependencies would fall into her hands without argument. The Argentine claim was based on geographical proximity, and the fact that a papal decree embodied in the 1494 Treaty of Tordesillas had allocated to Spain all new lands discovered west of a meridian thought to run from the southern tip of Greenland to the mouth of the Amazon – the title to which Argentina declared she had inherited.

The situation was further complicated when in 1940 Chile, unwilling to miss out on any pickings, also put forward a claim to a nearly identical area including all the Falkland Islands Dependencies. Her grounds were based not only on geographical proximity, but also on the somewhat specious argument that geologically the Antarctic Peninsula is a continuation of the Andes, and thus a concrete part of the motherland.

In 1942 an Argentine expedition in the *Primero de Mayo* visited Deception Island and on 8 February purported to take possession of the sector between 25°W and 68°34'W. This was formally reported to the British Government seven days later. As a result HMS *Carnarvon Castle* was ordered to Deception where, in January 1943, Argentine marks of sovereignty were obliterated, the Union Jack hoisted, and a record of the visit left behind.

This then was the political background of events which led the British Government, even in time of war, to take action to preserve the country's existing rights by occupying or re-occupying various sites within the Falkland Islands Dependencies. This is how FIDS began, although for the first two years it was a naval exercise mounted under Admiralty auspices and code named OPERATION TABARIN.

Party from HMS Carnarvon Castle *raising the flag at Deception Island, January 1943. (Royal Navy)*

I

OPERATION TABARIN
1943–5

Britain was at war but the Antarctic was not forgotten, for now it had strategic value and in 1943 plans for a naval operation were initiated.

Not only had the activities of German commerce raiders brought home . . . the strategic importance of Antarctica, but political developments within Argentina made it highly undesirable that that country should be in a position to control the southern side of Drake Passage. A small military force was therefore assembled under the direction of the Admirality, acting on behalf of the Colonial Office. This force was known for security reasons as OPERATION TABARIN, the name of a well-known night club being thought eminently suitable for a detachment which was intended to winter in the Antarctic darkness. The original intention was for two bases to be established, one to guard Deception Island and the other to occupy the position on the peninsula* of Graham Land. The detachment at Deception Island, while doing what it could to deny the use of the harbour to enemy commerce raiders, would be in a position to provide information on the activities of both enemy and neutral vessels.

HUNTER CHRISTIE, E. W. *The Antarctic Problem*, George Allen & Unwin, 1951.

1943   Once the decision had been taken OPERATION TABARIN went ahead rapidly. The first problem was to find available young men with any sort of polar experience. James Marr was a Boy Scout who had been taken south by Shackleton on his last expedition in *Quest*, and later he had worked as a biologist in both the Arctic and Antarctic. Now a Lieutenant Commander RNVR he was serving in HMS *Jay*, a mine sweeper stationed in the Far East. Admiralty signals flew, hastily recalling him to England. Tall and gaunt-looking, he was a dour Scot with a pawky sense of humour. Described by a contemporary as a genial man with a great gift for inventing jingles, he also enjoyed playing his mouth-organ at bar-room sing-songs and doing 'turns' with comical twists. He was a great host with a hard head – 'Let us now

---

*Originally the peninsula was known to the British as Graham Land, to the Americans as Palmer Land. In 1964 it was agreed that the southern half should be called Palmer Land, the northern half Graham Land, and the whole feature became the Antarctic Peninsula.

mortify the flesh,' he would cry, as he poured his guest half a tumbler of gin. On taking charge of TABARIN he was promoted Commander.

During the next hectic three months men from the Services and suitably qualified civilians were withdrawn from their wartime assignments all over the world, and brought home with appropriate 'cover stories' to ensure that neither their families nor friends became aware of where they were going. Fourteen recruits were assembled, all volunteers and greatly excited at the prospect before them.

Meanwhile the Admiralty had chartered *Godthaab*, a small square-rigged, wooden sailing ship of 250 tons with auxiliary power, owned by the exiled Norwegian Government in London. She was renamed HMS *Bransfield* in honour of Lieutenant Edward Bransfield RN who was the first to chart a portion of the Antarctic mainland in 1820. Stores and equipment were purchased, legally where possible but scrounged from naval establishments when necessary. Polar advice on both logistics and science was provided by an advisory committee of three: James Wordie, a veteran of Shackleton's *Endurance* expedition of 1914, Dr Brian Roberts, biologist on the British Graham Land Expedition, 1935–7, and Dr Neil Mackintosh, Director of Discovery Investigations. Appreciating from the first that bases established for political reasons could also provide platforms for scientific work, for many years these three were to preside like benign paladins over the general planning and organisation. Hence they were largely instrumental in

HMS Bransfield. *Photograph taken in 1929 when she was the Norwegian* Godthaab. *(V. E. Fuchs)*

ensuring that many of the young enthusiasts from the Services were qualified to undertake or assist in a variety of scientific projects.

Among those selected were Dr W. R. ('Finkle') Flett, geologist, and Dr Ivan Mackenzie Lamb, an authority on lichens in the Natural History Museum. Surgeon Lieutenant E. H. Back RNVR was appointed Medical Officer and later became senior meteorologist. Proposals for the meteorological programme were far-seeing, including suggestions for upper air work and automatic weather stations, but such refinements were too complex, and much too expensive, to achieve in the short time available before they sailed.

1943/4   In November 1943 *Bransfield* left Tilbury but on the 29th the Colonial Office learnt that she had sprung a leak and put into Portsmouth Dockyard. Owing to her very heavy load of cargo she now lay deeper in the water than she had done for many years and this had revealed the weakness. Repairs would take too long for the expedition to be established in the field during the coming Antarctic summer season – November to the end of March – so alternative means of transporting men and material had to be found quickly. No suitable ship was available in England but in the Falkland Islands HMS *William Scoresby*, a small vessel (326 tons) originally built for Discovery Investigations, had been diverted to war work as a mine sweeper in the south Atlantic and based at Stanley.

The Governor and Commander-in-Chief, Sir Alan Cardinall, offered her to the expedition, and ss *Fitzroy* (853 tons) was chartered from the Falkland Islands Company. In Britain most of the stores and all the men were hastily trans-shipped to the trooper *Highland Monarch*, sailing for the Falklands on 14 December to relieve the garrison in the islands. Remaining cargo was shipped to Montevideo in the French vessel *Groix* and the *Ragnhidsholm*, from where it was collected by *Fitzroy*. On 26 January *Highland Monarch* reached Stanley, the island's only town, and the men and all their material were together again.

1944   The plan was first to establish a base at Deception Island in the South Shetland Islands, then to land on Signy Island in the South Orkneys, leaving an official record of the visit, and lastly to set up a second base at Hope Bay at the northern end of Trinity Peninsula. On 29 January *Scoresby* and *Fitzroy* sailed in company, calling first at Goose Green, a Falklands settlement, to pick up mutton carcasses. The ships had no refrigeration so these were hung in the shrouds, where they gradually darkened under the influence of wind and weather but would, hopefully, remain fresh enough for later consumption. They pressed on through the boisterous seas in the notorious Drake Passage, both ships blacked out and maintaining wireless silence, for who could know, even so far south, whether enemy vessels were in the area?

HMS William Scoresby. *(J. B. Farrington)*

The early morning of 2 February found them in thick fog, which gradually lifted to reveal the rocky coastline of King George Island. Above, the snow slopes merged with the cloud; below, they swept down to steep dark cliffs of imposing grandeur. Next day they sailed past Livingston Island to starboard and Deception lay dead ahead. Only one or two old hands knew what to expect. Closer and closer they steered towards the coast where great waves spumed against the rocks, *Scoresby* leading. Then quite suddenly she turned almost at right-angles as a narrow opening appeared under a vertical cliff. Carefully nosing her way through, it seemed almost as if a man could reach out and touch the rock.

Deception Island is appropriately named, for it is only from a narrow angle that one can see where the coastline is breached by this gap, known as Neptune's Bellows, to a water-filled crater within. Suddenly they were in the calm seas of a gigantic land-locked harbour seven miles across. All around snow-clad slopes swept down to the water's edge, with here and there red or orange cliffs and grey-black screes revealing the volcanic origins of the island. This magnificent sheltered harbour was first seen some time after 1819 when the South Shetlands were discovered by William Smith in the brig *Williams*. No doubt it provided welcome shelter for many sealing ships during the nineteenth century, but it was not until 1910 that Deception

Deception Island. Neptune's Bellows in foreground. (BAS)

became a major whaling station, the shore-based operations continuing until 1931. With the outbreak of the Second World War British naval vessels combed the known harbours of the sub-Antarctic islands in search of enemy raiders. In March 1941 HMS *Queen of Bermuda* had visited the whaling station at Deception to destroy the remaining stocks of coal and to blow holes in the fuel oil tanks, thus denying them to any German ships which might take refuge there.

Immediately inside Neptune's Bellows the old station lay deserted on the shores of Whaler's Bay, and on one of the huge fuel tanks the Argentine flag had been painted. But was the place deserted? The expedition was unarmed and all eyes anxiously scanned the dilapidated buildings. Then a door slowly opened and shut; but as tension built up no one appeared. It was only the wind.

The first ashore toured the station, where great quantities of rusting machinery, tanks and boilers, stood among the wind-shattered factory buildings. Once roofed with corrugated iron, these were half filled with snow and ice which almost buried the rusty works within. Loose corrugated iron sheets clanked mournfully in the wind, and along the shore lay scattered the enormous bones of innumerable whales, bleached by the sun and picked clean by generations of skua gulls. As the tide fell, great billowing clouds of steam rose from the ash beaches warmed by the volcanic heat below. That,

Derelict whaling station, Deception Island. (Royal Navy)

and occasional hot springs, were the only remaining signs of activity on this quiescent volcano. The last actual eruption had been noted in February 1842 by the captain of a passing American sealer, the veracity of which has always been regarded as doubtful. In 1921 part of the shore subsided, and the water in Whalers Bay began to rise and fall becoming so hot that it is said to have blistered paint on the hulls of ships lying in the harbour. In 1930 there was an earthquake, and part of the harbour floor dropped fifteen feet taking the end of the wharf with it. Since then no further activity had been reported.

After lunch the whole shore party landed:

... a rapid survey was made of the area around Whalers Bay. For a time several of the landing party were actively engaged in the removal or obliteration of sundry items of evidence of disrespect shown to lawful British sovereignty by unfriendly visitors to the island. The halyards of the flag-pole erected by one of HM Ships the previous year had been removed. However, N. F. Layther, the base radio officer, volunteered to reeve new halyards, and after a climb rendered difficult by malicious mutilation of the flag-pole, he succeeded in doing so and the Union Jack was broken at the top by 4.30 pm on 3rd February. This simple but significant act af allegiance was loyally acclaimed by all those assisting at the ceremony.
Official report

Soon scow loads of stores were being ferried ashore. Two whalers'

ss Fitzroy *in Whaler's Bay, Deception Island. (Operation Tabarin)*

dormitories and the old magistrate's house were found in good condition, so it was not necessary to build a new hut. One of the dormitories became the base building, and soon began to fill up with stores under the supervision of Flett, the Base Leader. He was an Orcadian, scholarly and serious, with the dry wit that comes readily to the tongues of dour northern Scots. The hands of time lay lightly upon him for all his forty-three years, his silver-grey hair and ruddy complexion. Now suddenly he rivalled Pooh-Ba in the splendour of his titles for, to do justice to the seriousness of the British occupation, the Governor had appointed him Magistrate, Coroner, Deputy Receiver of Wrecks, Deputy Controller of Customs, and Postmaster in the South Shetland Islands. Captain Andrew Taylor RE, the surveyor, wrote of him:

With the assumption of his titles he seemed to grow out of the chrysalis we had known on the voyage out. The old Flett, with his jocular smile was no more, and in his place was an austere, almost despotic northerner, encased in unapproachable dignity.

Later in the season Jimmy Marr would take up similar dignified appointments in Graham Land itself. It was highly unlikely that they would involve much additional work, and their increased responsibilities did not bring any corresponding advantage in their salaries. No one could expect to make their fortune from their years of isolation for no 'hard-lying' money was paid. Salaries ranged from £840 a year for the expedition commander to £225 for the cook.

In three days the ships had been unloaded and the shore party well established. *Scoresby* and *Fitzroy* sailed for Hope Bay, entering Antarctic Sound between Trinity Peninsula and Joinville Island. In calm sunny weather the sea was dotted with small floes and icebergs, in which the cracks glowed as with some wonderful internal cobalt-blue fire. From the ships the icy walls could be seen plunging into the dark depths, while here and there cold green masses jutted outwards and downwards far beneath the surface. Many of the floes were occupied by basking seals, while in the water an occasional whale blew and little groups of penguins played follow-my-leader, leaping in and out of the sea.

The thin-hulled *Fitzroy* was not built to operate in ice and anchored some twelve miles off, while Marr in *Scoresby* sailed on into Hope Bay and landed a party to choose a base site. They found themselves in the middle of an enormous Adélie penguin rookery where some quarter of a million birds argued and squawked discordantly, waddling to and fro from the sea to feed their young. So late in the summer the chicks were as large as their parents, dressed in grey-brown down already moulting in patches.

Meanwhile Captain D. W. Roberts, Manager of the Falkland Islands Company, in consultation with Captain K. A. J. Pitt, Master of *Fitzroy*, had concluded that the uncertainties of the local ice situation were an unacceptable risk for, with a change of wind, the ship could only too easily have been locked in for the winter while still unloading. Therefore Captain Pitt weighed anchor and retreated to the safer waters of Bransfield Strait, still carrying half the stores for the new base.

Although Marr himself was satisfied that it would be feasible to establish a station at Hope Bay, he was now left without sufficient material to do so, and the plan had to be postponed for a year. He ordered *Scoresby* to rejoin *Fitzroy* and sail south along the west coast seeking an alternative site for the second station.

Captain Pitt, still nervous of taking his little ship into ice-infested waters for which no satisfactory charts then existed, was anxious to land a shore party at the earliest moment possible. Persistent fog forced the ships to heave-to for two days until, on 10 February, clear conditions enabled them to examine Charcot Bay; but no landing site could be found along its rocky coast. Beyond Cape Kater they reached Hughes Bay and attempted a landing, but this was unsuccessful owing to dense brash ice, heavy swell, and a precipitous rocky coast against which six-foot waves were breaking. Fending off large fragments of ice with oars, the boats kept clear of the towering 'bergs which presented an unforgettable sight. As the swell rose and fell around them, it appeared as if their gigantic masses heaved slowly but inexorably from the sea, water pouring off each ice-foot as it broke the surface.

The boat party glad to be safely back on board, the ships continued southward through Gerlache Strait to a small sheltered bay surrounded by high ice cliffs. This was Port Lockroy on Wiencke Island, which had frequently been visited by past expeditions and whaling ships. Here they anchored while a party went ashore to examine the few rocky islets near the entrance. On one they found painted the names of previous visitors – Wilkins Expedition, *Discovery*, *Scoresby*, British Graham Land Expedition. Rocks also bore the names of three Argentinians who had landed there from *Primero de Mayo* on 2 February the previous year. Where, they wondered, was the official evidence of claimed sovereignty? Sure enough, several days later the carpenter 'Chippy' Ashton, putting up boards for the hut, found a sealed brass cylinder with Argentine markings. This was duly sent back to Stanley and would doubtless trigger a formal protest to Buenos Aires.

Marr having decided that this was a suitable base site, the same evening stores began to go ashore. There was only a narrow ledge of rock on which

Map 1, opposite. *The British Antarctic Territory extends from the South Pole to latitude 60°S and is bounded by longitudes 80°W and 20°W. South Georgia and the South Sandwich Islands are British Dependencies of the Falkland Islands.*

Letters shown to designate the British stations are those which were used in official communications for many years. This practice has now ceased. Philatelists will be interested to note that the letters J, O and W appeared in the 1950s on the franks used for mail from these bases, because the franks were made before the actual sites for these stations were chosen. There was also some confusion over nomenclature – the following alternative names being used from time to time:

J = Prospect Point	O = Paradise Harbour	W = Detaille Island
= Ferin Head	= Danco Island	= Loubet Coast
= Graham Coast	= Danco Coast	

All three bases are now closed.

A	Port Lockroy	**G**	Admiralty Bay	**O**	Danco Island
B	Deception Island	**H**	Signy Island	**T**	Adelaide Island
C	Cape Geddes	**J**	Prospect Point	**V**	View Point
D	Hope Bay	**KG**	Fossil Bluff	**W**	Detaille Island
E	Stonington Island	**M**	South Georgia	**Y**	Horseshoe Island
F	Argentine Islands	**N**	Anvers Island	**Z**	Halley Bay

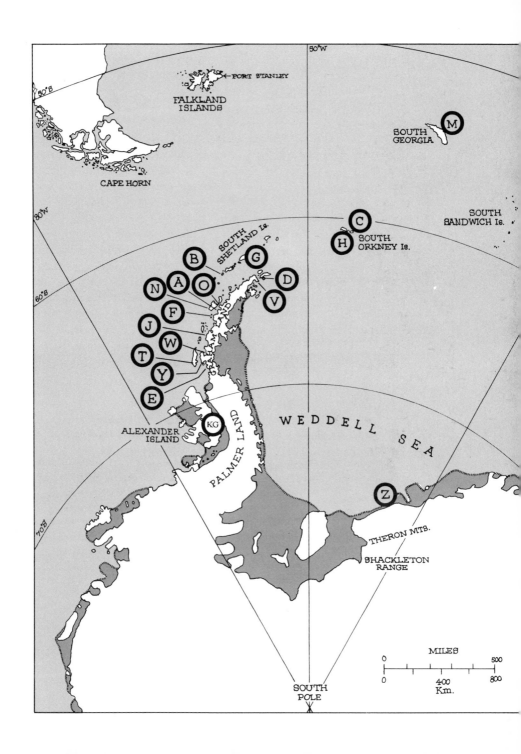

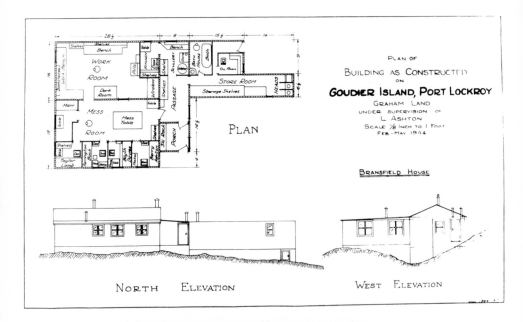

PLAN

PLAN OF
BUILDING AS CONSTRUCTED
ON
GOUDIER ISLAND, PORT LOCKROY
GRAHAM LAND
UNDER SUPERVISION OF
L ASHTON
SCALE 1/8 INCH TO 1 FOOT
FEB - MAY 1944

BRANSFIELD HOUSE

NORTH   ELEVATION

WEST   ELEVATION

Summer posting only! (Operation Tabarin)

to unload and no space to permit the sorting of boxes as they arrived. Everything had to be man-handled

... up the steep face of rock to almost the highest point of the islet, forty feet above the sea. Each case ... was handed up the slope from man to man and at the top ... some effort was made to sort out those articles required immediately. . . . To those of us who had enjoyed the comfort of the voyage out from England, the constant lifting and wrestling with the endless stream of cases that seemed to flow inexorably up from the loaded scows made an exhausting task, and told better than words of our poor physical condition. Davies called this part of the island 'Heartbreak Hill.' Many a case of fresh potatoes or tinned goods slipped from a pair of tired hands in this odd bucket brigade, spewing its contents down the grey, rocky slope into the sea.

Taylor's Journal

For five days unloading and building went apace. When the ships left on 17 February, the wireless had been working for two days and the hut was half up. The shore party now concentrated on finishing the main building, stacking away stores, unpacking and lighting the paraffin pressure lamps which were their main source of light. At night they threw down their sleeping bags on the bare floor, exhausted after the long days which began at 3 am. During the next month they finished the interior of the hut, built an annexe, and made cabin furniture for their personal needs and according to their personal tastes. This work was patiently supervised by Ashton, always ready with helpful advice and amazingly generous in allowing what he obviously considered 'a band of wood butchers' to use, lose and break his carefully cherished tools, His own thirty-six square feet of space were the showpiece of 'Bransfield House', gaily painted and boasting curtains of red and yellow bunting.

Mackenzie Lamb was undoubtedly the most admired and respected member of the small community. Tall and powerfully built, he had gentle manners and the best scientific brain. Taylor wrote of him:

He is one of the most unselfish characters I have ever met, a person it is a privilege to have known so well. Having a humour which at times approaches elfishness, he is a most sincere and earnest person who, while he is both logical and imaginative, has a realism about him which would not allow any sense of histrionics or dramatics to warp the steady judgement he possesses.

The naval flavour of the expedition, and particularly Chippy Ashton's influence, dictated the building jargon that developed. At first somewhat confused, the landlubbers soon learnt to speak of the floor as a 'deck', the front 'forepart', the rear as 'aft', whether discussing a building or a board. The latter were sawn either 'fore and aft' or 'thwartships', partitions were 'bulkheads', the ceiling the 'deckhead'. The outer edge of a piece of wood was its 'outboard' side, and posts or columns were 'stanchions'. Anything lying about outside was 'overboard' and when lost it was 'adrift'. The kitchen was, of course, the 'galley', rooms were 'cabins' and any cupboard a 'locker' in which 'gear' was 'stowed'. Disposable rubbish was 'gash', and the chap whose turn it was to clear up and keep the base tidy was the 'gashman' – words still used today.

Scoresby returned on 19 March with a second load of stores. Since by now the weather was usually bad, these were left in piles covered by carefully tied-down tarpaulins. Struggling in total darkness under such a cover to find some required article from the stack of cases was exasperating – as the muffled voice of 'Taff' Davies was heard to observe feelingly, 'a task for a bloody bed-bug'.

During the early months building and fitting out the station occupied so much time that little was left for scientific work. Meteorological observations were made regularly and passed to Stanley, but it was many months before Taylor could begin any survey, or Marr and Mackenzie Lamb could make more than desultory attempts at their zoological or botanical work. On special occasions after the day's labours they held a party, Marr reciting his most recently composed monologue, or accompanying their songs on his mouth-organ as alternatives to gramophone music. Ashton was a dab hand at making things, particularly little ships inside bottles on which he worked most evenings. The hard, awkward outside work, and the often foul weather, induced an excess of swearing. To counter this it was decreed that anyone using bad language at the dinner table should carry up an extra sack of coal from the beach. Soon their anxiety was lest the hut entrance become totally obstructed by the accumulation of sacks.

They had not expected to see a ship again until the spring, but in April they heard that *Scoresby* was again at Deception and would attempt to pay them a final visit. A few days later she arrived, bringing Flett and a visiting meteorologist from Stanley, together with such gifts as a long bath, bicycle wheels for use as sledge meters, mutton carcasses and, best of all, mail.

1944   On 24 April the BBC Overseas Service for North America carried a news item about this supposedly secret expedition. The localities of the bases were not mentioned, but it was stated that they would be occupied for a long time, with a view to exercising administration over British territory and carrying out scientific work. So much for the strict security which had been imposed on them, and under which they still lived, for all wireless messages, even stores lists, had to be sent in cypher.

Doc Back was not the only keen meteorologist. At Deception young Sub-Lieutenant Gordon Howkins soon showed his professionalism by dedicated application to his task, not only in making the observations, but in using them to develop theoretical considerations regarding travelling polar

Neumayer Channel from Wiencke Island. (Operation Tabarin)

anticyclones and other matters. From 1 July he personally undertook six observations every twenty-four hours, a formidable task for one man. He also acted as 'medical officer' to the base, 'devoting much of his time and energy to the work entailed . . . he carried out any emergency measures with confident competence'. Flett began his geological studies on 5 May, but one day when out 'chipping' with Jock Matheson they both fell heavily and took some time to recover from their injuries. No bones were broken, but this incident virtually put an end to serious geology.

At Lockroy Taylor did some local plane-table work and took rounds of photographs from surrounding high points. This was not easy, for the camera provided dated from 1903 and was somewhat erratic. Owing to war-time conditions, financial stringency and rushed preparations, this was not the only dubious piece of equipment sent south. Both base and field wireless sets were secondhand and certainly not built for low temperatures. The sledges came from the Army and had been designed for a very different type of operation. Before they could be used at all, considerable strengthening and modifications had to be made. There were no 'skins' for the skis. As these were essential on the steep snow slopes, seals were killed and skinned so that they could make their own. At one time they had tried attaching hinged, sharp-edged wooden flaps to the backs of the skis, but these 'galloping mouse traps' were not a success.

During winter the *Port Lockroy Prattler* appeared monthly and claimed to be the most southerly news-sheet in the world. It was the forerunner of a number of publications started by bases in later years, though none of them ever came up to the high standards set by the really beautiful *South Polar Times* produced by Scott's last expedition and lavishly illustrated by that great artist Dr Edward Wilson.

In June they heard about the invasion of Europe, but this major event of the war made little impact for already they had become parochial in their interests. The thoughts and reactions of isolated groups tend to relate far more to local circumstances, while the outside world becomes remote and great happenings have little relevance – sometimes they even seem a little absurd.

By mid-July the weather was warmer and penguins began to return to the rookery at Lockroy. On the 24th the sun peeped over the mountains for the first time and the tempo of preparation for spring sledging increased. Handlebars were being made for the sledges, a fitment for a large compass was constructed, tents were broken out and Eskimo seal-skin boots stretched to fit their owners. To measure the daily distance travelled they attached a bicycle wheel to each sledge, but unfortunately no cyclometers could be found in the pile of stores. To overcome this Ashton contrived an ingenious measuring device from an old ship's log left behind by *Scoresby*.

At last in September Marr, Davies, Taylor and Mackenzie Lamb set out, man-hauling two sledges up a steep glacier in thick fog. When this cleared they saw that the way round Wall Range to Luigi Peak led down a steep slope. At the bottom one sledge broke through the snow bridge of a crevasse but was recovered. A little further on their progress was impeded by large scattered blocks of ice which, they suddenly realised, had fallen from the 2,000-foot cliff towering above them. In all haste – but too late – they tried to extricate themselves. There was a report like a big gun being fired far above their heads, followed by deep distant rumbling like thunder. Then they saw it – thousands of tons of snow and ice hurtling down the cliff at speed. For a few seconds they stood gazing, hypnotised by the white curtain now descending, great blocks of ice seen dimly through a cloud of snow. Then throwing off their harnesses they ran like mad but had only covered a few yards when the horror was upon them. Casting themselves flat they felt a blast of wind, then everything was blotted out by fine powdered snow which forced itself into eyes, ears and mouth. After what seemed an aeon the wind dropped, the terrible thundering died away and they could see again – they had all escaped with nothing worse than bruises and a very bad fright. Hastily they hauled their miraculously undamaged sledges up to the crest of a ridge from which they could see the mountains of Danco Coast. The next few weeks were spent surveying and collecting rock samples and lichens, and by 18 October they were back at base. The ice slope on which they had so narrowly escaped disaster was later appropriately named Thunder Glacier.

1944/5   Eventually there was news about the expedition's future. For the coming season the Colonial Office had chartered ss *Eagle* (550 tons) in Newfoundland, primarily to establish the station at Hope Bay, while a zoologist, Captain N. B. ('Freddy') Marshall, had gone to Labrador to buy huskies. There were even rumours of an aircraft. Lockroy would be relieved entirely. Three new men, Sub-Lieutenant Jack Lockley RNVR, Norman Layther from Deception, and Charles Smith were expected to take over the station for the following winter. Among the new recruits coming out were Captain Victor Russell RE and Lieutenant David James RNVR, scions of

ss Eagle ; *cape pigeons feeding. (J. B. Farrington)*

Harrow and Eton respectively – an infusion of seemingly blue blood which particularly delighted Marr.

Taylor celebrated his birthday on 2 November, receiving from his companions a comb sawn from plywood and a brush in which nails formed the bristles, their tribute to the improved luxuriance of his hair while at Lockroy. Five days later *Scoresby* arrived, her holds full of stores, most welcome fresh fruit and vegetables, a number of living wild plants from the Falklands together with four hundredweights of peaty soil for acclimatisation experiments, and 'Gertrude'.

She was the most southerly pig that ever lived and came from the Falklands. Six weeks old, she was soon everyone's pet, fed all day from scraps from the galley, and living in a kennel made by Davies strategically placed in a sheltered position beside the front porch. Sure footed as a goat, the whole islet became her stamping ground. She reached her social peak on New Year's Eve when, as the clock struck twelve, she was invited to 'first foot' Bransfield House, being welcomed over the threshold with a saucerful of gin. One day when Ashton was painting the boats he forgot about Gertrude, and after lunch came upon a series of grey tracks all over the rocks below the hut. She was found covered in grey paint from the tip of her nose to the end of her curly tail, and Ashton claimed that even that did not account for all the paint which had been emptied from the pail, suggesting that she had drunk most of it. But when the time appointed for her demise came, her meat was not grey, neither did it taste of paint. All the same there were some among them who refused to discover this for themselves.

Mackenzie Lamb was soon engaged in making a small garden for the wild plants the ship had delivered, using the soil which had come with them. This was covered with wire netting to prevent depredation by birds. Twenty years later, under the conservation regulations contained in the Antarctic Treaty, such an experiment would have had to have been most carefully controlled to avoid the perpetuation of alien flora, but fortunately none survived to confuse the natural order.

Lockroy was finally relieved on 3 February 1945. As the old hands left the little hut which had been their home for almost a year, their nostalgia was assuaged by the prospect of new excitements. A few were going home, but most of them looked forward to new bases, new country to explore – and this time with dog teams. Next day they were back at Deception where they found *Eagle* waiting.

Eagle was the last of the Newfoundland sealers, a small wooden steamer with a clipper bow and a large barrel at her foretop. She was weak amidships and leaked for'ard, but she was commanded by a man with the heart of a lion who was to become a legend, long remaining in the hearts of the party she embarked at Deception to open Hope Bay. Captain R. C. Sheppard was fifty but looked years younger, with a soft voice and beautiful manners which belied his forceful character. On the voyage south he had fallen down a ladder and broken some ribs, which caused much anxiety about his fitness to continue in command, but despite his pain he insisted that he could carry on. Examining him, Doc Back was at last persuaded to declare him sufficiently fit to sail, provided he was not exposed to any bad weather conditions. Fortunately no one could foresee the hazards ahead.

Tom Carrel, the gnarled old bos'n affectionately referred to as 'Skipper Tom' was eighty-one, and he had served in *Theodore Roosevelt* from which Peary had landed in the Arctic for his last attempt to reach the North Pole in 1908. He had a powerful physique and apparently eternal youth, for he could still flense a seal or swarm up the mast to the crow's nest faster and more nimbly than anyone on board.

The plan had been that *Eagle* should establish Hope Bay, with Andy Taylor in charge and Flett as his number two. It was intended that after this Marr, with Matheson and three newcomers, would open a station in Marguerite Bay nearly 500 miles to the south. But Marr had been feeling unwell for some months and his health seemed to be deteriorating. He therefore asked to be relieved of command and suggested to the Governor that he should hand over to Taylor. This was agreed, but the Marguerite Bay project was abandoned, the extra stores and men being put into Hope Bay.

When the ship left Deception on 11 February she looked like an untidy Christmas Tree. On the fo'o'sle head were tethered the dogs. The deep welldeck for'ard was filled with lumber, anthracite, beds, benches, ladders and yet more dogs. On either side of the bridge a pound had been built, each heaped high with coal. Athwart the after hatch, and far too big for convenience of passage, lay the scow with lumber piled high around it and dogs inside, while aft, tied round the emergency steering wheel, were still more dogs. Four men slept aft, one on the saloon table, and the rest under the fo'c'sle head where Ashton had as usual ingeniously built eight forms two feet wide by partitioning two broad shelves with light boarding. None of this conformed with Board of Trade regulations, but then none of the Base Leaders were official inspectors.

Next day they reached Hope Bay, relieved to find that this time the bay was free of ice. The shore party split up to examine the area for the best site, while Mackenzie Lamb took his cameras over to photograph the old improvised stone hut built by the three castaways from Nordenskjöld's unlucky expedition who had wintered there in 1903. His purpose was to ensure a proper record before any later intruders visited it and possibly collected souvenirs.

The new base needed to be on a level area large enough for the erection of buildings, accessible to a landing place, the maximum distance possible from the local Adélie penguin rookery, to avoid both noise and stench and, if possible, near a good summer water supply. Ultimately they chose a flat moraine overlooking Antarctic Sound, behind which an ice slope rose smoothly to several hundred feet. This would enable parties to sledge at any time of year from their back door. At one side of it a small summer melt stream cascaded merrily down to the sea.

The first load to come ashore was a corrugated iron hut, prefabricated at Lockroy by Ashton, to serve as a temporary galley while building was in progress. This was promptly dubbed Uncle Tom's Cabin. It also provided space where men remaining ashore overnight could lay out sleeping bags. At the end of five days of virtually non-stop work, with dories bringing in load after load while the good weather held, seven men were sleeping regularly in the Cabin and three in a tent pitched alongside. The main hut joists were laid, the concrete mixed and poured for the piers. A dump of non-essential food and equipment was landed a mile away in Eagle Cove, thus named after the ship. This would be sledged up to base later.

They were difficult days and Taylor, the new overall Field Commander, was uderstandably critical of the London administration which had given no thought to providing *Eagle* with proper landing facilities, nor had the cargo been sensibly stowed in Stanley.

It was not until 25 February, or twelve days after discharging began, that such essentials as radio equipment, kitchen utensils and the nails and hut hardware were landed. As a consequence Farrington [the radio operator] was not on the air . . . until 27 February, [while] Berry cooked for a dozen men throughout that period with a single pot, and Ashton was continually confronted with difficulties in the erection of the house.
Taylor's Report

The previous year they had submitted a requisition for 'one sixteen-foot sturdy motor boat, with stouter planking than before, decked in and complete with pulling and sailing gear'. *Eagle* had a heavy scow, weighing in itself about five tons, which required very careful handling in order to move it on and off the ship as it all but overtaxed her derricks. It was roughly twenty-five feet along with a ten-foot beam, drawing four feet fully loaded, on which occasions it would be carrying some ten tons. In addition London had sent a very light fifteen-foot open boat with a single cylinder engine – apparently a secondhand pleasure craft with *Jeanry* II painted across the stern. Taylor considered this so dangerous that he returned it to Stanley.

Fortunately, after serious arguments, he had managed to acquire a motor boat which authority had intended for Lockroy, but even so landing operations in such difficult waters were a nightmare. In a glowing tribute to the crew who bore the brunt of them Taylor wrote:

I would like to state that if the establishment of this base proves of any political significance, and further, if the ensuing year's work of the members . . . should prove to be of any scientific value or interest, I consider that the credit for these opportunities is entirely attributable to the efforts of the *Eagle*.

Twenty-five dogs were also landed and allowed to roam at will, living contentedly off the penguin rookery where they did untold damage, and were a considerable nuisance, running loose among the busy and often exasperated builders. In those early days before the need for the conservation of wild life had made its impact, such methods were not recognised as wanton. Freddy Marshall, who had travelled out in charge of the dogs, felt himself so inexperienced in their management that he had sent a signal ahead warning Taylor of his ignorance. Later, to enable him to concentrate on his scientific work, they were made David James' responsibility and dog spans were laid, but this was more for convenience of the men and the safety of the animals than in the interests of the penguins. James made great efforts to acquire enough seals to provide four pounds of meat for each dog every other day, but there was insufficient time available to achieve this, and it was still thought necessary to allow between four and seven huskies to run free daily to find their own dinners in the rookery. Since 1946 strict control has been exercised throughout the FIDS bases, and it became unthinkable that dogs should be allowed to run free.

Very soon the weather became atrocious, often high winds and rough seas made it impossible to run boats. Even at the beginning, when the men were still putting up the Cabin, the strong winds had made it necessary to guy the metal framework, but one evening a high gust dragged an anchoring boulder and the whole edifice collapsed, bending the framework, shearing the bolts and pulling them out of their concrete beds. There was nothing for it but to take the whole thing to pieces and start all over again.

During these building activities a loud report was heard from the direction of the ship, followed by the appearance of a sinister column of black smoke rising into the sky. Two anxious shore parties raced off, one to the dinghy, the other to the headland, but the ship was still there. Later they learnt that Captain Sheppard had brought some black powder from Deception in case it became necessary to blast a way through ice. This had been left on deck and a careless smoker had ignited it. Very fortunately it was unconfined and flashed harmlessly.

That same night a gale force wind arose and *Eagle*, lying at anchor, was forced to use her engines to ease the strain on the cables. Suddenly a huge iceberg bore down on her. There was no time to weigh anchor and absolutely nothing Sheppard could do quickly. As the great mass slowly towered over them, Skipper Tom turned and said quietly, 'Well Captain, I guess this is the end'. Yet as he spoke the 'berg must have grounded, for it stopped, turned to

Building Hope Bay – flag flying on Uncle Tom's Cabin. (I. Mackenzie Lamb)

one side and pivotted off to starboard. Sheppard saw his chance, spun the wheel hard-a-port and, as the ship sheered away, the 'berg glided harmlessly by within a few feet of her. It was a breathless moment, which could have ended very differently.

Gradually the base was assuming recognisable form. The mess-room was set in the centre, surrounded by eight compartments each eight feet square, six of them with double berths, one a combined cabin and office for the Field Commander, the other the wireless room. An annexe contained the laboratory, galley, carpenter's shop and bos'n's store. By 15 February the roof was on, and for a few minutes all work stopped while a battery of cameras took pictures of Jock Matheson raising the first Union Jack at Hope Bay, on a staff made from one of the poles which had supported the roof of Nordenskjöld's hut. He had fastened this to the peak of the roof of Uncle Tom's Cabin.

With politics ever to the forefront, Matheson was also making four large signs, each consisting of legs supporting a metal sheet on which was painted BRITISH CROWN LANDS. These were intended for later erection at strategic points along the coast as further tangible proof that the British claim was being maintained.

During those first busy weeks all administrative traffic between the Field Commander and Stanley or other bases was passed through *Eagle*'s wireless room. Considerable anxiety was felt when Deception went off the air for a week. As soon as the ship's holds were empty she prepared to return there for a second load, and Flett took passage to find out what had gone wrong.

As she left in a strong gale, the temperature ashore dropped to 19°F and a blizzard drove a fine powdering of snow through the cracks in the Cabin, falling steadily onto the dinner table. By supper time they ate wearing a variety of oilskins, parkas, coats and balaclavas, while Ashton and Davies struggled to plug the gaps with newspaper, 'sisalcraft' and even Berry's dishcloths. As the wind gusted to sixty knots the Cabin strained alarmingly and the corrugated iron roof vibrated as though it would tear away at any moment. Ashton sat up all night waiting for something to give, but the others took to their sleeping bags on the principle that if the building was going to blow away nothing would be achieved by staying awake to wait for it. By morning the weather moderated, but the main hut they were building was over a foot deep in snow, all of which had to be dug out. The Cabin was hastily shored up with six-inch baulks of timber.

Meanwhile *Eagle* had reached Deception and reported that their wireless silence had been due to a fire in the engine-room which had burnt out both the motor and the generator. These had now been repaired and normal contact resumed.

The provision of seals for dog food led, at the beginning of March, to the first scientific specimen being found when a bright salmon-pink foetus, perfect in every detail even to tiny claws on its flippers and whiskers on its face, was taken from inside a leopard seal. This was preserved for Marshall's collection.

At Deception *Eagle* took aboard thirty tons of coal, thirty tons of ballast and twenty tons of lumber, all of which had to be ferried out in small dories, a Herculean task for the crew. By 12 March she was back at Hope Bay and, when weather permitted, once more from dawn to dusk scowload after scowload of material was landed at Eagle Cove. For four days the motor boat towed 'trainloads' of dories to the beach where the 'coolies' disposed of it. During these operations Captain Sheppard had developed a bad cold and found coughing excruciatingly painful.

St Patrick's Day, the 17th, dawned with the wind at gale force, a high unsteady glass and thick driving snow reducing visibility to twenty yards.

When Tommy Donnachie switched on the walkie-talkie for his mid-morning wireless schedule with the ship, her signals were very faint and he learnt that she was at sea. Struggling against atmospheric interference the operators somehow maintained contact:

The blinding gale was still blowing with a roar that reverberated through our empty wooden building, which seemed to act as a sounding board to amplify its screaming noises. We heard 'Sparks' talking . . . in his customary cool, laconic voice, repeating every few words to make certain that we got it all . . . 'Hello Tommy. Hello Tommy. Harold calling Tommy . . . In the gale this morning we were forced to cut the scow adrift to avoid damage to our rudder and propellor. We have lost your small dinghy. We have lost our anchor and eighty fathoms of cable. We have drifted out to sea and are now in the lee of some land. We think we are to south'ard of you, but do not know for sure. We have had two collisions with icebergs in the poor visibility and we have lost our bow and part of the foredeck. We cannot tell what the exact damage is but we do not seem to be taking much water. That is all Tommy. That is all'.
Base Journal

It took some time, and many repetitions, to get all this. A party had immediately rushed out into the gale to Eagle Cove but could see no sign of the ship, nor did they find any of the cargo which they had hoped to salvage. In an hour *Eagle* was calling again to say that she was coming back into the bay and would try to anchor in the cove. The wind still raged furiously while everyone hovered anxiously round the wireless. Presently Sparks was back again:

Hello Tommy. Harold calling Tommy. We have now lost our last anchor. We have given up all hope here now. Captain Sheppard has practically decided to beach the ship. I have an important message for Captain Taylor from Captain Sheppard. He wants you to send all the men you can spare to Eagle Cove where the beaching may be made. They are to bring ropes and any other tools they may think would be useful. Did you get that Tommy? Over.
Base Journal

Doc Back was already collecting first-aid equipment, two sledges were prepared for the injured, one of them loaded with a light and a heavy line, an empty can with which to float the light line off to struggling swimmers, and nine men set off into the teeth of the gale, wading through what had now become deep soft snow. Leaving Donnachie to keep wireless watch, they reached a high point from where they could see the ship in the middle of the bay facing out to sea. But James turned back to collect a forgotten piece of equipment, and then came hurrying out with the news that a further message had just been received saying that, despite the damage, Sheppard had decided to attempt a run to Stanley. It was a brave decision. Eagle Cove was but a rock-strewn beach where the ship would almost certainly have ripped out her bottom, and it would have been difficult indeed for men to get ashore in the wind and sea had she broken up before the gale moderated.

With relief the shore party watched her go, their fingers tightly crossed and a private prayer on their lips. All were conscious of their debt to the gallant little ship and her indomitable crew who had worked so unflinchingly to establish them ashore under dire conditions. Now she steamed slowly away, her sides deep coated with ice and her bow stove in. Sheppard, cool and unruffled, stood on his bridge with old Skipper Tom still beside him, without anchors, short of water, and bunkers running low. She had made a proud voyage and they wished her all the luck she now so badly needed.

It is impossible to put into words the feeling we all have here towards Captain Sheppard . . . [he] has shown himself a determined and efficient seaman, intrepid and fearless, willing to cooperate with us to the extent of jeopardising his own health . . . risking his ship for us when he felt the hazard warranted, and determining his course of action just as decisively when the predominant danger was to his crew . . . a truly gallant gentleman and a loyal dependable friend, he has won for himself a high place in our esteem and affections.
Taylor's Report

A message was immediately sent to Stanley asking that *Scoresby* should put to sea to stand-by.

1945   The shore party returned to base, first to list the stores they would now have to do without, for only one-third of *Eagle*'s second cargo had been discharged. These included a second Nissen hut and corrugated iron sheets needed to complete the Cabin, all the linoleum for the floor of the main hut, some stoves and heaters, some twenty-five tons of coal, boats, much of the lumber required to complete the annexe, most of the acid for the storage batteries which supplied power to the wireless station and the lighting unit, a year's supply of boots, and a miscellaneous assortment of food and scientific equipment. Maybe *Scoresby* would be able to bring some of them down before the season ended. If not, at least they had sufficient to survive and were ready for rationing if necessary.

Towards the end of March they were ready to assemble the cooker, a source of headaches over the years as new bases were established. This one had a small brass plate attached to the water tank at the back which read, 'For eight officers and twenty men', and was considered just right, the fourteen members of the base being hybrids of these extremes. The first blow was when they discovered that the boiler required a pressure water supply system and a hot water storage tank before it could be used – there was no immediate prospect of acquiring either. The second shock came when, standing knee deep in an intricate mass of queer-looking parts, it transpired that the assembly instructions referred to another type altogether, and there was no mention of hot water boiler attachment. Furthermore, none of the asbestos cement or piping for the chimney had arrived, and in the end there was 'one piece left over' for which no one could think of a place. It was finally hung on a nail 'in case of brainwaves'.

After supper Taylor and Berry hopefully lit it. Smoke poured from almost every orifice except the chimney, and at the end of the bout they emerged from the galley feeling and smelling like smoked hams, to report thankfully that the fire was out, but a black tarry liquid was dripping through those openings which did not emit smoke. In the end several days had to be spent on improvised modifications before the beast gave in.

On 15 April Alan Reece reported from Deception that Sam Bonner, a Falkland Islander, was worrying about his health and had requested permission to return to Stanley as soon as this was possible. He was a heavy smoker who had already had medical treatment for nicotine poisoning. Now he had developed recurring earache and a bad cough, chronic headaches and breathlessness. He was also worrying about wintering at a base without a doctor and with only limited medical facilities. For a time daily messages about his condition were passed to Doc Back, who supervised his treatment over the wireless, and *Scoresby* was sent from Stanley to bring *Eagle*'s missing cargo to Hope Bay and to evacuate Bonner from Deception. But she ran into heavy ice in Bransfield Strait which it was impossible to negotiate and, to everyone's dismay, was forced to turn back home. Throughout the winter Bonner's health slowly deteriorated.

At Hope Bay Davies and Berry made an inventory of the food stocks and found that the tinned meats which were being used to provide two hot meals daily were going to last only until mid-July. Their routine was immediately cut to one hot meal and later, as winter drew in and the heavy outside work was completed, they lived on only two meals each day. Taylor, always conscious of the possibility that at worst the base might not even be relieved until the spring of 1947, warned everyone of the pressing need for economy and thrift in using any kind of material, in particular their clothing. He also announced the liquor arrangements – one bottle of port and one of sherry every Saturday night, a bottle of whisky every first and third Saturday of each month, with rum on the table every evening.

The doctor had already been husbanding a small private supply of beer. He discovered the error of this philosophy when one morning he found that four of his six bottles had frozen and burst forming little mounds of glass and ice on the floor of the wireless room. He drank the two erect bottles the same evening, appearing the picture of affluence as he sat sipping luxuriously while reading *The Times* of 29 August the previous year.

At the end of April security was slightly relaxed as the cyphering staff in Stanley was being reduced. It was a great relief to the bases when the Governor gave permission for certain categories of messages to be sent *en clair*.

Early in May they received news of the German capitulation and this provided legitimate excuse for local celebration. In order to facilitate Donnachie's participation in the festivities, Back and James undertook the subtractions in the cypher traffic which had to be passed that day; but they began their task too late in the evening, for after the transmission it was found in Stanley 'that their batting average was roughly one mistake in every four groups'.

VE Day (8 May 1945) was as much a holiday in the Antarctic as it was at home. The bases listened to the Prime Minister's historic announcement, then to the King's speech, after which Taylor signalled the Governor: 'In these lonely outposts His Majesty's loyal subjects from England, Scotland, Wales, Ireland, the Falkland Islands, New Zealand and Canada join with the Empire to celebrate this historic day'. But this time their celebrations were nostalgically muted, memories returned to other places, and to companions with whom they would have given much to have spent that day. . . . It took a little time to settle down to work again.

On Midwinter Day the first *Hope Bay Howler* appeared, edited by Back, containing news items and articles, and letters from the other bases. To pin-point how they saw themselves it carried a sardonic 'advertisement':

Bright young man for the Antarctic. Must have knowledge of botany, zoology, ornithology, surveying, taxidermy, geology, oxometry, etc. German and French essential. Must be able to type, operate wireless set, light fires, clean drains, build houses and drive dogs. Sound knowledge of huntin' shootin' and fishin' expected. Salary despicable, prospects nil. Please write and state any additional qualifications.

An inter-base chess tournament had been organised in which Port Lockroy was routed, but their own account of this débâcle in the *Howler* explained that, 'On reflection we attribute this to our impetuosity in making a board and men in ten minutes or so from a piece of lino, some corks and pins'. Lockroy had also tried fishing for fun, but the one specimen secured was of such horrific appearance that it went to science without a murmur of protest from anyone.

By this time the Hope Bay dogs had been sorted into two teams and training began. Every day, weather permitting the 'Big Boys' and the 'Odds and Sods' made three trips to Eagle Cove each morning, and one after lunch, to haul back loads of coal and other material dumped there. One or two weaker animals had already been lost through fights, and four well matched dogs, 'Gin', 'Whisky', 'Punch' and 'Bitters', known collectively as the

'Drinks', had gone off on a foraging expedition from which they never returned, probably blown out to sea on loose ice. Happily these losses were counterbalanced by both 'Beauty' and 'Pretty' producing families.

The naming of Pretty's litter, a dog and two bitches, became a burning issue – everyone had suggestions but no one liked anyone else's. Influenced by the General Election going on at home, they finally agreed that a decision must emerge from a majority vote. From a field of fourteen 'candidates' the final runners were:

The Temperatures – Fahrenheit, Centigrade and Zero
The Jews   – Reuben, Rachel and Rebecca
The Sitwells   – Osbert, Edith and Sacheverall
The Isles   – Eigg, Rum and Muck
The Churchills   – Winston, Sarah and Diana
The Drinks   – Whisky, Sherry and Ginny

Much to everyone's surprise the Temperatures romped home an easy winner, but this caused a riot among the dog drivers, now faced with cries of 'Wheet Fahrenheit' or 'Owk Centigrade'. After much argument and a heated letter to the *Howler*, democratic principles were thrown to the winds and the pups became the Jews, Reuben, Rachel and Rebecca.

A later edition of the *Howler* carried an assessment of the dogs reflecting the exasperated affection in which they were held by the scientists:

The Husky has a most diabolical sense of humour, a positive genius for trouble . . . I wonder if the dog who found out that he could falsify the amount of precipitation in the rain gauge kept the secret to himself or told the joke to his friends? Did Rover first wait for a sunny day before pillowing his head on the globe of the sun recorder? Which of our dogs dislikes surveyors? It was an ingenious idea to wait until the glass on the sledge had broken and then to alter the position of the pointer by a rub of the nose . . .

On 23 June Back was urgently summoned to the wireless room for a medical 'sched' with Deception, where Bonner had apparently had a sudden stroke and was lying comatose. He gave Reece detailed instructions of tests to be made which would confirm the diagnosis, and told him how the patient must be nursed. For several days wireless watch was kept almost around the clock as under the doctor's long distance supervision Bonner slowly returned to consciousness, without any memory of what had happened. From then on he was only allowed to potter gently around base, doing no heavy work and kept as quiet as possible until the arrival of the first relief ship.

As the days gradually lengthened the men's spirits quickened. At Hope Bay everyone turned their minds to the summer sledging problems. At last they would be able to test themselves and their equipment in the field, developing techniques for serious travelling – an art in which none of them had any experience.

Their first idea had been to travel south over the Larsen Ice Shelf and try to find a route up to the plateau of the Antarctic Peninsula. Then realising their inexperience, they felt it would be foolhardy to be too ambitious and it was decided to go only as far south as Cape Longing, and then eastward to Snow Hill Island where they hoped to find Nordenskjöld's old base which might even still be habitable. Returning along the eastern and northern coasts of James Ross Island would entail a reasonably testing traverse of 270 miles.

Bonner's precarious health required that the doctor remain near the wireless, so the original party of six was cut to four, Taylor as surveyor, James in charge of the teams and meteorological observations, Vic Russell responsible for the field radio, the commissariat and glaciology, and Mackenzie Lamb the botanist, who would also collect such geological specimens as opportunity offered for the later attention of Flett at Deception.

It was therefore with some dismay that James observed signs of what might be mange in a number of dogs. Many signals were exchanged with the senior veterinary officer in Stanley on both diagnosis and treatment. Meanwhile Matheson busied himself making sixty-four canvas 'dog boots' in various patterns, which they intended to use if rough surfaces made travelling painful for the animals with unprotected feet. By 8 August the sick dogs had recovered and it was time to start.

The whole base helped to get the sledges up the steep glacier to the pass above. From there each was hauled by a seven-dog team, James and Russell with the Big Boys, pulling a nine-foot Nansen weighing 900 pounds loaded, and Taylor and Mackenzie Lamb with the Odds and Sods, recently more decorously renamed the Chromosomes, hauling a twelve-foot sledge weighing 800 pounds. These were heavy loads for untrained teams with inexperienced drivers, and the hard uphill work on the soft surfaces encountered during their first week reduced the daily average to only five miles. It was particularly tough going on the Big Boys who were hauling 130 pounds per dog on the smaller sledge, and also breaking trail. During this period they also found that they had used forty per cent of the paraffin which was intended for a journey planned to last twenty-eight days. So some more useful lessons were learnt the hard way. Dogs should not normally be asked to haul more than 110 pounds per animal, the greater load should be carried on the larger sledge, the lighter one breaking trail, and careful discipline must be applied to daily fuel consumption.

A camping drill had been developed, which set a pattern for travelling that has hardly changed in the succeeding thirty years. On halting at the end of the day each sledge was picketed fore and aft. The two men sharing a tent then divided the duties turn and turn about as 'inside' and 'outside' man.

Nordenskjold's hut, Snow Hill Island, 1945. (A. Taylor)

Both erected the tent, then the inside man laid out a ground sheet while the outside man unharnessed the dogs, clipping them back onto the centre trace of the sledge. When the inside man was ready the current food box, the utensil box and the sleeping bags were passed in to him. He immediately started the Primus to prepare a hot drink, while his companion outside fed the team, unloaded the sledge, turned it over to clear ice from the runners, dug blocks of snow to hold down the tent skirt, and generally secured the camp for the night. Snow blocks which would be melted down for water were placed between the inner and outer tent flies on the left of the entrance sleeve, the fuel can on the right. Finally he crawled into the tent, carefully brushing surplus snow from his clothing, and happy to find a hot cup of tea awaiting him. The inside man then prepared supper, while wet foot gear and socks were hung up in the apex to dry. Next day they swapped routines. The importance of such a common drill was quickly recognised, for it ensured that everyone knew precisely what to do, nothing was forgotten, snow was kept out of the tent, and no discussion or arguments regarding procedures arose when different men found themselves travelling together.

On 14 August, in Prince Gustav Channel, they put down a small depot against their return, also caching all but one pair of skis, which was later to cost them dear. They then set off for Cape Longing, constantly being diverted by high ice ridges, chasms and moraines, where the men had to haul with their teams. On James Ross Island they found a depot left by Nordenskjöld from which they took tea, sugar, sardines, paté, pea flour, sausages and butter, together with some dried vegetables, apple rings and prunes. All were in good condition after forty-three years. But four days later at Snow Hill their hopes of some indoor comfort were dashed, for although the hut still stood, the windows were broken and it was largely full of snow.

Moving on to Seymour Island, where many fossils were collected, they found the depot left by *Uruguay* when she rescued Nordenskjöld's party in 1904. Although most of the tins were rusted through they were able to add corned beef, rice, beans and sugar to their already dwindling supplies. Next morning they paused at Cockburn Island to collect lichens and fossils, noting that Mackenzie Lamb was the first botanist to visit the island since Sir James Hooker had been there with Sir James Clark Ross over a hundred years before.

By this time they were concerned about the diminishing supplies of paraffin, and had only one-and-a-half days' dog food left to see them through the last forty-four miles back to base. Though the weather was deteriorating they had to keep moving, for they could not afford to lie-up. As they headed for Sidney Herbert Sound the surface became increasingly soft and deep, and apprehension began to build up. Only the man wearing skis, which they used in turn, could move at all easily, the others sinking knee-deep at every step. With dismay they now recognised their error in depoting the other skis, but there was nothing to be done but plod on laboriously, getting very tired indeed.

On 2 September they covered only four miles, and there were only two fills left for each Primus. Two days later to save weight they jettisoned the wireless set, sledge repair kits and everything else they could spare, books, cigarettes, extra clothing. Still labouring to keep moving at all cost, Taylor was wearing a pair of snow shoes, Russell and James taking turns on the skis, while Mackenzie Lamb most unselfishly insisted on floundering through the soft snow all day, and became correspondingly exhausted. To help the dogs they all man-hauled when they could but for another three desperate days the surface grew ever softer and stickier, until they were sinking to their

waists. At times they were even crawling on their hands and knees. On the third day they covered only three weary miles, the next day less than five.

Temperatures had ranged between −20° and +40°F and the dogs, working so hard on half rations, were exhausted too. Once stopped it was difficult to get them to start again. By now there was only a little corned beef left to feed them, and the men faced the painful necessity of having to kill the weakest to give the remainder a chance. On the 7th both teams failed completely, several animals had to be carried on the sledges. That night 'Mutt' was shot, providing more than two pounds of meat for each of the others.

Next day, quite suddenly, their troubles were virtually over. The dogs had gained strength dramatically on one good feed, the temperature rose to +5°F, the surface improved with less snow cover, and they at last reached the depot laid on their outward journey. There was fuel and food for everyone, and a pair of skis for each man. On the 10th, very thin and worn, they were back at base – the first dog sledging journey had been accomplished.

If it had been a hard experience, much had been learnt. They had travelled 271 miles in thirty-two days (averaging 7.7 miles a day) which was four days more than the twenty-eight for which they had provisioned themselves. The average distance covered was just two miles per day less than they must have calculated when they set out. So they learnt the need to build a reserve into calculations for future journeys.

Before the end of the year Taylor, Mackenzie Lamb, Russell and Davies made other journeys, notably one of 500 miles in fifty-one days, which improved techniques and laid the foundations of the highly efficient sledging for which Hope Bay was to become renowned during the next nineteen years. Even without the benefit of experienced supervision the men were becoming drivers and the dogs were being welded into efficient working teams.

Meanwhile at Deception man-hauling parties had been laying depots at strategic points, and a number of short exploratory journeys had been made around the island. During one, steam was found rising from a hill at a height of 1,000 feet where the ground was +46°F – hotter than the ambient air temperature. This caused some alarm, for perhaps the emanation presaged a new eruption.

As the year drew to a close everyone was increasingly anxious for news of the men coming south to replace them, particularly for some estimate of their date of arrival so that intelligent plans could be made. But unhappily an

Map 2, opposite. Hope Bay/James Ross Island area

impenetrable shroud of secrecy prevailed. This almost total lack of communication from London caused considerable irritation, which was bad for morale. Undoubtedly those at home were lacking in imagination, but this is a pattern which in varying degrees has been repeated throughout the history of the Survey. Even with today's teleprinters, when plans, ships' itineraries and the names of newcomers are routinely sent to all bases, they still feel they are being kept unfairly in the dark. At home it is recognised as the 'No one ever tells me anything' syndrome.

Perhaps inevitably this attitude will always persist, for however much information is given, more is always expected. Yet there must be a limit to the detail which can be sent to people who cannot know the thinking that prompts many decisions, and it is certainly unwise to communicate plans which may later have to be changed, for this also gives rise to dissatisfaction and loss of confidence. At home the country was perhaps over security-conscious, having become accustomed to wartime secrecy, but clearly it was not recognised how very out of touch isolated groups feel, and how quickly a head of steam can build up. So when relief ships arrive, they do not always find the warm welcome they might expect.

TABARIN was mounted at short notice in the middle of a war, and was surely a fine example of the British genius for instant improvisation. The presiding trinity, Wordie, Roberts and Mackintosh, were a strong group with the right background, and with men drawn from both Service and civilian sources, the assortment of small ships from Canada and the Falklands Islands, the whole hotch-potch was somehow welded into an effective unit, despite the secrecy of the operation which often militated against efficient organisation.

In two years, three regularly reporting meteorological stations had been established. At Deception a start had been made in examining the geology and glaciology, while at Lockroy some biology and topographical survey had begun. At Hope Bay, where the strongest team was established, considerably more had been achieved. The various sledge journeys, already totalling several hundreds of miles, had greatly improved and extended the mapping of this area. Geological reconnaissance had laid the ground for future detailed work, successful tidal observations had been made, marine biology begun, and an extensive botanical collection greatly extended the knowledge gained by the few earlier visitors. They could all justifiably feel proud of what had been accomplished.

2

FIDS is born
1945–7

1945 With the ending of war, steps were taken to transform a naval operation into a civilian organisation. The nearest established British administration was in the Falkland Islands, the bases had been set up in the Dependencies, so in July 1945 OPERATION TABARIN was officially renamed the Falkland Islands Dependencies Survey – FIDS. Basic supplies still came from naval stores but were now paid for from the Colonial Office Development and Welfare vote. Recruiting became even more complicated since the majority of the new men were still serving officers. None of them could accept appointments without agreement from the Service to which they belonged, or the civilian body to which they would return when demobilised. Some of those particularly needed could not be spared, others were found medically unfit for polar life.

Some strange anomalies arose, such as that which resulted from a new agreement between the Admiralty and the Meteorological Office which prevented naval meteorologists from working at land stations. In any case the Navy was short of trained men, and the Meteorological Office was uninterested in extending its work to Antarctica. However, both tried to be helpful and Brian Roberts, still the active agent in organising the annual relief, secured a number of professionals who, aided by enthusiastic though untrained amateurs, could keep the established programmes running. Geologists and surveyors were another problem, and special arrangements had to be negotiated for their release from the Services.

Lacking a proper office organisation, and with such a multitude of logistic complications, the newly convened FIDS Advisory Committee was hard pressed to meet the sailing date. It was necessary to acquire specialised stores, formulate proper *Regulations and Scientific Instructions* for the growing baby, organise the establishment of two new stations, obtain more huskies and, above all, find an ice-worthy ship to replace the *Eagle*.

Their first step was to appoint a new Field Commander to relieve Taylor, and FIDS was fortunate indeed that for this post the Navy seconded Surgeon

Commander E. W. Bingham RN. Ted Bingham was well known in the polar community, having served with the British Arctic Air Route Expedition 1930–1, and shortly afterwards wintered in Labrador with the *Challenger* Survey Expedition during which he travelled extensively with the Eskimoes. More importantly, he had spent two years with the British Graham Land Expedition and was in all ways a most competent field man.

He was a small, sturdily built Irish doctor, with keen blue eyes and radiated energy. His experience and enthusiasm made him an ideal choice for coping with the still haphazard and disjointed administration, and as soon as he joined he sat with the committee. At once he used his knowledge of how the Services worked to pressurize or cajole shocked and reluctant naval store-keepers into giving him what was needed without wasting time going through normal channels—frequently without the blessing of official sanction. If he was the bane of the authorities, his name soon began to be used as a threat in the naval victualling department, for the Commander always wanted everything 'by this evening please', and was no respecter of regulations which he delighted in ignoring.

Assisted only by a young typist, who soon left under the pressure of her working conditions, he cheerfully presided over the whole logistic scene from a small office in Northumberland Avenue. This was cluttered with skis, driving whips, food samples, dog pemmican, polar clothing, and telephones which never stopped ringing. When not interviewing recruits he would disappear to places like Chatham Dockyard where he just happened to know that he could find specially strengthened claw hammers, anchors, and a variety of equipment impossible to come by honestly in the stringent aftermath of war. Marshalling the most unconvincing arguments, he would talk the chap guarding them into allowing him to remove them at once – mercifully it is not recorded how much just 'got lost' and had unaccountably to be written off.

In the evening he returned to the paper work. His unfortunate bride of only a few months soon recognised the wisdom of joining those one can't beat, and happily sat with him into the small hours checking stores lists or typing orders for the hundreds of items still required. All this was still further confused because of uncertainty regarding the number, or even location, of bases to be supplied. Three were already occupied, four more were planned but how many would it in fact be possible to establish during the coming summer season?

1945/6   A charter was signed with the Canadian Ministry of Transport for MV *Trepassey*, a wooden ship of 325 tons, and to everyone's delight she was under the command of Captain Sheppard. She first sailed to Labrador carrying Surgeon Lieutenant Stewart Slessor and Sub-Lieutenant Tom O'Sullivan RNVR, sent there to obtain more huskies. Twenty-two were

MV Trepassey. *(W. M. Sadler)*

bought at Nain, eleven from Hopedak and the remainder in ones and twos at other places along the coast rejoicing in such names as Kamersuk, Kauk and Mehkovik. Dogs cost $7.50, bitches $10 each, and most were in poor condition resulting from lack of food and care from their Eskimo owners. However, with a regular diet of fresh cod, and occasional feeds of salted seal, they quickly improved, and later on the voyage south eight puppies were born. Together with the twenty-five animals already at Hope Bay, these dogs were to found the colony of Antarctic huskies which served FIDS so well for thirty years.

Effforts to find passages direct to Montevideo failed, so the new recruits flew to Lisbon where they joined ss *Empire Might*. Bingham himself flew to South America, his wife sworn to silence as to his whereabouts, her friends believing that he had gone to Korea. The secrecy which had shrouded TABARIN was to continue.

On 21 December *Empire Might* arrived in Montevideo, and the *Paraguay* brought in the bulk of the stores. *Scoresby* was already there waiting to embark eight men for Stanley that afternoon. Five days later *Trepassey* came in, and left loaded to her gunnels with dogs tethered all over her foredeck. The remainder of the men and the rest of the stores were picked up on the 28th by *Fitzroy*. By 4 January 1946 everyone and everything had reached Stanley and had been allocated to appropriate ships, all of which sailed in the next few days to begin the relief.

1946   Bingham's first tasks were to relieve Deception Island and Hope Bay, and to search the coasts of the South Orkney Islands for a site on which another base could be built. On 14 January *Scoresby* reached Hope Bay on her second attempt, took off Taylor and all the wintering party except for Vic Russell who was left in charge, the only old hand with seven new men.

On the same day Bingham arrived at Deception in *Fitzroy*, the stores were unloaded and personnel changed over, Sub-Lieutenant John Featherstone RNVR being left in charge. On the 15th Bingham transferred to *Trepassey* and sailed for Hope Bay, sending *Fitzroy* to relieve Port Lockroy. Everything went as planned and three days later *Scoresby* and *Trepassey* were battling their way out of Hope Bay through close pack ice lying to the north. Once clear of this they joined *Fitzroy*, the three ships sailing in line ahead making a brave little convoy. *Trepassey* with her sails set was in the lead, followed by *Fitzroy* with *Scoresby* bringing up the rear, wearing respectively blue, red and white ensigns. On receipt of a message that Bonner was again in need of medical attention, *Fitzroy* was diverted to Deception to evacuate him to hospital in Stanley. The other ships ploughed on through ice to the South Orkneys.

At many points the coastline was too precipitous for unloading; others offered only exposed anchorages. There were no charts of these waters and *Trepassey* found at least one dangerous rock the hard way. On the southern side of Laurie Island, an Argentine meteorological station had been maintained in Scotia Bay since 1903, when Dr W. S. Bruce had handed over to them his Scottish National Antarctic Expedition base. It was politically inexpedient to build a British station in close proximity, and Bingham finally chose a site at Cape Geddes.

On 21 January unloading began but it was not to be easy. Day after day high winds and a heavy swell alternated with fog or rain and sleet, and sometimes the jostling brash ice heaved against the boulder-strewn landing place, making it impossible to use boats. Constant frustrations finally led Bingham and a few hardy volunteers to stay ashore in the cold, unheated, half-built hut, so that at least some work could continue despite weather conditions. In ten days the base was up and the Post Office, the outward and visible sign of official administration, was open for business. The new Base Leader, M. A. ('Mac') Choyce, and the three men who would winter with him moved in. Next morning the ships sailed. The isolation of this small party became total, for soon their wireless broke down and, after two separate occasions when successful repairs were made, they finally went off the air until the base was relieved the following season. It says much for Choyce's leadership and their high morale that every man volunteered for a second year south.

On the 22nd *Fitzroy* arrived at Scotia Bay, and Commander Bingham and Captain Sheppard donned their best uniforms to pay a courtesy call on the

Argentine station Orcadas in Uruguay Cove. They were greeted by nine friendly men who escorted them proudly round their brand new hut which boasted a central heating system, a long bath, and a WC with a septic tank alongside the furnace, luxury indeed in Antarctica. Language problems happily inhibited communication, which was convenient for it precluded both sides from having to answer awkward questions of sovereignty which should officially have arisen. In return some of the Argentines were entertained in *Trepassey*, a man with chest trouble being treated by the doctor. Thus strained relations were left to the politicians, and a cordial atmosphere established between at least two parties in the field.

Before leaving the South Orkneys Bingham landed in Sandefjørd Bay at the western end of Coronation Island, where a partially completed hut had been built by a party from *Scoresby* the previous season. Stores were put ashore for emergencies, but he discovered that the building stood in the middle of a large penguin rookery, the rising stench making it uninhabitable. It was never occupied and was later dismantled. One must assume that during the ship's original visit the penguins had been absent, but no one could understand how such a site was ever contemplated. It certainly pointed the error of leaving such decisions to the inexperienced.

Arriving back at Deception, *Trepassey* at once began loading stores for a new sledging station in Marguerite Bay. The dogs which the ship had brought south had spent the last month running loose ashore, as a result they were now fit and hardy, and had formed themselves into congenial groups which Bingham observed closely, for later he would combine these into disciplined teams. When the ship's holds were crammed to the limit, thirty tons of cargo and forty drums of fuel were lashed down on deck. The large unloading scow was secured athwartships, and into this went the motor boat for a new station. As usual every remaining nook and cranny harboured a tethered dog. Once again accommodation did not conform very closely to Board of Trade requirements, for four members of the expedition inhabited the tiny saloon, three slept in the galley, and the rest in the wireless room or the engine room.

While still at Deception Duggie Mason, the incoming surveyor, had spent some weeks surveying two air-strips, one 800 yards long, the other an emergency alternative of 350 yards. Neither coincided with the landing strip used by Sir Hubert Wilkins in 1928, for this had deteriorated and much of it had slumped into an adjacent crater. It was to be some years before Mason's work proved its worth, for it was not until 1959 that the Survey was able to obtain its own aircraft which would fly from Deception.

Trepassey finally sailed on 17 February, called first at Port Lockroy where Bingham found the new wintering party in good heart, their only real problem a stubbornly leaking roof. They sailed through the sheltered waters

British Graham Land Expedition hut; picture taken in 1946. (W. M Sadler)

of the Neumayer Channel where seals abounded, lying in lazy groups on the floes, while penguins porpoised through the sea, leaping into the air to land on the ice and watch the intruders go by. A group crowded on the very edge of an ice cliff peered anxiously into the depths for their enemy, the leopard seal. A front runner inevitably got pushed in, then observing that no ill befell him, the others cascaded happily after him, and so away about the serious business of feeding.

At the Argentine Islands the old British Graham Land Expedition hut was found in good condition – but the Argentine flag flew over it! On the door was written '1°/de Mayo, Marina de Guerra. Republico Argentina, Febrero 1942'. Removing these signs of encroachment, a depot was left in the building under an official British notice nailed to the wall. For Ted Bingham it was a nostalgic return. A 'Welcome to Brighton' poster still hung above his old bunk and the stone shelters he had built for his dogs still stood, silent and empty. Sensitively his companions left him to his thoughts while the building was sealed against the elements, and a dory of freshwater was taken out to the ship to supplement their very meagre supply, for *Trepassey* lacked the luxury of a distillation plant.

As she sailed out through French Passage the uncharted rock-strewn waters became an alarming hazard. Two men were posted on look-out in the crow's nest, while the motor boat was lowered and driven slowly ahead of the ship towing a sweep, as cautiously they picked a way through the reefs. Once in the open sea the way was clear. By 23 February they were entering Marguerite Bay, so often inaccessible in later years but now happily free of ice. As Captain Sheppard felt his way carefully into Neny Fjord in a strong gale, the Chief Engineer chose this inauspicious moment to announce an impending engine failure, but their luck held just long enough for the ship to anchor safely at Stonington Island.

During the 1939/40 season the United States Antarctic Service Expedition had built their East Base at Stonington (West Base was on the other side of the continent at McMurdo Sound), a complex of buildings which now presented a sorry sight. All around, the summer melt revealed the debris of two years' occupation. Here a kitchen midden of rusting tins, there a pile of ageing stores, and nearby lay the still-tethered carcases of dogs hurriedly shot before the Americans departed when Congress suddenly discontinued the funds which supported their work.

The buildings themselves were in complete disorder, even the washing-up water lay frozen in a basin. The doors had been left open, either by the expedition when they were prematurely evacuated by air or by later visitors, and some of the huts were full of snow. Outside, the canvas covering which had sealed the joints between the panels had been torn away by wind to such an extent that the dark windowless rooms were lit by narrow shafts of light. It was a depressing and, to the newcomers, a shocking sight.

Since it was Bingham's plan to live in one of these buildings while the British base was erected, the first task was to clear sufficient space and get the stove going to dry out the interior. The site chosen for the new station was 250 yards distant, and as soon as the first scow loads of material had been landed building began. While the weather held the men worked a strenuous eighteen hours each day, snatching cat-naps between boatloads, even falling asleep while eating. John Tonkin, a particularly energetic and irrepressible character, once woke up only when his cigarette had burnt its way through windproof trousers to his thigh. In less than three weeks the base was completed.

With her holds empty, *Trepassey* now needed ballast. Her Newfoundland crew took the scow across the water, made fast to the foot of a steep unstable scree, and then loosened the lower stones. A mass of rubble thundered down filling the scow. This unusual method certainly saved a lot of time and an immense amount of work, and the Newfoundlanders remained happily unperturbed by the very real dangers of causing a major landslide which could have sunk them without trace.

The day before the ship sailed Bingham relented and declared a 'holiday' so that everyone could write their last letters home. But inactivity went against his busy nature and soon, with twinkling eyes, he was suggesting a series of 'voluntary' jobs for anyone with moments to spare. Both the letters and the jobs got done, but throughout the following year, whenever some particularly unpleasant or difficult task arose, the wicked cry would go up for another 'public holiday' on which to tackle it. On 14 March they held a last night party, and next morning Sheppard gave three cheerful goodbye toots on his siren as *Trepassey* sailed away.

So ended the shipping season and the bases settled down for the winter. At the small stations, Deception and Lockroy, the regular meteorological observations occupied the men fully, as they did at Cape Geddes, although there the failure of the wireless made it impossible to transmit the results. Hope Bay in its second year was in the happy position of being equipped to mount extensive exploratory journeys. Vic Russell was teaching his new team to drive dogs and planning the first training sledge journey on the Taylor (now Tabarin) Peninsula.

1946   At Stonington the engine house remained to be finished, a store house built, and the great pile of stores which had been landed had to be separated into two dumps, each to provide supplies for one year. These tasks completed, Bingham set about teaching everyone to drive dogs, and this time there were no 'following leaders', for all the leading dogs were trained to hold a course under the orders of the man behind the sledge. The teams had been chosen and organised, but to his chagrin sea ice failed to form until late in the year. Even by midwinter there was no safe solid ice around the island, and all training was perforce restricted to local runs or up onto Northeast Glacier, which was hardly suitable for beginners owing to extensive crevassing. The age gap between Bingham and his men, plus his wide field experience, made him an admired father figure and under his leadership they quickly became an efficient team.

On 2 April Lockroy reported an exceptional tide that rose three feet above normal, accompanied by a powerful current in the confined waters which displaced numerous grounded icebergs. Later this was related to a tidal wave which had probably originated in the Aleutians and moved southward along the west coast of South America. It was lucky that no one had been left to occupy the British Graham Land Expedition hut at the Argentine Islands for the following summer it was found to have completely disappeared. At the time there were dark thoughts that the Argentines had somehow removed the building without trace, but there is little doubt that it was swept away by the surge of the tidal wave forcing its way through the narrow channel beside which the base had been built.

The lack of sea ice around Stonington compelled Bingham to revise his plans for the next season's work, both north and south of the station. It was clear that a way must be found up the steep slope leading to the plateau which stands over 5,000 feet above the base twelve miles to the east. This was a major challenge for not only were the glaciers which run down the escarpment heavily crevassed, but if any worthwhile journeys were to be accomplished, a very substantial depot of supplies would first have to be established at the top.

Continual blizzards caused by cold air pouring down from the plateau dramatically reduced the number of days on which dog teams could move at all. Only the most dedicated persistence enabled the men to haul three tons up to 1,400 feet by the beginning of August. Then parties began prospecting for a route over the upper reaches of Northeast Glacier, and by the 18th they had raised the depot to 3,000 feet. Ahead they could see a very steep slope leading to the top. It soon became known locally as 'Sodomy Slope', a pseudonym for an even ruder name, but as neither was acceptable in polite society, the less descriptive, but more respectable, 'Sodabread Slope' was eventually substituted. From this may be judged the problem it presented to heavily laden sledges. It was apparent that it would be necessary to use block and tackle to haul them up and already the men were beginning to live on the

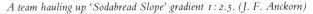

A team hauling up 'Sodabread Slope' gradient 1 : 2.5. (J. F. Anckorn)

depot supplies, so they all returned to base to reorganise and bring up more material.

On the 24th Bingham took out a party – Tonkin, Mason and Kevin Walton – in an attempt to find an easier route up to the plateau, this time above Square Bay to the north. They were almost immediately faced with disaster. Less than a mile from home, on the well known track they had so often followed, Tonkin was walking ahead to encourage the labouring teams when he just disappeared, leaving a small hole on the surface. Immediately overturning his sledge and roping himself to it, Bingham moved forward cautiously and was greatly relieved to hear Tonkin shouting to him. He had fallen into an unseen crevasse, and was now tightly jammed by his chest some forty feet down with his legs dangling over a bottomless pit, hardly able to breathe.

As the second sledge came up they dropped a double rope to him with loops made for his arms, but he could not get these under his armpits. Mason raced back to base to fetch help and more rope, returning with Doc Slessor and 'JJ' Joyce, but all their combined efforts to dislodge Tonkin failed. Walton then volunteered to go down to him. He was lowered carefully, but at thirty feet the crevasse suddenly narrowed to eight inches, and he too was jammed. They hauled him back to the surface and moved sideways to try again at a different point. At their second attempt Walton found himself totally jammed between icy walls, but at least he could now see enough to know what needed to be done. Back once more on top, he broke off the spike of an ice axe to make a tool with which he descended again, and this time managed to chip his way still further down until he reached Tonkin.

The space in which they were both confined was so small that Tonkin could not even turn his head, but chipping away carefully Walton gradually won sufficient room to adjust the ropes and free his chest. With the combined pull from those above and his own strenuous efforts, Tonkin suddenly came free like a cork from a bottle and was hauled up. He had been imprisoned for three hours and was very, very cold. Wrapped in blankets on a sledge they hurried him home, where the doctor found that the ropes had damaged the nerves of his hands and wrists. To his bitter disappointment it was the end of his sledging for the rest of the season. Walton was later awarded the Albert Medal for saving his life.

John Tonkin had been a paratrooper who had had an eventful war. Having escaped from an Italian prisoner-of-war camp, he was dropped into France a week before D-Day. There his party was ambushed, thirty of them were shot and five were never seen again, but the remaining fifteen got back, bringing one man under arrest for mutiny. Now, if he chafed under his enforced restraint, he never allowed his depression to show, and his companions have paid tribute to his cheery courage. To keep his hands exercised, each day he would tip out a box of small nuts and bolts, then spend many weary hours forcing himself to pick them up one at a time until he gradually regained his dexterity. It took him six months.

Two days after the accident the sledge party set out again, Reggie Freeman replacing Tonkin, but they soon agreed that the northern route to the plateau was quite impracticable – it would have to be 'Sodabread'. But before they could turn back they found themselves pinned down for thirty-six hours by one of the great down-draught winds referred to locally at Stonington, in politer moments, as the 'fumigator'. Every two hours they crawled out of their tents to cut new snow blocks with which to hold down the tent skirts. Gusting to 100 knots, the wind eroded the surrounding surface until the tents were perched on pedestals and increasingly in danger of blowing away. On the second day of their lie-up it quite suddenly died away, and they broke camp to set out for base over a completely changed surface of enormous wind-cut *sastrugi*.

From this time on all their efforts were concentrated on tackling 'Sodabread' with its gradient of one in two-and-a-half. For a month the weather was against them and twenty-four days were spent lying-up in tents. When it was possible to work, the system was for three men and one dog team to haul downwards attached to a rope passing through a block at the top, while three others and the second team hauled upwards attached to the loaded sledge. At first this presented interesting problems, for as the teams approached each other every dog tried to take advantage of this unexpectedly splendid opportunity to join battle. Only wild shouts and threatening whips prevented bloodshed, but mercifully even the dogs were soon too tired to engage in their favourite pastime. It was gruelling work and only on 26 October was the whole three-ton depot carried to the top, across a feature known as the 'Amphitheatre', and deposited on the edge of the plateau itself. They returned to base confident that it would support all the exploratory work they hoped to achieve.

Bingham planned to use two parties, both working northward from the depot – he himself with Freeman and Walton on the west side of the plateau, Slessor with Sadler, Joyce and Mason on the east side. But delayed yet again by impossible weather, it took them nine days just to climb back up to the depot. Then, after one good day in which they covered fifteen miles, dense cloud enveloped them for the next four. Not only were their hard-won supplies dwindling uselessly but Bingham was almost immobilised by a severely strained back, and the doctor strongly advised him to return to base. Eventually his pain forced him reluctantly to agree and his party retraced their steps leaving Slessor's group to go on alone.

They quickly learnt the bitter lesson that cloud and drift are normal on the plateau, and they could only expect to travel one day in every four or five – a fact of life which has plagued every plateau sledging party since. In the end Slessor's party covered 300 miles and reached a point just north of Wilkins' erroneously named Crane 'Channel', arriving back at base on 9 January 1947.

By April 1946 the Hope Bay newcomers were also ready for their first long journey. To begin with, Russell established Bill Croft, a geologist from the Natural History Museum, with Dick Wallin to help him, at the Naze on James Ross Island. Fossil plants had been found there the previous November and Croft intended to make extensive collections.

Russell, with John Francis, Dr Jimmy Andrew and Tom O'Sullivan, then returned to reconnoitre a route over the Trinity Peninsula through what was still unknown country. Travelling over sea ice, their progress was constantly hindered by open water and slush. Then, as they headed up into the mountains, day after day they encountered gale force winds or falling snow, and progress was difficult even on the few days when it was possible to travel.

Today, such conditions are expected along the spine of the Antarctic Peninsula, but to those who pioneered the routes they came as an unpleasant shock. Visibility was so bad that the surveyors could achieve little, but they did at least prove a route to the top, and were able to see the possibility of a descent to the west coast. By returning down the glacier now known as the Russell East Glacier, they also proved an overland route from Hope Bay to the southern part of Prince Gustav Channel, which could be used in the event of open water preventing travel over sea ice.

All this took so long that food ran short and they became increasingly anxious about getting back. By 10 May, thirty-five days out from base, men and dogs were on half rations. Originally they had planned to return to the Naze for Croft and Wallin, but as the dead-line passed these two would realise that they must man-haul back to base. On the 15th they were fifteen miles from home, camped on sea ice near View Point, and the dogs were fed the last of the pemmican.

Next day the drift was so heavy they could only see a few yards and resigned themselves to lying-up, the teams curled into neat balls gradually disappearing under the snow. At midnight O'Sullivan woke up to find his sleeping bag wet, with water seeping through the floor of the tent as accumulating drift weighed the ice down into the sea. High winds prevented them from re-pitching their tent, so he and Andrew moved in with Russell and Francis for a crowded night, sharing in turn the two dry bags.

In the morning the abandoned tent was half buried in accumulated drift and, worse still, one of the dogs was so deeply covered that he was suffocated. As they set about digging up sledges one was four inches below water level, and as they dug, the strong wind filled the hole with drift almost as fast as they could clear it. Paddling about in leaking seal-skin boots, they made so little progress that Russell decided to abandon it. They turned their efforts to a second sledge where water was only just above the runners, and raised it to the surface.

Meanwhile their second tent was slowly flooding. Working frantically they managed to keep the two sleeping bags dry, but had to strike the tent, and in doing this in the howling blizzard one of the poles was broken. Somehow it was re-pitched on the surface, now three feet above its original level, and a sorry sight it was. But they were only too thankful to crawl into its shelter, with the welcoming roar of the Primus that promised at least a hot drink.

The following morning although the wind still raged, they tried hard, but unsuccessfully, to raise the third sledge. Climbing the rocks of View Point, Russell could see above the drift, and satisfied himself that it was reasonable to attempt the crossing of Duse Bay, for now it was imperative that both men and dogs got back to base. Selecting the strongest animals to haul the one remaining sledge they let the others loose. By the time they finally left 'Swamp Camp' two of their sledges were entirely buried and only two feet of the abandoned tent stood above the surface.

With the wind behind them they made good speed, the loose dogs scampering ahead until, just before dark, they reached the coastal ice cliffs on

'Swamp Camp'. (S. J. Francis)

the far side of the bay where they camped, too tired to go on. That evening the dogs went hungry and the men ate their last crumbs of food. On the morning of the 19th everything except their sleeping bags and tent was depoted before they started up the hill on the last leg. The surface was very soft and even snow shoes sank deep. Francis and O'Sullivan pulled with the dogs, while Russell and Andrew shoved behind the sledge. They all reached the top exhausted, even one of the dogs having to be given a ride. But after that conditions became easier, and nine hours after they had set out they reached Hope Bay – and wonderful steaming hot baths. Each dog was given as much seal as he could eat.

Three days later Croft and Wallin came in, having man-hauled back from James Ross Island where they had left all their specimens for later collection. After a week of recuperation a recovery party left base, Reece replacing O'Sullivan who had suffered frost-bitten hands. This time aided by good weather and fast surfaces the party split, two to recover the tent and sledges awash at Swamp Camp, and two to pick up the fossils which had been collected and left on James Ross Island.

Reunited once more at Swamp Camp, the party looked forward to a fast run home. But that night 'Pretty' seemed very noisy and wouldn't settle. Knowing she was pregnant Russell got out of his sleeping bag to release her from the span thinking she might be looking for somewhere away from the team where she could whelp privately. The same thought had evidently occurred to her, for by the time he got back to his tent he found her already inside, happily snuggled down on his sleeping bag. Much against her will he turned her out, whereupon she spent the next half hour trying to get into the other tent. Eventually she returned to Russell's, to eat her way through the outer and then the inner flaps of the entrance sleeve. Woken by ripping canvas, he was just in time to see her nose coming through. A second later she was in, and once more making herself comfortable on his sleeping bag. Both realised she had won, so she remained curled up at the foot of the bag while he squeezed himself in at the top and tried to sleep.

Presently he heard infant squeaks and by torchlight he watched the litter arrive. By morning there were five, and he generously shared his breakfast porridge with the proud mother – after which she produced a sixth, to be rewarded with his bacon too. As the men broke camp, Pretty and her family remained in the tent until the last possible moment, and were then transferred to a prepared nest on one of the sledges, to ride triumphantly back to base.

In July Croft left to study the geology of Seymour Island lying southeast of James Ross Island, this time accompanied by O'Sullivan. Their major anxiety was the uncertain state of the sea ice, with the possibility that they

Cretaceous fossils from the James Ross Island area. (BAS)
Top: Gunnerites *sp. – Vega Island*
Left: Inoceramus pictus *– Tumbledown Cliffs*
Right: Lahillia sp. *– Lachman Craggs*

could be cut off until one of next season's relief ships could reach them in January or February. They accepted the risk, deciding that they would be able to live on the penguins which would have returned by the time their food ran out. Yet their trip was completely successful and they returned having accomplished much useful work. They brought back a collection of fossil penguin bones from a site discovered by the Swedish South Pole Expedition 1901–3, and from other localities. Subsequent studies showed these to be similar to fossils found in Australia and New Zealand. Though very incomplete specimens, they represent Miocene birds which may have been as much as six feet tall.

Simultaneously Russell, Andrew, Francis and Wallin set out on a more complicated survey traverse which took them south to the Russell East Glacier, westward through unknown mountains to the west coast of Trinity Peninsula, then north to Mount Bransfield, and so back to Hope Bay. They travelled 472 miles, and Russell's report included detailed descriptions of the mountainous areas through which they pioneered a route. In later years these were of inestimable value to successive parties which followed them. They visited Cape Roquemaurel, and at Cape Legoupil discovered the only landing place on the northwest coast which provides access to the interior. This was where, two years later, the Chileans established their Base Militar Bernado O'Higgins.

The party had its share of bad luck. On the fourth day out Doc Andrew found that he had mysteriously broken a rib. Although he carried on sledging valiantly for another six days, Russell then had to take him back to base and return with Reece in his place. Six weeks after this Wallin fractured an arm when his sledge turned over, although at the time he did not appreciate what had happened. Despite constant pain he continued travelling for another four weeks until 19 October when he began to suffer severely. Even then they diagnosed only a bad attack of rheumatism. It was nine days later, when the party returned to base, that the doctor found the fracture, which by that time was almost healed.

Soon after this Andrew himself was in trouble once more. While moving about the roof of the hut he was struck by the spinning propeller of the wind generator. The propeller shattered and he received a deep gash on the head. Between periodical relapses into unconsciousness, he instructed poor O'Sullivan in the art of stitching wounds, and under his cautious but devoted ministrations the doctor made a good recovery. The propeller was not so fortunate and had to be written off.

Russell's last journey, with Francis, Reece and O'Sullivan, began on 16 December. The party had intentions of sledging south to Pitt Point on the sea ice, and then of seeking a route up to the elusive plateau south of Russell

East Glacier. With the advancing season and higher temperatures they once again had great difficulty in travelling over the slushy surfaces of the ice in Prince Gustav Channel. Often deep in melt-water they spent hours finding even sufficient space to pitch a tent, and it took them three weeks to reach the plateau via the Aitkenhead Glacier.

There they were on a gently undulating ridge, so narrow between valleys falling away on either side that the route had continually to zig-zag within a width of little more than a mile. The ground fell away so steeply that there was no possibility of any effective surveying. Nevertheless, they were hoping to find a suitable route to the south, when the attempt was precluded by a message from Bingham ordering them back to meet the ship which was expected to reach Hope Bay during the third week in January.

They returned in much more propitious weather conditions. On their last run in they covered fifty-seven miles in twenty-four hours. The purist will not count this as a single journey for they stopped to sleep for five hours. But it was still a considerable achievement in those early days of Fids sledging.

1946/7 Miles (later Sir Miles) Clifford had taken over as the new Governor in Stanley, and for the next seven years he was to exert a great influence on the fortunes of FIDS. For the 1946/7 season he appointed John Huckle, a young wartime naval officer newly recruited to the Survey, to act as his liaison officer with Bingham, still Field Commander at Stonington.

For some anxious weeks Deception had been off the air. The first ship to reach the island was *Trepassey*, now commanded by Captain E. Burden, who arrived to find that the base had been burnt to the ground in September. The men were living as refugees in an adjacent factory building where they eked out a frugal existence. The cause of the fire was never clearly established. It could have been triggered by a hot coal falling from the stove, but it seemed more likely that drying clothes had been hung too close to the stove pipe. Only the cook was in the building when it happened, and by the time he discovered the blaze the whole corner of the room was in flames already out of control. Only a few stores had been saved.

Huckle was charged with establishing small parties in Admiralty Bay and in the British Graham Land Expedition hut on the Argentine Islands. At Admiralty Bay he put up a temporary base with timber taken from the Deception whaling station which, that year, was to be occupied only during the summer. On 7 January he arrived at the Argentine Islands to find that the old base had vanished. All that remained was an upturned dory attached to a metal ring set in concrete which had originally been inside the building. He therefore hastily erected a new hut made from material taken from Port Lockroy, and Frank Elliott was left there in temporary charge of the small party. A few weeks later much of the snow covering disappeared, and they found many bits of the old building deposited well above high water mark on Skua Island. This finally confirmed that it had been destroyed by the tidal wave reported from Lockroy.

Fitzroy had again been chartered to help with the relief. Her newly appointed Captain, F. W. ('Freddie') White, was a stocky, lively man, extrovert and always ready for a party, but very competent at his job. He became a well known and greatly admired figure to many generations of Fids, and finally an Elder Brother of Trinity House. Also on board was James Wordie, sent out on a summer visit to assess the progress being made at the bases. It was his first return to the Antarctic since his ordeal on Elephant Island in 1915, when he had been stranded with Shackleton's party for four-and-a-half months after *Endurance* had been crushed by ice.

Others in the ship included Gordon Robin, an Australian physicist, ten years later to become Director of the Scott Polar Research Institute in Cambridge, and Ray Adie, a South African geologist, aged twenty-one and seeing snow for the first time. Robin had been designated the new Base Leader to take over Cape Geddes from Choyce and initiate a radar research project. Adie had been selected with a view to gaining experience which he could use when South Africa was in a position to mount her first Antarctic expedition. Instead he was destined to become Deputy Director of the Survey.

A party of three from the Ealing Film Studios had also come out to shoot genuine polar scenes for use as background in *Scott of the Antarctic* which was then being made. Two of them were the camera team while David James (ex-Hope Bay) had returned as technical adviser. The cast were working in Norway and Switzerland, but neither location could provide the broad sweep of polar scenery needed to give the film its authentic atmosphere.

Besides *Trepassey* and *Fitzroy* a fleet of foreign ships was in the area. From Argentina two frigates, *King* and *Mureruera*, the *Chaco*, *Patagonia*, *Ministro Ezcurra* and a small whale-catcher, *Don Samuel*, all visited Deception Island. The Chilean frigate *Iquique*, followed by the transport *Angamos* arrived from Valparaiso, with the declared intention of reaffirming Chile's claim to the sector between longitude 50°W and 90°W. A Russian whale factory ship, *Slava* (previously the British *Empire Venture*), was also operating, but this was a purely commercial enterprise with no political implications, for the Soviet Union, like the United States, neither claimed nor recognised claims to any part of Antarctica.

International encounters were friendly if formal, except for the occasion when men from *Ministro Ezcurra* removed all the glass from the windows of the whaling factory at Deception, together with the mattresses and some

Signy Island hut, 1948. (G. de Q. Robin)

tools. The Naval Commander promised to return them but he was only able to discover one workshop vice, which he duly sent back. Other items quickly disappeared – doubtless overboard – as official enquiries started. It was also rumoured that a private American expedition was coming south to occupy East Base on Stonington Island. It was further rumoured, though hardly believed, that they were bringing WOMEN!

The relief proceeded with all the usual problems of plans and counter plans, and general post among base members as they either embarked for home or transferred to another station for their second year. It was suddenly considered politically inexpedient to maintain the British presence at Cape Geddes as it was close to the Argentine station on Laurie Island, so the base was closed and Robin's party was established on Signy Island instead. Unhappily after the ship had left he discovered that some of the essential parts of his equipment had not been landed. Unable even to begin his planned experiments, he sensibly turned his abilities to other useful scientific tasks.

Both ships carried stores for Hope Bay. On her way there *Fitzroy* sailed past Elephant Island, and Freddie White offered to put Wordie ashore to revisit the spot where he had spent such hard and anxious months, but he would not

'But you can be Leader next time.' (R. V. Gill)

hear of it. 'There's no time', he insisted; 'we must hasten to our rendezvous'. Had it been me, I doubt that I could have resisted it.

Frank Elliott who relieved Russell, was an expert mountaineer who had been specially selected, for the extensive sledging journeys had already shown the need for men with his kind of experience and skills. He quickly proved himself an energetic and competent field man. Only two weeks after his arrival he led a party (Francis, Adie and Choyce) on a four-week traverse when temperatures were already constantly below zero and often in the minus thirties. Later they embarked on a successful 352-mile journey to lay a depot at the Seal Nunataks, for the following season they planned an exciting project – to travel from Hope Bay right down the Antarctic Peninsula to Stonington, and for this a well stocked depot along the route was essential.

When fifteen miles from base the men were amazed to see 'Captain' 'Dainty' and nine puppies streaming out towards them across the ice of Duse Bay, having apparently followed their tracks. Allowing the visitors but a short rest, the men ordered them sternly to go home, fearing that a sledge would have to be detached to make sure it was executed. However, Captain was quick to appreciate that he had done the wrong thing in promoting the escapade, and collecting his brood he led them off the way they had come. That evening the sledge party broadcast the event to all bases, but wireless conditions were bad and no one picked them up. Hope Bay began organising anxious searches, and it was not until two days later that a very tired Captain, followed by his hungry charges, plodded wearily home from their illicit excursion.

The Chilean *Iquique* had sailed south to Marguerite Bay, and on 20 February she arrived at Stonington. The previous winter the Fids had cleaned out the American buildings, and spent much time sorting and packing specimens and valuable equipment which had been abandoned in 1940, with a view to shipping them back to the States. On arrival *Iquique*'s Captain declared himself impressed by the orderly state of the buildings, and invited all Bingham's party on board. While they were enjoying his hospitality the Chilean crew were allowed ashore. At 5 am some of them were seen lighting a fire on the floor of a hangar which the Fids had built in anticipation of receiving a small aircraft. The following day a visit to the American huts revealed a chaotic scene of boxes broken open, their contents scattered. Personal belongings, sleeping bags, blankets, tools, even welding equipment had all been removed. The sailors had enjoyed an orgy of looting.

The Fids were appalled and angry. Once more the whole area would have to be tidied up. But this did not end the problems, for on 8 March *Angamos* arrived, and sent a party of fifty men ashore for recreation. A little later the Commodore, the Captain and the First Lieutenant landed. In the American buildings they found their sailors already busy opening up the remaining unrifled boxes, chiefly medical supplies. After strong British protests the First Lieutenant was ordered to stop the pillaging, but the men appeared to take little notice of him. When the officers made some effort to prevent American material being carried back to the ship, this merely resulted in large piles of looted equipment being left scattered on the beach.

When at last all the visitors had departed the state of chaos was indescribable. Every box in the American huts had been ransacked, the floors were littered with smashed crates, torn clothing, medical drugs, chemicals, food and cooking utensils. This was the unhappy scene when, on 12 March, Commander Finn Ronne USN finally brought in the Ronne Antarctic Research Expedition to reoccupy East Base.

3

The Americans come to Stonington 1947–8

1946/7 Finn Ronne was a polar veteran. The son of a Norwegian-American who had served with Amundsen over some twenty years, he had also been a dog driver with Byrd's first Antarctic expedition in 1928. Finn had taken part in Byrd's second expedition in 1933, and later he had been second-in-command of East Base. Good looking, tough and enthusiastic, with Antarctic exploration in his blood, he was now the proud commander of his own expedition, conceived and mounted by his own efforts, despite untold difficulties and setbacks. His wife Jackie was his staunchest supporter, and had worked endlessly to raise the necessary money.

Harry Darlington, Chief Pilot and third-in-command of the party, had married only a few weeks before the expedition sailed. Ronne had allowed Darlington's bride and his own wife to sail down the South American coast in his ship, *Port of Beaumont*, to see the expedition off from Valparaiso.

There he unexpectedly decided to take his wife south and this led to much argument, some members of the crew even threatening to leave the vessel. A compromise was reached when the ship's company agreed, some very reluctantly, that two women would be preferable to one, and Ronne invited Jennie Darlington to go too. But Darlington was a naval officer of the old school, and felt strongly that women had no place on an all-male expedition. Only very unwillingly was he persuaded to agree to the arrangement. Thus, to their great surprise, Jackie Ronne and Jennie Darlington were to find themselves the first women ever to winter in Antarctica.

Ronne had many sterling polar qualities and total dedication to the task in hand, but it was his role to issue the orders, others' to obey, and he brooked no alternative suggestions. *Antarctic Conquest* (Putnam & Sons, New York, 1949), his official account of the Ronne Antarctic Research Expedition (RARE), includes the following somewhat surprising passage:

While Amundsen had investigated his men for six months before picking them for one of his trips, I hadn't time to observe the temperamental suitability of my people before choosing them. As a result I got a sharp-tongued fellow who sneered at everything, a couple of prima donnas concerned entirely with their own glory, a jolly kleptomaniac, a modest hard-working member who brooded unhappily the whole time, a spoiled youth who flew into tantrums when he couldn't have what he wanted, a brilliant individualist who insisted on doing everything his own way even when it was the wrong way, a lazy cuss who did little besides sit around and talk sex, a politician who demanded a vote on every decision. . . . So it is not suprising that we had some long-smouldering feuds, quite a few open quarrels, and a couple of cases of disciplinary action.

The picture he paints is so bizarre that it comes as a shock when he concludes: '. . . from what I've seen of explorers I know I could have done much worse in my selections. And compared to some expeditions I've been on, I assure you that our party was one big happy family.'

On arrival at Stonington Ronne strongly resented the British presence, and was understandably appalled at the state in which he found his old base. He flatly refused to believe Ken Butler's account of how it had all come about, and accused the Fids of having lived in the huts almost up to the time of his arrival. He refused to credit that they had already wintered at Stonington, on the grounds that their own hut was much too clean and well cared for to have been occupied that long! The North American Newspaper Alliance which had partly sponsored his expedition, and for which Jackie was to supply regular articles from the field, was graphically informed about the depredations committed by perfidious Albion.

Ronne immediately issued a decree that there would be NO FRATERNI-SATION between the two parties, their bases sited some 250 yards apart in a wilderness of snow, and their members speaking the same language. In *My Antarctic Honeymoon* (Frederick Muller, 1957), a racy account of her experiences as told to Jane McIlvaine, Jennie Darlington speaks delightfully of Anglo-American relations and the problems they posed. All the following excerpts in this chapter are from her book:

Arguments over the 'facilities' took time to resolve. Although the British had set up their own hutments they still maintained a territorial toehold on the American-built plumbing at the American-built camp. The Anglo-American toilet became a major issue. Following a meeting of what we termed the island's 'privy council' Major Butler admitted that his party had yet to fully abandon the privy, built by the United States government on United States territory . . . the presence of women did play a part in bringing about an amicable settlement. It was explained that twenty-one men and two women sharing facilities with eleven Britishers could . . . lead to the friction prophesied. Despite the fact that the British resented giving up what they called 'the county seat', the colonial body was unseated.

In the end, after a few cases of frostbite, but without perceptible loss of face, British sovereignty was upheld. 'On behalf of His Majesty's Government' the British Colonial Office duplicated our facilities from the architectural drawings in *The Specialist*. Thus additional American plumbing was brought to the polar regions.

Stonington Island huts in 1947, hangar in left foreground. Mt Nemesis in background.
(BAS)

The Ronne expedition had brought three aircraft and the oddest assortment of dogs ever collected into one group. Originally they had left Beaumont with forty-three huskies, but distemper had broken out during the voyage and by the time the ship reached Valparaiso half the animals were dead. In Punta Arenas Ronne had acquired anything he could find with four legs and a tail. He arrived south with the surviving huskies supplemented by sheep dogs, cross-breeds, even something described as a 'hairless whippet', which felt the cold so badly that it had to be put down.

The way of life at the two stations was in striking contrast. The Americans lived cafeteria style in their large, windowless buildings, making little attempt at homely standards of tidiness or household cleanliness, while the Ronnes remained withdrawn from the others in their own small and separate bunkhouse. The Fids, exercising the national genius for making a home from home in any uncomfortable circumstances, made gaily coloured curtains for their windows, the living space was decorated with family pictures and carefully tended bulbs brought out from England. They ate at a dinner table properly clothed and laid, and maintained a regular routine of scrubbing out the whole base each week. Every day they gathered for afternoon tea, and woe betide the cook-of-the-week unless home-made scones and cakes appeared on the table. The Base Leader took his turn at all the household chores, asking no favours.

Across the way the non-fraternisation edict was bitterly resented, and after a time gradually ignored. Surreptitious parties of Americans began creeping guiltily over the hill by the back way where they were unseen. They were as delighted as surprised by the home comforts, and soon caught on that tea was a recognised social event at four o'clock, which then became the favourite visiting hour. While the Americans quickly appreciated that the Fids presented a solid front of youthful enthusiasm and efficiency, they themselves appeared to lack a sense of combined purpose and soon divided into a number of cliques each with its own point of view. Nor did they keep their internal troubles between themselves, every opportunity being taken to relieve their stresses by discussion with the 'enemy' over the hill.

During February a FIDS party returned from a long sledge traverse during which they had been cut off from news. Jennie Darlington remembered:

Walking over the hill I came upon the FIDS tethering line. On our arrival several of the Britishers had been away . . . Now one . . . just back from the trail, was tying up his dogs. If he heard my approach the man gave no indication of it. After a quick desultory glance he turned his back on me. In that wilderness as far from conventional mores and civilisation as it was possible to be, I stood nervously debating whether I should speak or take flight. The Britisher finished tethering the dogs and began to unload his sledge. Nobody said a word. I could have been a snow statue or a mirage. Then, pushing a shovel at me, he issued a clipped command, 'Say, hold this a moment will you?' 'Certainly', I answered automatically.

At the sound of my voice the man started. He slowly straightened up from the sledge, turned, stared at me, his eyes going from the ends of my long green and white knitted stocking cap, from under which the pigtails protruded, to the tips of my regulation boots. Then his eyes widened. His mouth dropped open. Astonishment, embarrassment, and a certain confused fear flashed across his weather-beaten face. Involuntarily he reached out, grabbed the shovel, looked at it an instant, and then glanced back at me. Without another word he turned and fled to the British bunkhouse.

While I stood considering Anglo-American relations, two men emerged from the hut, my acquaintance from the tethering line escorted by Tommy Thomson, the British Auster pilot. As though stalking a she-bear, they advanced within earshot. 'No need to take on so', Thompson was saying. 'Just thought we'd have an absolute smasher waiting for you when you got back.' 'But a blonde with pigtails', gasped the man. . . . At sight of his friend's panic-stricken face he burst into peals of laughter. . . . Dr Butson's relief at finding me real was beautiful. Like a man encountering an orange trail marker after being lost, he said, 'Thank God! . . . I thought I'd gone round the bend. I do apologise. After mucking about on a glacier for several months I mistook you for a mirage'.

On 31 March *Fitzroy* and *Trepassey* arrived on the last call of the season,

'Ice Cold Katy'. (A. R. C. Butson)

bringing the new Governor to visit his parish. Some weeks earlier *Trepassey* had delivered an Auster aircraft to Stonington. The enormous crate which encased it had been floated ashore on a raft made from forty empty fuel barrels, and it was then hauled up the beach with block and tackle. Within two weeks the plane had been assembled and named 'Ice-cold Katy'. With the arrival of the two ships the parties at Stonington had between them assembled in one place the greatest fleet of transport yet seen in Graham Land – three ships and four aircraft.

Port of Beaumont was securely anchored in a sheltered spot in Back Bay; later she would become frozen-in for the winter, but the intended stay of the British ships was unexpectedly extended when, on the night of 1 April, it was discovered that *Trepassey* was on fire for'ard of the engine room. At the time Jennie Darlington and Jorge di Georgio (RARE) had by invitation treacherously rowed across to visit Captain Burden in *Fitzroy*, 'our act of treason disguised by a mantle of darkness'. Now the ship quickly moved nearer to her stricken sister to give what assistance she could. Amazed by the calm way in which the Limeys were fighting the fire, the American visitors were further overcome by the sight of:

Governor Clifford directing operations on deck wearing an outfit that was worth the trip. A cloth golf cap, muffler, tan polo coat, overshoes, mittens, and holding a pipe. All that was missing was an umbrella.

Port of Beaumont. *Roman Four Mountain in background.* *(BAS)*

Presently it was announced that both the British ships were on the rocks, and negotiations opened for American assistance from *Port of Beaumont*, both in pulling the ships off, and for all the fire extinguishers she could spare. The 'task force' despatched for the extinguishers returned with just one under his arm, but luckily by then the fire was under control, while both ships had floated free on the tide. 'The Limeys never said a word – either then or later!'

The night before the ships' second scheduled departure a storm blew up.

At one in the morning Mac noticed that the 65-mile-an-hour wind was blowing the three ships against the glacier. He awakened Ike, who ordered the *Beaumont* moved. As the ship swung to starboard, the two British ships acted accordingly. In a tangle of dragging anchors, fouled lines, and crashing gear, the only three ships in the vicinity of the Antarctic continent all decided to occupy the same spot. In the engine-room Woody lifted the after-hatch and saw the *Fitzroy*'s bow looming over him. Ducking back down the ladder, he slammed the hatch behind him. 'Holy Gee', he said, 'the ships haven't got the word on non-fraternisation. I'm getting the hell out of here.'

The British ships sailed that afternoon amid heaving anchors and sighs of relief. We had been told not to send any mail home. The reason given was that our letters would bear a British postmark. . . . Time passed. . . . The rebels became more defiant of the Commander. The cold war continued. Daily, at tea time, the iron curtain was penetrated. Now nobody bothered to take the circuitous route around the island. After a series of interviews with Major Butler, Commander Ronne finally 'agreed in principle to co-operating'. Finally the ban was lifted. People came and went openly, and the British were forced to lay additional places at their tea table as part of the daily programme.

As winter came on, both stations were planning next season's field work. Ronne, with three aircraft, intended to undertake extensive air photography for survey purposes, but for this ground control was essential, and he had only one efficient dog team. On the other hand the Fids were highly efficient sledgers, rich in experience and with the right equipment. In the friendly climate now sanctioned it was agreed that a joint Anglo-American sledge party would travel to the east side of the peninsula, and southward to the head of the Weddell Sea, and planning began.

All this time the other FIDS bases were also being relieved. During the first three months of the new year several Argentine and two Chilean ships called at Deception Island on a number of occasions which added up to twenty-three visits. Doc Andrew, who had temporarily succeeded Featherstone as Base Leader, was kept very busy dealing with so many visitors, and ensuring the delivery of all the 'protest notes'★ as a preliminary to the hospitality he then offered. At the same time he kept a wary eye on all moveable items, both at the base and the whaling factory.

Bingham had handed overall command to Major Ken Butler at Stonington, but he undertook a last tour of the whole area before going home, including a visit to the South Orkneys, where he selected the site for a new base on Signy Island at 100 feet above sea-level. This of course was to replace Cape Geddes, and in a week the hut was up, Robin moving in with three companions.

At Admiralty Bay Reece and 'Nick' Nicholson were embarked, having been landed there in January to occupy the embryo base which was to be properly built the following season. The wisdom of installing them early was vindicated when they received a visit from some Argentine officers from *Don Samuel*, their presence establishing the priority of British occupation.

Once more back at Deception, Bingham installed Huckle as the new Base Leader, going on to call at the Chilean station which had been established in Discovery Bay on Greenwich Island. Again he changed into naval uniform to go ashore and deliver the official protest, a procedure which by this time had become a tiresome irritation.

Setting out in *Trepassey*'s ancient and very shabby motorboat, he saw a large number of grinning Chileans lining the shore to receive him. At this

---

★ On Government instructions Base Leaders presented Notes of Protest to foreign base leaders or ships' captains whenever these were encountered on land or at sea in the area claimed by Britain. In 1952 this mutual practice was abandoned.

inauspicious moment sadly the engine petered out, and they were in imminent danger of being cast ingloriously ashore among the jostling boulders of brash ice along the beach. Frantic efforts to re-start it in time to prevent an ignominious rescue by the enemy succeeded in the nick of time, and they achieved some semblance of a dignified landing.

Then the language barrier provided insuperable difficulties, for Bingham, in his non-Spanish, failed utterly to discover the Chilean Base Leader's name. At last Commander Kopaitic relented. He smiled and said helpfully in excellent English, 'May I make it easier for you by suggesting that you use my second name, which is O'Neal'! The visit was protracted and friendly, Bingham observing with interest that the base boasted five live sheep destined to provide fresh meat during the coming winter.

So ended the 1946/7 season as the ships returned to Stanley.

1947   With the descent of winter the bases settled down with some relief to their scientific work and, at the travelling stations, to preparations for their spring journeys. At Hope Bay Elliott was drawing up detailed plans for the 600-mile traverse along the east coast of the peninsula to Stonington. This would be the first time that anyone had travelled south of Cape Disappointment, which Nordenskjöld reached in 1902.

At Stonington Ronne and Butler were refining the details of the Anglo-American traverse still further southwards along the east coast. It would be over two months before either project could be set in motion, and meanwhile Ronne was anxious to establish meteorologists at 5,600 feet on the plateau, to assist his flying programme later in the year.

To this end, on 15 July he set out with a party of five, including Peterson and Dodson chosen to be the first two observers. In two days they had set up the little camp, but a five-day blizzard with winds gusting to ninety knots delayed Ronne's return to base. When he finally got back he learnt that there had been only one wireless contact with the campers, followed by silence. Anxiety grew as the base operator made continual unsuccessful efforts to get through.

For four days bad weather precluded all flying, but as soon as he could take off Darlington flew up to the camp. There was nowhere he could land but he buzzed the tent half-a-dozen times without eliciting a response. That night the Americans were entertaining some Fids at their weekly film show when Dodson, white and frozen, burst into the hut gasping, 'Pete's down a crevasse'. Gulping down boiling coffee he blurted out his story between chattering teeth.

They had not been able to make their wireless work, their tent had begun to rip to pieces in the high winds, and so on the 25th, during their first spell of reasonable weather, they had started back for base. They travelled unroped and trailing their skis, not wearing them. About eight miles from home Peterson suddenly disappeared leaving a gaping hole. Dodson could hear him calling but was unable to reach him, even with a rope nearly 120 feet long. He had then raced for help as fast as he could.

Following John Tonkin's accident the previous year, the Fids had given much thought to rescue techniques and emergency gear was kept ready in the front porch. Butler was quick to offer assistance, and the Americans thankful to accept it. Within an hour thirteen men, including the doctor from each base, and two teams of FIDS dogs left with Dodson as guide. But on arrival at the scene of the accident, even in the dark it was only too clear that they must hunt in an area riddled by dangerous crevasses.

Roped together in groups, they swept the surface by torchlight but it took three hours before they at last found the hole. Both doctors were sure that by this time Peterson was dead, but each of them volunteered to go down. Butson was chosen as the smallest man present, while Freeman ran a rope through a block beneath a sledge straddling the yawning gap.

Butson asked, 'If I find him dead, what shall I do with the body?' The direct question, breaking into the midst of the silent men grouped about the chasm, brought home the full extent of the tragedy. Commander Ronne decided that the body would be left there until Pete's parents were notified. Then, if possible, the matter would be handled according to their instruction. 'Righto', said Butson, 'Lower away.'

At 120 feet he found Peterson, head downwards jammed between the icy walls, with his rucksack lying on the back of his neck.

Everybody waited, scarcely daring to breathe. Dark bearded figures, dogs and sledges clustered around a hole in the white wilderness. Then came the unbelievable words, 'He's alive'. Butson became brisk. . . . 'Pass me down another line. Put a loop in the end for a harness.' Again a long wait. Then the lowered lines quivered. 'Pull.' The men pulled. Nothing happened. Their boots slid in the snow. Their breath shortened to gasps. Pete was so tightly wedged . . . that the doctor had to untie the knot in the line . . . wind the rope around Pete's body, and retie the knot. Again the men pulled. Suddenly, like a cork yanked from a bottle, Pete was jerked free. Foot by foot the rope returned to the surface. . . . Pete's head rose. . . . In the dimness the streakes of frozen blood from the scratches criss-crossing his face gave him a ghastly appearance. Harry [Darlington] caught his rigid body.

Peterson had been down there twelve hours. While the doctors tended him in a warmed tent, the other men stamped about outside for the rest of the night to preserve their circulation. No one wanted to pick a way back through the crevasses until daylight.

In the morning Peterson and Dodson, both well wrapped up, were brought back to base on sledges. Peterson confessed that he had not expected to live, but his relief on hearing the searchers tramping about on top was somewhat tempered by overhearing the conversation regarding the disposal of his body.

They also planned a major geological trip, the route to lead south on the west side of the Antarctic Peninsula to Cape Jeremy, then down George VI Sound. This party consisted of three Americans, Bob Nichols, Bob Dodson and Art Owen, with Kevin Walton from FIDS who would be the only one with sledging experience. On 30 August they set out, Walton taking his own dog team, the seven 'Orange Bastards,' and FIDS equipment, while the Americans drove a fifteen-dog team and used their own gear. It was intended that Tonkin (FIDS) and Nelson McClary (RARE) should support them for the first ten days, and later a RARE Weasel (an ex-wartime tracked vehicle) would follow up with additional supplies.

This journey was doomed to failure from the beginning. First, one of Tonkin's dogs, essential for the coming east coast journey in which he was also to take part, was badly injured in a fight and he was forced to turn back on the second day. Then it became apparent that the untrained RARE dogs were not hauling efficiently and the single-skinned American tent was bitterly cold in driving winds. Both dog and man pemmican proved unsuitable, and the party itself recognised that it was not an efficient unit.

Contrary to British advice, but to meet Ronne's plan for the season's air support programme, they had started too early. In any event they found themselves travelling on an ever narrowing belt of fast ice and, with an offshore wind, there was imminent danger of the whole party being driven out to sea. Also, conditions were quite unsuitable for the Weasel waiting to follow them south. Reporting their predicament, they went off the air before a reply could be received, and turned back. So ended the abortive west coast journey which had been planned to cover 1,400 miles.

1947/8   A month later Nichols and Dodson made a shorter trip to the northern end of George VI Sound. This time they used FIDS tents and sledges, and the dogs were better trained. The result was a successful and useful geological reconnaissance lasting ninety days.

The southern journey along the east coast was undertaken by two Americans and two Fids, using FIDS dog teams and equipment, and supported by American aircraft. The planes also carried out the air photography of the area, for which the sledgers supplied ground control.

Three main depots had to be laid, one on the plateau, another at Cape Keeler and a third near Mount Tricorn. The first of these was established by 10 September, supplies being flown in by Tommy Thomson in 'Ice-cold Katy', and Chuck Adams flying the American Norseman. On his last sortie Adams nearly lost his life when trying to break out the skis of his machine, for suddenly he slipped and fell into the turning propeller. By enormous good fortune he suffered only a two-inch cut in his scalp and a nasty headache, and was still able to fly the aircraft back to base. Perhaps he is the only man ever to have survived being struck on the head by a turning propeller.

The Cape Keeler depot was to be put in 150 miles from Stonington by 'Ice-cold Katy', again flying in company with the Norseman. The arrangement was for the Auster to land first to lay out a strip with flags and flares for the larger load-carrying plane. On 15 September Ronne decided the weather was good, and told Butler that the Norseman would be ready to fly 'in a few minutes'. Twenty minutes later 'Ice-cold Katy' took off, and climbing high Thomson could see that the far side of the peninsula was cloud-free. Since he was flying the slower aircraft, he decided to go on to Cape Keeler without waiting for the Americans, where he came down and marked out a landing strip.

The Norseman did not, in fact, take off for nearly three hours, and returned the same evening having failed to see either the Auster or the flares lit for it by the Fids. But that night the Auster did not return, and the notorious 'fumigator' began to blow. Anxious as they all now became, it was two days before conditions eased up to allow an air search.

The Americans used every possible opportunity to fly, and to aid the search a wireless station and a fuel depot was established on the east coast. No one found any trace of the Auster for four days, but on the 22nd Jim Lassiter, flying back to base along the west coast, suddenly saw three dark specks moving slowly across the sea ice. Landing to investigate, he found Thomson and his passengers, Freeman and Bernard Stonehouse, walking home, hauling the Auster's petrol tank as a sledge on which to carry their pitifully few belongings.

They were tired and very hungry, but otherwise unharmed. It transpired that when the Norseman had failed to rendezvous they had waited an hour and then decided to return to base. The down-draught from the mountains had forced Thomson to cross the plateau at a lower elevation further south, and by the time they reached the sea ice on the west coast it was almost dark and snowing hard. With no hope of reaching base, Thomson had to land. In the poor visibility a ski hit a protruding lump of ice and 'Ice-cold Kay' turned over on her back.

Miraculously unhurt, the men picked themselves up and recovered their emergency gear from the plane, then camped for the night. In the following days of bad weather they could only march three of four miles each day, sleeping three in a two-man tent, sharing in turn one sleeping bag, and eking out their food by rationing themselves to 500 calories a day. The dedicated flying by the Americans in extreme conditions had saved them, but it had been an uncomfortably close shave.

On 9 October the sledge party set out, their first task on reaching the ice shelf on the east side of the peninsula being to lay a small depot requested by Elliott from Hope Bay. This was to support the last leg of the Hope Bay–Stonington traverse, and at Hope Bay news that the depot was in place was anxiously awaited, for the long journey down the coast could not start until these final supplies were ensured. After many lie-ups in driving blizzards, and the replacement by air of two Americans because one had a broken collar bone and the other knee trouble, the depot was duly put down.

The sledgers – Mason and Butson (FIDS) with Owen and Wood (RARE) – set course south through unknown country towards Cape Keeler, where Butler flew in to replace Butson, and Walter Smith took over from Wood. On their final outward leg they reached Nantucket Inlet at 74°30′S and then turned home. By the time they arrived back at Stonington on 21 January 1948 they had covered 1,196 miles in 105 days. This journey demonstrated the value of combined air and ground operations and, more important, Ronne's aircraft had photographed the new coastline, while Mason had provided at least a skeleton ground control for the area.

By September preparations for the long awaited Hope Bay–Stonington traverse were in full swing. Hope Bay sledgers would rendezvous with a party from Stonington sent out to meet them at Three Slice Nunatak, some 350 miles to the south, and together they would cross the peninsula on the final leg. It was the first journey between two bases, and originally the final stages were to have been observed from 'Ice-cold Katy', now sadly a tangled heap on the sea ice.

The day appointed for departure was 17 October, but scarcely were the sledges loaded than the wind rose to gale force and lasted for forty-eight hours. Two days later they tried again. Elliott, Francis, Choyce and Adie were up early, and ready to leave by nine o'clock, when the exhuberant leading team suddenly turned of their own accord and charged down the hill. Other means having failed to stop their wild career, Elliott turned the sledge over, whereupon the 'cowcatcher' buried itself in the snow and broke. Three hours later they were once more ready to start.

Their troubles were only beginning. Four days out and north of Cape Longing, they discovered that five bridges on two of the new sledges had broken. So perforce leaving their main loads, they returned to base for repairs. More bad weather then prevented a fresh start until the 27th, by which time abnormally high temperatures had produced large areas of melt water all over the ice in Prince Gustav Channel.

Often they were hard put to find a dry camp site and had to seek raised snow drifts in the lee of icebergs. Then followed a period of tremendous winds blowing down from the high plateau. On occasion they had the

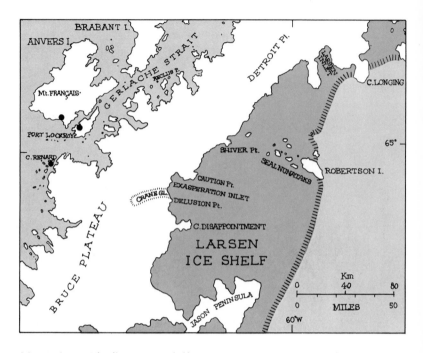

Map 3. Anvers Island/Larsen Ice Shelf area

remarkable experience of being peppered with agglomerations of ice crystals up to an inch in diameter. Many were heavy enough to hurt both men and dogs, and they were relieved to clear the area.

Picking up the Seal Nunataks depot they found themselves travelling across water pools thinly frozen over. The ice bore the weight of dogs, but the drivers and their sledges were hauled through the sludgy mixture of snow and water. At one point Adie's leader, 'Joy', broke through into a deep pool and was totally exhausted by the time he was able to retrieve her.

However, that evening as they made camp, she produced a record fourteen puppies, and next day was working again apparently quite unaffected and full of beans.

By now they were in country new to Fids. Only Nordenskjöld had penetrated further south and the pressures began to mount. Ten days behind schedule, and facing the problems of an unknown route, it was necessary to push on as quickly as possible which, of course, militated against the interests of both the survey and geological work. Indeed, these themselves were incompatible, for Adie needed to reach the rocks along the coast, which often proved to be inaccessible when they got there, while Francis could not survey satisfactorily if he was close in under the cliffs and glaciers. The

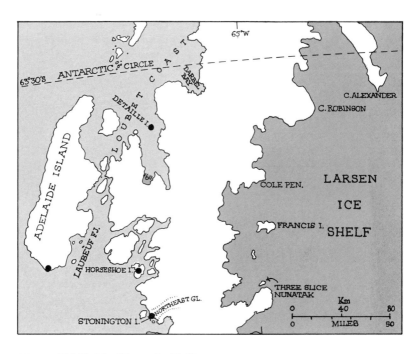

Map 4. Adelaide Island/Larsen Ice Shelf area

conflicting needs led to frustrations, especially for Elliott, who as leader had constantly to consider their rate of progress in relation to their dwindling supplies.

The names of features which now scatter the coastline – Shiver Point, Caution Point, Exasperation Inlet, Delusion Point – reflect the mood of the party. Even Cape Disappointment, Nordenskjöld's furthest south, must have seemed bitterly appropriate as they struggled on.

Nevertheless, the latter was one of the places where Adie succeeded in reaching rocks, which proved to be strikingly banded Jurassic rhyolites. In them he found quantities of fossil wood, many of the tree trunks still standing as they had been when overcome by volcanic outpourings some 165 million years ago. How lush the climate was then, before the Antarctic continent drifted into its present cold environment.

At three points, now known as the Jason, Churchill and Cole Peninsulas, heavy crevassing forced them to leave the ice shelf and climb up over the land. Beyond them they had expected a clear run to their rendezvous, where the Stonington party must have already arrived. But on the day appointed they still had fifty miles to cover.

Travelling in low, dense mist, they were surprised to find themselves climbing steadily until suddenly halted by a wide crevasse. Quite unexpectedly, they had found what is now known as Francis Island. The descent to the ice shelf posed considerable problems and took another day. The dogs had to be thrown, one by one, across the narrowest part of the crevasse, while the laden sledges were laboriously manhandled over.

Next, the descent was so steep that everything had to be lowered by rope, which went well until Adie's sledge broke away and shot off at tremendous speed. Luckily there was no crevasse at the bottom and it careered out onto the level ice without even upsetting. The only damage was an aluminium survey pole which snapped in two. Exhausted after this effort, they camped and prayed for clear weather the next day.

Meanwhile Freeman and Thomson (FIDS), with Donald MacLean (RARE) had left Stonington for Three Slice Nunatak during the second week in December. *En route* they picked up McLeod (FIDS) and di Georgio (RARE) who had spent four months manning the weather station which had been re-established on the plateau. These two had been living a troglodyte existence for the snow surface lay three feet above the top of their tent, with a labyrinth of tunnels extending all round it. All five then sledged to the rendezvous scheduled for 28 December. The appointed date arrived with no signs of the Hope Bay party, and with no communication facilities they could only sit and wait – and hope.

But two days later specks were seen moving in the distance, and soon the two groups met amidst a babel of voices and greetings. With everyone talking, and apparently no one listening, Thomson gleefully handed round a rum punch he had brought for the occasion. Choyce, not to be outdone, magically produced cigars which he had carried secretly all the way from Hope Bay. It had been a long haul, with constant bad luck, but it added up to an outstanding journey – even by Fids standards.

Five days later they could see Stonington, where a great welcome awaited them. This is how Jennie Darlington saw their approach:

When the trail party from the British base at Hope Bay arrived, I sensed the time-honoured romance and appeal of long polar journeys. That day in 1947 those of us watching, as team after team poured off the glacier, saw a sight that may never be seen again. Six dog teams and ten men who had travelled hundreds of miles exemplified an old-fashioned art that may soon belong to the polar past.

In silence broken only by the creak of the runners on snow the huskies swept down off the glacier. The men's faces were fine-drawn, gaunt, wind-burned almost to blackness. The dogs, though still galloping and gallant, were obviously tired, sinking down into the snow to sleep on arrival. Equipment was worn from hard use. Windproofs were torn and weathered.

Yet as they came down, the dogs waving their tails like plumed banners, their coats rippling like multicoloured waves against the whiteness, an awed stillness descended on us. Matched step by step by magnified blue shadows, the weary dogs, the bearded men, signified the pioneer concepts of strength, simplicity, and survival.

The journey had taken seventy-one days, and over 200 miles of new coastline had been surveyed. Everyone felt pleased. But some wondered if a ship would ever reach Stonington through the pack ice which showed absolutely no signs of breaking up. It was already January, and *Port of Beaumont* was still held fast. If relief proved impossible they would all be committed to another winter.

At East Base there was special reason for anxiety and their doctor was frantic. He had done his homework well, and brought with him drugs and instruments for every possible contingency – except the one which he knew least, and which he now faced. Jennie Darlington was expecting a baby – perhaps they would stand godfather to the very first real Antarctician.

1948

4

We go to gain a little patch . . .
1947–9

We go to gain a little patch of ground,
That hath in it no profit save the name
Shakespeare

Wordie had been my tutor at Cambridge and, in 1929, it was as a young
geologist that I had gone to East Greenland with him, my first experience of
expeditions. Though bitten by the polar bug, an opportunity in 1930 to join
an East African expedition was irresistible. During the next ten years I was
first a member and later the leader of four African expeditions, and my
disappointment at missing Gino Watkins' Arctic Air Route Expedition and
the British Graham Land Expedition had faded. War service filled the next
six years, and when it ended I spent a further year in Germany in Military
Government.

After such a time lapse, and under rapidly changing conditions, there
seemed to be little immediate opportunity to go back to African work, so on
returning home in 1947 and hearing about FIDS, I told Wordie I would like to
be considered for a geological post. He was totally discouraging; 'You were
making your way in African work, you should stick to it', he counselled. But
1947 undeterred, I applied to FIDS and was called for interview in June.

Bingham was home again, and busily engaged once more in finding new
recruits and stores to send south next season. He was a member of the
Selection Board I faced at the Colonial Office, as was Juxton Barton, who
had been Colonial Secretary in Kenya when I worked there. My interview
concluded, I walked out hopefully, but was totally astonished to be called
back within minutes and offered command of the Survey. I think my age,
already thirty-nine, and my previous expedition experience were considered
relevant factors.

Accepting the post with alacrity, I set about trying to discover the
whereabouts of the scientific specimens already collected by Fids. They
seemed to be scattered throughout the country, from Glasgow to the

Natural History Museum in London. Apart from this I received no directive about the general programme, nor the work to be done from Stonington where I was to be based. It was indicated that as much survey, geology and meteorology as possible should be done, and to this end I began collecting and reading past scientific papers, but soon discovered that very little had been published about TABARIN or FIDS. The upshot of this was that we went into the field with virtually a blank cheque to plan our own programme.

When visiting Stonington the previous season, Governor Clifford had seen Ronne's *Port of Beaumont*, and had agreed with Bingham and Captain Burden that a similar kind of vessel was badly needed for FIDS operations. His report to the Colonial Office was followed up, and by August Wordie was in the United States searching for one. He finally found a boom defence ship, then designated AN-76, which had been returned to the American Navy under the lease-lend agreement, having served during the war as HMS *Pretext*. Built of pitch pine, she displaced 1,015 tons, had a length of 194 feet, beam 34 feet, and draft 14 feet. Her twin diesel-electric engines developed 1,200 horse power, giving a service speed of 12 knots.

By the end of October she was in London and refitting under the auspices of the Crown Agents, a task which took considerably longer than expected and during which, for some reason, I was never allowed to go near her. On 15 December Mrs Creech Jones, wife of the Colonial Secretary, re-named her *John Biscoe* in honour of an Enderby Brothers' sealing skipper who circumnavigated the Antarctic continent and annexed Graham Land for the Crown in 1832.

Sailing day was 18 December, and I went aboard at Tilbury to a scene so chaotic that it is impossible to describe it adequately. It was half-past four, and dark. Crates, bales, half-opened boxes and miscellaneous paraphernalia of every kind strewed the decks, while the newly arrived Fids struggled with their luggage, seeking helplessly for somewhere to put it down. To add to the confusion, it was an hour before the keys to the quarters aft could be found, which left the hopeful occupants wandering frustratedly about the ship cursing. None of us had met before, and I wondered how many might already be having second thoughts. When at last the keys were produced, we drew lots for the bunks.

There was one double cabin, the rest were to sleep on canvas strips slung in three tiers between steel uprights extending from deck to deckhead. Eighteen men occupied one closely packed space amidships, the remaining seven crawled into a similarly equipped cubby-hole entered through a hatch on the after deck.

Hundreds of cases, ship's stores and FIDS cargo all jumbled together regardless of whether it was for the hold or deck stowage, had been dumped aboard by the dockers. Since they were paid by the ton, they cared little whether things were properly stowed. The sight was so appalling that in the evening some of the crew suddenly jumped ship, convinced that she would turn over once we left the river.

Without a full complement the Board of Trade refused us permission to sail, so the Captain hastily went ashore and press-ganged a number of unlikely-looking characters standing about on the dockside, including a Latvian and a very large, fierce-looking Estonian – of whom more later.

On 20 December, by the grace of God and only five weeks later than originally hoped, we finally sailed down river and the Fids set to stowing the mountain of deck cargo. Our most dangerous job was extracting twenty-five crates of sulphuric acid from the aeroplane cases on the for'ard hatch. These had been stacked on their sides, upside down, even on edge balanced precariously among other boxes. We very gingerly moved them aft where, if any broke, acid would not, we hoped, be sprayed all over the ship by the wind.

Biscoe was not a passenger ship, so we were all officially signed on as 'supernumeraries' and quickly discovered the implications of this. As soon as some semblance of order was achieved and the decks scrubbed down, we began to play a regular part in the ship's routine. Daily I posted names for working parties in every department: to work in the galley, four men; bos'n's party, four men; Second Officer's watch, two; watchkeepers, six; catering assistant, one; cleaning wash-place, two. So it went, and throughout the voyage the unofficial crew played their part in running the ship – only too often struggling against sea sickness as well.

We hardly ever saw the Captain. The first evening he invited me to his quarters for a very stiff drink, assuring me that of course he never took a drop at sea, but this was only the river wasn't it? I reeled out of his cabin to make friends with the First Officer who turned out to be a very small and very charming Irish peer, Lord H. He had a large bald head, and a happy knack of handling men which was to surprise us all. He ran his polyglot and somewhat ruffianly ship's company with consummate tact and soft words, always ready to turn away wrath and soothe down the drunks or the wild ones.

Of the twenty-seven Fids who made this first voyage, only Doc Slessor (ex-Stonington) had had Antarctic experience. He had volunteered to come south for the trip to initiate me into my new responsibilities, and was indeed a great strength. He was a sturdy, active man, who always found something that needed doing and then did it. His equable temperament suited admirably our rather strange conditions. Purposeful, sensible, helpful, never did he overplay his hand.

Our first port of call was St Vincent in the Cape Verde Islands, where we needed water and fuel. Needless to say we arrived on New Year's Eve, to be told that nothing could be done for us for twenty-four hours. So both the crew and the Fids were given shore leave, departing exhuberantly in small boats to share local festivities. Perfect peace descended on the ship, where Slessor and I settled down to some quiet fishing over the stern. The officers, too, were ashore, only the Third condemned to sit out the jollifications in his lonely cabin.

It was a beautiful, warm, moonlit night, but presently he was disturbed from his contemplations by the totally unexpected arrival of the water boat, shortly followed by the oil barge. The latter managed to discharge a large quantity of diesel fuel onto the deck, which no one noticed in the darkness. Soon the shouting died away and once more peace reigned. Some time later we observed the bos'n and members of the crew returning – and suddenly there was an empty boat secured alongside.

Concerned to protect the belongings of those ashore, Slessor and I dashed down the companion way, to hear loud laughter and female voices in the bos'n's quarters. Hastily summoning the Third Officer we opened the door, whereupon a number of black people rushed out and up to the deck. A very large woman suddenly decided she would not leave after all, but remained clinging like a limpet to the companion way rails, while the Third Officer pushed her broad backside upwards with all his might. Seeing that he was getting nowhere, I added a judicious judo grip, and up she went – straight into the bum boat. As the visitors rowed away, we began the arguments with a very drunk bos'n who clearly resented our stuffy, moralistic attitudes. We put him to bed, still swearing volubly.

So back to our fishing – but not for long. Soon we were interrupted by the arrival of a sailor who reported that we had now acquired a Canadian stowaway, and what should he do? The man turned out to be a tough-looking character, very drunk, very belligerent and demanding a job. Telling him that regretfully we had no vacancies just then, I realised that I was going to find myself in a fight fairly soon, so began edging him towards the rail.

Suddenly, out of the dark, little Lord H appeared. Immediately grasping the situation, he smiled warmly, shook our unwelcome visitor by the hand, and linking arms affectionately he led him gently back to the gangway. 'My dear fellow, how really nice to see you! Of course it isn't quite the moment to talk about jobs. But you get some sleep now and come back to see us in the morning. I'll see what can be done.' Totally confused by this friendly approach, the obstreperous Canadian went meekly over the side and disappeared in a rowing boat.

This story had sequels, for when we sailed next day we saw a great commotion going on on the top deck of an anchored American freighter, towering over us as we put to sea. Four men were swinging a body which they finally hurled expertly into space where, turning over and over, it fell fifty feet into the water with a mighty splash. It was our friend, trying his luck with less courteous hosts.

The final sequel came seven years later, when I was again in St Vincent, in MV *Theron* carrying the Trans-Antarctic Expedition south. A stately bum boat rowed out ceremoniously, and sitting proudly in the stern, sheltered by a gigantic umbrella and smoking a cigar, was our Canadian stowaway. He had remained in the islands after all, and was now the prosperous boss of all the bum boats trading in the harbour.

But to get back to New Year's Eve. Slessor and I returned to our fishing lines. Presently a boatload of happy Fids arrived out of the darkness, singing gently. As they clambered nimbly enough up the side of the ship and over the rail, each in turn met the unseen oil slicks deposited earlier. The deck was suddenly a mass of very surprised, slimy figures, picking themselves up off their hands and knees, now deeply suspicious of the potent qualities of the hooch they had enjoyed ashore.

Hardly had peace been restored than the air was shattered by blast after blast on the ship's siren – the New Year had arrived. The other nine ships in the harbour all joined in, vociferously sounding off on their hooters, firing rockets or Very pistols, and generally making the night hideous. *Biscoe's* siren may have been weaker than some, but our searchlights, signalling lamps and rockets were more spectacular. The cacophony brought out all the Fids, and assembling on the monkey island we sang *Auld Lang Syne*, which swelled dramatically across the suddenly quiet and astounded harbour.

Thereafter activity languished until about three o'clock, when the Captain returned with a party of visitors, all in fancy-dress. As the Mate went to receive him over the side, someone pressed the fire alarm bell which set off enough noise to wake the town. Unfortunately no one knew where to turn it off. Endless minutes passed and still *John Biscoe* made her presence felt, while frantic figures sped all over the ship turning or pressing every little knob and switch. The control was finally discovered on the aft mess deck and suddenly we could talk again. It had been quite a night – and Slessor and I had not even one fish to show for it.

Next morning the last of our supplies came aboard and we sailed for Montevideo. Now our daily chores included painting the entire superstructure a pale blue-grey, a very great improvement. For entertainment we organised lectures and discussions, sessions of *Twenty Questions*, a ship's concert and a 'Crossing the Line' ceremony.

Once the engines stopped, and we found the ship turning in a swirling circle. The steering gear had failed. For different reasons this kept happening

1 RRS John Biscoe *at old Grytviken whaling station, summer. (C. J. Gilbert)*

2 *Millerand Island seen from Stonington Island. (M. R. A. Thompson)*
3 *Recovering men who fell with collapse of ice cliff – no wet feet! (V. E. Fuchs)*

all day, first it was a fuse, then twice because of burnt out contacts, and finally because a small metal spring one inch long broke – and of course there was no spare. This could have been bought anywhere for a penny, but now we had to set to and make one. It seemed ridiculous that the entire ship was controlled by so cheap and insignificant a vital part.

The night before we reached the River Plate I was sleeping on deck and was suddenly woken by someone falling over my bedding. Rubbing my eyes I was astonished to find that our Estonian greaser was apparently chasing the ship's electrician with a large carving knife. Hastily setting off in pursuit, I lost him in the dark so rushed off to find the First Officer. As I was speaking to him the huge Estonian appeared, still brandishing his weapon and towering menacingly over little Lord H.

'He calling me Estonian bastard', he shouted. 'I kill him'.

With instant aplomb Lord H mastered the situation.

'But my dear old chap', he smiled, 'you *are* an Estonian bastard. In England that is a term of endearment which we only use to our best friends. What more can he say to you?'

Confused by this direct and innocent approach, the greaser wavered long enough to be led quietly away and to bed. The First Officer had won again.

But not for long. A few hours later our trouble maker was on the rampage once more, and this time he had to be forcibly restrained until we reached harbour. Here he was handed over to the local police, and when last I saw him he was spread-eagled face downwards, being carried away by the gendarmerie, two on his arms, two to his legs, while a splendid officer with drawn sword marched solemnly ahead.

On 25 January 1948 we arrived in Stanley. The Governor himself was away, but the ship was to be officially welcomed by Mrs Clifford, who was waiting as we moved slowly in. Unfortunately, in coming alongside we ran hard and fast onto the mud, and despite agonised cries of 'Hard-a-port' and 'Hard-a-starboard' from the bridge, the ship remained stuck just twelve feet from the end of the jetty. In the end a single plank was rather shamefacedly rigged across the intervening water, and the Governor's lady bravely made an assisted, but rather perilous passage on board. Thus, a little ignominiously, ended the first voyage of the *John Biscoe*.

1947/8   Six days were spent in Stanley sorting cargo and refuelling, then we sailed for Deception in violent, steep seas. So violent were they that abreast of Pembroke Lighthouse the Captain decided to turn back and shelter in Sparrow Cove, beside the hulk of Brunel's *Great Britain* which had been beached there for many years. As we came about *Biscoe* almost lost steerage way and, wallowing in the troughs, she rolled through more than ninety degrees. For some minutes the crashing of crockery and everything else that

Admiralty Bay huts in 1948. Flagstaff Hill in background. (BAS)

could move echoed round the ship. Even the normally stable pots and pans were dislodged and careered round the galley, leaving the cook wading about in a boiling swill of gravy, meat and vegetables.

When at last we were entering the shelter of the cove a naval tanker, HMS *Gold Ranger*, passed us coming in. She tersely signalled, 'Windy, what?' Somewhat shamed by this, we at least spent a comfortable night, and sailed again in reduced seas next morning.

At Deception we found the Governor, taking passage in HMS *Snipe* for a cruise round his territory. As we began unloading stores, she sailed for Signy and South Georgia. Our first task was to build a raft on which to land our de Havilland Hornet Moth (a replacement for 'Ice-cold Katy'), since its two large crates prevented access to the hold. We still lacked skis for the plane but hoped they would arrive from Canada. Some time later the case apparently containing them was brought in by *Snipe*, on her second cruise, but when opened it proved to be full of unwanted stove pipes. We never did discover what had happened but being useless without skis, the crated Hornet Moth remained hauled up on the beach until it was taken back to Stanley a year later.

Unloading completed, *Biscoe* sailed for Signy to embark Robin and his men, leaving behind Dick Laws, the new Base Leader, to winter with Ralph Lenton and Derek Maling. All three were new to the Antarctic, but in the next two years each made a significant contribution to FIDS work. Laws was assiduous in his study of the elephant seal population, which resulted in monographs which have become standard works on the subject. Maling, although the meteorological observer, also made a preliminary survey of the island, while Lenton proved himself invaluable. Officially the wireless operator, he was an excellent cook and a very competent carpenter. In later years he was reappointed to take charge of building at a number of stations.

Our next call was at Admiralty Bay, King George Island, where we built a permanent base in place of the temporary shanty set up the previous season. There we found a small Argentine hut about twelve feet long, erected just eighty feet from ours and occupied by four men. They proved friendly enough, but we swapped the customary Protest Notes before the social exchanges could begin. In three days our new station was sufficiently weatherproof for occupation, and we left Eric Platt with four companions to complete the interior and winter there.

Back at Deception I received a message from Butler suggesting that we make for ice-bound Stonington with all possible speed. This would enable us to take advantage of the channel which two American icebreakers were then cutting in order to free *Port of Beaumont* and enable the Ronne expedition to go home; Mrs Darlington was not to make Antarctic history after all. Hastily adjusting our plans, we remained at Deception only long enough to take on water.

On arrival we had secured alongside an Argentine mine-layer which was also watering from our well, sunk into ground warmed by volcanic heat. During this operation there was a sudden flash, followed by a loud explosion near an old wooden whaling barge lying 300 yards along the beach. This was loaded with boxes of black powder once used by the whalers. It transpired that two Argentine sailors had been amusing themselves by extracting some of the explosives and setting it alight. Both were badly burned about the face and one man's clothes caught fire. He rushed into the sea, which extinguished the flames, but the cold was an additional shock on top of the explosion. Their ship carried no doctor but fortunately in *Biscoe* we then had three – Slessor, Bill Sladen destined for Hope Bay, and David Dalgliesh coming to Stonington with me – and all went over to treat the injured men.

Meanwhile the American icebreakers had broken through to Stonington, and another message from Butler was urging us to hasten. We sailed that evening, but hardly had we cleared Deception than the Captain arrived in my cabin to enquire if by chance I happened to have any charts of the Antarctic Peninsula area? Not having regarded this as my part of the ship, I

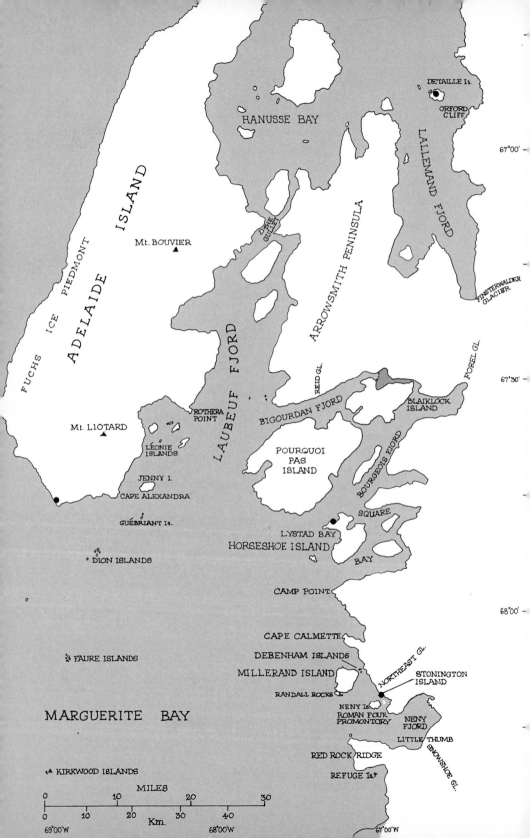

HANUSSE BAY

DETAILLE Is.

ORFORD CLIFF

LALLEMAND FJORD

67°00'

ADELAIDE ISLAND

FUCHS ICE PIEDMONT

Mt. BOUVIER ▲

ARROWSMITH PENINSULA

FINSTERWALDER GLACIER

THE GULLET

FOREL GL.

67°30'

Mt. LIOTARD ▲

ROTHERA POINT

LAUBEUF FJORD

REID GL.

BIGOURDAN FJORD

BLAIKLOCK ISLAND

LÉONIE ISLANDS

POURQUOI PAS ISLAND

BOURGEOIS FJORD

JENNY I.

CAPE ALEXANDRA

SQUARE

GUÉBRIANT Is.

LYSTAD BAY

BAY

HORSESHOE ISLAND

DION ISLANDS

CAMP POINT

68°00'

CAPE CALMETTE

FAURE ISLANDS

DEBENHAM ISLANDS

MILLERAND ISLAND

NORTHEAST GL.

STONINGTON ISLAND

MARGUERITE BAY

RANDALL ROCKS

NENY Is.

ROMAN FOUR PROMONTORY

NENY FJORD

LITTLE THUMB

SNOWSHOE GL.

RED ROCK RIDGE

KIRKWOOD ISLANDS

REFUGE Is.

MILES

0   10   20   30

0   10   20   30   40

Km.

69°00'W   68°00'W   67°00'W

shook my head in appalled dismay – apparently he had forgotten to provide himself with anything south of latitude 63°S. Something had to be done fast. We scoured our luggage until someone finally dug out a school atlas, while I found some small-scale maps of the *land* areas. With only these rudimentary aids, Second Officer Brown was to bring us safely through ice and shoals to Marguerite Bay.

On 21 February we arrived in the bay, having been hindered by heavy ice off Adelaide Island. *Port of Beaumont* had been released, and was lying alongside the icebreaker *Burton Island* at the Faure Islands, together with her sister ship *Edisto*. *Biscoe* in turn secured to *Beaumont*, handed over long-awaited mail to the American ships, and I went aboard to meet Ronne's outgoing party.

That evening dozens of curious American sailors invaded our little ship. Many of them were anxious to be on their way home, one in particular complaining bitterly at the length of their voyage. He turned out to be *Burton Island*'s postman. He hadn't had a goddam letter to deliver for three months, and was being kidded daily by his companions for his failure to produce non-existent mail.

Next day we arrived at the channel cut through to Stonington Island, but discovered it filled with huge blocks of impenetrable ice already refrozen. As the United States were determined not to get involved in national disputes, the American ships were officially forbidden to assist us. But *Burton Island* had a friendly Captain who now found occasion to return to Stonington on his own affairs, and we most gratefully fell in behind him.

That evening we anchored in Back Bay, working frantically throughout the night to get our sixty-five tons of stores onto the sea ice by 6 am, which was as long as *Burton Island* could convincingly remain. So it was in a great hurry that I took over from Butler, who was destined to take charge of the FIDS office in Stanley, where he worked directly to the Governor. As we waved goodbye and watched *Biscoe* go, I noticed a fringe of splintered wood floating around her water line, splinters up to two feet long weaving gently like seaweed along the length of her hull. This was the result of ice abrasion of the pitch pine hull which, in places, had cut in to a depth of two inches. Clearly she would require the protection of greenheart sheathing before she came south next season.

1948   At Stonington we now numbered eleven: five old hands and six newcomers. Dave Jones, Bernard Stonehouse and Terry Randall had already spent a year there, Adie had sledged down from Hope Bay, and Huckle had come with

Map 5, opposite. Northern Marguerite Bay

RRS John Biscoe *(originally* HMS Pretext*) at the Argentine Islands. (BAS)*

us after a year as Base Leader at Deception. As I pondered my administrative duties I felt the time was appropriate for those of us who had come from the Services to drop our rank. I circulated a message to all bases that in future men would be placed in charge of projects, journeys or the home station according to their suitability and regardless of their Service seniority. In Britain our language had by now become contaminated by our American cousins, and the 1948 relief parties had brought down the term 'radio'. So we now dropped the 'wireless' with our ranks.

For a time we continued to hope that *Biscoe* would return to Stonington with the aircraft and its skis, for the plane was to play a large part in the journeys we planned. The dogs also needed seal meat from the Argentine Islands if they were to be kept alive and healthy. Then we heard that the ship had developed engine trouble, and although the Governor once more chartered *Fitzroy* to help us, the ice situation precluded her from coming further south than Lockroy. Captain White hopefully remained there as late

Stonington Island hut 1949. (D. G. Dalgliesh)

as 9 April, when he finally signalled his inability to reach us and returned to Stanley. We were on our own for the winter.

Bad ice conditions also affected three other bases, for I had intended to supply Admiralty Bay, the Argentine Islands and Lockroy with a minimum amount of equipment from our slender stocks to enable them to do at least some travelling. This was now impossible. At Signy, Laws had planned to survey part of Coronation Island and to make an extensive elephant seal census, but without the hundred man-days' sledging rations they were to have received from us, his plans too had to be severely curtailed. Hope Bay was, of course, well supplied, and by 17 April Frank Elliott was ready to take out a party on a surveying and geological traverse in the James Ross Island area.

It was therefore doubly frustrating at Stonington to see open water to the horizon in Marguerite Bay, for without firm sea ice we had to wait in patience until after the winter before we could mount a major journey.

However, there was still much to learn at base. One day there was the dreaded cry of 'Fire', but our fortnightly practices stood up to this first test. Everyone seized extinguishers, axes and buckets of water as we tore down the smoke-filled passage to the bathroom, and in three minutes the fire was out. It had been caused by boxes and other inflammable material being pushed against the unlagged chimney pipe in the space above the ceiling.

Next Bob Spivey was caught out wearing the wrong footgear on a short trip during which the temperature dropped thirty degrees in two hours. He was severely frostbitten and nearly lost all his toes, their horrible blackened appearance remaining an anxiety for many weeks.

Huckle and I learnt another lesson after making the mile-long crossing to Neny Island in a small boat. On our return two hours later there was a flat calm and a thin slush of ice crystals was forming on the sea. The outboard motor would not start, so we rowed off in fine style for the first 200 yards. There the ice was thicker, in places over-rafted, and we were quickly in trouble. By the time we were half way across the oars would no longer break it, yet it was not strong enough to bear our weight if we left the boat. We could have been held half a mile offshore indefinitely. Standing in the bows I spent nearly two hours smashing the ice ahead with a boat hook while Huckle rowed for dear life. As we at last approached the ice foot there was much jeering and applause from our unfeeling companions, assembled on the shore and happily betting on our progress. Lesson: never go boating in low temperatures.

Alone among us I was a Cambridge man and had looked forward to listening to the Boat Race. My solicitous friends called me to the radio room where the commentator was already describing a very poor performance. Cambridge was nearly four lengths behind at Barnes Bridge. The speaker's voice was being drowned by the noise of the helicopter from which he worked, and the next thing we heard was an all too vivid description of the Cambridge boat sinking with all hands.

Suddenly realising that my consternation was not being reflected in the faces around me, I became aware that they were all grinning and that Stonehouse was missing. In fact he was perpetrating the convincing commentary in the engine room, the generator providing the very realistic helicopter noises. Having had their fun in full measure, they put the clocks back to normal and half-an-hour later we reassembled to hear the real race – in which Cambridge won by five lengths. Oddly enough the real helicopter was grounded by engine trouble.

Every Fid who has served at a sledging base will spend the rest of his life recounting his dog stories, and on arrival a first priority is for the new men to learn to drive a team. I was particularly fortunate at Stonington to have Adie

4 *Break-up of sea ice at Signy Island with a Great Skua in foreground.*
(D. D. Wynn-Williams)
5 *Mount Edgell, Palmer Land (left), with Alexander Island in far distance.*
(C. Swithinbank)
6 *(Overleaf) Shackleton's Cross at King Edward Point, South Georgia. (C. J. Gilbert)*

7 *and* 8 *'Krill' (Euphorbia superba) the food of whales, seals and birds; a potential source of protein for man. (C. J. Gilbert)*

as my instructor. 'Darkie' was leader of the team I took over, and I shall never forget his friendship and intelligent cooperation. Huskies are exuberant, rumbustious animals who fight each other with or without provocation, just for fun. However, they love humans and are always eager to be petted, fondled and made much of. Some are stupid but work hard, with their heads well down but never seeing the crevasses into which they inevitably fall, others are lazy and quickly learn to keep their traces just taut enough to fool an unsuspecting driver that they are pulling their weight. All are great characters, but only a few are sufficiently intelligent to use their wits, break trail, and keep a true course in a wilderness where there are no landmarks. These become the team leaders, not only willing and sensitive to a driver's commands, but ever alert and ready to look after both him and the team when, in his ignorance, he gives a wrong one.

When sledging parties are in the field, one of the first things drivers have to come to terms with is the ritual of the Evening Chorus. After camp is made and the dogs have been fed, one of them – usually a bitch – will point her nose to the sky and give a long-drawn-out h-o-w-l, which is immediately taken up by all the teams. They sit, every nose pointing upwards, and 'sing' in unison. Suddenly it stops, then every ear is pricked awaiting an answer. The silence persists for about half a minute before they put on a repeat performance, which is again followed by an expectant pause. When yet another reprise fails to produce results they finally give up, and curling into balls the teams sleep.

However, should another party be working in the same area and happen to make camp within a radius of, say, five to six miles, and there is no wind to drown sounds, it is a different story. As the first chorus dies away it will elicit an immediate response from 'over the hill', and when this in turn ends, the original teams will again take up the refrain. Chorus follows chorus, each 'silent' interval yielding a distant reply, and very soon exasperated drivers at both ends will be adding their infuriated cries to the general cacophony – but with no effect at all! The alternating howling will continue until at last the dogs themselves decide that enough is enough.

In my eyes, as a leading dog Darkie was unique. He did not give friendship lightly and he never permitted liberties. Anyone trying to pet or fondle him was put in his place with dignity. When, after many months of travelling together, he had taught me many lessons and saved me from disaster more than once, he would finally acknowledge the affection between us by standing quietly against my leg, pressing it gently and perhaps allowing me to stroke his ears – never more than this, and it was always a very private arrangement between us.

In every team there are two special dogs – the leader and the King Dog. The leader is appointed by the driver (and may sometimes be a bitch), but the

King Dog has won his position by strength and cunning. Only rarely will another challenge him, and then only when he thinks he has a chance to oust him from the supreme position.

It is obviously preferable to have a leader who is also the King Dog, for when the driver calls a halt the leader stops, and none will dare to over-run him. If the King Dog is only one of the workers he, or the rest of the team, will all too often try to reach the leader to settle an old score. Thus the leader will be unwilling to stop, and the driver can have difficulty in bringing his sledge to rest.

A good driver must learn to be a real part of his team – the 'top dog' – and to establish that no one challenges his orders. But to achieve this he must understand things from the dogs' point of view, following their line of thought, even seeing the terrain ahead from their eye level.

Darkie was both leader and King Dog but my first efforts to control the team were a dismal failure for, despite his high reputation, he completely ignored my commands. It was Stonehouse who finally suggested that my voice was much deeper than that of his previous driver, and indeed as soon as I raised the pitch he began to respond intelligently. Sometimes too intelligently for my *amour propre*.

Once when I approached a line of small rocky islets, I knew that there was only one route between them for a sledge – but where? I decided to go round the last one but Darkie immediately objected, constantly looking round at me reproachfully as I persisted with my orders. As he turned the point we suddenly arrived at open water! Darkie just sat down and gazed at me disdainfully, clearly saying, 'I told you so'. Duly humbled, and feeling a little foolish I stopped trying to be clever, 'Owk', I cried, and without hesitation he turned back along the edge of the islands, and without any command suddenly steered left. This took us up and through the gap which he had obviously known about all the time.

Lacking seals, dog feeding was a considerable problem. On 28 May we had for our animals only fifteen bales of stockfish, forty pounds of pemmican left behind by the Americans, one-and-a-half seals, three seal skins and blubber, together with fifteen gallons of seal oil which we had rendered down. There was also our dog pemmican, but this had to be conserved for travelling. We decided to feed them one pound of pemmican each on three consecutive days, the next day a stock fish soaked in seal oil and half-a-pound of pemmican, followed by a day on which they got nothing – then the cycle was repeated. Thus they lived through the winter until we were once more able to hunt seals.

At the end of July a message from the Governor told me that the Chileans were reported to have established a base to the west of Hope Bay. I asked

Elliott to go out and look for it, but the terrain he faced involved travelling over fifty miles across the mountains of Trinity Peninsula to reach the alleged site. His party (Elliott himself, O'Hare, Green, McNeile) found the station at Cape Legoupil where, after the exchange of the prescribed Protest Notes, they received a warm welcome from the surprised occupants.

The Fids had proved that an inland route existed, but even more important at that time, they had also shown that they were active in the area claimed by Britain. The only Chilean activity appeared to be daily weather reporting, but it transpired that they had already made the risky attempt to reach Hope Bay over the coastal sea ice. They were forced to turn back on finding open water only five miles from Legoupil.

On 27 July Adie, Huckle, Spivey, Stonehouse, Brown and I left for Alexander Island with five sledges and a total load of over two-and-a-half tons, in order to lay a depot for the long summer journey we planned. Although the return distance was only 220 miles this proved the hardest traverse any of us was to make. For twenty-five days we struggled southwards in deep soft snow, driving drift and mists which obscured the coastline. Navigation was necessarily by dead-reckoning for it was impossible to see anything. Sometimes the surface was so bad that sledges were constantly overturning. On one day Adie righted his twenty-five times in one mile. It was also gruelling work for the dogs, which were fed only one pound of pemmican each day. After 110 miles 1,050 pounds of food and fuel were put down about three miles from the ice cliffs of Alexander Island, and became known as Cape Nicholas Depot (now Cape Brown).

I intended to return via Mushroom Island, where we had left a small depot for the purpose, but Darkie now had quite other ideas. For the first five miles I had a really tough running battle with him, for he just would not keep the course I was steering. So determinedly did he pursue his own way before finally giving in and doing what I asked, that in our tent that evening I took the trouble to plot not only our actual journey but also the course which he had so persistently tried to follow. His was seven degrees off mine – and headed absolutely directly back to base still 110 miles away!

In marked contrast to the outward journey, we returned in cold, clear weather with surfaces hardened by constant wind, and took only six days. As soon as I got in I was called to the radio room to talk to George Barry, Base Leader at Lockroy. He was a worried man, for Ken Pawson, John Blythe and Bill Richards had set off four days earlier in a dinghy to visit Doumer Island. They had rowed out into Neumayer Channel and disappeared round a headland intending to spend one night away. Now they were three days overdue, and alone at base Barry was talking of building a raft to go after them. This courageous but foolhardy proposal was quickly quashed – tidal current, wind and drifting ice would have made it a highly dangerous undertaking.

There was no immediate practical help we could give – Hope Bay and Stonington were each 250 miles away, and in any case there was no known route down to the coast near Lockroy. The Argentine Islands station was only forty miles from them, but help from there would entail a very risky boat journey with scant hope of success in the prevailing conditions. We finally planned to attempt sledging a boat to the area from Hope Bay, but happily on the 28th and six days overdue, the wanderers turned up safely. Rashly going further than they had intended, drifting pack ice had closed in behind, cutting off their retreat. Worried about the possible length of an enforced stay, they had killed two seals to augment their food supplies and to provide blubber for fuel. Then their luck turned; a change of wind dispersed the ice and they were able to row back, though only with considerable difficulty and in the teeth of half a gale.

Poor Ken Pawson – even at base he was accident prone, and tells in his journal the following story against himself:

One night after a period of pretty hectic outdoor activity running behind sledges I developed quite a sore, chafed area around the rectum. I could not get to sleep, and not wishing to disturb anyone by switching on lights, reached up to my shelf for a small tin of vaseline near my medical kit (used mostly for my ice axe). Removing the lid I applied a liberal amount in darkness to the affected area. Five minutes later I sat up with a yell – I was on fire and switched on the light. I was amazed to find my hands black, the sheets the same – in the darkness I had grabbed a tin of Cherry Blossom boot polish.

The boys of course roared, showing no sympathy, and Dan Jardine swears I went out and sat in the snow to cool off . . . I must admit it was a night never to be forgotten, and I might add that I find it difficult even now to reach for anything in darkness. This episode generated the sophistry recorded in our base *Line Book*: 'Use Cherry Blossom boot polish – brings up boots like a baby's bottom.'

On 16 September the Northern Party (Stonehouse, Blaiklock, Dalgliesh, Spivey) left with three teams in an attempt to reach Darbel Bay 100 miles to the north. The route led over the sea ice and through the narrow channels separating Adelaide Island from the mainland. Adie and I supported the first stages with two more teams, he towing two twelve-foot Nansen sledges, the last one carrying a flat-bottomed dory for use where open water was to be expected. When we reached The Gullet between Adelaide and the mainland we found it filled with thin ice or frozen slush, on which it was dangerous to travel even with an empty sledge, and it was impossible to launch the dory. Plans were therefore altered to include a survey of the east coast of Adelaide and the adjacent islands. Adie and I took back the redundant dory, making a sketchy geological reconnaissance of the coast *en route*.

On Jenny Island the Northern Party discovered a long bamboo pole iced into a raised beach, heavily eroded on its windward side and surrounded by rocks which had once formed a cairn. They believed it to be the cairn left by Gourdan of Charcot's *Pourquoi Pas?* expedition in 1908–10. Blaiklock computed the height to be sixty feet, very different from the ten metres quoted by Charcot. But their major discovery was a small emperor penguin rookery on the Dion islands where 100 adult birds were found with seventy chicks. This was only the third such rookery known, one at Cape Crozier discovered in 1902 by Scott's first expedition, the other thought by the German South Polar Expedition 1901–3 to exist at Gausberg, because of the large number of birds seen in the area. Both these were on the other side of the continent.

While investigating the islands Spivey and Blaiklock, with the leading sledge, broke through some thin ice and began to sink slowly. Dalgliesh threw a rope, while Stonehouse rushing up on skis to help also fell through. Then a bridge of skis was made and the swimmers crawled out. Next a rope was fastened to the semi-floating sledge, the team cut free and, together with Dalgliesh's team, were exhorted to haul it out.

Suddenly Stonehouse's dogs realised that they were missing something, and came pounding up to find out what. At the same moment Spivey and Dalgliesh's teams started a war, until two of them fell through. One dog managed to escape and made off in pursuit of a penguin a few hundred yards away. By this time the sledge was almost water-logged but Spivey, working half immersed in the sea, frantically unloaded it, and finally all the supplies were recovered. The only casualty was the poor unsuspecting penguin. This party returned to base after fifty-six days, having covered 500 miles, done much useful survey, and bringing back geological and biological collections.

Meanwhile on 22 October the Southern Party (Huckle, Brown, Adie, Fuchs), with three sledges, had left for the Cape Nicholas Depot, intending to make a geological reconnaissance, survey the northern coasts of Alexander Island, and select a suitable site for a proposed new station at its northern tip. But examination revealed that high unbroken ice cliffs precluded any possibility of establishing a station from the sea, so we turned south to continue survey and geology in George VI Sound. Dividing into two groups, Brown and Huckle concentrated on linking their survey with that of the British Graham Land Expedition at Ablation Point, while Adie and I carried the geological reconnaissance to the point we called Keystone Cliffs, south of Fossil Bluff. After journeys of 550 and 940 miles respectively, we were all back at base by 20 January awaiting the arrival of the ship.

At Hope Bay too they had had a busy year. When Elliott returned there in

Adélie penguins leaping ashore. (Operation Tabarin)

Biscoe he found himself with an entirely new party, of which only Oliver ('Dick') Burd, transferred from the Argentine Islands, had previous Antarctic experience. Numbers were reduced from nine to seven. During April, May and June four men (Elliott, Green, Burd, Jefford) undertook a fifty-one day journey in order to fill a gap in the survey along the south coast of James Ross Island, and to make a geological reconnaissance of that area. Strong winds with melting drift and a slushy surface slowed them up, and soon they were picking their way through pools of water lying on the surface of thin ice, only four to five inches thick. They were relieved to reach Church Point and camp on land, then climbing to a vantage point they saw open water to the south extending from the mainland to the islands in the east. Their only hope of progress was to force an overland route.

Despite poor visibility, they followed a tortuous route among the wide crevasses of the Russell East Glacier and finally climbed 500 feet above Pitt Point. There they were hit by hurricane winds gusting to over 100 knots, and for two days had constantly to replace the fifty-pound ration boxes being used to hold down the tents. Frank Elliott recorded in his journal:

It was impossible to walk in the wind, all one could do was to crawl between fierce gusts. We opened a tin of dog pemmican and crawled along putting a block in each dog's mouth; even then most of the food blew away as they crunched it. They made no attempt to stand. In one extra strong gust I was blown more than fifty yards before I could stop myself . . . Jefford was blown along but managed to grab a sledge as he passed. The loaded sledges were swinging to and fro on the pickets with every gust. I have weathered many storms but never one so bad. I have a very great respect for the design and strength of the Pyramid tent.

When the storm subsided they continued their work as far as Hamilton Point on James Ross Island, where open water in Admiralty Sound forced them to turn back. The return was also hard going. Three or four feet of snow had fallen, masking all obstacles, and every few yards the sledges bogged down. This soft snow was too deep for skis, even for snow-shoes, yet a man had to 'wade' ahead to break some sort of trail for the labouring teams. When they eventually reached home they had travelled 354 miles and experienced almost every hazard that sledging can provide.

The subsequent journeys culminated in November when a party of four (Elliott, Jefford, O'Hare, McNeile) set off to work along the Cape Roquemaurel/Cape Kater coast. On the eighth day out, when they were ascending the Russell East Glacier, 'Gert' fell through a crevasse bridge and they could see her lying on soft snow 100 feet down. She was apparently uninjured, for when they called she climbed to the top of a snow pinnacle rising fifty feet from the bottom of the crevasse. Since the hole was in the centre of the thinnest part of the snow bridge, another one was dug close to the edge. An abseil rope and life lines were run over a sledge, and Elliott descended fifty feet to swing himself onto a ledge on the side of the crevasse. From there he traversed to a position from which he could climb onto the pinnacle, where Gert gave him an affectionate welcome. By the time she had been hauled up to the surface and he had climbed out again with the aid of prussik slings, the rescue operation had taken three hours.

On 18 November they had reached a point 1,500 feet above sea level inland from Cape Kjellman. In the distance lay Cape Kater, apparently separated from them by a deep valley glacier, and a complex of rock ridges and buttresses. That evening I was still working in George VI Sound and spoke over the radio to Elliott. We both knew that no one had been able to make contact with Hope Bay for ten days, and we were worried. Was it just a breakdown in the equipment, or were they in some kind of serious trouble? We agreed that it was time for Elliott to return and find out.

A few days before this anxiety I had been greatly shocked to receive a report that Eric Platt, Base Leader at Admiralty Bay, had been out in the field with

The spring return to Hope Bay. (H. J. Dangerfield)

Jack Reid when he suddenly collapsed with a heart attack near the top of a pass. Reid tried desperately to carry him home, but single-handed this was impossible. Racing back to base in the dark, he met a search party which had already set out to look for them. Together they climbed back to the top of the pass, but when they got there Platt had died. Greatly distressed, they carried him back and he was buried near the base. The cross which marks his grave still stands today.

Elliott's party made all speed back to Hope Bay, covering eighty-five miles in five days – thirty-nine on the last day. As the base gradually came into view they were surprised to see a tent, instead of a mound of snow with chimneys standing through it, a large, gaping, black hole. This was a bad shock. The whole place seemed strangely silent, despite the noise now being made by the few dogs that had been left behind. No one came out to meet them, no puppies were bounding around, and even their own teams were quiet and subdued. On arrival it was clear that the tent had not been used for some time.

Elliott walked straight over to the rookery camp which the doctor, Bill Sladen, always used for observing penguins, confidently expecting to find three men. But only a very strained Sladen came out, and with difficulty told him that the base had been burned to the ground. Both Dick Burd and Mike Green had died in the flames. He had kept his solitary vigil for sixteen days,

Emperor penguin and chick, Halley Bay. (G. Lowe)

10 *King penguins, Royal Bay, South Georgia. (M. G. White)*
11 *Emperor penguin rookery, Halley Bay. (C. Johnson)*

unable to make any radio contact. He was in a state of deep shock, and that night it was mutually agreed that no one would talk about the fire.

In the morning details of this terrible tragedy were gradually unfolded. The fire had occurred while Sladen had been working over at the rookery. It is best described in his own words:

The first thing I saw was a dense cloud of smoke, most of which was coming from the north end of the hut. The snow was dark with soot on the leeward side . . . I found the door with difficulty and tried to push my way in . . . billows of smoke rushed out . . . the door was half drifted up . . . I just managed to scramble out again . . . I tried to force my way through the w/T window but was compelled to come out as the fumes were so hot and suffocating. There was no answer to frantic shouts made between breaths inside the window. As I ran round the south end of the hut I noticed a glow at the junction of the engine shed, back porch and main building. Snow was falling away around it and flames were being fanned by the gale. I tried pushing snow down into it but to no avail. . . . Smoke was coming out of every chimney . . . the roof at the south end was ablaze and . . . I had to give up all hope of rescue. . . . The sinister silence; the dark smoke torrenting down to the sea, pressed low by the gale and drift; the feeling of complete and utter helplessness; worse still, the thought of Dick and Mike with no one to save them was the most terrifying thing I have ever experienced.

The main roof collapsed at approximately 0300. . . .

Between 0230 and 0300 I was moving all dogs at the east end of the spans to the west end. They were already blackened by the smoke.

At 0330 a piece of burning wood set light to the store dump for the new base on Hut Point nearly two hundred yards away . . . I could do nothing as the sparks were rushing down in that direction. At 0345 the north extension of the hut was aglow and this roof fell in at 0400. At 0500 the hut was still burning and the store pile [fire] spreading rapidly. I went to investigate, but some ammunition exploded. I also remembered that there was a store of explosives on the Point.

At 0600 the smoke was less and it was possible to go into the Tin Galley ['The Cabin', saved from the fire because it was buried under snow] for a short rest out of the wind. I did not stay long for fear of fumes. The floor beams [of the hut] were still burning . . . tins of condensed milk . . . were bursting continuously. The stores on Hut Point were now burning with less vigour, but small ammunition was still exploding.

At 0700 the temperature was 13°F . . . the wind . . . was mostly gusting to 40–50 mph with some drift. I walked around trying to keep warm until 0800 by which time I was satisfied that there was no danger of anything else catching fire. I rested for three-and-a-half hours in my observation tent at the [penguin] rookery.

He pitched a tent near Andersson's hut at Seal Point and daily made unsuccessful attempts to contact Elliott on his field radio set. In an effort to divert his mind from the tragedy he continued his penguin studies.

. . . the heavy depression that seemed to well all around me; a feeling of great loneliness and deepest sorrow; the grim sight of utter desolation that greeted me every time I passed the still smouldering hut; the work we had struggled to do to the best of our ability under very trying conditions. Seven of us instead of nine (in 1947) . . . the reports so carefully prepared and containing so much of interest and experience. All this seemed as nothing when my mind turned back to the two companions we would never see again. Their quiet and unruffled outlook on life had never ceased to impress me. I felt much in need of those qualities now.

These two tragedies, which actually occurred on the same day, cast a sombre shadow over all the bases where we felt them keenly. At Hope Bay the remaining five men could only settle down as well as they might in their tents to await relief.

Back at Stonington a wide pool had now appeared in Neny Fjord, and by the end of January this extended to the western end of Red Rock Ridge. Soon Neny Island was surrounded by water and we could launch the motor boat. Reconnoitring by sea we found a small, ice-covered, rocky island which looked like a low iceberg south of Neny, and a rock lying only two feet beneath the surface. This had not been discovered previously because there had always been an iceberg grounded on it. Now these obstacles constituted real hazards, for they lay in the direct path of ships approaching Stonington.

Although our main interest was in the break-up, life was still very busy – painting the hut, maintaining engines, sealing, trawling for biological specimens, enlarging the hangar to accept the bigger plane, which we still expected from Deception. On 11 February I climbed to the top of Roman Four Mountain and, from 3,000 feet, could see through binoculars a thin line of water stretching along the western horizon – but between this and Neny Fjord there still lay some forty miles of unbroken fast ice.

By the last week of March real doubts about our relief assailed us, particularly the five (Adie, Stonehouse, Huckle, Jones and Randall) who faced the possibility of being the first men to experience a third consecutive Antarctic winter. We had rations for another year, but coal would be short, and if the same ice conditions prevailed again, who could know if the ship would be able to reach us even next season.

Biscoe, with the Governor on board, had arrived at the Argentine Islands 200 miles to the north, but sea ice, snowfall, mist and gales prevented her moving further – she could not even get to Port Lockroy. On the 30th she made one final attempt to sail south, but after only eight miles reached impenetrable pack ice. Then on 1 April the Governor signalled that they could do no more, and the ship turned back for Stanley. At Stonington the sea was beginning to freeze, with temperatures already dropping to $-30°F$. At last our fate was confirmed – it would be another year before we saw a new face.

5

The Lost Eleven
1949–50

1949 By the end of the season *Biscoe* had taken off everyone from Hope Bay, and Port Lockroy had closed down. Deception and the Argentine Islands were now solely occupied with meteorology, while at Signy biology was the main concern. At Admiralty Bay Jardine took up Platt's geological work, Jefford (ex-Hope Bay) began a survey of King George Island, and Geoffrey Hattersley-Smith, the new Base Leader, started glaciological studies for which he had been training in England for some time.

At Stonington we decided to improve our home comforts by converting the large workshop into a 'quiet room' to which anyone could retire from the general hurly-burly. This provided immediate action, and had a therapeutic value in diverting our thoughts from our disappointments, but once completed I never remember anybody going there to be quiet.

Early in April I submitted plans to the Governor for a geological and survey journey to the southern end of George VI Sound, and the establishment of a three-man party for six weeks (this ultimately turned into ten weeks) to observe the emperor penguin rookery discovered at the Dion Islands the previous summer. Since Sir Miles Clifford was taking no chances, and proposed to obtain an aircraft to fly us out the next summer if this became necessary, all field parties had to be back at base by early January. In fact we did not expect a plane on floats to be able to land in Marguerite Bay until after the ice broke up, hopefully in late February.

Emperor penguins hatch their eggs during winter, so on 1 June Stonehouse, David Dalgliesh and Dave Jones, with Spivey and me in support, left for the Dion Islands. Judging from Cherry-Garrard's account in *The Worst Journey in the World* we believed that egg-laying would not begin before the second week. In three days we were at the rookery where, to our disappointment, we found many birds already carrying eggs on their feet as they slowly strutted about the bare ice. This was a serious blow, for Stonehouse hoped to collect a timed series of embryos throughout the incubation period – something which had never been done before. Its

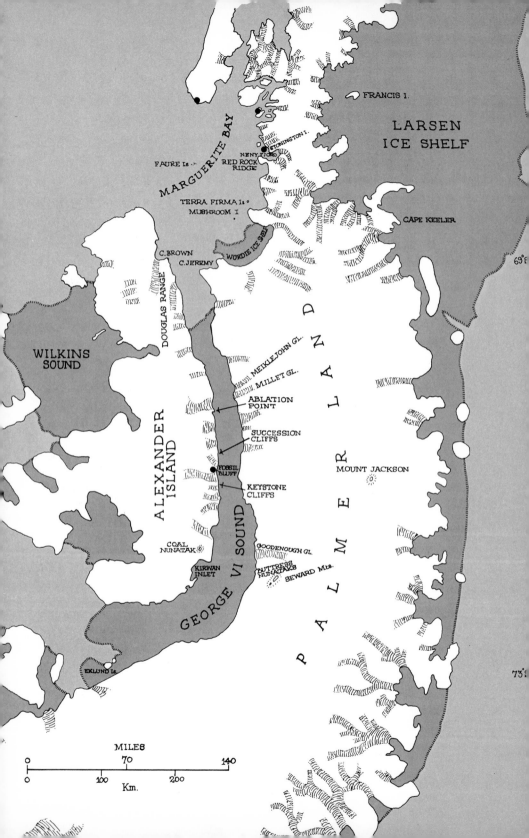

LARSEN
ICE SHELF

FRANCIS I.

MARGUERITE BAY

FAURE Is.

RED ROCK
RIDGE

NENY FJORD

STONINGTON I.

TERRA FIRMA Is.
MUSHROOM I.

CAPE KEELER

63°

C. BROWN
C. JEREMY

WORDIE ICE SHELF

WILKINS
SOUND

DOUGLAS RANGE

MEIKLEJOHN GL.

MILLET GL.

ABLATION
POINT

SUCCESSION
CLIFFS

ALEXANDER ISLAND

FOSSIL
BLUFF

MOUNT JACKSON

KEYSTONE
CLIFFS

P A L M E R   L A N D

COAL
NUNATAK

GEORGE VI SOUND

GOODENOUGH GL.

KIRWAN
INLET

BUTTRESS
NUNATAKS

SEWARD Mts.

EKLUND Is.

73°

MILES

0   70   140

0   100   200
Km.

importance lay in the belief that emperors might be a particularly primitive bird and the embryos could reveal unusual stages of development. This idea was later found to be erroneous, but he wanted to prove the point one way or the other.

The outstanding characteristic of the rookery seemed to be the peace and quiet prevailing, there were no squabbles going on, no bickering of any kind. Many birds seemed to be unpaired, but those that were, kept together. Periodically the one without the egg would begin a croaking ululation, which was taken up by its mate who, at the same time displayed the egg by teetering back on its heels and raising the lower abdominal curtain of feathers. At this the 'enquirer' appeared satisfied and both would settle down once more, standing quietly side by side.

Every bird had an overpowering desire to hold an egg, or indeed any object of similar size. On one occasion a Leica camera was found to be missing, the thief being discovered only when we saw a penguin waddling off with a leather strap trailing between its feet. Perhaps this innate urge to hatch something is valuable in preserving the species, for an unprotected egg or a newly hatched chick would quickly perish unless sheltered from the cold. A few eggs which had somehow been abandoned were frozen hard and cracked. However, they made excellent omelettes and we believed ourselves the first people ever to eat emperor penguin eggs.

Spivey and I spent two days mapping and geologising around the islands, and then travelled some fifteen miles south to the Faure Islands for a one-day general reconnaissance. These proved to be an extensive group of perhaps fifty small islands and rocks, and we marvelled that Charcot's *Pourquoi Pas?* could have survived an involuntary storm-driven passage through them in 1908. In contrast to the Dions, where we had found numerous seals, penguins and blue-eyed shags, the Faures presented a desolate, eerie scene with no life of any kind. We turned for home, reaching base in time for the midwinter celebrations.

By this time the British press, sensing a good story in our enforced extra year, had blown us up into 'heroes'. Headlines at home spoke of 'Trapped Men on Ice', 'Marooned Scientists' and, more dramatically, 'The Lost Eleven', a name which stuck to us through many years. The BBC beamed special monthly programmes to us, on which our families were invited to send personal messages and choose a favourite piece of music.

As our plight became more and more exaggerated, another current radio cliff-hanger was keeping the nation enthralled each week. This was the heroic adventures of Duncan Carse as 'Dick Barton, Special Agent'.

Map 6, opposite. Alexander Island/George VI Sound/Palmer Land

Becoming increasingly irritated with the absurd build-up about us, Carse got himself into trouble with the newspapers by stating publicly that all the fuss was totally out of proportion, and that we were perfectly all right – which indeed we were – but it spoilt the whole picture. As the controversy developed, the press scathingly suggested that it was time for this fictional hero to produce some real action himself. But in fact Carse, who had spent two years in the Antarctic with the British Graham Land Expedition, and was later to lead three expeditions to South Georgia, was well qualified to express an informed opinion on our situation.

In June 'Jumbo' Nicholl, Base Leader at the Argentine Islands, set out southwards with Dennis Farmer and 'Jock' Tait, intending to reconnoitre a route into Darbel Bay, 100 miles north of Stonington. As the base was not equipped for travelling – they even lacked sleeping bags – this was a considerable undertaking. Unhappily for them the temperature stayed below −40°F for the five days, with the minimum reading of −51°F, a record low for the Antarctic Peninsula area. As they were unable to transmit because their batteries froze, we began to be anxious about their safety, but on 7 July they were back home, having been forced to return without achieving their objective.

Shortly after this I received a message from the Governor saying that because of the difficulties of access, he had decided to close Stonington after our relief next season. To compensate for this Port Lockroy was to be reopened. This was a bitter pill, for we all felt that we had opened up a valuable field of geological work on Alexander Island. I wrote in my journal at the time:

Somehow it seems . . . that all our efforts here are to bear no future fruit. In fact we have accomplished as much in our time as an expedition could be expected to do, but somehow in a concern of this nature it seems like the dying of a family through failure to produce a new generation to carry on the good work. I am desolate!

We put a brave face on it, but became stubbornly determined to use our last sledging season to advantage. The main journey could not begin until early September, but meanwhile there was still plenty to do. The Dions rookery party had to be brought back, we made soundings through the ice to find a new ship channel north of Neny Island, and numerous short journeys enabled us to complete the local survey and geological work.

On 14 August Adie and I set off for the Dions with light sledges, for we hoped to bring back all the seal meat we could carry to nourish our dogs after their lean winter. To fatten them up, we stayed at the islands for two weeks, our time well spent in survey and geology. My bitch 'Lizzie' was a great favourite but a headstrong girl who gave us plenty of trouble. She was very

Leaving the Dion Islands, −41°F, note condensation from dog's breath. (D. G. Dalgliesh)

lovable but a real old trollop with no morals at all. When in season she always contrived to get off her span, and then went round visiting every dog she could before we caught up with the situation. We never had the faintest idea who was the father of her endless litters.

But on this occasion it was not love that was on her mind. She managed to get loose just for fun, and was found happily chasing penguins, who by now were all holding tiny chirruping chicks. A number lost their young in the scramble, and all of us spent a lot of time, in the dark and a high wind, trying to collect them. The live ones were brought back to the tents, to be kept warm until we could return them to the rookery next morning.

Settling down for the night, we had hardly got to sleep when a vociferous cheeping woke us, which was obviously going to continue indefinitely. At wit's end, we suddenly thought of feeding them with premasticated herrings in tomato sauce, the only fish we had. Soon we were all busy munching and dropping small, unsalubrious lumps into tiny ready-gaping beaks, after which silence prevailed. It was not long before we were to sympathise with penguin parents, for every two hours throughout that very long night the whole pantomime had to be repeated if we were to get any sleep. At dawn we thankfully relinquished our fostering, the chicks were returned to the rookery and immediately adopted by eager adult birds.

On the 18th the little winter camp was broken, and the five of us left for base carrying 550 pounds of seal meat and a large plywood box containing four emperors and three tiny chicks. They were intended for the London Zoo. The adults did not need to feed (they had not been observed to do so since 4 June), yet they were constantly able to regurgitate food for their young. Unhappily only one chick survived the journey, for the others were trampled on by their parents as the sledge swayed from side to side.

By the time we left for home, six months later, the chick weighed 35 pounds, and our fishing commitment had become three fish per man per day, for the birds required thirty-three every twenty-four hours. We caught them by hand-line or in fish traps made from chicken wire. One stormy night their wire enclosure filled with so much drift that three adults simply walked up and over the top. So in the end we brought back only two birds; sadly they did not have sufficient resistance to survive in England and died of aspergillosis.

Without an aircraft to lay depots the long southern journey was a most complex operation. A four-sledge advance party (Huckle, Brown, Spivey, Toynbee) left on 8 September to establish depots at the Terra Firma Islands, Mushroom Island, and finally as far south as conditions would allow them to travel. At the appropriate time Spivey and Pat Toynbee were to hand over their remaining loads and make a fast run home, leaving the other two to put in the final depot before carrying on the survey begun in George VI Sound the previous season.

According to the progress made by the advance party, Adie and I would leave two or three weeks later and travel as far south along the coast of Alexander Island as supplies would permit. In fact we set out on 1 October, knowing that bad conditions had so delayed the first depot-layers that we would be lucky to reach even the southern end of the Sound.

The previous year we had got as far as Keystone Cliffs, so named because it was there that we felt we had at last the key to the geological structure of the Sound. We planned therefore to travel as fast as possible to this point and continue work from there onwards. The main interest lay in the Jurassic and Cretaceous sediments which form Alexander Island, which we already knew to be fossiliferous and heavily folded. Both the rocks and their structure were entirely different from the older dioritic rocks which formed the east side of the Sound only thirty miles away. In the interpretation of the relationships lay the answer to the origin of the Sound itself. In addition to geology, we also mapped the coast, made meteorological observations every three hours, and collected any botanical material (mosses and lichens) we encountered. They were busy days.

After three days we came to the deep, soft snow which had so hampered

Ablation Point, melt pools between pressure ridges. (BAS)

the advance party, and day after day were forced to 'relay', taking forward part-loads, returning for the rest – thus achieving only one mile forward for every three we travelled. Seventeen days out, and 102 miles from base, we met the first support party returning.

That night we all camped together, and during the radio 'sched' with base learnt that Captain Harry Kirkwood had reported that *Biscoe* was already off Spain, and this time he was looking forward to reaching us. It all seemed very remote. We were only at the beginning of our journey, and it would be another three months before we returned to the comforts of base, and perhaps mail from home at last.

Meanwhile Huckle and Brown still struggled south in appalling conditions. Speaking to them by radio on the 21st I agreed to their leaving our last depot at Ablation Point, seventy-five miles short of the planned position. It was essential that they should at least reach Ablation in order to tie-in their survey with that of the British Graham Land Expedition where an astronomical fix had been made.

A week later we were at the ice cliff which marks the front of the floating ice shelf filling George VI Sound. Conditions at last improved, and on 2 November we reached Ablation Point, just missing the surveyors who had already crossed to the east coast. Once we thought we saw their sledges coming towards us and hastened forward to meet them, but about 400 yards further on were astonished to find we had been deceived by some miraged empty dog pemmican tins left at one of their old camp sites.

As we travelled, the great Douglas Range to the west extended as far as we could see, the highest peaks rising to 10,000 feet. At our halts we never tired of gazing at this magnificent panorama, with its peaks, spurs and great tumbling glaciers pouring down to the Sound. By the 6th we were at Keystone Cliffs and our real work began.

Soon we found ourselves among high ice ridges which were impossible to distinguish in the 'whiteout', a diffuse light condition when the overcast sky appears to merge with the snow surface. There are no shadows, no horizon, and perspective is lost. Scouting about for a way through, I probed ahead with a six-foot ice chisel. Suddenly I felt nothing in front of me, and stopping rather hastily I became aware that my skis were projecting over an invisible but sharp edge. Retiring cautiously to firmer ground, we made camp to await better visibility. Next day when it cleared, my ski tracks could be seen ending at the edge of a fifteen-foot drop to a snow slope down to the bottom of a rift forty feet below.

Extricating ourselves from this confused area we followed the coast, expecting to find the ice promontory shown on the map as ending in 'Cape Stephenson'. Instead the coast ran back into an embayment now known as Kirwan Inlet, thus on the map the area of Alexander Island was reduced by 300 square miles. We then set course for Eklund Island, sixty miles distant.

Now forty-four days out from base, I was becoming increasingly worried about the dogs who were clearly very tired. They were getting only one pound of pemmican each day, and the endless vista of snow provided nothing encouraging for them to run towards. The dejected state of these usually over exuberant creatures even affected us, for it was both depressing and tiring to drive them, when every ounce of pull seemed to be exerted by one's own will-power. At every slight rise or soft patch they had to be exhorted afresh while we also pushed, or the sledges stopped at once. As these occurred every few yards, the shouting was well nigh continuous for hours on end. It certainly sapped our energy.

That night we decided to feed all the remaining blubber we had during the next two days, thereby giving each animal about half-a-pound extra in addition to the pemmican ration. Next morning the snow became increasingly deep and soft, so we waxed our wooden sledge runners. There was also an astonishing improvement in the teams after their first blubber feed, and we began to feel that when it was finished we would just have to feed dog to dog if we were to get home.

As we travelled, there was suddenly a black spot on the horizon, winking at intervals, then disappearing. Eklund Island, now thirty-seven miles off, was appearing and disappearing with the varying refraction of the atmosphere. As soon as it remained steady I tried unsuccessfully to get Darkie to hold course towards it, until bending down to his eye level I realised he could not yet see it. It seemed incredible that an angle subtended by only three feet could make so much difference at so great a distance. But a mile further on the whole team saw it and, pricking up their ears, broke into a rapid trot.

The surface was increasingly undulating with occasional rifts in the hollows. Halting on one of the ridges to rest the teams, the dogs suddenly jumped up, trying to turn back along our track. A quarter of a mile away, unbelievably, we saw eleven Adélie penguins plodding steadily across the ice shelf. Every now and then they stopped to look around as though getting their bearings. Our debilitated animals badly needed food. Hurriedly unloading Adie's sledge, we raced back in hot pursuit. Killing is never pleasant, but this providential gift was all the more extraordinary coming at such a crucial moment, for we never saw another penguin until we returned to Marguerite Bay one month later.

With the appetising scent of the birds on the sledges being wafted over their heads by a following wind, the dogs perked up, and soon we came to the steeply drifted-up front of the ice shelf, separated from Ekland by sea ice. This was a surprise, for about thirty miles of the shelf must have broken up and drifted away since Ronne and Carl Eklund had been there nine years earlier. Descending a steep drift-slope to the sea ice, we made for the nearest of nine small rocky islets which surround Eklund Island and camped.

There we cut up the penguins and each dog got half a bird, about five pounds of food. When they had finished feeding, just five tail feathers remained on the snow – beaks, claws, flippers, everything had been consumed.

During the four days spent at that camp we examined a number of the small islands, which proved to be granite or diorite, and were also able to climb to the top of Eklund itself. There are in fact two tops, the highest a snow ridge of 1,400 feet, the second a rock pinnacle 500 feet lower. To reach this we cut some 200 steps down the inside of the surrounding windscoop, and after a steep climb up the rock itself we stood beside a substantial cairn which had been built by the Americans.

Intent on finding the United States Claim Sheet which Ronne was reported to have left there, we began dismantling the cairn stone by stone, until at last, adhering to the underside of a boulder from the lowest layer, we found a specimen bag labelled FINDERS KEEPERS. Inside was a piece of paper letter-headed *United States Department of the Interior, Washington*, on which was written:

This peak in Georg [sic] VI Sound was climbed this day by the Southern Party of the United States Antarctic Expedition 1939–41. Its base is in Marguerite Bay close to Neny Fjord.
Carl R. Eklund   Tomahawk, WISC. USA. Naturalist.
Finn Ronne   Leader this party and Chief of Staff USAS.
Dec. 14 1941

The date should have read 1940, for Ronne's party were evacuated by air from Stonington in early 1941. There was no other record, and this did not seem to us to constitute 'one of the Claim Sheets issued by the State Department'. Rebuilding the cairn, we left a note recording both the American visit and our own, taking the original with us.

Our intention to leave Eklund on 22 November was baulked by a rising wind and heavy drift, so we settled down in our tents to see out the storm. During our two years at Stonington Ray Adie and I had sledged many, many miles together, and I always marvelled at his imperturbability and constant meticulous attention to detail. At the end of each day's long and often weary march he always gave me a written statement of exactly how far we had travelled, how much food and fuel we had left, and the actual weight carried by each sledge. Despite his youth he had already developed the habit of precise thinking which was later to make him one of the best scientific editors in the country.

By now our two books had been read and re-read, but Adie was not to be defeated. I was suddenly astounded to find myself listening to him expounding the virtues of a brand of sausages. With care and attention to proper emphasis, he was reading aloud the label on the tin – every stop and comma. Next it was pea flour, then the tin of peaches we were keeping for Christmas Day. To such is one reduced when, during months of isolated travel, everything has been said, and each man knows every detail of the other's family life and the nooks and crannies of his home.

More profitably, we discussed the possible geology of the country beyond our logistic capacity to reach. This led us to thoughts of bigger and longer expeditions to the interior of the continent. So, in a snow storm, originated the idea of crossing Antarctica, and that evening I set to with a stub of pencil to outline the concept of such a journey. We even began working out logistics. Five years later it came true, and the betting fraternity at Stonington lost their wagers. But Adie who had shared the first dreams was not able to be one of my party. He had taught me to drive dogs – I would like to have returned the compliment in a Sno-Cat.

We finally left Eklund on our fifty-third day out, 420 miles from base, although with the necessary relaying we had covered 620 miles. With eighteen days' food left before we would have to reach a depot left in latitude 72°S, there was time to make for the rock bastions 123 miles away in the southeast corner of the Sound (now Buttress Nunataks). They had never been visited.

For seven days we suffered only head winds and low drift, but on the eighth we were in a field of enormous *sastrugi* where large, open and bridged crevasses reduced our travel to six miles. That night we made camp two miles away from the 2,000-foot faces of the nunataks, and next day were able to reach two of them. Unlike the Cretaceous sedimentary rocks of Alexander Island on the other side of the Sound, here they proved to be older, somewhat metamorphosed intrusives, which tied in with previous knowledge of the rocks on the east side. Continuous barometric readings showed that we were at the lowest level of the ice shelf – indeed at sea-level, which seemed remarkable. At Eklund I had sounded the sea depth near the ice front and found sixty fathoms, with a strong current running under the shelf. Now it seemed possible that the scour of the current in the bend of the Sound was sufficient to thin the ice from beneath.

Four days later we had crossed to the western side of the Sound and were camped at 1,250 feet on Alexander Island, among a group of three nunataks composed of fossiliferous shales and sandstones. A seventy-knot blizzard gusting to ninety knots hit us, and we hastily built a protective snow wall around the tent, remaining fully dressed all night, our backs supporting the bending tent poles. Fortunately the wind died in the morning and we spent three days working among some twenty nunataks in the area. One of them – Coal Nunatak – contained thin lenses of coal besides fossil remains.

On 8 December, with only one day's dog food left, we set off for the depot. Conditions were clear, with a bright midnight sun giving a distant scene of great grandeur. One hundred miles to the east–northeast, behind the heavily crevassed Goodenough Glacier, we could see Mount Jackson* (8,600 feet), to the east lay the Buttress Nunataks, and beyond them the as yet unvisited Seward Mountains.

For some miles the dogs raced joyfully down the steep slopes. Then, after negotiating the ridges, pinnacles and walls of pressure ice at the edge of the Sound, we reached the ice shelf and soon found our depot. We now had six days' dog food to carry us the ninety miles north to Ablation Point.

Biscoe was already in Stanley. It was time to head for home, but we determined to fit in all the work we could before the New Year deadline. The previous season we had tried to achieve more work by travelling for six hours, sleeping four hours, working four hours, then sleeping again for four hours and travelling another six hours. Thus we had tried to achieve twelve

---

*The first ascent of Mount Jackson was led by J. C. Cunningham with W. Smith, D. T. Todd and J. L. Gardner on 23 November 1964.

Early Cretaceous fossils from Coal Nunatak, Alexander Island about 105 million years old. (BAS)

Above left: Gonatosorus *sp. (fossil fern)*

Above right: Sphenopteris *sp. (fossil fern)*

Opposite: Leaf of an early Ginkgo tree

hours' travel and four hours' work in every twenty-four, but had soon found the regime too much. This year we realised we could work only if we travelled fast.

On the way back we stopped for a day at Ablation Point, and each spent twelve hours working separately in the hills. We thought there was tidal movement in the embayment, and if indeed there was a tide, the bay itself must be filled with sea ice, not ice shelf. This would provide a useful datum for survey purposes. But it would certainly be surprising, indicating that the adjacent ice shelf must thin out towards the coast at this point. (In 1970 this was proved correct.)

Leaving on 15 December, the teams were soon involved in the crevassed zone which had caused us trouble the previous year. Then we had nearly lost

Adie's Mutt when his trace broke while crossing a crevasse. Peering into the depths we had seen him quietly standing on a bridge of ice twenty feet down.

... we pushed the sledge back over the crevase to act as a bridge ... about 20 feet down I came to rest on ice spanning the crevasse ... Mutt stood quietly without so much as looking round ... amidst a shower of tinkling icicles which plunged on past,

and speaking gently to him I fixed the rope to his harness. Then Ray, who had tied my life line firmly to the sledge, began to haul the 100 pound dog slowly upward . . . While this was going on I had the opportunity to study the magnificent sight of the narrow, cavernous place in which I found myself. Everywhere hung huge icicles 10 to 15 feet long, with bases as much as 18 inches thick. Of these I had to be careful, for a piece could easily be dislodged and could have knocked me out . . . The walls were hung with an amazing lace-like curtain of ice crystals, the individual crystals being an inch in diameter and linked together to form glittering pendants.
Author's journal

Remembering that experience, this time I tried to keep as far east as possible, but we were confined by great pressure ridges sweeping out into the Sound from Albation Point. Thaw conditions are the worst possible for travel in crevassed areas and we soon found that where the bridges had not already fallen in, they did so immediately the sledges crossed.

It was interesting to observe Darkie's technique. He advanced cautiously, somewhat in the fashion of an heraldic lion or leopard, each paw extended as far as possible to test the surface in front of him. In this way he found every crevasse and successfully crossed the majority, whereas those behind went blundering into them in spite of the obvious holes he had made. Others would suddenly dash sideways to avoid an imaginary crevasse which was no more than a surface marking in the snow, which Darkie had ignored. Indeed with him ahead, be it on glacier or thin sea ice, I can move forward with the greatest confidence.
Author's journal

On the seventy-ninth day of our journey we were once more back near the depot left on the edge of the ice shelf, with only one day's dog food left and still 150 miles to go. There we were shocked to find that the shelf had calved, and our supplies now lay on what was an iceberg, with sheer forty-foot walls descending to open water. Below us, and some 400 yards away on the sea ice, lay a seal we had killed and left for the return journey, separated from us by a belt of open water. I set off along the high front of the ice shelf, seeking a way down onto the sea ice, and eventually recovered the seal, but it cost me eighteen miles to provide the dogs' dinner which had been lying so close to us.

After that we still had to recover the depot. With considerable relief we found a point where the iceberg was still only ten feet from the cliff on which we stood. This we bridged precariously with a twelve-foot sledge, by building a snow mound on the very edge of the chasm, to act as a fulcrum, so that our combined weight could hold the sledge tilted in the air as it was pushed across. Once in position, we anchored it securely at both ends, and then laboriously brought across the second sledge to pick up the cache lying a few hundred yards away.

The last leg home led past Cape Jeremy, Mushroom Island, the Terra

Firma Islands and the Refuge Islands, clearing the depots as we went. During this period came high temperatures, mist and fog, and for a time we were all coated with white rime. Each black, doggy face looked distinctly odd through this white mask and the long hair on their backs and tails drooping with its weight seemed to be covered in delicate white lace.

Then the temperature dropped and we made better time, covering thirty-one miles on each of three successive days. Despite this, however, travelling was far from straightforward, for it was high summer and the ice was deteriorating fast. On 28 December we made our final run in, not a day too soon for we were only just able to cross Neny Fjord. First we became involved in a series of diversions due to long tide cracks, and then found ourselves in a maze of melt pools, between which we had to drive with scarcely enough room for the sledge to balance on the ridges between them. The dogs, deeply suspicious of the water, refused to run through the pools, always trying to find a winding route which kept them on dry snow.

The inevitable happened. My sledge tipped sideways and turned over in a foot-deep pool, then Adie's did the same, then mine a second time. All our gear, and worse still our maps and notes, were sodden, while the wind blew across our course at thirty knots, with strong gusts which made the teams unwilling to run sideways to it. It was useless to try and keep clear of pools so I headed into wind, but we made little progress despite throwing some of the dogs into the water hoping they would lose their disinclination to get wet. After a few hours of this we were very hot from our struggles, and decided to drop 600 pounds to be picked up later in more propitious conditions. Providentially we did this just in time, for within 400 yards I went straight through the bottom of a pool to the sea beneath. Adie perforce followed, and had he been heavily laden the remaining ice below could well have broken.

The wind increased, sometimes carrying clouds of flying ice particles, the teams hardly able to move against it, and ski-ing was out of the question. So we plodded on behind the sledges, pushing when necessary and caring nothing for the water. Presently the pools froze lightly, the dogs could step warily across although the sledges ploughed through, running on rotten ice below. When two miles from home we were seen, and Jones and Blaiklock came out to guide us in.

The base had laid out mile-long strips of a mixture compounded of soot, black diesel oil and sea water, aimed at hastening the melt so that a water strip would be available for the expected sea-plane. This had worked only too well, and now they led us along the only route past long parallel lines of open water. So we arrived home, after covering 1,084 miles in ninety days. Steaming baths were ready, a considerate gesture extended to returning sledgers, made partly in self-defence for they never realise how evil they smell!

During our absence Jones and Blaiklock had sledged north to complete the survey work in Bourgeois Fjord, and had discovered that it was connected with Bigourdan Fjord by a channel filled by an ice shelf. This was probably the last remnant of a shelf which must once have extended through all the fjords, and perhaps the whole of Marguerite Bay. Its presence supported the earlier deductions of Launcelot Fleming, who had been both geologist and padre with the British Graham Land Expedition.

1949/50   Even more important for us, *Biscoe* had brought out two sea-planes, a de Havilland Norseman and an Auster. The former had been procured in Canada by the Governor himself who was determined on a successful relief, by air if necessary. This was the last Norseman ever built, for the type was soon to be replaced by the Beaver, two of which Sir Miles had ordered for later Government use in the Falkland Islands.

By early January 1950 the planes were at Deception and ready to fly, but it was planned that they would try to reach us from the Argentine Islands, over 200 miles nearer to Stonington. However, ice prevented *Biscoe* from getting there until the 28th. Meanwhile we too had our part to play in the operation. Appropriate flying loads were packed and weighed, regular radio 'scheds' and meteorological flying forecasts maintained, boats prepared to take us out to a plane if evacuation became necessary, ice conditions carefully observed, both locally and from the top of Neny Island as far as the horizon, and the base prepared for closure.

The first large pool of water, some 700 yards long, appeared in Neny Fjord, gradually extending to over a mile within two days. On the 28th Port Lockroy had been reopened, and two days later we were in hourly communication with the Governor, who despatched the Norseman on a reconnaissance flight. That afternoon the red and silver plane flew in from the north, soon it was circling base, dropping our mail and a welcome leg of lamb. Then Pilot Officer Pete St Louis RCAF flew off to investigate conditions in Neny Fjord. From base it looked as if the melt area had again been covered by jostling ice floes, and we were greatly astonished to hear that he was coming down.

What a scurry – everyone tearing hither and thither, dressing, loading a sledge, rushing off across the ice. John (Huckle) and I were first away to get the dory we had placed at Neny into the water. Then followed Stonehouse, Randall, Jones and Adie with the sledge. Looking back we saw that it had sunk, later it transpired that this happened a number of times, soaking the personal gear and records.

Meanwhile Huckle and I strode on, launched the boat and had it waiting for Randall and Stonehouse, the first to arrive. The aircraft seemed a long way off and we could see no open water, nothing but a heaving mass of brash and floes, but apparently decreasing in quantity further out. It was clearly necessary to hasten yet avoid overloading the dory, which would have to be lifted in and out of the water to

The Norseman arrives to relieve Stonington. (V. E. Fuchs)

pass the heavy ice near shore. I therefore sent off Huckle, Stonehouse and Randall without waiting for the others or any of the gear to arrive. I hoped that (Ken) Butler, due to join us from the plane as relief radio operator, would be able to bring the boat back to the heavier ice where we could have gone out to help him. But conditions proved to be so bad further out that this was impossible, indeed it took the boat nearly two hours to reach the plane. Rising wind and increasing overcast forced the pilot to take off immediately with Stonehouse and Randall, leaving Huckle who volunteered to return with Butler.
Author's journal

That evening we drank the last carefully preserved bottle of gin to celebrate Ken Butler's return to Stonington – the first new face we had seen in two years. There followed a further wait of eight days due to bad weather, but on

6 February the Norseman arrived, again piloted by St Louis, and this time able to land close to the ice edge, so loading was easy. The outgoing passengers were the last of the three-year men, Adie, Jones and Huckle, together with the penguins, and assorted specimens and records. It was a great relief to know that they at least would now get home, come what may.

Meanwhile Flight Lieutenant John Lewis RAF was using the Auster to reconnoitre the ice situation for *Biscoe*'s attempt to reach us, and three days later she was making good progress southward. That evening we paid our last visit to the observation point on Northeast Glacier. Through glasses we saw innumerable icebergs breaking the line of the darkening horizon, among them the intermittent winking of the ship's masthead light as she wove an erratic course through ice invisible to us. In a few hours she was gliding silently down Neny Fjord, past Neny Island, her dark hull twinkling with lights.

After the first greeting, final plans were made for embarkation during the next two days. Our most painful duty was the necessity to put down all but thirty-seven dogs, the maximum number we could take out in the ship. It was something we had dreaded for they were our friends and had shared our lives. To them we owed our achievements, sometimes even our survival, and now we were going to break the mutual trust which had built up between us. Quietly, in the night, a few of us steeled ourselves for the inevitable, our only comfort lying in the knowledge that as each animal in turn enjoyed his last meal isolated from his companions, none of them knew what was about to happen. It was a terrible thing to have to do.

Of the remainder, most went to live at other bases. A team of nine came back to England, to play their part in the Polar Pavilion during the Festival of Britain. There Darkie and his followers gave over 2,000 sledging performances for the public, living isolated in the grounds under special quarantine conditions. They were a great draw. Two drivers lived with them, and each morning the team was exercised in harness, hauling a sledge around the grounds before the public were admitted.

When, after six months, the Festival ended, Darkie came to live with me in Cambridge where he became a well-known figure. He always wove a careful course through the traffic as he hauled me on a bicycle, ever punctillious in obeying commands regarding the lights. But it took a long time to teach him not to jump the white lines, which *he* knew to be 'crevasses' in the tarmac.

By the evening of 11 February 1950 the chimneys, windows and doors had all been boarded up and we said goodbye to Stonington. It seemed extraordinary, but we were truly sad at leaving – the beginning of a nostalgia which has remained with all The Lost Eleven ever since.

6

Kaleidoscope
1950–8

1950–59 With both Hope Bay and Stonington closed, the Survey's activities were greatly reduced and for a time our story becomes less coherent. The reader must forgive me if I ignore chronology. Geology and glaciology at Admiralty Bay ceased with the departure of Jardine and Hattersley-Smith, and although six stations remained open, the work was reduced to meteorological recording, except at Signy. Here Sladen returned for a second tour as Base Leader and to study the penguins.

A new base was established at Grytviken, South Georgia, under Danny Borland, a professional meteorological forecaster who took over from the amateurs at the whaling stations. In 1951 he was succeeded by Laws, who re-engaged for a second tour to continue his work on elephant seals. When he left, the Government took over the station from FIDS, and Borland returned – to remain there almost continuously for over twenty years, soon becoming the uncrowned king of South Georgia.

The men were not idle, nor did they fail to create their own personal adventures in competing with the environment, but the Colonial Office still had no long-term plan for Antarctic work, and scientific direction was inadequate. The total field staff was only twenty-six, and the annual budget for all purposes, including ships' operations, £149,000.

At home the battle for the expansion of polar research continued, waged by the FIDS Advisory Committee, and in particular by Brian Roberts and Neil Mackintosh who, between them, gradually extended the *Scientific Instructions* which were to give direction to future field parties. When Sir Miles Clifford took personal control of the Survey, he had appointed Ken Butler (ex-Stonington) as Secretary, FIDS – always known colloquially as SECFIDS – to head a small administrative staff in Stanley. He had also charged the Crown Agents in London with responsibility for purchasing and shipping all stores, the supervision of *John Biscoe*'s refit, and the annual recruitment of scientific and support staff.

Like the Advisory Committee, the Governor was determined that there should be scientific productivity, but from his point of view it was important that there should also be some advantage to the whalers, whose taxes paid for the Survey in the early post-war years. This meant an emphasis on meteorology, which to some extent conflicted with the views of the committee members who were anxious to promote topographical survey, geology, biology and glaciology. Nevertheless, he recognised the opportunities in these other fields, and a broad scientific plan finally emerged.

Alas, the system did not work very well, for despite the lack of any scientific advisers in the Falklands, the Colonial Office required the Governor to propose the annual plans. By the time these were received in England, there was little opportunity to modify them in keeping with the scientific proposals put forward by the committee. Thus coordination of administration and science was difficult to achieve. Furthermore, there was still no established means of prosecuting research based on the information and material obtained in the field, often at great cost.

All this was recognised by the committee, although the Colonial Office members were unimpressed by demands for a scientific organisation. They paid lip service to science, but it was not in their original brief to make any substantial contribution. Nor were they personally interested, scientifically orientated, or aware of the possibilities.

A harassed senior official, when I challenged him that the only interest seemed to be in finding some immediate return like gold or uranium, exclaimed in horror, 'Heaven forbid – that would only make things much worse – think of the international trouble it would cause!' So what were poor scientists to do? To find something valuable would make trouble, to soldier on without proper facilities was a travesty of science, yet the word itself was being used to cloak the real reason for Britain's return to Antarctica.

There was already a considerable accumulation of records and specimens, and by 1950 some means of handling them was becoming increasingly urgent. Pressed by Roberts, scientific members of the committee, together with some of the scientists who had returned from the bases, met Dr N. B. Kinnear, Director of the British Museum (Natural History), to discuss what should or could be done. Mackintosh, as Director of Discovery Investigations, had been receiving most of the reports, and had undertaken to keep at least some order in the mounting mass of material. A possible course of action was for Discovery Investigations to become responsible for the custody of specimens and records, and their distribution to specialists to work up, but this could only be a temporary expedient, for the future of that organisation itself was uncertain.

Then the Natural History Museum agreed to store the specimens, recognising that they would remain the property of the Governor of the

Falkland Islands unless and until he released them for incorporation in the Museum collections. The Museum was also asked to consider the publication of a series of scientific reports which would include all subjects except meteorology and survey. These would be the responsibility of the Meteorological Office and the Directorate of Overseas Surveys respectively.

Hardly had these matters come under discussion than Sir Miles Clifford sent home a plan for the development of a Falkland Islands and Dependencies Meteorological Service. He proposed that it should have its own Director and integrate the meteorological work of the Falklands, South Georgia and the Antarctic stations. Provided the necessary manpower and money could be found, the Meteorological Office favoured this idea, but considered it was too soon to begin upper air work, as proposed in the Governor's scheme. For the Colonial Office the plan would ensure continuity of occupation without incurring additional expenditure on other work.

The last point made the suggestion unacceptable, as it stood, to the scientific members of the Advisory Committee. They still stressed the urgent need for continued mapping, the extension of geological and biological work, glaciology and other studies, recognising that there was so much to be done, if only the Government was not too parsimonious in providing the means.

Finally Mackintosh strongly recommended the establishment of a small separate office to handle material arriving back from the field, under a scientist with Antarctic experience. This was agreed, and when I returned from Stonington in April 1950 I was offered the post. Under the unwieldy title of Falkland Islands Dependencies Scientific Bureau (FIDSC Bureau) we set up a proper scientific organisation in London. This opened on 19 June in Queen Anne's Chambers, Broadway, and I was given a place on the Advisory Committee.

Our original offices consisted of two bare rooms containing two wooden tables, two chairs and two steel cupboards, crammed with some hundreds of field reports. My instructions were to buy a typewriter and some stationery, and an armchair for visitors. Later it was hoped that I might be able to employ a typist, and even look forward to a time when I could acquire an assistant.

My brief was to interview the returning scientists and decide where, and how long, they should have to write up their results. I was also to negotiate with the Natural History Museum regarding the publication of our scientific work, and to act as the centre for the distribution of specimens and information. It also fell to my lot to deal with innumerable queries which were already arriving from the public.

In the course of time I recruited my assistant, Miss Evelyn Todd, a

Geography graduate from Cambridge who has been with us ever since. As our typist was called 'Eve', I arbitrarily decided that she would become 'Anne' – and thus she has been known to successive generations of Fids for nearly thirty years.

With Anne's assistance my task was greatly eased. I soon realised that her meticulous accuracy and capacity for taking pains enabled me to hand over to her the stream of enquiries which poured into the office. When later we began publishing, she became the first editor of our scientific reports, and as time passed her small office was so congested with incoming publications, the photographic library, and hundreds of Base Reports that she could hardly move round it. So far the office has moved six times and each move was an increasing nightmare as Anne contemplated the mass of paper to be sorted out again at the other end. The stacks of files are still growing higher, but when a Fid is seeking some obscure fact from the past his first thought is 'Anne will know' – and she always does.

Our daily grind was sometimes enlivened in unexpected ways. During the late Antarctic winter of 1950 one of the men at a small base became increasingly withdrawn, spending most of his time sharpening a knife for no apparent purpose. When questioned by his Base Leader he was unable to explain this, but volunteered the information that he did not really feel responsible for his actions, even suggesting that it might be safer if his companions tied him up. So they lashed him to his bunk, and for some weeks until the relief ship arrived, he remained happily under restraint, only being released for meals. *Biscoe* was specially diverted to fetch him out to be sent home for treatment.

At Montevideo the shipping company refused to carry him unless accompanied, so another Fid was detailed to travel home with him, and as soon as they arrived in England the escort reported to me at the Bureau. I learnt that on one occasion during the voyage the patient had woken up and asked his friend to please lend him his soul in order to fetch back his own which, he alleged, had left their cabin. 'What did you do?' I asked with considerable curiosity. 'Well, I hardly liked to lend him mine', was the bizarre reply, 'I wasn't really sure I'd get it back'. The trouble seemed contagious!

Although meteorology and survey were specifically excepted from my responsibilities, it was not long before I inevitably found myself involved in both. Neither the Meteorological Office nor the Directorate of Overseas Surveys had direct knowledge of Antarctic affairs, nor was there any easy means of communication with the Governor. At that time no planes flew to the Falklands, and there were only ten mailing opportunities each year. Thus an exchange of letters took two to three months.

The Bureau was not officially concerned with the annual recruitment of staff, but the Crown Agents asked me to sit in on interviews for the selection of scientists. It was soon clear that advertising scientific posts was not the best method of getting men temperamentally suitable for Antarctic life. To improve this situation the Colonial Office was persuaded to second a 'Personnel Officer', and in 1956 W. O. (Bill) Sloman joined the Bureau, one of the best things that ever happened to the Survey.

He began regular annual visits to all the major universities throughout the country, lecturing with slides in the relevant departments, and explaining to qualifying graduates the opportunities for both professional experience and high adventure. This quickly paid dividends and the procedure has been followed ever since. Every year, from October to Easter, the personnel staff make the round of universities, and as a result the Survey has never been short of recruits. For over twenty years Bill himself bore the full brunt of this annual exercise, always establishing and cultivating invaluable relationships in the departments he visited. During the (English) summer the candidates came for interview and Bill always chaired the Selection Board, specialist scientists or technical staff sitting with him as appropriate to the categories being recruited. This established a continuity of judgement over the years, and did more than anything else I know to try and ensure compatibility among young men facing two years of isolation together.

Since FIDS had no laboratories or library, it was necessary to go cap in hand to various university departments and persuade professors to accept a geologist here, a biologist there, to work under their supervision. This made it difficult for me to keep proper contact, but had the advantage of bringing to notice, in many parts of the country, the Antarctic work that was going on. The Survey owes a great debt to the many heads of departments who helped in this way. Other work was farmed out to appropriate specialists in the Natural History Museum or in universities at home and overseas.

By 1951 I had discovered that the Museum was not really in a position to publish the amount of material which was coming back to the Bureau. This led to the idea of starting our own series of scientific reports. Negotiations were opened with the Cambridge University Press but Her Majesty's Stationery Office insisted on their right to publish Government-sponsored work. I based the format and style on the *Discovery Reports*, and when all the arguments regarding size of print, type of paper and photographic reproduction had been resolved, *Falkland Islands Dependencies Survey Scientific Reports No. 1* appeared. Thereafter it was usual for the scientific results to be published in this series, although contributions to *Nature* and other specialist journals were encouraged when the subject matter was appropriate.

By 1961 difficulties over the specialised nature of our reports led the Stationery Office to agree that we should use a private printer, and in 1962 when the name of the organisation had been changed, the series became *British Antarctic Survey Scientific Reports*. Soon after this the need arose for a vehicle in which to publish shorter papers, as a result of which the first copy of *British Antarctic Survey Bulletin* appeared in 1963.

By 1954 a number of things were happening simultaneously. Internationally, there were incipient scientific plans to hold a Third Polar Year during 1957–8 (following those held in 1882–3 and 1932–3), but this time the studies were to be part of a global investigation, not confined to the polar regions. The period was therefore to be known as the International Geophysical Year (IGY).

Meanwhile Brian Roberts, who had been advocating aerial photography of the Antarctic Peninsula for a number of years, now saw the possibility of this being realised and plans were in the making. At the same time I was personally preoccupied with plans for the Trans-Antarctic Expedition (TAE), a project which had been in my mind since the last year I spent at Stonington.

For the IGY, twelve nations undertook to maintain stations in the Antarctic. Taking into account all the existing political disputes, and the participation by nations not in dispute with anybody, special arrangements were necessary to ensure that the planned scientific programmes could go ahead without hindrance. It was agreed that for the duration of the IGY all claimant countries would permit anyone to mount programmes anywhere in 'their territory', and that all information obtained would be freely exchanged.

The coordination of the scientific activities became the responsibility of the Special Committee for Antarctic Research (SCAR), working under the aegis of the International Council of Scientific Unions (ICSU). SCAR had no executive function, but was to provide a forum for discussion, and hence advice, regarding the value of proposed research and the means to be employed in carrying it out.

During the IGY forty-four Antarctic and sub-Antarctic stations were occupied, the Americans putting in a base entirely by air at the South Pole itself, while the Russians established themselves at the Pole of Relative Inaccessibility, the point on the continent furthest from any coast. The principal objectives of the IGY were the examination of the earth and its atmosphere, and the effect of the sun upon them. Studies were made of aurorae, cosmic rays, geomagnetism, glaciology, ionospheric physics, meteorology, seismology and gravity. Some countries included biology, geology and oceanographic work.

Particular attention was paid to meteorology, for the wide, though sparse, distribution of stations on the continent made it possible for the first time to gain a comprehensive picture of the southern weather systems. The network was broken down into groups of 'daughter stations' reporting to 'mother stations' and so to the IGY Weather Centre, established at Little America on the coast of the Ross Sea. There, a team drawn from six countries compiled upper air and surface charts, issuing daily weather forecasts which were invaluable to the flying programmes. Thus an overall picture of Antarctic weather began to emerge.

As far as possible all FIDS stations were geared to contribute to IGY programmes. In 1954 we had already begun to replace the old Argentine Islands station, known as Wordie House, by a new geophysical observatory on Winter Island. This was to handle geomagnetism, seismology, upper air observations, ozone measurements and tides. Ralph Lenton, who by then had wintered at Signy, Admiralty Bay, Deception and Port Lockroy (at the last two as Base Leader), was sent to take charge of the building. He was faced with the complex problems of constructing a non-magnetic hut, and installing a Dobson ozone spectrophotometer and a seismograph. By 1955 all these were operational, and when six years later Port Lockroy was finally closed, the ionospheric programme was also transferred to the observatory.

Sir Raynor Arthur succeeded Sir Miles Clifford as Governor in 1954. He too was anxious to promote increased scientific activity at the bases, although not solely in the interests of IGY. This resulted in the establishment of two more stations in 1955, at Anvers Island north of the Argentine Islands, and Horseshoe Island in Marguerite Bay. The following year two more bases were built on Danco Island, Danco Coast, and on Detaille Island off the Loubet Coast in Lallemand Fjord. Yet one more was opened at Prospect Point, on the Graham Coast in 1957. Of these five stations only Detaille and Horseshoe, where surface meteorological observations were maintained, contributed to the IGY geophysical programmes, the others being mainly concerned with topographical survey and geology.

Since none of the FIDS bases lay to the east of the Weddell Sea, which was a key area in establishing broad geophysical coverage of the continent, the Royal Society decided to build a station on the Caird Coast. It was to be named Halley Bay in honour of the man who discovered Halley's Comet, and was destined to make the major British contribution to IGY.

Meanwhile, my proposals for a Trans-Antarctic Expedition, with its need of Government financial support, had appeared to Roberts as a competitive threat to his proposed aerial survey. I was in an invidious position, for as Director of the Scientific Bureau I also had a vested interest in his scheme. There were many arguments as he and I pressed ahead with our respective plans, but in the end both were successfully achieved, for TAE received a

Government grant of £100,000 (towards the total cost of £725,000), while £250,000 was provided for the air photography.

This was undertaken on contract by Hunting Aerosurveys Ltd under the direction of Peter Mott, Technical Director of the company, with John Safferey as Flying Manager. It became known as the Falkland Islands and Dependencies Aerial Survey Expedition (FIDASE), and extended over the two summer seasons 1955/6 and 1956/7. Using a chartered Danish ship, *Oluf Sven* (950 tons) the FIDASE base was established at Deception Island near the FIDS station. Two Canso flying-boats, the amphibian version of the Catalina, were flown down from Canada, because their endurance of thirteen hours would enable them to work as far south as Marguerite Bay. But as much of the area rose steeply to between 4,000 and 8,000 feet, their limited operational altitude of 14,000 feet was a disadvantage for photographic mapping. Nevertheless, good coverage was obtained, extending from the tip of Trinity Peninsula as far as the southern end of Adelaide Island, a distance of some 500 miles, and in addition included the South Shetlands and other islands lying off the mainland coast.

For ground control FIDASE used two helicopters to establish eighty-four fixed points as far south as Cape Renard, but in the second season they only had one, and this unhappily crashed on Tower Island though neither of the occupants was injured. They were then reduced to man-hauled sledges for ground control on King George Island until another helicopter could be obtained five weeks later. By that time little of the season remained, and the area over which control had been established was only 6,000 square miles out of the 37,000 for which vertical photography had been flown.

In later years FIDS surveyors using tellurometers established control throughout the length of the Antarctic Peninsula, and this has made it possible to use much of the remaining air photography for map production.

My TAE plans finally took shape in 1955, calling for the establishment of a base in roughly the same area as the Royal Society had chosen for their IGY station. Although the two expeditions were completely separate operations, we originally hoped to set ourselves up at one site if possible. The Royal Society party sailed south in MV *Tottan* and reached the Caird Coast first, but as their Captain considered the ice further south to be impenetrable, their Leader, David Dalgliesh who had been with me at Stonington, decided to land in latitude 75°35'S on a floating ice shelf some 500 feet thick.

The Caird Coast is bounded by continuous ice cliffs up to ninety feet high,

Opposite: (top) Danco Island hut.
(bottom) Rongé Island in middle distance, Danco Island in foreground. (F. E. Wooden)

and Dalgliesh's first problem was to find a breach where it would be possible to unload stores. There was a small embayment where the winter sea ice still remained fast, from which a long slope of drifted snow rose gently upwards to the level surface of the ice shelf 100 feet above sea-level. A mile inland from here they began building Halley Bay. Huts erected on ice shelves pose great problems, for the ice is constantly being eroded from beneath by currents, while snow and drift accumulate on top. Therefore any building soon disappears below the surface, where tremendous pressures are exerted turning the snow to ice, which then deforms and flows under its own weight. Their main hut was of the same design as that developed for TAE. First a 'carpet' of expanded metal was laid down on a levelled area, and on this the building was erected. The most unusual feature was a series of V-shaped struts of nine-inch timbers which extended every eight feet from the centre of the floor to the roof. This not only gave great strength but would, it was hoped, prevent the usual upward arching of the floors of huts put up on ice. In those days the mechanics of this were not understood.

Three weeks after *Tottan* landed her party, the TAE arrived in MV *Theron*. Halley Bay was nearly 200 miles short of where we had planned to build our base, and air reconnaissance showed heavy crevassing inland, which would seriously impede our proposed journey to the Pole. So after a short visit I decided to try and push further south. Owing to the daring and determination of Captain Harold Marø we finally succeeded in establishing Shackleton Base at the head of the Weddell Sea.★

By 1954 *Biscoe* was ageing, and could not be expected to service the increased number of bases. To meet this situation Colonial Office approval was given for the laying-down of a new steel ship to replace her. In addition, the purchase of a year-old Swedish vessel *Arendal*, built for work in the Baltic ice, was also authorised. After being modified to carry more passengers she was re-named RRS *Shackleton*, and sailed south for the 1955/6 season under the command of Captain W. (Bill) Johnston. The new *John Biscoe* was launched at Paisley, and also given the status of a Royal Research Ship. (The old *Biscoe* was sold to the New Zealand Government to become HMNZS *Endeavour*; she was used in support of the New Zealand group of the TAE.) In 1956/7 Captain Norman Brown (ex-First Officer of the old *Biscoe*) took over *Shackleton*, while Bill Johnston became the senior Master in command of the new *Biscoe*.

Meanwhile the Royal Yacht *Britannia* had carried HRH The Duke of Edinburgh on his world tour, which included a visit to Australia to open the

★An account of TAE is not part of the FIDS story but may be found in *The Crossing of Antarctica*, Fuchs & Hillary, Cassells, 1959. Among the sixteen members of the Crossing Party were David Stratton (ex-Hope Bay), Ken Blaiklock (ex-Stonington & Hope Bay), Ralph Lenton (ex-Signy, Admiralty Bay, Lockroy, Deception and Argentine Islands), and John Lewis who had flown in to rescue us from Stonington in 1950.

Canso flying-boat at Deception Island (FIDASE). (F. E. Wooden)

1956 Olympic Games, and a visit to the British Antarctic bases. On 1 January 1957 *Britannia* arrived off the Antarctic Peninsula, but since she was not ice-strengthened she could not take the risk of entering ice-filled waters. Prince Philip, accompanied by Sir Raymond Priestley and Edward Seago the artist, together with some members of the suite, therefore transferred to *Biscoe*, which was also carrying the Governor, Bill Sloman from London headquarters, and Crawford Brooks, that season's American Observer to the FIDS stations. Sir Raymond, who had been south with both Shackleton and Scott at the beginning of the century, was already sixty-nine years old. He was wonderful company, a born *raconteur* with an inexhaustible fund of anecdotes which endeared him to all.

Their first call was to Detaille Island, and notable for the first game of tennis ever played south of the Antarctic Circle. It transpired that Crawford Brooks was such a tennis enthusiast that he never went anywhere without racquets and balls. These he suddenly produced like rabbits out of a hat, as he saw his opportunity for a really original game. Because the balls would not bounce on the snow surface, the rules were appropriately modified to 'continuous volleying', and he challenged Sloman to an experimental match. Seeing what was afoot and not to be outdone, Prince Philip promptly challenged Sir Raynor Arthur to a game. Soon his equerries, and even Sir Raymond, never one to be left out, were testing their skill. So was formed the first, and possibly the last, Antarctic Tennis Club. It was suitably commemorated when Brooks returned to America and sent each member a special tie embellished with penguins and crossed racquets.

  Biscoe next called at the Argentine Islands, and then visited Anvers where Peter Hooper had laid on a dog sledge ride for the royal visitor. One recalcitrant member of the team was an animal named 'Duke', and for weeks prior to this visit base members had spent much time coaching each other never to urge him on with shouts of 'Duke, you bastard – PULL'. The royal

RY Britannia *and* HMS Protector *at Port Lockroy. (Royal Navy)*

suite have a knack of hearing about things like this, and the Duke of Edinburgh came ashore for his ride eagerly watching for the system to break down – but the Fids kept their cool, and their manners were impeccable.

  It was a fairly difficult ice season, and the skilled efforts of Bill Johnston and 'Digger' Ward, the Chief Engineer, in keeping the ship moving in the intricate maze of pack ice did not go unnoticed. They were to be Antarctic shipmates for many years, and later Bill used to describe events as BC (Before Chiefie) or AD (After Digger). At Lockroy they found *Britannia* and HMS *Protector* waiting. Before returning to the Royal Yacht the Prince visited the station, sheltering beneath the towering crags of the Fief Mountains. There the ionospheric recordings were becoming of increasing importance, as the base was now part of the IGY network.

  That evening all three ships sailed for Deception, making a brief call *en route* at Danco Island. On arrival visibility was too bad for *Britannia* to enter

Prince Philip and Sir Raymond Priestley at Anvers Island. (BAS)

Neptune's Bellows, so the royal party suffered a rough passage by launch to reach the base. On the way in they passed the hulk of a Salvesen whale-catcher, the *Southern Hunter*, which had been wrecked three weeks earlier on 31 December.

Although not entered in the records, the story goes that the catcher had entered Whaler's Bay, cruised around, and was seen to disappear on her way out through Neptune's Bellows. Apparently she met an Argentine ship coming in through the narrow channel and, to avoid collision, altered course to starboard. Almost at once she struck the reef which lies near the middle of the Bellows. Immediately her siren was sounded, the Norwegian crew started shouting and waving to the Argentinians for all they were worth. Unaware of the catastrophe the latter returned the compliment by hooting and waving back. Under the happy impression that they were the recipients of New Year greetings, they sailed serenely on, leaving the castaways to their fate. Fortunately another Norwegian catcher soon appeared on the scene and took off the crew. The wreck remained on the reef for many years as a grim warning.

Owing to its position, and the excellent harbour facilities, Deception always achieved more callers than other bases, and a custom had grown whereby visitors were invited to sign an immense board in the lounge, at the same time being relieved of some personal memento to be pinned beside their signatures. Prince Philip was not excused this ritual. A length of his tie was ceremoniously cut off midst much jubilation, but his ever vigilant staff had demonstrated intelligent anticipation, for within moments Commander Michael Parker produced a duplicate from his pocket. Two girl secretaries from *Britannia* each lost a lock of hair removed with a blunt penknife. Years later I was to admire these trophies, proudly displayed as the cream of an unusual and treasured collection.

Escorted by *Protector*, *Britannia* paid a final visit to Admiralty Bay where the Prince went ashore to inspect the base, and so ended his tour of six FIDS stations. It had been eagerly anticipated by young men spending two years of their lives in isolation and was a great boost to morale. It had also been great fun – one hopes for Prince Philip too.

The Anvers base had been set up as the result of a visit by an old Falkland Islander to the Bureau in 1953. He showed me a nodule of copper ore (47% copper) which he claimed to have collected at low tide among the boulders at the foot of ice cliffs on the western side of the Lemaire Channel. The site lay below the green stained rocks of Copper Peak, and with this somewhat dubious evidence of mineralisation we had decided to investigate.

So it was that Ken Blaiklock (ex-Stonington and Hope Bay), in overall charge of the 1954/5 summer operations, had found himself in a chartered Norwegian ship, the *Norsel*, searching the coast of Anvers for a possible landing place and building site, which also provided access to the interior. Sailing along the south coast it was not long before he recorded that they had 'entered an almost land-locked harbour formed on the outer edge by a string of low islands'. Inland there was a good level area, and behind that a snow ramp leading up to an ice piedmont and the towering massif of Mount Français (9,060 feet) in the distance. Two days were spent in manhandling seventy-five tons of stores ashore, and two more in building concrete foundations for the hut. Then *Norsel* sailed, leaving Peter Hooper, geologist, in charge of a six-man party which included two surveyors.

For two years they travelled extensively over the island, making fourteen separate sledge journeys. Their first venture to the north end and over the piedmont revealed that there were only two places where they could break through into the mountains to the east. These were exploited to the full, but

MV Norsel. *(J. A. Exley)*

they also received welcome assistance from Port Lockroy. On several occasions Bob Whittock took a small boat across the Neumayer Channel to move Anvers men along the coast, and in this way they were able to work the Copper Peak area, which was otherwise inaccessible.

A major achievement was the first ascent of Mount Français, from the top of which they hoped to photograph the whole area. Stanley provided regular weather forecasts, without which it would have been foolishly dangerous to attempt the mountain, especially as the last leg entailed many hours of continuous climbing. Unhappily, just as they reached the summit they were enveloped in cloud, and had to beat a hasty retreat with few pictures of any value.

Sir Raynor Arthur was a very tall, distinguished-looking and impressive figure, sometimes daunting to the shy on first acquaintance. He was also a friendly man and when, a few months later, he arrived on his official tour of the bases, he clambered ashore at Anvers with a beaming smile and outstretched hand. 'Hullo! I'm Arthur', he announced. The nearest diminutive Fid sent down to meet the boat warmed to him, grasping his hand and pumping it up and down, he responded, 'Hullo to you – I'm Bill!' His successor, Sir Edwin Arrowsmith, arriving at another base, once found himself being introduced all round as 'Mr 'arry Smith'.

By the end of 1957 the geology and survey was finished and the base closed. We never found copper.

When later the Americans were looking for a site on which to build their Palmer Station, our abandoned hut on Anvers Island was lent to them as

Port Lockroy huts. (A. H. Swain)

temporary accommodation. They decided on the nearby Bonaparte Point where a large complex was erected for summer biological and glaciological work. In winter it was occupied by a small naval maintenance staff. As they had no experience of polar life, in the interests of safety they were not provided with skis or camping equipment, nor permitted to use the boats.

At the time we were using the high ice piedmont 1,000 feet above the shore station, as a summer airstrip, because from there men and material could be flown south long before our ships could expect to reach the southern bases. Each season we stationed two experienced men, usually mountaineers, at Anvers for the summer. They received the parties brought in by ship and guided them up through the crevasse zones to the airstrip. They were always warmly welcomed by the Americans.

As a small return, we suggested to the authorities in the States that we could perhaps contribute something by training their wintering men in polar techniques and crevasse rescue, so that they could be given more freedom to move around the island. The idea was gladly accepted, as the frustrations of men pinned down to an area only a few hundred yards round Palmer Station had already been recognised.

In 1971 Mick Pawley and Graham Wright were landed on Anvers for these purposes, and also asked to repair and paint our hut. While working in the loft a blow-torch dropped into a completely inaccessible corner, quickly setting alight the wooden wall. In minutes smoke and fumes drove them outside, where they could only stand and watch the conflagration. Every timber was consumed, and when two years later I visited the island, only a scatter of rusting metal marked the site of our old base.

Danco Island, Prospect Point, and Detaille Island were not well chosen for science. In each case this all important decision had been left to the Master of *Biscoe*. He had little knowledge of the needs of field workers and, not unnaturally, was chiefly concerned to ensure easy access by ship in later seasons. So it happened that they were built at places where access inland was restricted to a few miles or, in the case of Detaille, was cut off by open water for a large part of the year. By the end of the 1958/9 season everything that could usefully be done had been achieved and the stations closed. They are mentioned briefly here because the area was part of Prince Philip's tour, but are discussed in more detail in Chapter 9.

To return to the IGY. This experiment in scientific cooperation between nations proved so successful that, when it ended, the international scientific community persuaded the participating countries to continue working together for a further twelve months. Many did so, and this period was called the International Year of Geophysical Cooperation (IGC). It was not only valuable for science but also in prolonging the time during which political disputes were laid aside. This provided the opportunity for lengthy international discussion, which finally resulted in the drafting of an Antarctic Treaty. In December 1959, after sixty-four preparatory meetings, the proposals were initialled by twelve nations (Argentina, Australia, Belgium, Chile, France, Japan, New Zealand, Norway, South Africa, United Kingdom, United States, USSR).

Two years later this treaty was ratified and signed in Washington by the participating Governments. It is to last for thirty years before revision, during which all national territorial claims remain in abeyance, 'frozen' in fact; but they could quickly re-emerge if the treaty breaks down or is not renewed.

At last the freedom of science in Antarctica had been assured for a commendable period, and it was largely the cooperative efforts of scientists themselves that had led to this happy result and the possibility of a long-term solution to political problems in the area.

7

Intermission
1953–70

Here I must ask the reader's indulgence for a short 'Intermission' in the FIDS story. Both the mechanics of Antarctic life and the increasingly sophisticated science which today is its justification require central organisation and direction. For the record I must set down how the administration gradually expanded and developed, for it is the backcloth against which the rest of this book must be seen. To make it as painless as possible I have covered the whole seventeen years in one chapter, and it may even be omitted by any who may find it a boring interruption to the thread of what is, after all, offered as a polar odyssey.

Before I sailed with the Trans-Antarctic Expedition in the autumn of 1955 Sir Raymond Priestley came out of retirement to take over the Scientific Bureau. More than that, he was made titular head of the whole Survey until my return three years later. As a young geologist he had been a member of both Shackleton's *Nimrod* expedition, 1907–9, and Scott's *Terra Nova* expedition, 1910–13. In later life he had been Vice-Chancellor, first of the University of Melbourne, and then of the University of Birmingham.

He was an ideal person to direct and expand our scientific work, and rapidly endeared himself to the Fids. For the rest of his long life, until 1974, he was a constant guide, philosopher and friend to generations of young men who found him an inspiring, and always entertaining link with the past giants of Antarctic exploration. He had himself spent one of the hardest winters ever endured down south and his Antarctic stories were legion.

In 1953 Frank Elliott had taken over from Ken Butler as SECFIDS, remaining in Stanley for the next six years with John Green (ex-Deception and Argentine Islands) as his assistant. When Elliott retired Green became SECFIDS and Eric Salmon (ex-Signy, Deception, Argentine Islands and Detaille) joined him in the Stanley office.

Green was an enterprising character, with an endearing but sometimes expensive tendency to 'test' new equipment. This was not always a success, as when one of our newly introduced Muskeg tractors became completely bogged down in a distant Falkland stream before it ever got as far as the Antarctic. On ceremonial occasions he acted as the Governor's ADC, complete in tight trousers, spurs and wearing aiguillettes. Apart from the energy he put into the organisation of FIDS activities, he will long be remembered in Stanley for his part in a mischievous naval deception.

HMS *Nereide* was arriving to take over the role of guardship in the Dependencies, and before leaving the station the officers of HMS *Burghead Bay* were intent on perpetrating some hoax on their successors. In the absence of Sir Miles Clifford who was on leave, the Colonel commanding the Defence Force was Acting Governor, and was persuaded to look the other way while plans were hatched – even to the 'borrowing' of his uniform. Green was co-opted because no one in the Wardroom could fit into his ADC's uniform.

The ground was laid by a signal informing *Nereide* that the Acting Governor would visit the ship as soon as she anchored, and *Burghead Bay* would provide the boat to take him across the harbour. They were privately warned that he was a stickler for protocol, and would expect to be received on board with an eighteen-gun salute and a guard of honour.

As the ship came in, a by-now-slightly-nervous Green, immaculate in uniform, reported to the 'Acting Governor', played by the First Lieutenant of *Burghead Bay* resplendent in the Colonel's uniform. He was promptly placed in charge of a case labelled *Genuine Tussac Wine, vinted and bottled by the Falkland Islands Company. Produce of the Falkland Islands*, to be taken on board as a present. They were pulled across the harbour by six smartly dressed sailors – the 'Acting Governor' disliked motor boats. Received ceremoniously, 'His Excellency' was escorted to the Captain's quarters and Green down to the Wardroom, where the native wine was greeted with delight and profuse thanks. His unease was soon assuaged by several gins, until it was time for him to rejoin the Captain before attending the 'Governor' on his departure. Green wondered what had been going on above,

. . . but judging by the burst of laughter which greeted me as I knocked, all was well. They were both in tremendous form. The Captain embraced me with one arm and proffered a large gin with the other. A further flow of sallies from the 'Acting Governor' continued to convulse the Captain, and somehow induced a fit of hysteria in me. With tears steaming down my face, I shall never forget the relief with which I heard the words 'Governor's boat alongside, Sir'; and the despair which followed when the Captain said, 'Tell it to wait. One for the road, Sir?'

At last we emerged into the blinding sunshine of a bright Falkland's day. Up went a sword in salute, and we descended to the shrill of the bosun's pipe and entered the boat. Halfway between the two ships all was revealed when the men groped into a variety of boxes. In seconds Very lights and rockets were whizzing up from our boat in all directions, accompanied by a similar display from the foredeck of *Burghead Bay*. Back on board the scene in the Wardroom was indescribable. My earlier hysterics were mild by comparison. The Captain broke out champagne, and Number One was chaired round the decks for his impeccable performance.

The final dénouement came later when the case of Tussac wine was opened in *Nereide*. It was a wonderful golden brown, and tasted of peat water – which it was!

When I returned to the Bureau at the end of 1958, Priestley suggested to the new Governor, Sir Edwin Arrowsmith, a complete reorganisation of the administration. The Crown Agents were still responsible for our logistics, and housed a small FIDS stores office manned by Barbara Wells, who worked direct to SECFIDS providing a liaison with the relevant departments. Sir Raymond proposed that this should be merged with the Scientific Bureau and the whole organisation directed from London. Broad agreement in principle was reached on this, but it took time to achieve full amalgamation.

As a first step I was appointed Director of the whole Survey, with the formal responsibility of keeping the Governor fully acquainted with our affairs, and through him the Colonial Office. In practice this meant that in most matters I dealt directly with them since in fact they were just around the corner.

Anne Todd, Bill Sloman and I moved offices to a tall, narrow Crown Agents' house in Gayfere Street, and I took Eleanor Honnywill from my TAE office with me as my personal assistant. The adjacent building housed Barbara Wells on the second floor but there was no central communication between the two, and no lifts. To visit the stores office next door we could either go down to the ground floor, into the street and up again, or up and across the top floors and down again. Either way we took plenty of exercise.

We were soon joined by Joe Farman and David Simmons, both geophysicists who had been together for two years at the Argentine Islands. In his second year Farman became Base Leader, and carried responsibility for all the base programmes during the IGY. They were given house room in order to sort out and put in order the field geophysical observations, for as yet there was nowhere more appropriate where this work could be done. Farman was a man of parts, whose erudition on many subjects often baffled us, with highbrow tastes in music and a connoisseur's judgement of wines which was often generously put to good use on behalf of others.

Eric Salmon came as Finance Officer on six months' probation, for he had been a meteorologist at five bases and then Establishments Officer in Stanley, but lacked financial experience. The understanding was that the Colonial

Office Finance Department would show him what was required, but his appointment would only be confirmed provided he proved his competence.

A tall, slightly stooping figure, with a serious mien which belied a mischievous sense of the ridiculous, he had a wide reputation for practical jokes. In Stanley people dined out on his spare-time escapades. Once when invited to a wedding, he and Clements, with chosen cronies, employed the hours while the bridal couple were enjoying their reception, in removing every stick of furniture from the home they were going to that evening. On arrival at an empty house the distraught bridegroom called in the police – who knew exactly what must have happened but could find no witnesses. A bargain was struck in which they offered immunity and a blind eye, providing everything was back in place within the hour. It was.

But now the Sword of Damocles hung over Salmon, and his high spirits disappeared as he laboured to acquire accounting skills. We sadly watched him brood, morosely struggling with his figures as he sought to make a responsible impression on his mentors. The first intimation of possible recovery came when practical jokes were resumed. Soon he was automatically suspected of being the instigator of all the peculiar enquiries which reached us, though many – including letters from 'flat-earthers' – turned out to be genuine. In due course his appointment was confirmed and he became an excellent Finance Officer.

Salmon's close rival in enliving our days was Sloman, who had the ability to make improbable pronouncements with such an air of dignified authority that everyone felt compelled to believe them; though the girls really should have known better than to accept that one of the Survey's aircraft had inadvertently been supplied with two left wings.

In 1963 the post of SECFIDS was abolished and John Green came back to London, where the office had moved to larger premises in Gillingham Street. There he worked as Operations Officer for three years. In Stanley Ted Clapp (ex-Argentine Islands and Hope Bay) who had been Communications Supervisor, became Officer-in-Charge of our advance headquarters. He controlled our radio station working to the bases, processed the relief ships as they passed through Stanley, issued polar clothing to the new recruits, and handled the local requirements and problems emanating from the bases. He was ably supported by Ray Clements (ex-Deception), the Supplies Officer, who took over the Office when Clapp came home on leave.

Communications were still primitive. Besides the ten mailing opportunities to Stanley each year, there was a daily exchange of about ten to twenty telegrams, with all the opportunities for misunderstanding which 'telegraphese' encourages. We could never maintain close touch with bases until many years later when teleprinters were introduced, but Clapp talked directly to them every day. In moments of trouble or triumph he was always there to encourage, guide, congratulate or commiserate. They found him a tower of strength.

When isolated communities are living in what can sometimes become stressful conditions, it is a bad thing to allow oneself the luxury of anger with a companion. But it can be good for local morale to enjoy a grumble, and particularly to have someone all can blame or hate. London headquarters was the obvious target, and often poor Clapp got the backlash – usually from both ends and sometimes simultaneously. He was the unfortunate pig-in-the-middle and fulfilled a unique but often thankless role. In moments of crisis, when the seat grew too hot, he would resort to biblical references. One morning his telegram read, 'See *Ecclesiasticus*, Chap. 4, v.3':

To a heart that is provoked add not more trouble:
and defer not to give to him that is in need.

Shortly after Green's arrival Derek Gipps, a member of the Crown Agents staff who worked in the department concerned with our supplies, also joined us. He had already spent a season south touring the bases and had become expert in our specialised needs. His boundless energy and quick-fire thinking were breath-taking, and his experience of logistic planning and procurement invaluable.

He quickly established a highly efficient Stores Section, soon joined by Maurice Sumner and Paul Whiteman, both of whom had been Base Leaders at Halley Bay. The Section took over all our logistic needs, from food, clothing, sewing machines and libraries to specially designed prefabricated huts, sophisticated scientific equipment and aircraft.

Gipps had his own unique, and often unusual, methods of getting our ships away on time, even when Southampton Docks were strike-bound and the *Queen Mary* herself could not move. Furthermore, he could somehow get them through South American bureaucracy despite the fact that they had arrived at a weekend or during an extended national fiesta, when no office was open and no decisions could be taken or clearances granted.

He was not above collaborating in Sloman's machinations. On one occasion it was known that the Survey was to have a Staff Inspection by the Civil Service Commissioners, which is a normal procedure whereby the permanent executives are assessed and their individual responsibilities scrutinised. By some devious means Sloman obtained a sheet of appropriately headed notepaper, and early in March a letter arrived stating that this time there would also be an inspection of the junior office staff on the morning of 1 April. To save time on the individual interviews the girls were instructed to bring with them a detailed statement of their skills and office functions.

We had no normal Civil Service demarcation lines. All the girls did everything as required, and then a bit more when necessary, but this summons generated sufficient anxiety for them all to compete in compiling ever longer lists of even the most trivial tasks which they performed so uncomplainingly, as they laboured over their job specifications.

Meanwhile Gipps was lining up a buddy in the Crown Agents with a poker face to play the Staff Inspector, and it was 'leaked' to the girls that it would create a good impression if they appeared for their interviews 'well dressed and properly groomed'. On the morning appointed, all the men were stunned when they appeared – where was the party!

At ten o'clock the Inspector arrived, wearing pin-stripe trousers and complete with bowler, brief case and umbrella. He must have felt nervous, for his first pronouncement was that he never interviewed women unchaperoned and Sloman must sit in with him. Each girl was summoned in turn, and subjected to a series of preposterous questions which got wilder and more irrelevant as the morning passed. Each came out flushed with indignation at the ineptitude of 'that perfectly odious and idiotic man who knows absolutely nothing'; but so good was Sloman's control that not one of them remembered the date, until noon struck and the culprits came into the office with a bottle of champagne and eight glasses. These were not even empty before plans for revenge were brewing.

Each year members of the home staff toured the bases to keep touch with the work and see first-hand the logistic problems which constantly arose. To the wintering men these visits by the 'Permafids' were known as 'summer charlies', but the annual encounters provided opportunities for the bases to let off steam; although the following winter inevitably produced another brew of grievances, for it was impossible to convey to those in the field the frequently complex reasons for decisions being taken or altered.

Later we arranged for men re-engaging for a second tour to work for a few months in the office prior to their departure. This paid many dividends, not least their ability to see, and later explain to the bases, the problems in the context of the home situation. Many of them were to return south as Base Commanders.

Since the beginning of TABARIN each base had had its Leader, the time-honoured title of the man in charge of an expedition, but as the years passed and the number of stations increased, the mantle of responsibility began to fall on younger men, very often with little experience. I became aware that leadership was sometimes giving way to a cabal, and there were even instances of men not accepting, or even realising, that final decisions lay with the Base Leader. In 1966 this led me to change the title to Base Commander – a term which leaves no doubt about who has the last say.

On the science side, a major innovation by Sir Raymond Priestley had been the formation of a Geological Section under the direction of Ray Adie, who returned from industry to take up the appointment. Priestley achieved this by persuading the University of Birmingham, and in particular Professor Fred Shotton, who was then Head of the Department of Geology and Geophysics, to accept a small group of FIDS geologists to work up their results. All were paid by the Survey but facilities were provided by the department, a contract being negotiated for five years at a time.

This proved so successful that when I became Director I sought to repeat the pattern with the other sciences. A Geophysical Section, supervised by Joe Farman, went to the Department of Natural Philosophy in the University of Edinburgh with the personal encouragement of Sir Edward Appleton, then the Principal. This department handled geomagnetism, ozone, solar radiation and seismology. The ionospheric studies remained in the hands of Roy Piggot at the Radio and Space Research Station, Slough, for he had been guiding this work since its inception. At Edinburgh Farman's knowledge of wines soon became known, and for many years he was sent regularly to the continent to spend considerable sums of money stocking up the University cellar.

For zoology another Section was set up under Martin Holdgate, and accepted into his department by Professor Eric Smith of Queen Mary College, University of London. I soon realised that botany was being neglected, yet there were abundant bryophyte and lichen floras in Antarctica, and more complex communities of flowering plants in South Georgia. To remedy this we established a Botanical Section under Stanley Greene, and Professor John Heslop-Harrison accepted it into his department in the University of Birmingham.

Topographical survey remained the responsibility of the Directorate of Overseas Surveys, where W. D. C. Wiggins, Deputy Director and later Director, received our returning surveyors. There they computed and plotted their field work under the guiding hand of Miss Barbara McHugo, and the Directorate drew and published the maps on a variety of scales.

During the 1950's glaciology was a minor activity and came within the purview of the Geological Section, but in 1963 Gordon Robin (ex-Signy), by now Director of the Scott Polar Research Institute in Cambridge, and I reached an agreement whereby the Survey would financially support the post of Assistant Director of Research in Glaciology within the Institute, and Dr Charles Swithinbank was appointed. Apart from his responsibilities to the Institute, he also supervised and promoted increased glaciology for us. Eight years later it became possible to negotiate a contract to establish a formal Glaciological Section based at the Institute, and Swithinbank became its Head.

This led to considerable expansion and, among other activities, he initiated a long-term radio-echo ice-sounding programme using equipment designed by Dr Stanley Evans, a member of the Institute staff. Basically it was a transmitter fitted in an aircraft, which made possible photographic records of the thickness of the ice over which it flew. Signals were beamed downwards from an antenna under the plane and echoes came back, both from the ice surface and the bedrock below. Thus they revealed the depth of ice cover and also the topography of the underlying surface.

Another line of research developed at this time was the study of human physiology for which the Antarctic environment is particularly suitable. Not only is the climate extreme, but isolated bases provide captive (and usually co-operative) groups ideal for experiments which can be conducted without intrusion from the outside world and under known conditions. Because there is little illness in Antarctica, it had always been difficult to recruit sufficient medical officers. As an inducement to join it was therefore decided to offer doctors the opportunity to do physiological research.

In 1956 the Medical Research Council agreed to train our medical recruits in their Division of Human Physiology before they went south. At the bases they each had a specialised project, and on return were guided and supervised in analysing their results. This scheme proved highly successful, and led to many of our young doctors gaining higher degrees. The Survey owes much to Dr Otto Edholm and his staff for all the help they gave in promoting and guiding the research.

Meteorology was in a category of its own. When in 1950 Sir Miles Clifford had set up the Falkland Islands and Dependencies Meteorological Service, Gordon Howkins (ex-Deception), who became Director, was also made responsible for the meteorological work at the Survey's bases. Advice was available from the Meteorological Office in London, but the mother station in Stanley was paid for by FIDS – apart from a small subvention of £500 a year from the colony.

When later the Survey came under the control of the Natural Environment Research Council, it was no longer possible to justify the cost of the Stanley station against the science vote. It was therefore closed, and our Geophysical Section took over the Antarctic meteorology. Transmission of the daily observations to the World Meteorological Organisation network became the responsibility of our radio station in Stanley.

The Survey had also supported and provided facilities for a variety of work promoted by universities all over the world. Among these was the Scotia Arc Project, in which Professor D. H. Griffiths and his team at Birmingham University studied the structure and development of the island arc for a number of years. They used seaborn magnetometers, gravimeters and seismic shooting.

Another activity which extended over some fifteen years was the regular recording of VLF signals ('whistlers') on behalf of Professor M. Morgan of Dartmouth College in the United States. This was first a commitment at the Argentine Islands, then since 1970, at Halley Bay. Similar work in the same field has been done at Halley Bay for Professor Tom Kaiser of the University of Sheffield, as a surface control for his satellite studies of VLF signals.

Besides such long-term projects, individual scientists from Britain, the United States, Japan and the Soviet Union have spent periods of up to a year at our bases working on their own particular projects. Such visits, together with those by senior scientists invited to the stations each summer, were valuable in providing both advice and inspiration to young workers. Many Fids have obtained higher degrees by making special studies of particular problems, while at the same time contributing to the long-term programmes.

Once this general pattern of scientific administration had been established, there were only two major changes. In 1966 Martin Holdgate left us to join the Nature Conservancy and was succeeded by E.A. (Ted) Smith. When three years later he left to take up a career in music, the Zoological and Botanical Sections were merged under the overall direction of Dick Laws (ex-Signy and South Georgia), who returned to polar work from Africa where, for many years, he had been studying large mammals. On my retirement in 1973 he was to succeed me as Director of the Survey.

In our early years the major difficulty was a total lack of 'prospects', and no permanent posts to which men could be appointed with a degree of security. Returning scientists were given a contract lasting a year or two to write up their results, so continuity was impossible. No sooner had a man gained Antarctic experience in his subject than he was forced to move to some other organisation. Increasingly we found ourselves training scientists who then went back to work in polar regions for other nations.

To solve this problem efforts were made to turn the Survey into a Public Office, which would make it possible to provide a number of permanent, pensionable posts, both in science and administration. But while this rather protracted battle was still in progress there was a change of Government, and the Treasury suddenly proposed the closing down of all British Antarctic work as part of the national economy drive.

This threat to our very existence made it essential to seek and coordinate support from all possible quarters. In its dying days the Commonwealth Relations Office, which had replaced the Colonial Office, had little stomach for supporting an organisation of which it had always had limited understanding. Their lukewarm recommendations were hardly helpful. The Ministry of Defence offered more favourable opinions of our worth, but these were not pressed very hard because they had long since decided that they had no direct interest in Antarctica.

On the other hand, the success of the IGY, which in 1961 had led to the ratification of the Antarctic Treaty, could not be ignored. The Foreign Office was keen to see Britain play her proper part in this embryonic but exciting new development in international relations. It therefore strongly supported the continuance of our work. The Royal Society also backed us to the hilt, for the scientific interest which had been aroused by their own highly successful IGY party at Halley Bay had since been maintained through the Society's own National Committee on Antarctic Research. By then this committee had also accepted responsibility for advising the Secretary of State regarding the Survey's scientific programmes.

When all the opposing arguments had been heard by the appropriate Cabinet Committee, our fate was referred to the then Council for Scientific Policy (CSP). There followed a series of cliff-hanging meetings at which various bodies and important people gave their views. I, too, was summoned to present our case to the best of my ability, very conscious that failure on my part could spell our dissolution.

In the end we were vindicated. The Council advised the Government that, on our scientific fruitfulness alone, we ought to continue to work at the existing level of activity. There is little doubt that the strong Royal Society support, so ably expressed by Dr David (later Sir David) Martin who was then Executive Secretary, was a major factor in this decision.

The Council further proposed that responsibility for our affairs should be transferred from the Commonwealth Relations Office to the newly formed Natural Environment Research Council (NERC), set up under the aegis of the Department of Education and Science. NERC agreed to accept us as one of its component bodies on the understanding that we brought with us the annual sum of one million pounds, as recommended by the Council. The CSP also supported the need for additional funds to build a new ice-strengthened ship to replace both *Shackleton* and the Danish vessel we chartered annually for the relief of Halley bay. The Cabinet agreed.

The Survey was formally transferred to NERC on 1 April 1967 – perhaps an appropriate date after so many alarms and excursions. We were legitimate at last.

Fortunately for many of the staff, our long struggle for recognition as a Public Office had ended in victory just twenty-four hours earlier. This meant that all the years of service under contract could now be counted as pensionable. Under NERC, additional permanent posts were approved. At last a proper structure had been achieved, which has since ensured a nucleus of experienced men, and consequently the possibility of properly planned continuity in the scientific programmes.

RRS Bransfield. *(S. Vallance)*

As so often happens when a change of control takes place, there followed a difficult period of adjustment, largely due to the fact that the Survey was the only NERC organisation whose interests were rooted entirely outside Britain. Even our southern hemisphere summers happened during English winters, and this meant that administrative methods developed for home-based Institutes could not easily be applied.

There was also the anomaly of including atmospheric sciences under the NERC umbrella, for normally these would have become the responsibility of the Science Research Council. Yet it was obviously impracticable to divide control of our activities between two masters, for in the Antarctic the field organisation and logistic support for all disciplines were inextricably linked.

Furthermore, there were some in high places in NERC who felt strongly that all its effort should be devoted to science in this country, and seemed unwilling to appreciate the need to look outward in a global context. Workable solutions had to be found, and in time the value of Antarctic science came to be better understood. Now the Survey enjoys the fullest NERC support, and coming under its mantle has proved invaluable in furthering Antarctic work.

Once it was agreed that we should have a new ship, the first thing to decide was the capabilities which should be built into her. I called an office meeting, with members of the Crown Agents Shipping Division in attendance, to discuss our requirements. We agreed on the need for a vessel capable of carrying 1,500 tons of cargo, a helicopter, and ninety-nine men including a crew of thirty-six. Her endurance should be fifty days at twelve knots. We proposed a length as little as possible over 300 feet with a beam of sixty feet to ensure manoeuvrability in ice, a necessary alternative to providing the power of a true icebreaker. To allow her to operate in reasonably shallow water a draught of twenty feet was suggested. The preferred propulsion system would be a single variable-pitch propeller, driven by twin diesel-electric engines. A particular requirement was an enclosed crow's-nest where duplicate steering, engine controls and gyro repeaters would be located.

The naval architects chosen were Graham and Woolnough who had designed the new *Biscoe* in 1955. The final dimensions they produced were quite remarkably in keeping with those we had proposed:

Length overall	325 feet
Beam	60 feet
Draught	20 feet 6 inches
Gross weight	4,816 tons
Displacement	6,900 tons
Horsepower	5,000
Service speed	$13\frac{1}{2}$ knots

Tom Woodfield, Master-elect, went to Leith to stand-by during the building at the Robb Caledon Yard. In December 1969 he watched the first welding of preconstructed units on the slipway. Later, when the engines were being installed, he was joined by Lieutenant Commander (E) Tony Trotter RN who was to sail as Chief Engineer.

Woodfield had come to us in 1956 as Third Mate in *Shackleton*, tranferring to *Biscoe* as Mate three years later, and in 1964 he became Master when Bill

Johnston had to retire through ill health. Now his experience of polar
vessels and the conditions they had to contend with proved invaluable.

Handling ships in ice requires a special skill, even a special instinct, which
can only be acquired by practical experience, and such opportunities are
rarely open to officers of the Merchant Navy. The Survey owes a great deal
to all the officers and men who have served for such long periods in our ships,
for without them no permanent parties could ever have been put ashore, and
no bases would have been built. They are the front line of attack on the
defences of Antarctica.

It has been our good fortune that so many have remained with us for
many years. John Cole joined *Biscoe* as Third Mate in 1960. Successive
promotions saw him serving in both *Biscoe* and *Shackleton*, until in 1969 he
was given command of the former, remaining her Master until he resigned
in 1972 to take up a home-based post with the Scottish Marine Biological
Association. Another man who has remained with us since joining *Biscoe* as
Second Mate in 1964 is Malcolm Phelps; he became her Master in 1972.

In the course of so many years of service such officers have encountered
the many special hazards of Antarctic waters. The ice floes that suddenly
close on a ship and hold her fast, the unstable iceberg that turns over, or the
unexpected rapid freezing of the sea in which ships are so often beset. On
these vessels, and the supplies they carry, the bases depend. Rarely have the
ships failed them, and then only in circumstances when even an icebreaker
could not have fought a way through to a station. Only skilful handling and
a long experience of the ways of ice can sail them safely through to their
destinations – our Captains have indeed served us well.

Throughout the building of the new ship Gipps was our representative
through whom all decisions were conveyed. It was a task after his own heart
and his energy knew no bounds. We felt, each time he disappeared to
Scotland, that he could be building her single-handed, and certainly his
quick appreciation of problems solved many a difficulty – and many there
were too.

Inevitably we suffered delays. For example, the large electric motor,
weighing fifteen tons, rolled off the transporter on its way up to Scotland
when the driver took a roundabout too sharply. Traffic was held up for miles
around, and it had to be returned to the makers.

The ship was launched without a hitch on 4 September 1970. Over a
hundred people, including most members of the Natural Environment
Research Council and their wives, and all our office staff, except Eleanor
Honnywill who stayed behind with the teleprinter to the bases, were flown
from London to Leith. With great glee Gipps had proved conclusively, to
the astonishment of the authorities, that it was far cheaper to charter an

aircraft for the return trip than to pay rail fares and hotel expenses, so the gala occasion took on the air of a festive day-trip to the seaside. My wife was invited to christen the ship *Bransfield*, in honour of the first man ever to have charted a portion of the Antarctic mainland in 1819. Fids have known her affectionately as 'the Brantub' ever since.

Fitting-out produced a new crop of difficulties, particularly on the occasion of her first tentative trial when an arc developed on the main switchboard only a mile or two from her berth. In a few moments the whole thing had fused into a twisted mass of metal. Fortunately a passing tug quickly brought her back alongside, but it was yet another set-back to delay her delivery.

Bransfield was finally handed over to us three months later, after very brief trials. To the dismay of the Hogmanay-minded Scots, she sailed from Leith on New Year's Eve 1971, arriving in Southampton on Saturday, where she loaded on Monday and left for the Antarctic on Tuesday.

8

Hope Bay reopened
1952–64

1951/2   The most serious field incident between Britain and Argentina regarding Antarctic claims occurred three years after we lost the base at Hope Bay. By that time the Argentines had moved in and built a station only a few hundred yards from our burnt-out hut. In February 1952 George Marsh was Base Leader and medical officer of the party sent to put up and occupy a new base. Frank Elliott, by then SECFIDS, was also on board *Biscoe* when she anchored in the bay.

As the first boatload of material went ashore, a fusillade of shots from automatic weapons whizzed over the heads of the landing party. Unloading began, but Elliott and Marsh hastened up to the Argentine base and requested the Station Commander to stop the 'firing practice', pointing out that it was rather dangerous. He in turn expressed strong objections to the British return, and very soon armed men, clothed in white, were seen spreading out around the area. Fids were being ordered back into their boat at pistol point. As they arrived alongside *Biscoe* Captain Bill Johnston re-embarked the men but firmly refused to reload the stores, and reported the incident to the Governor.

Sir Miles Clifford ordered him to keep the ship where she was and sent an immediate signal to the Colonial Office. Without waiting for their reply – perhaps even guessing what it might be – he at once sailed for Hope Bay in HMS *Burghead Bay*. Even before she dropped anchor a boatload of Royal Marines was on its way ashore, and Argentines were seen hastily abandoning their base to retreat into the inhospitable hinterland. There was of course no intention to harm anyone, but the thought of perhaps being shelled was apparently an efficacious deterrent. Too late, a message came back to Stanley ordering the Governor to take no action until he received further guidance, as the dispute was being dealt with between Governments.

Meanwhile the new British base was going up under naval protection. In the diplomatic exchanges which followed this sorry episode, it was regretted that the Argentine Station Commander had exceeded his instructions, and

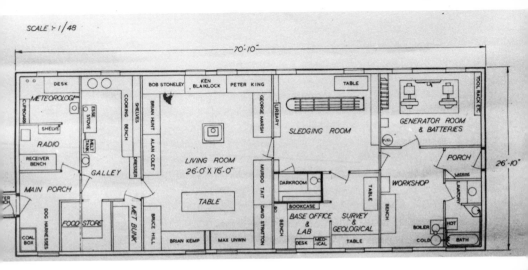

SCALE ÷ 1/48

70'-10"

METEOROLOGY — DESK — BOB STONELEY — KEN BLAIKLOCK — PETER KING — TABLE

CLIPBOARD — SHELVES — SHELVES — ESSE STOVE — COOKING BENCH — BRIAN HUNT — GEORGE MARSH — LIBRARY — SLEDGING ROOM — GENERATOR ROOM & BATTERIES — TOOL RACK ETC.

RADIO — MELT TANK — DRESSER — ALAN COLEY — LIVING ROOM 26'-0" X 16'-0" — FUEL — PORCH

RECEIVER BENCH — GALLEY — MURDO TAIT — TABLE — DARKROOM — WORKSHOP — LATRINE — LAVATORY

MAIN PORCH — FOOD STORE — MET BUNK — BRUCE HILL — TABLE — DAVID STRATTON — BOOKCASE — BENCH — BOILER — HOT

COAL BOX — DOG HARNESSES — BRIAN KEMP — MAX UNWIN — BASE OFFICE & LAB — SURVEY & GEOLOGICAL — DESK — MED-ICAL — TABLE — COLD — BATH

26'-10"

Top: the new Hope Bay. (BAS)
Bottom: the living room (1956). (P. B. Thompson)

he was withdrawn. Sir Miles Clifford then suggested to the Colonial Office that it was time to end the childish games of political protest in Antarctica and soon afterwards, to the great relief of the field men, the Governments finally agreed that this would be discontinued on both sides.

Happily, the first Argentine naval vessel to visit Hope Bay the following season was commanded by Capitán Rudolfo Panzarini, whose tact and friendliness healed the breach which had so sadly arisen. In later years he was to be a popular and valuable member at our international scientific meetings where he did much to enhance the image of his country.

Eleven men re-occupied the base including one geologist, Bob Stoneley, and two surveyors, Ken Blaiklock (ex-Stonington) and David Stratton, who later was to be my second-in-command during the TAE.

The first priority was to procure sufficient seals to feed the dogs through the winter. Owing to the large expanse of open water that season there were few to be seen. Each sighting of one lying on a drifting floe led to a wild scramble for a boat in which to reach it before it slid back into the sea.

One day Stratton ran into the hut shouting that he could see a Weddell 'with a curiously deformed head'. Neither he nor Marsh, who rushed out to help capture it, had as yet seen many seals, but the odd appearance of this one was perhaps a scientific challenge. Shooting, unless it is very accurate, is liable to result in the escape of a wounded animal, so the more humane method of stunning them with a blow on the head was the normal practice. The hunters rowed out to the floe, and Marsh clambered onto it and dealt the seal a heavy blow. It just shook its head, and far from any thoughts of retreat, proceeded to take avoiding action with considerable agility. Then, turning the tables, it sank its teeth into Marsh's arm and held on. Horrified at this turn of events, Stratton climbed out of the boat to the rescue, tried to stun the seal, and missed – but it let go and slid quietly back into the water.

Rushing Marsh back to base with all speed to have his arm stitched, Stratton remarked that he must be the first man who had ever been bitten by a Weddell. On arrival they were aghast to be told by more experienced companions that the 'curiously deformed head' had in fact belonged to a leopard seal, a highly dangerous predator. Marsh had been extremely lucky not to have lost his arm or been dragged into the sea. He still carries his scars.

Despite all efforts it was impossible to build up an adequate supply of dog food, nor was *Biscoe* able to find more seals further afield. A quantity of good old 'meat and veg' Army rations was brought ashore, but even this

1952   contribution was short-landed by over 100 cases, and by April the dogs were losing condition fast. One pound of pemmican or two tins of meat and veg on alternate days was a totally inadequate diet. By May many were in a state of semi-starvation and three had died.

During blizzards every animal was checked several times day and night.

Sometimes three or four were found collapsed on the spans, and had to be taken into the hut for several days to recuperate. If there was to be any kind of sledging programme in the following spring and summer their rations had to be increased.

Excavations deep into the ice around the old base brought to light thirty cases of dog pemmican, supplemented with vitamin tablets, but even this bonus would make the food last only until July. Marsh decided that a party must travel south to search for seals in Duse Bay. As none of the dogs were fit enough for even such a short journey, the party would man-haul.

The first attempt failed, but Marsh and Stratton at least put down a depot for future use. On 2 June, in the short hours of daylight, Stratton, Stoneley and Jock Tait tried again, immediately running into impossible weather. Twice the sledge they hauled was blown over, the second time landing on its runners after rolling over three times. Stoneley then kept it stable during gusts by throwing himself across it.

During a lull they made camp, but no sooner were they inside the tent than a 'whirlie' passed over, sucking it up and scattering the three men. While in the air the inner tent was torn from the outer, and both blew away quickly followed by the ground sheet, pegs and other paraphernalia. Searching around they recovered almost everything, but the tent itself was so torn that it was dangerous to travel with it and impossible without it. Disconsolately they returned home, being blown off their feet by eighty-knot gusts at intervals. But visibility was good, and aided by bright moonlight they were back at base eleven hours after they had set out.

Two days later they tried again, Max Unwin replacing Stoneley who had a cut hand. By then some of the dogs had recovered strength on their improved rations and they took a team. This party ranged over the sea ice between View Point, Beak Island and Seven Buttresses for ten days, returning triumphantly, leaving thirty-six seals along the route for later collection. July was spent bringing in the carcasses, feeding up the dogs and establishing a depot on Beak Island.

By mid-August they were ready to embark on the first working journey around the southern end of James Ross Island, where Blaiklock and Stratton filled in gaps in the previous mapping, while Stoneley, assisted by Marsh, made a geological reconnaissance as far as Snow Hill and Seymour Islands. A further journey to the Sobral Peninsula completed the year's sledging.

1953   The following season parties made a number of journeys – the longest covering 720 miles during the winter of 1953 – from late April to mid-July, when the survey and geology of Jason Peninsula (then thought to be an island), Robertson Island and the Seal Nunataks were completed.

1953/4   Perhaps the most enterprising was the summer survey of Joinville Island by Stratton, John Standring, Blaiklock and Julian Taylor. Because it could

Camping on sea ice at Cape Obelisk, James Ross Island. (BAS)

only be reached by sea, no one had previously worked on this island. The party was landed there on 7 December 1953, and spent fifty-nine days in completing the map and visiting almost every rock exposure, a most satisfactory result.

1954   Standring was a geologist who, when working at The Naze on James Ross Island, made the remarkable discovery of a *Plesiosaurus* vertebra. This dated back to the Cretaceous period, and was the first vertebrate fossil other than penguins to be found in the Antarctic. Unfortunately it lay on the surface and could not be ascribed to any particular stratum. Although he, and indeed other parties, searched the area, no other specimens have been found, but the sediments abound in Cretaceous ammonites and mollusca.

At that time 'continental drift' was still a suspect theory. Its many supporters were hoping that representatives of the great Jurassic/Cretaceous reptilian fauna would be found in Antarctica, thereby supporting the proposition. Unhappily plesiosaurs were marine reptiles, and could easily have swum into the area. It was to be nearly twenty years before David Elliot, an ex-Fid working with Americans on the other side of the continent, found the land reptile *Listrosaurus*, but by then the continental drift hypothesis had already become respectable.

Nineteen fifty-four was also the first of two years during which Julian Taylor studied the work output of huskies, using electrically recording strain gauges which showed that the maximum pull of a nine-dog team was 300 pounds. Weight for weight this was almost the same as that produced by the rowing eight which won the Olympic Games in 1924.

As a part of this project he determined the energy input in the form of food, and found the ration insufficient for long journeys. As a result not only was it increased but the constituents of dog pemmican were drastically changed, with very beneficial results.

In his published report he drew attention to what every dog driver knows – mental stimuli are as important to dogs as to men. Driving a team where mountains or icebergs lie ahead provides few problems, but if the terrain is flat open snowfield to the horizon they will soon lose interest in working. Drivers have different ways of overcoming this. Some send a man ahead on skis, but this is hard work and it is also difficult for him to maintain an accurate course. He has to travel an appropriate distance ahead of the team – too far and the dogs lose interest, too close and they are liable to overrun him.

Personally I found that whistling or singing produced remarkably increased performance. Although it is easier and more efficient than singing, whistling for hours into the teeth of a cold wind is quite difficult. Fortunately dogs are friendly, if undiscerning critics, always ready to overlook wrong notes or a raucous voice, and romp along with renewed vigour. For me *Onward Christian Soldiers* always called forth their best efforts, perhaps because it was one of the only two tunes which I can roughly reproduce. The other is *Show me the way to go home*.

1954/5   By now Hope Bay had achieved an enviable reputation as a major sledging station. Survey and geological work were steadily extended, and whole books could be devoted to each wintering party in turn. Indeed, two have been written – *Expedition South* by W. (Bill) Ellery Anderson (Evans Bros, 1957) covering 1955–6, and *A World of Men* by Wally Herbert (Eyre and Spottiswoode, 1968) covering 1956–7. Here I am able to touch only briefly on some of the highlights.

Bill Anderson was Base Leader at a time when relations with their Argentine neighbours were cordial. The Argentine presence was a political gesture but they were not equipped to travel and did very little scientific work. Anderson noted:

Our mutual exchange of gifts with the Argentines was greatly appreciated on both sides. They liked our pickles, curry powder, tea, jams, tinned spaghetti, and occasionally a bottle of Scotch; and we always welcomed the chilled mutton and beef from their refrigerator, with its donkey-engine that, believe it or not, chugged away all through the Antarctic winter.

I had no political embarrassments to cope with, as Major Moreno, after his first attempt, did not try again to discover my plans: nor did he make any territorial claims for Argentina. But he did keep pestering me for a 'Protest' – I think he wanted to show his government how assertive he had been. To satisfy him, I wrote out a protest for every Argentine hut and refuge in my area, nine in all, and handed them to him. He was delighted, and we drank to international friendship.
Expedition South by Ellery Anderson

1955   Anderson planned a journey south to Cape Alexander in latitude 66°44'S, to close gaps in the existing map, particularly the Evans Inlet area. For this it was first necessary to enlarge an existing depot at Cape Longing, and while he and Norman Leppard were on their way to do this they came upon a surprising scene near Lagrelius Point. Before them lay three pools of open water, the largest about six miles square, in which some 200 whales, mostly lesser rorquals, many killers and a few bottle-nose, were swimming. On the surrounding ice lay a thousand or two crabeater seals – truly an oasis full of life and sound in the silent, sterile desert.

Weddell seal. (C. G. Collop)

They concluded that the animals must have been trapped when the sea suddenly froze round them. Further on they found other smaller pools, one about a hundred yards long by fifty wide. Astonishingly this contained Adélie penguins, crabeaters, a leopard seal and a number of killer whales, all swimming happily together. They could scarcely believe their eyes, nor account for the complete lack of fear in both penguins and seals in such close proximity to their predators.

The main journey was made by Anderson, Taylor, Leppard and Tait, and on 15 August this party also visited the 'whale pools'. By now the smaller ones had frozen over, the largest was reduced to two stretches of water, each two or three hundred yards long. There were still about 150 whales 'blowing', and some 600 crabeaters, many with pups, were lying on the surrounding ice. One lay half submerged in water, unperturbed by the presence of killers. If these approached within a few feet, the seal put its head under water and snapped until they retired discomfited. After a while it slid into the sea among them, lackadaisically reappearing a few yards away. Anderson, always adventurous and enterprising, promptly inaugurated 'The Fids Whale-patters Club'. The animals appeared so harmless that the men reached down to pat them, first somewhat cautiously with ski-sticks and then, as confidence increased, daringly caressing them by hand.

Two months later, their work completed, the party sledging home were once more back at the pools. Now only about fifty by fifteen yards of open water remained. In this four whales were 'blowing', but for two or three

Founding The Whale Patters' Club. (A. F. Lewis)

miles around lay a few healthy Weddell cows nursing pups, surrounded by the bodies of 2,000 dead crabeaters, many already covered in drift. It was a terrible sight. Three days later they reached Red Island, where again they found many hundreds of dead crabeaters lying half buried in snow, among them one solitary Weddell with her pup, both alive and well.

Shortly before their return Dr Paul Massey and Phil Mander had sledged through the same area and recorded fifteen hundred dead or dying crabeaters. Massey reported that all the affected seals, whether dead or comatose, had oddly swollen necks and a trickle of blood running from their mouths. On dissection he found their guts empty, their livers a palid colour, and pus oozed from the neck glands when an incision was made. Since he too found a few live and healthy Weddells, he thought the mass death must have been due to some infection peculiar to crabeaters. Specimens were collected from five seals and sent home for investigation, and a number of others were examined externally.

At the Scientific Bureau in London we were receiving reports about the dead seals with perplexity, and all kinds of suggested explanations were put forward. Perhaps there had been a submarine volcanic explosion, though there was no known source for this? Perhaps it was a virus, but where from, and how was it communicated to such a large number of animals? Why were the Weddells apparently immune? One theory was that some planktonic species, such as a poisonous dinoflagellate, had 'bloomed' in enormous numbers and then been eaten by krill, a major food source for crabeaters, but not touched by Weddells. Many people discounted such a possibility and favoured the idea of a virus infection. The specimens sent home did not reveal a cause – indeed we never found an explanation.

1955/6   Early in 1956 the first ships into Hope Bay were the Argentine icebreaker *General San Martin* and the cargo vessel *Bahía Aguirre*. As unloading proceeded, a peculiar object looking like a propeller-driven sledge was seen being dragged from the shore. Some curious Fids went over to investigate, and returned with the amazing news that it was a wind-machine, brought out by a film team. They also made the unbelievable discovery that two tons of soap flakes had been unloaded. With help from the former, the latter were to provide artificial blizzards, through which intrepid Argentines would tramp to immortality before the cameras. Later they watched, fascinated, the system successfully operated, and for the sake of the *amour propre* of their Argentine Antarctic friends, hoped that it was actors who were facing the balmy blast of the soapy blizzard.

1956   At the end of the season 'Lofty' Worswick (ex-Signy and Admiralty Bay) succeeded Anderson as Base Leader. None of the journeys that year passed through the areas of the dead seals, but evidently the cause, whatever it had been, had persisted, for on 31 August Dr Hugh Simpson, Roger Tufft and Mike Reuby found a similar situation when man-hauling around James Ross Island. Just west of Lockyer Island, in an area about eight hundred by four hundred yards, they came upon hundreds of crabeaters. Many of them were swimming in small pools, but about a hundred lay dead on the surrounding ice, while a considerable number were lethargic and dying. The symptoms were the same, 'parched mouth, glazed eyes, blood trickling from the corners of the mouth and numerous aborted pups'. Nothing like this has been reported since, but although many parties in subsequent years travelled through the area, they saw only Weddell seals.

Simpson's party were on a month-long man-hauling trip to enable him to study the varying level of eosinophils (one of the groups of white cells) in the blood of those acting as his guinea-pigs on the journey. Urine samples were taken as they travelled, and Simpson hoped to show that the recorded changes were related to the varying stresses they experienced. Later he was to repeat the experiment on Lee Rice, Dick Walcott and Tufft during a sledging journey which lasted eighty-six days.

Having established normal levels for each man over a period at base, he found that just before they started out they dropped by twenty-five to forty per cent and remained low, with minor variations, while they travelled. The rebound came either just before, or immediately after their return, amounting to between a hundred and fifty and two hundred per cent, and then gradually returning to the original norm.

At first it seemed that here was a practical, and more precise method of measuring an individual's reaction to stress than any subjective psychological assessment, but unfortunately Simpson also found that the complexity of other factors which influence the eosinophil level was too great. So we continued to judge a man's potential by the time-honoured methods of experienced interviewing, and observation during training.

After he left FIDS Simpson again repeated this experiment when crossing the Greenland ice cap, with similar results. Therefore one cannot help feeling that, however complex the factors, environmental stress does produce a variation in eosinophil level and is an overall reflection of each person's reaction. If future work should resolve the difficulties of interpretation, the method may still provide a useful tool for the selection of men.

1957   The main journey planned for 1957 was to cross the Antarctic Peninsula from Hope Bay to the small Reclus Peninsula on the west coast, where a field hut had been built. Apart from mapping a new stretch of country, it was hoped to find a practical route between the east and west coasts for future use.

To this end a support group from Paradise Harbour – Denis Kershaw, Dick Foster and Ray McGowan – were landed by ship at Reclus to find a way up to the plateau. They had no dogs, so back-packing and man-hauled sledging were the order of the day. Of the fifty days this party were in the field, thirty-nine were spent pinned down in their tent by dense cloud or driving blizzards.

It was not an easy task. After six miles of undulating snow fields they forced a way 1,000 feet up a steep slope at the head of what came to be known as the 'deadly cwm'. Then came a one-and-a-half-mile traverse across another precipitous slope beneath a dangerous cornice, where a man could have slid 2,500 feet into the sea below. When at last they reached the plateau at 7,000 feet they built a snow cairn and left directions for the guidance of the Hope Bay party. For another eighteen days the weather forced them to lie-up before they could retreat to the shelter of their depot 1,500 feet below, to await the dog teams.

Meanwhile Lee Rice, Wally Herbert, Ken Brown and Pat Thompson set out from Hope Bay and had been making their way over the well-known sea ice route to Pitt Point, then overland past Simpson Nunatak to the Detroit Plateau via a heavily crevassed glacier, with its inevitable delays. Once up on the plateau they were in new, gently undulating country, which should have been easy going.

They had bad luck. Persistent mist made navigation difficult, and the deep soft snow slowed them down until their average had fallen to three miles a day. When good visibility returned they could see what looked to be a second plateau to the south, apparently with no connection to the one they were on. If this was so, they had little chance of ever reaching Reclus.

Reconnaissance proved that the two plateaux sloped down to a point where they were joined by a very narrow snow-covered ridge which they called 'the catwalk'. Its domed surface was just over a hundred yards long, and the ground fell away 1,500 feet on either side. It was a dismaying prospect.

The safety margin for travel was no more than twenty feet on either side of the summit line. If the dogs were permitted to run only slightly off course, the sledges would slide down the slope and over the edge . . . we stopped the teams short of the steep drop down on to it, and put rope brakes under the sledges. I fastened a line to the front of the dog trace and, wearing crampons to get a good grip . . . led the first team down . . . while Lee stood on the brake and controlled the descent. . . .

Even as we struggled with double teams to haul the first sledge up . . . on the southwest side of the col, cloud started pouring over it once more; the catwalk had closed the route behind us.

A World of Men by Wally Herbert

They had been on the plateau thirty days and travelled eighty-eight miles.

They had another thirty to go before they could hope to see the Reclus party's cairn. The question now was whether they had enough food. More days of mist and travelling 'blind', then suddenly visibility improved – they could see the Reclus Peninsula lying 7,000 feet below them. Sweeping the area around them with binoculars they picked out a tiny dot: the cairn at last.

Another six miles and they were there. Tied to a marker flag was a bag containing directions on how to reach the encampment below, and two miles later they could see the dark speck of a tent at the foot of a mighty drop. With rope brakes again fitted, the drivers standing on the sledge brakes, the teams tore down the slope.

Unstoppable in their headlong rush, the dogs overran the welcoming party, knocked over the radio mast, and ended up in a tangled mass along the guy ropes of the tent. It was, to say the least, a boisterous meeting – but when finally order had been restored there was time for thankful greeting, and later in the tents the swapping of adventures went on late into the night.

Next morning they faced the hazards of the last sixteen miles which the Reclus party had so laboriously overcome on their way up. One day was spent back-packing the loads across the mile-and-a-half traverse of a slope too steep for a heavy dog sledge. First the men trod down a track wide enough to accept the sledges, then a few dogs were tied on to the 'uphill' side of each sledge, where they instinctively pulled diagonally up the slope against its drag, the forward motion being provided by man-haulers. Safely across they pitched camp with some relief, and only one day's food left. The final run down to the 'deadly cwm' was easier, and the journey was accomplished – The Hope Bay contingent had covered 280 miles in 54 days. They had also proved the possibility of crossing the peninsula, but the difficulties had been such that it was unlikely the route would ever be used except in dire emergency.

1957–9   The two years when Don McCalman was Base Leader saw an increasing emphasis on survey because of the need to provide ground control for the air photography flown by FIDASE. Most of the many journeys undertaken were devoted to this although geological work continued, and in 1959 a geomagnetic survey was initiated by John Ashley. The reason for this was to trace the submarine and sub-ice extension of the James Ross Island volcanics towards the older rocks of Trinity Peninsula.

The same year Ian Hampton, physiologist, and Dr Neil Orr began both a two-year human physiology programme and a dietetic study of the dogs. The former entailed the measurement of temperature gradients within the tent, internal body temperature and the temperature gradient through clothing, using an electrically recording wire vest. Wind speeds, air temperature and humidity were concurrently recorded to determine the cooling effect of the environment. All these measurements were maintained throughout the twenty-four hours, no mean task when added to the normal trials of a dog-sledging day.

The dog food trials demonstrated that the new type of pemmican, Nutrican, developed as a result of Taylor's previous work, was clearly an improvement, but even this was insufficient to maintain the dogs' body weight and stamina. They did, however, return to normal within five days when fed on seal meat.

Unfortunately the weight penalty of feeding meat on any long journey precludes this, and dogs, like the men, have had to be content with concentrated rations of small bulk. That this is not permanently injurious has been demonstrated by the many long journeys completed at Stonington and Hope Bay, from which the teams have returned thinner but still healthy. Indeed, it is probable that like the men, the dogs leave the luxury of base overweight, and are only really fit after the first strenuous days in the field.

1960   In 1960 Hope Bay was again threatened by fire discovered at two o'clock one morning in the harness room. There had been too little insulation under the stove and the smouldering of a joist spread to the wall behind. A repetition of the 1948 disaster was prevented after a tough fight lasting two hours. By good fortune there was no wind to fan the flames, and only one interior wall and the lavatory were lost.

Neil Orr had become the new Base Leader and during that year twenty-two journeys were mounted and much useful work was done. On two occasions there were incidents which could have ended badly. When Dick Harbour was out surveying with two General Assistants, Keith Allen and Ron Miller, they camped two miles from View Point. Next morning Miller left the tent before the others, and when they emerged thick drift had reduced visibility to a few yards and he was nowhere to be seen. Concerned for his safety, they tried for two hours to find him. Then thoroughly alarmed, they left the camp standing and set out for View Point to report and get help.

They were met by Miller himself, who said that he had lost sight of the tent and could not find his way back to it. After two hours of wandering he had sensibly made for the sea ice and followed the coastline hoping to find the View Point hut, though he had never previously been there. Fortunately he saw it looming up through the drift. Once again the lesson had to be learnt that one must never wander out of sight of camp or base in bad visibility.

In July, when a surveying party of six was extending the triangulation among the mountains above Larsen Inlet, a snow bridge suddenly collapsed under Hampton's sledge, which fell and then swung some fifteen feet below the surface. His lifeline slipped off the handle bars and he dropped seventy feet to a snow bridge further down.

The dogs were able to hold the sledge steady until his companions arrived. Hampton was dazed, but sufficiently conscious to tie himself to ropes lowered by Chris Brading, Ron Tindal and Bill Tracy. Meanwhile John Winham and Harbour quickly pitched a tent in which they could treat his injuries. He was hauled to the surface and found to have a severely lacerated scalp, a flap measuring four by three inches hanging over his right ear, and a dislocated elbow.

After trimming his hair they sewed his scalp back and worked to stop arterial bleeding. Then, splinting his arm, they tried to call Hope Bay, but without success. However, Signy heard them, relayed their request for medical advice from Stanley, and radioed Hope Bay asking Orr to go to their aid – but he himself was out sledging north of base and could not immediately be contacted.

On the fifth day they learnt that Orr and Keith Allen were at last approaching, so leaving Tindal to look after the patient, the others set off to intercept and guide them to the site. Their later reports indicated that their return over the hidden crevasses behind the sick camp was made with considerable trepidation, for they all suffered from what they termed 'a severe attack of craven crevassitude' – as well they might. The doctor's own account reads,

. . . a sledge party had to come and find us. I picked up Keith Allen at Hope Bay and the two of us, with two teams, set off on a compass course . . . in the most appalling conditions (the only time I had lain in a tent clutching on to the emergency cord as I was certain that the tent would blow away during the night).

Hampton had an eight-inch gash over his left ear, a Bell's Palsy – paralysis of the left side of his face – and a fracture dislocation of the left elbow. The repairs on his scalp had healed beautifully and, after the infection in his ear had cleared, the paralysis resolved . . . when he returned to base I gave him a general anaesthetic and Ron Tindal and I reduced his elbow. He quickly regained full mobility, and was sledging again by the end of the season.

On the way back we had another minor mishap when Tindal, who was driving Hampton, wrapped in a sleeping bag and strapped to the sledge, fell down another crevasse . . . The sledge handle bars jammed and Tindal was suspended by his safety-line. Hampton was unhurt but complained bitterly of the snow which was trickling down the back of his neck.

1960/1   Ian Fothergill became Base Leader in his second year and held the post for a third, one of the few Fids who have wintered three times consecutively. When planning the base programmes he was relieved of the tedious task of major depot-laying which had so often delayed the scientific work in previous seasons. To everyone's relief, the aircraft by now based at Deception established a large depot at Cape Longing in May 1961, and another at Pedersen Nunatak in October. In December further flights replenished both these caches to support the 1962 sledging programme. Had this not been possible, it is doubtful whether any more useful work could have been done from Hope Bay, for the field areas were now far from base. As it was, they were profitable years.

Harbour and Tony Edwards carried the triangulation down to the Seal Nunataks, and filled in the detail of the Crane Glacier between Cape Disappointment and the head of Beascochea Bay on the west coast. Neil Aitkenhead, Phil Nelson, David Elliot and Mike Fleet completed the geological mapping of the James Ross Island volcanics, the west coast of Trinity Peninsula, and the extensive area between the Drygalski Glacier and Cape Disappointment.

In 1961 conditions had been good and the cold weather ensured safe travelling over sea ice or well bridged crevasses on land. In contrast, 1962 began with warm winds in January and these continued intermittently throughout the year. The sea ice broke up and crevasse bridges became unstable or disappeared, making almost any journey a dangerous undertaking.

A bonus was that *Shackleton* was able to penetrate further south than ever before, and laid a much needed depot near Striped Hill on the mainland to the west of Egg Island. This provided at least some support for the final year's operations.

1962/3   The only field work planned was an extension of the magnetic survey, and the new Base Leader, Noel Downham, applied himself assiduously to the deployment of his nine men to best advantage. Weather was generally cold and clear, good for travelling. But now the trouble was the seemingly erratic movement of numerous large, tabular icebergs in Prince Gustav Channel. These broke up the sea ice making the normal route to the south unreliable, if not impossible. Though forced to use the much more laborious land routes, the Fids made ten journeys during which 800 vertical magnetic stations were observed, extending the magnetic survey as far south as Cape Disappointment, and westward via the Russell West Glacier to Charcot Bay.

1963   In April Downham, John Mansfield and Mike Wilkinson were camped near the Aureole Hills when the rising wind tore out three dog pickets, together with an ice axe holding one of the sledges and its dog team. All were blown into the tent and into the other team, causing complete chaos. Before anyone could get out one of the dogs was strangled by a guy rope, the tent itself was torn and the poles bent.

For three hours they sat, fully clothed, two of them in the time-honoured position – backs against the windward poles. Then, despite two ice axes, two shovels and three survey poles holding the guys, the tent collapsed over them. Disentangling themselves, it was impossible to stand but they managed to swivel the apex of the tent into the wind. Crawling in with what gear they could salvage, they settled down to see out the night.

Next morning they discovered that one of the second team's pickets had held, and the tangled mass of seventeen dogs and two sledges had swivelled down wind from it. After digging a hole and erecting the small emergency 'pup' tent in it, they sorted themselves out before starting a hunt for missing gear. Some items were never found, others were recovered up to a mile away. Four days and fifty miles later they reached the safety of the View Point hut.

Everyone hates to see his own base closed. I still remember the sadness with which we battened down the windows and closed off the chimneys of the Stonington hut in 1950. However stark an Antarctic base may be by home standards, it represents comfort and security to those who live there. The knowledge that there will be no more comings and goings, that the dogs' last Evening Chorus has died away – such thoughts cast a gloom over the days before departure. Only the memories remain, and fortunately it is always the successes, the happy times which stand out, while frustrations, risks and boredom are miraculously forgotten. When the final parting comes we all find that we have great affection for the small hut which has been our home for so long.

Perhaps for Downham himself the sense of finality was not so great, for he went to take command of Stonington before the actual evacuation. That was left to Rod Walker, Roger Robson, Mike Wilkinson and Mike Smith, who had the dubious privilege of officiating at the last rites when we arrived in *Shackleton* on 13 February.

1963/4 We found 1,000 cases ready to be manhandled down to the rocky shore. A strong wind and melting snow made it a slow and unpleasant task, while very low tides made it impossible to bring boats in for seven hours at a stretch. Major Toledo, Commander of the Argentine station, wished us well with the assurance that his countrymen would look after our hut. Nineteen years to the day after Hope Bay had been opened by OPERATION TABARIN in 1945, we finally sailed away from this famous sledging base.

9

The best laid schemes . . . 1952–60

We have seen how by 1950 the scientific effort had been reduced to no more than meteorological observing at six stations, but soon there was gradual recovery until by 1957 there were twenty-five scientists and surveyors, and twenty-nine meteorologists, distributed among eleven stations.

1952–3   Admiralty Bay was a small meteorological station where a constant source of interest was the nearby gentoo penguin rookery. In February 1953 a fine day encouraged George Hemmen, Roger Banks, John Raymond and Arthur Farrant to make a boat trip to the rookery, and also to check a depot which lay seven miles across the bay. Because they landed at a very sheltered point, they failed to notice that a rising wind was whipping up high waves in the open water. After a few hours ashore they started back, and sailing out from behind sheltering rocks they suddenly realised that it would be impossible to reach base in their small boat. Hastily they turned back to shore.

Unwisely they had set out without a tent, and though they had taken a radio transmitter it failed to work. There was no way of reporting their now uncomfortable situation, and the prospect of spending a night in the open was hardly cheering. Hauling up the boat above the apparent high water mark, they turned it upside down and huddled miserably beneath it, hoping eventually to sleep.

The wind continued to rise, and by nine o'clock was gusting to seventy-five knots. The snow had turned to rain, and soon it was obvious that there was going to be an exceptionally high tide. Four times during the night they dragged the boat yet higher up the beach, the wind constantly threatening to blow it away. Their concerted efforts only just held it down, but with each move they gained experience, finally achieving a reasonable shelter by resting it on food boxes taken earlier from the depot and using the floor boards to sit on. A wall of old whale bones and boulders collected from the beach gave additional protection, and when the larger holes were filled with seaweed most of the draughts were excluded.

They had a Primus, and had already picked up fuel and four-year-old rations from the depot which they intended to take back to base to sample. A cooking pot placed outside caught the rain, and presently they tried to brew-up but without success.

The next day was equally miserable with alternating hail, rain, snow and a blustering wind. By evening they were all much colder, but a heavy snowfall blocked up the remaining gaps in their make-shift shelter and this was deemed a blessing. No one slept much. By tea time the wind had dropped and they rushed down to the beach to launch the boat, but no sooner were they at sea than the weather again deteriorated, and when they cleared the headland the waves were seven feet high – too high to turn the boat across them and regain the shore.

They were forced to cross the bay to a beach four miles away, but since they were now being driven towards the open sea, they could only try desperately to edge on to course for a few moments every time the boat rose to the top of a wave:

It seemed obvious to me that the only hope of survival was to take each wave dead astern and ride with it . . . I had to concentrate all my attention and energy on the battle . . . I was mighty glad I was at the tiller, for I had no time to think of what would happen should we not make the crossing. . . . What the others thought I hate to imagine, what with being in such a little cockleshell, and with their lives in the hands of a novice . . . one good wave breaking over us and that would have been that. *George Hemmen's Journal*

A hundred yards away from the shore the engine ran out of petrol. Two men seized the oars struggling to keep the frail craft from broaching-to, while the third hastily slopped fuel into a heaving tank. The engine reluctantly spluttered into life again, and they came slowly inshore.

Another miserably cold night under the boat followed. In the morning they collected moss to light a smudge-fire near which all four stood, hoping that base would notice them. They also wrote BOAT OK in letters three feet high made out of rocks and boulders laid on the snow, in the hope that with the x70 magnification of a theodolite telescope base would read the signal.

The evening that the party failed to return, the base had alerted Stanley, and on the third day they had seen the men attempting a crossing though the boat was frequently lost to sight in the rough seas. They had also spotted the signal fire, and rescue was being organised. As the marooned mariners were preparing for another attempt to put to sea, HMS *Snipe* suddenly appeared round the headland and dropped anchor. Almost immediately a motor boat towing a whaler was chugging towards them. The whaler came in close, the rescue party leapt ashore, and there were relieved introductions all round.

The Fids had been living with an improvised lamp made from a cigarette

Admiralty Bay hut, 1950. (R. H. W. Nalder)

tin with a string wick; now their faces and clothes were black from smoke which accentuated their broad white smiles. While the whaler returned to the ship, the motor boat took them in tow and soon they were safely home, four days overdue, cold, tired and hungry, but with no lasting effects worse than some minor frostbite suffered by Banks.

To everyone involved this episode caused much anxiety, and emphasized the point that small boats can be used only with great caution in Antarctic waters. It was emphasized tragically three years later when a dinghy leaving *Biscoe* after dark overturned and Ron Napier, on a visit from Signy to Admiralty Bay, was drowned. His body was never found, but it was thought that he hit his head as he fell and had been unable to help himself.

1954/5   Ken Blaiklock (ex-Stonington and Hope Bay) went south again in the *Norsel* for the 1954/5 season in charge of the summer operations. Having established Peter Hooper's party on Anvers Island (Chapter 6, p. 149) he had continued south to Marguerite Bay, where a new station was to be set up to replace Stonington, so often inaccessible to ships in the past. A suitable site was found on the northwest coast of Horseshoe Island.

Horseshoe Island hut. (BAS)

It was already 11 March and temperatures were dropping, so speed was essential. In forty-eight hours the ship was unloaded and building begun. But on the fifth day the sea started to freeze and *Norsel* hurriedly weighed anchor, ploughing her way through six inches of new ice to the Faure Islands, where they found open water only just in time. Another couple of days and she would have been frozen-in for the winter.

Eight men under Ken Gaul wintered at Horseshoe. At first they lived in tents, cooked on five Primus stoves and ate in a 'shanty' built from ration boxes. Snow and constant wind made building arduous and slow. Just occasionally the weather relented and the luxury of ordinary conversation was possible between the tents.

After eight weeks' hard slogging they moved into their hut, but though now protected from the weather, conditions were still very primitive:

By the time I got the water into the bath it was tepid, when I put the first foot in it was cool . . . by the time I'd finished it felt as if my bathwater was beginning to resemble the bucket of frozen water kept there. Consolation – I am the first man on base to have a bath in twenty-eight degrees of frost. They revived me with whisky and lime.
Derek Searle's Journal

1955   Despite long cold periods, gale force winds regularly blew the new ice out
before it was strong enough to travel on. This frustrating sequence persisted
throughout the winter, upsetting all plans for field work. Not until 9 July
were conditions stable enough for a party to visit Stonington. *En route* they
called at the Argentine station on the Debenham Islands where, despite
language problems, they were royally entertained. In a mixture of German,
French, Spanish and English they learnt that it would be impossible ever to
reach Stonington, and next morning while a gale blew they watched a black
area of open water rapidly extending towards them. Hastily they beat it back
to base before the fast ice broke up.

Confined to their island, life was still sometimes enlivened by locally
devised entertainment. Radio hoaxes are not an original idea, but the one
perpetrated at Horseshoe that winter is probably the longest ever sustained
by Fids.

Derek Searle and Gordon Farquhar, the radio operator, devised a situation
whereby the 'domestic' receiver in the bunkroom would be tuned to a pre-
arranged frequency – when lo and behold! there would be music. It was to
come from the record player and their meagre supply of discs.

This limited selection made it virtually certain that some men at least
would soon find it strange that the surprisingly loud and clear radio station
only played music which they already had at base. Accordingly, variations
were introduced. Farquhar could play the bagpipes and had brought a
chanter with him, he was also a creditable performer on the mouth organ.
By switching rapidly from one to the other he managed a convincing
imitation of the Jimmy Shand Show, a programme then popular in
Scotland.

Fairly soon two members of the audience twigged what was happening and
joined the hoaxers. Becoming more ambitious, the four of them started a
request programme purporting to come from Stanley, and broadcasting
requests from fictitious people at other bases. They also broadcast news
bulletins containing incredible, if not horrific items—Marilyn Monroe was to
lead a women's expedition to climb Mount Everest, an interview with
Duncan Carse (Dick Barton in the current radio series), in which the
admissions made would have brought a blush to his cheeks.

As it all became more and more unbelievable, gradually all but one
unsuspecting innocent tumbled to what was happening, but no one spoilt
the fun. The final broadcast took place the day before everyone except the last
victim was to leave on a sledging trip, he being left behind as caretaker of the
base. The 'news' received that evening, reported that there had been a
revolution in Argentina where fighting had broken out between the Army
and the Navy. It included a warning that the likely conflicts which would
follow at Argentine Antarctic stations could well lead to the losers seeking

political asylum at the nearest British bases, and called on everyone to keep calm and use their heads.

By this time the 'caretaker' was relaying the dire tidings all over the base, alarmed and very upset, desperately working out how to handle the arrival of an unknown number of refugees from the Argentine station on the Debenham Islands. What should he do, and how should they be treated?

There was a great temptation to prolong the hoax even further but the victim's anxieties were now so painful that the hoaxers confessed. His reaction is not recorded.

1955/6 On the anniversary of the establishment of Horseshoe, *Shackleton* arrived with the Governor on board and Searle was told that he had been appointed Base Leader for his second year – a popular choice for he had shown much restraint and great understanding of individual foibles during the past difficult winter. Unhappily similar weather patterns were repeated the

1956 following year, successive periods of high temperatures and gales which broke up the ice. On 20 July it even rained. Only on a few occasions were they able to reach the mainland, but conditions there were always so bad that it was impossible to achieve any substantial work.

1956/7 For this reason when *Biscoe* relieved Horseshoe in March 1957, the opportunity was taken to put up a small hut on Blaiklock Island as a stepping stone, so that bad sea ice conditions would not in the future prevent work on the mainland. As it happened, however, the 1957 winter provided a solid freeze-up which enabled Peter Gibbs and John Rothera, the relief surveyors, to establish a control network extending from Adelaide Island, over Laubeuf Fjord, Reid Glacier and Bigourdan Fjord, a very considerable advance on what had previously been possible.

Early in 1956 a new station under Tom Murphy was established on Detaille Island. It was near the entrance to Lallemand Fjord on the Loubet Coast, seventy miles north of Horseshoe. At first this was known as Lent Island because it was during Lent that building began. Then Eric Salmon (ex-Signy, Deception and Argentine Islands) discovered that Charcot had already named it Detaille Island in 1909, and this old name was adopted. The purpose of the station was to facilitate topographical and geological surveys of the Loubet Coast and Lallemand Fjord, neither of which was easily accessible either from Marguerite Bay to the south, or from the Argentine Islands to the north.

At Horseshoe Searle was perturbed, feeling that the range of his field activities would be restricted by the work of Detaille surveyors, but in the event travelling conditions from Horseshoe proved so difficult that this competitive situation never arose. It was soon found that travelling from Detaille was also greatly restricted by unstable ice, and parties working on the mainland were repeatedly cut off for long periods. Just as the Blaiklock refuge had been built for workers out of Horseshoe, another refuge was established at Orford Cliff, Lallemand Fjord, for Detaille parties.

It was there that *Biscoe* landed Lieutenant Angus Erskine RN, the new Base Leader, with Denis Goldring, Jim Madell and John Smith, on 3 March 1957. After a month's work on the plateau Erskine and Madell, who had separated from the other two, found it impossible to get back to Detaille so made their way via the Finsterwalder Glacier to the Blaiklock refuge. There they were met by Gibbs, who took them back to Horseshoe where they had to wait until midwinter before the ice was safe for them to return to their own base.

Meanwhile Goldring and Smith were having their own adventures. While searching for a depot of dog food they had cached their camping gear, and by the time they found it increasing wind had raised so much drift that they could not find their way back. Each spent the night in his own snow hole with only Nutrican dog pemmican to chew on. By morning so much snow had fallen that although they got back to their cache, they failed to find their gear – so returned to their holes for a second night, and more Nutrican. On the third day they spotted the upstanding tip of a ski and knew that their equipment lay buried deep in the accumulation. It was a lucky escape.

1958/9   At the end of 1958 Detaille was closed. Ironically, the winter freeze had for once produced solid ice in Matha Strait and that season it did not break out. Even with the assistance of two Americans icebreakers *Biscoe* could not reach the station. So having secured it against the elements, Brian Foote's party sledged their belongings out over thirty miles of sea ice to the ship. As the dogs were being hoisted on board 'Steve' escaped and refused to be caught. Instead he set off for home along their sledge tracks, thus sealing his fate for there was no time to organise a round-up. It was a very sad ending, and the drivers who had loved and worked with him felt it keenly.

Nearly three months later everyone at Horseshoe was astounded to see Steve running happily over the hill, fit and well, and delighted to be the centre of such an enthusiastic welcome. From his good condition it was clear that he had returned to Detaille and lived on the old seal pile from which the dogs had been fed. As midwinter approached and still his friends failed to return, he must have decided to go and look for them. He could have gone west to the ice edge or he might have turned north or east. Instead he surely remembered making the sixty-mile sledge journey to Horseshoe the previous season and confidently set off south. Since no vestige of a trail could have remained, he had to remember the intricate route, across the sea ice of

Detaille Island hut. (J. S. Madell)

Lallemand Fjord, over the glaciers of the Arrowsmith Peninsula, down into Bourgeois Fjord, and so to Horseshoe Island and the base lying in a bay on the west coast.

In winter there was no food along the route, and it is astonishing that a dog should take a conscious decision to seek company and abandon his larder on the strength of a past memory. So much for those who believe dogs cannot think.

1955/6   The station on Danco Island had been set up fifty miles north of the Argentine Islands solely for reconnaissance in a geologically unknown area, and to establish ground control for the aerial photography then being flown by FIDASE from Deception. It was therefore particularly unfortunate that Danco should have been chosen, for it was quickly discovered that there was no access inland. In consequence, throughout its occupation, from early 1956 to the end of 1958, all the work was based on boat journeys, carried out with considerable risk, over an area extending from Cape Murray some seventy-five miles to the north, to the Miethe Glacier twenty-five miles to the south.

At various points attempts were made to reach the plateau on top of the Antarctic Peninsula, notably along the spine of Reclus Peninsula, where parties spent many weeks but to no avail. To the south, a probe inland up the Miethe Glacier brought them no further than seven miles from the coast, but despite this, persistence did bring some results, and Brian Bayly and Graham

Hobbs, geologists, returned home with at least something concrete for their great efforts. John Ketley, Leslie Harris and David Evans, surveyors, succeeded in establishing some of the ground control.

In late 1956 a base was established at Prospect Point, fifty miles south of the Argentine Islands. Here, too, it was soon found that access inland was impossible, geological and survey work was perforce restricted to the coast
1957 and the off-lying islands. From May to September Ron Miller and his five companions travelled across sea ice as far as Leroux Bay some forty miles to the north, and south to Cape Evensen fifteen miles distant.

During the whole period the ice was seldom more than six inches thick, and frequently the burden of snow caused flooding, with consequent slushy surfaces. Often open water and leads prevented access to many of the islands – no wonder they scrupulously obeyed the rule 'always camp on land'. Their journeys were highly dangerous, and their determination not to stagnate at base highly commendable. At the end of 1958 the base was closed.

In April 1957 Edwin (later Sir Edwin) Arrowsmith became Governor. He was also to become the first High Commissioner for the British Antarctic Territory in 1962 when that area was separated from the remaining Falkland Islands Dependencies.

His first tour of the southern bases in *Protector* during 1957 was enlivened when we nearly lost *Shackleton*, then commanded by Captain Norman Brown. On the 25th she sailed from Signy *en route* for South Georgia but was quickly stopped by ice. For four days Brown fought his way slowly towards Powell Island, making painfully slow progress. Then a piece of heavy ice tore a hole in the port bow. Twenty minutes later there were six inches of water in the main hold, and they were in bad trouble. Ballast and bilge pumps were started, and a portable pump was brought into action but it proved a losing battle. Attempts were made to construct and rig a collision mat but after two hours in appalling conditions, icy cold and wet, it was clear that this was having little effect.

Brown had already altered course towards Uruguay Cove on Laurie Island, where he planned to beach his ship. Cargo was jettisoned to lighten her, while the boats were cleared away ready to be lowered. Suddenly they were in impenetrable ice and hopes of beaching her had to be abandoned. Boats were lowered as they prepared to abandon ship.

While all this was going on, a second collision mat had been made from the canvas scow cover. The ship had now listed twenty degrees to starboard but despite this the second mat was successfully placed, and by five in the

Opposite: RRS John Biscoe *following two American icebreakers. (US Navy)*

morning the hard pressed crew thankfully watched the water level slowly going down. This made it possible to move sufficient cargo to get at the damage from inside, and after two hours' labour temporary repairs had been made. The boats were brought in, the engines began to keep the ship clear of ice, and by midnight, when the whale-catcher *Southern Lily* arrived to stand by, they were making slow passage towards South Georgia.

Their troubles were not over. On 1 December a rough sea and a heavy swell forced the Captain to seek refuge in the lee of a convenient iceberg, where they awaited HMS *Protector*, also on her way to offer help. On arrival she embarked all the Fids, and *Southern Lily* then resumed her whaling. Freed of passengers, *Shackleton* sailed cautiously on but next day water was once more gaining on the pumps, and again they had to find an iceberg to shelter behind. *Protector*, sailing in company, sent her helicopter over with a shipwright and more materials with which to repair the damage. This time they had better success and by next day the nightmare was over, the ship having berthed safely in Stromness Bay, South Georgia. From there she moved into the whaling factory's floating dock where welding was possible. There have been only too many occasions when our ships have suffered ice damage or found unchartered rocks, but apart from *Eagle*'s hair-raising voyage from Hope Bay to the Falklands in 1946, this was the only time when there was real danger of losing a vessel.

It had been decided to re-open Stonington, but though *Biscoe* repeatedly tried to break through the ice, it was already 6 March 1958 before she finally succeeded in reaching the station. The six men who were to re-occupy it, with Peter Gibbs in charge, were landed with their stores as quickly as possible, and the ship sailed again for more open waters.

1958   To their dismay they found that the intervening years of melt and freeze had covered the floors of the hut with a layer of ice over a foot thick. This gave a peculiar 'low-down' look to their home, for the chair seats were only four or five inches above the surface, while all the smaller objects like buckets were completely hidden, and the cross beams supporting the roof were just about head high.

They set to chipping out ice and after ten days of hard work most of the floors were clear. Then a sudden rise in temperature brought water cascading through the window frames to lie several inches deep on the floor. Frantically they baled, for if it once froze they would have to start all over again.

To aid the baling process pits were dug through the floors where water could accumulate, then a trench round the outside of the hut to help drain off what they threw out. Later two major drainage trenches eight feet deep were dug and roofed over to prevent them filling up with drift.

It was a long struggle to conquer the problems, and the many hours of physical work hindered the scientific programmes for which they had come. Even so at least one new arrival found an element of romance in their sorry conditions.

... for me the hut possesses a fascination far above any of the other well-groomed base huts; the fact that we have pulled her through from her impending decay and nursed her back to warmth has rooted an affection within us which could never have occurred on arrival at an inhabited dwelling. Apart from this attraction, the shadows of history still linger over Stonington Island – Bingham, Fuchs, Ronne and the two ladies have left their impression on the place. Often I wonder what it was like when there were twenty other chaps just over the hill, and when at any moment Mrs Ronne might walk into the bunkroom.
Peter Forster's Journal

Journeys were mounted as quickly as possible. The two surveyors, Gibbs and Forster, succeeded in extending the mapping in the mountainous area between Mobiloil Inlet and the Wordie Ice Shelf, while Nigel Procter worked on the coastal geology.

Dr Henry Wyatt started his programme on human physiology and dog nutrition. His particular interest lay in energy expenditure measured against food intake when sledging, and this necessitated measurements of skinfold thickness and body weight, together with water intake and urine output while travelling. He also made measurements to determine whether the men suffered any marked degree of dehydration out sledging, an effect which physiologists had long claimed to occur.

To these ends his companions acted as guinea-pigs during numerous journeys of ten to fifty-nine days' duration. It is to their credit that they suffered without complaint the inconveniences involved on top of the normal stresses of sledging. Wyatt's work was far more detailed and complicated than I have indicated here, and his results were of considerable interest to his professional colleagues when he got home.

On 3 June Gibbs and Wyatt were returning home after a six-week survey journey on the plateau when they learnt from a radio 'sched' with base that a strong wind had broken up the sea ice on 28 May, while Stan Black, Dave Statham and Geoff Stride were travelling from Horseshoe. They had sledged to the emperor penguin rookery on the Dion Islands, about thirty-seven miles to the west, to observe the hatching period. The trip had been planned for four men but at the last moment Ray McGowan, the radio operator, was having trouble with his transmitter and had stayed behind to mend it. He was very disappointed, but the decision saved his life for the three-man party which set out on 27 May was never seen again.

There are many records of inexplicable or mystical events occuring to people in times of great danger. John Paisley was then Base Leader at Horseshoe, and at two o'clock that afternoon he watched his party apparently negotiating a lead about a mile-and-a-half from Pourquoi Pas Island without misgivings.

> . . . a few minutes after nine [that evening] I was overcome by an unbelievable feeling of calamity. The force of this was such that contrary to my nature I was compelled to get onto my knees and pray. Such a compulsion has never happened before or since.
> *John Paisley's Journal*

Many months later when Paisley returned home, he was shown a letter dated 28 May 1958, written by his aunt to his mother saying 'John has been involved in a terrible accident with loss of life, but he is safe himself'. His own experience in the field was vivid enough to cause him intense anxiety when the sledging party did not come up on the radio on the 28th or 29th. On the 30th he had written:

> Paddy woke me early and confirmed a horrible premonition that has been with me since the night of the 27th – the ice has gone. I walked to a good view point along the rocks . . . All the way I was thinking what I might see, but in spite of that I was totally unprepared for the shock. I was appalled . . . that ghastly expanse of black water from the ice edge to the horizon. I returned to the hut stunned. Only that they had reached their camp site was the whole world. . . . But for my feeling of concern last Tuesday night I should not doubt their safety. Tried the radio again tonight but without luck.

Next day SECFIDS (John Green) in Stanley was told of the situation and he, rightly, ordered Paisley to take no immediate action because the three men at Horseshoe with only one dog team would be too weak a party to mount a search. All bases were alerted to keep a radio watch, but nothing was heard. On 2 June John Rothera, based at Danco and surveying in the Arrowsmith Peninsula area to the northeast, broke in on a radio 'sched' to say that his party would search Laubeuf Fjord. By the 4th they were travelling along the north shore of Pourquoi Pas Island but found nothing.

On the night of the 6th 'Yona', a bitch from the missing teams, returned to Horseshoe exhausted and still wearing harness. For hours they searched for her tracks with lanterns, but it was only next morning that they could follow them out into Lystad Bay where they disappeared. She seemed to have been coming from the south, which was ominous for it might indicate that the lost party had drifted in that direction on broken sea ice.

By this time the Stonington field party had got back to their base, and Paisley asked Gibbs for help. His response was immediate, but it was a daunting undertaking for winter darkness was upon them, and the sea ice was in a very treacherous condition. They knew there was open water only sixteen miles to the west and a wide lead extended from Pourquoi Island to Camp Point, which could cut them off from Horseshoe.

Gibbs, Procter and Wyatt searched northwards, their first stop the Argentine station on the Debenham Islands where they learnt that two dogs had been seen but could not be caught, when men approached they ran off towards Millerand Island. They decided to investigate that area first and soon saw the dogs, but they in turn were unable to get near them. An Argentine field party camped on Millerand reported that six days earlier 'Chloe' had arrived, ravenous and very iced-up.

Quickly moving on they next sledged to Randall Rocks, Stipple Rocks and Pod Rocks in very treacherous ice conditions. Everywhere there was heavy new pressure ice and at any moment a shift of wind could have set it in motion. Nothing was found and by the 15th they were back on the mainland coast at Cape Calmette, where they heard that 'Elma' had now returned to Horseshoe.

Joint plans were made between the two bases to search the rest of the mainland coast and the east side of Adelaide Island. On the 17th the two uncatchable dogs seen at Millerand arrived at Stonington, turning out to be 'Ruth' and 'Angus'. Both were wearing harness, but Angus' trace had been cut or bitten while Ruth's harness was complete with trace and attaching ring. It is possible that the ring twisted clear of the cliphook, but more likely that she had been released. If so, it followed that the traces of harnesses on the other dogs had probably been cut by men, not sheared by dogs' teeth.

On the same day Gibbs found 'Cocoa' and 'Umiak' in Square Bay, well to the north of Stonington. Cocoa was in fair condition with two bits of ice on his coat but wearing his harness, which had been chewed in two places and the trace cut six inches from his collar. Gibbs remembers that two or three other dogs which returned also wore harness (though he did not see them), so it could be deduced that an accident occurred while the party were travelling, but the trace clipped to Cocoa's *collar*, not to his harness, indicated that the men had stopped for some reason.

At that time a custom had developed of leaving the dogs in harness overnight, which would account for both the trace and the harness being bitten through. But the fact that the traces were clean cut raised the question of whether perhaps the men had had time to cut the teams loose from whatever danger was threatening them – we shall never know for certain.

On the 29th 'Bessie' and 'Cocky' came back to Horseshoe. This made nine animals home out of the fourteen that had set out as two teams – six from one, three from the other. When a search of the islands and fjords in northern Marguerite Bay revealed nothing, the parties turned their attention to eastern Adelaide Island and the Dions to the south, where again the sea ice was precarious. No clues were found. Beyond lay the Faure Islands, right in the path of any ice blown out by northerly winds – clearly the last hope for the lost men.

By now instructions had been received from Stanley *not* to risk life by extending the search over areas of new ice. The two Base Leaders called their parties in, but could not accept the order personally. They felt strongly that at least the two of them *must* make the attempt – a very courageous decision in view of the darkness and unstable ice. It was 8 July, forty days since the party had disappeared, and even if they were on the Faure Islands it was doubtful whether they could have survived so long. Yet there was just a chance in a thousand – and it had to be taken. Both were determined to make sure that no doubts remained.

On 9 July Paisley and Gibbs gingerly made a four-mile test run onto the thin ice and then returned. Next day, with 800 pounds on the sledge, they set out. Good weather held, and apart from some new pressure ridges, they covered the first eleven miles fairly easily. But the last five took two-and-a-half hours of manhandling the sledge over heavy pressure ice by a circuitous route, constantly having to find gaps between old rafted floes.

On approaching the nearest islet they found the way blocked by great pressure belts, but ultimately they forced a way through and camped inside the island group with considerable relief. As they rested, the sun just peeped over the horizon for the first time for many weeks, shedding a low golden light across the frozen sea, 'its warmth felt through the eyes rather than the body'.

Next day the wind rose to gale force and driving drift made any sort of search impossible. Conscious that any blow could break up the new ice, and prevented by thick drift from seeing what effect the wind was having, the men suffered an anxious time, their minds concentrating on food problems: 'Unless we find seals we will be hungry in three weeks' time.'

The following day was very cold but the wind dropped and they immediately broke camp, sledging through the maze of some fifty islands, islets and rocks, but found no sign of the missing men. The great risks they had so willingly run only proved that the party had never reached the islands. This last effort had failed, yet at least they had done everything possible. Now it was high time to look to their own safety.

Sunday 13 July was the day they were to return to the Dions, but once again the weather was deteriorating and a decision to travel gave them much to ponder:

I woke up, the tent a web of ice crystals, lit the Primus and waited until they had melted away. I then sat up and put snow in a pan to melt, and was adding the oats when my mother came in through the sleeve entrance of the tent. She looked at me and said quite calmly that she knew I was very concerned about the journey back. She admitted not knowing what my worry was, but if I left here today then everything would be all right.
John Paisley's Journal

Today Paisley recognises that many may think this episode fanciful, but for him the reality of it still remains. Whatever view one takes, it emphasizes the stresses which he and Gibbs were experiencing. They had an anxious discussion on whether they should risk the weather, but Paisley confidently insisted they must go.

Breaking camp, they sledged cautiously back through the labyrinth of pressure until reaching the level ice five miles out, they found it had cracked into large floes during the gale that had held them in their tent, and this meant that it was liable to go out with any strong wind.

With ten miles to go we were therefore taking a large chance on trying to press through; a chance, too, on not meeting any wide leads between us and the Dions. The alternative of returning to the Faures and sitting-out the ensuing bad weather, with the strong possibility that it would clear the ice and maroon us there, equally did not appeal. So praying for luck we sledged on as fast as I could drive the dogs. A crack had opened up in a line from the Faures to the Dions, and at right-angles to this we crossed two leads four feet wide, where the dogs behaved very well. The visibility decreased, as we knew it would, but fortunately no wind sprang up.
Peter Gibbs' Journal

Three hours after setting out they reached the safety of the Dions. It had been a gallant attempt. The two Base Leaders had deliberately taken severe risks, and one can only admire their persistence and cold-blooded courage in face of such very apparent dangers, tragically to no avail.

So ended the last hope of finding the lost men and we shall never know exactly what happened to them. There is little doubt that circumstances, perhaps the darkness or rising wind and drift, forced them to camp before reaching the coast of Adelaide Island. Then, possibly very suddenly, high winds could have broken up the sea ice into individual floes separated by ever widening leads of open water, and they would have been unable to break camp and get moving in the short time available. They probably cut the teams free to fend for themselves and the dogs jumped the leads in the general direction of home.

My reasoning as to the cause of this terrible accident is based on an occasion nine years earlier when five of us were sledging out to the Dions from Stonington to establish a camp at the emperor penguin rookery so that Bernard Stonehouse could study the birds. Some thirteen miles from the islands we found ourselves in an area of very hummocky ice, and on 3 June 1949 I had written:

. . . we struck an area of what once had been heavy brash and had now become frozen and drifted up in ridges at right-angles to our course. As the windcrust on the ridges was so hard that it would not break down under the sledge, we were continually hauling steeply up till the sledge was poised on the six-inch to a foot wide apex, the

runners arching ominously before the whole load crashed down on the far side. So far
we have covered nearly four miles of this, which is hard going for men and dogs –
besides being very bad for the sledges.

4 June . . . by lunch time we had covered less than three miles . . . the sledge
continually getting stuck on the steep drift slopes which are windcrusted to such a
thickness that it is impossible to break them down with shovel and ice axe. The first
catastrophe was Dave Jones being thrown backwards over Spivey's sledge-wheel,
which had something of the comic strip about it as Jones sat there among the debris
with a bemused smile on his face and a mangled wheel and twisted fork around his
neck . . . then Dalgliesh's sledge quietly 'sat down' and refused further service. Every
one of the bridges on either side had broken and the runners lay limply outwards.

In 1949 these conditions had resulted from winds whistling down Laubeuf
Fjord and breaking out an embayment in the edge of the fast ice, which later
filled with hummocky brash that refroze and became snow covered. Such an
area would remain unstable in gale force winds and similar conditions could
be repeated in any year. Anyone caught in a break-up of this kind of ice
would find it virtually impossible to escape quickly to safer surfaces.

Twice later these conditions are known to have been repeated. In 1960
Peter Forster and Dr Tony Davies, sledging from Horseshoe, reported a
nine-mile wide belt of brash and bergy bits frozen into the ice southwest of
the Guébriant Islands. In October 1963 Jim Shirtcliffe, Ivor Morgan and
David Nash, sledging from Adelaide to Horseshoe, also encountered
pressure ridges and refrozen leads in the same area.

After the tragedy a cross of oak was made in Stanley on which a brass plate
commemorates the names of Stan Black, Dave Statham (meteorologists)
and Geoff Stride (diesel/electric mechanic). It was several years before we
were able to reach the Dion Islands by ship, but it was finally erected high on
a stone cairn, an isolated memorial in a vast panorama of ice, to remind those
who come later that these islands were the objective of three gallant young
men in their last great adventure.

There is always a certain risk in being alive,
And if you are more alive there is more risk.
Ibsen

By mid-August Gibbs and Forster were on a man-hauling reconnaissance of
the head of Neny Fjord, trying to find an easier route to the plateau than that
via the steep slopes of 'Sodabread'. They established that it was possible to
get up a precipitous ramp from the sea ice onto the Snowshoe Glacier, but
deep soft snow and perpetual gusting winds prevented them from finding a
way up the glacier itself. Disappointed, they turned for home and that
night camped on Postillion Rock, a little islet raising its low rounded surface
only a few feet above the sea ice.

The following account of what happened then was written by Forster when he got back to Stonington after enduring a sixty-hour battle with the katabatic winds in Neny Fjord – the dreaded 'fumigator'. It also aptly represents the many occasions when travelling Fids have been similarly caught:

The scene was Postillion Rock. . . . During the night the wind rose, raising vast quantities of drift. When Pete (Gibbs) went out to tighten the guys, he returned with the bad news that the snow around the tent which was holding the pegs was rapidly eroding. As the day progressed the gale developed into a full blizzard, which was frighteningly amplified by the loneliness of our poorly pitched tent. Midday arrived, and it was my turn to crawl from a damp though relatively comfortable sleeping bag, don all possible protection and, tied to a climbing rope, push through the sleeve entrance – the gate to another world.

A world of such contrast that the first moments were spent in bewilderment at the harshness of the scene. No longer did the pleasant rocky knolls surround the tent, nor did the impressive cliffs of Roman Four appear above the blue ice cliffs. Gone was the berg-flecked sea ice extending to mountains that reach for the sky . . . Instead there was a world of hectic motion, a fuming cauldron, in which rearing stinging drift spiralled past, driven by the fantastic power of the wind; the drift and cold not only affected sight and hearing but one's very mind, even here in the comfort of base, to me the drift still swirls over Postillion. Such were my impressions on first emerging from the tent.

Then the task of inspection, which showed that the surrounding snow had been scoured by the blast, leaving the tent perched on a pedestal. The boxes which had originally rested on the canvas skirt had fallen away, leaving it flapping wildly in the wind. It was obvious something would have to be done soon if the tent was not to blow away. Under the conditions even tying a simple knot took minutes because it was out of the question to take gloves off. With Pete's help from inside we managed to tie ropes and secure the guys by various unorthodox means, and still the blizzard had not reached its worst.

Before darkness fell it was Pete's turn to do battle outside, and he found that by then it was only possible to crawl against the wind. Then we sank our crampons deep in the centre of the floor, froze them in with whatever liquid we could muster, and fastened a central cord to them to hold the tent down. Not even the sense of false security obtained from cotton wool ear plugs could bring me sleep that night.

Gradually . . . the tent shrank as drift filled the space between the outer and inner walls, thereby weighing down the inner walls. By morning things were in a shocking state; one side of the tent outer was flapping freely and rapidly tearing; Pete's side had been undercut by about four feet. I didn't think it would last much longer. Soon the overhang on Pete's side fractured and drift poured into the tent through a nine-inch gap at ground level. This Pete plugged with his bedding.

By now all was prepared for the worst – all clothing put on – food in pockets – compass – survival plans discussed. With all possible done we sat and waited; without, the increasing blizzard – within, our thoughts. Thoughts of a sudden gust, a crashing tent, the bubble bursting leaving nothing but cold drift penetrating the sleeping bag. Then dreams, dreams of one thing only – peaceful sleep . . . Then hopes – then prayers – even, perhaps, a little faith.

Then the blizzard eased, just short lulls between lengthy blasts, then longer lulls, then silence. Unfortunately dusk was already falling and another fourteen hours of suspense had to be endured. By now the tent had shrunk until there was barely room for us to crouch side by side, and making it impossible to sleep because of the cramped position. In the end luck was with us, and by two that afternoon we made a thankful return to base. Never before have I so enjoyed such physical and mental relaxation as I am getting now.

Of the other journeys made that year the longest was a fifty-eight-day survey traverse undertaken by Gibbs and Forster accompanied by Wyatt. They travelled south to Mushroom Island over the sea ice, then up onto the Wordie Ice Shelf, over the Fleming Glacier, across the plateau and home via the Traffic Circle and down 'Sodabread Slope'. While still in the field they learnt of difficult ice conditions, which would almost certainly prevent a ship reaching Stonington – that meant that they would all have to be evacuated by air from Horseshoe.

This unhappy forecast proved true. Even with assistance from the American icebreaker *Northwind, Biscoe* could not fight a way through to Stonington. On 7 March 1959 the whole base sledged up to Horseshoe, from where they were picked up by American helicopters and flown out to where *Biscoe* was lying in heavy ice off Adelaide Island. Once again the Marguerite Bay defences had won – and once again Stonington was abandoned.

At Admiralty Bay 1959 was a terrible year. On 23 April Russell Thompson and Alan Sharman went for a walk on the slopes behind base with two dogs for company. While they were negotiating a snow patch the excited dogs rushed past them, knocking over both men, who then slid out of control and fell over a rock cliff. Thompson was badly bruised, but when he had picked himself up he was horrified to find Sharman lying perfectly still. He had hit his head and been killed instantly.

All such terrible misfortunes are keenly felt in the small close-knit polar community, but as if this was not enough for the wintering party to absorb, only three months later they suffered further bereavement. Jeff Stokes, Ken Gibson, Colin ('Dick') Barton and Denis ('Tink') Bell were out on a surveying and geological journey. Ascending a glacier, Bell and Stokes were breaking trail a long way ahead of the second dog team. They had negotiated a crevassed area lower down, and believed that at last they were in the clear. The deep soft snow made the going difficult and the dogs showed signs of tiredness. To encourage them to persevere Bell went ahead, but unwisely without his skis. Suddenly he disappeared leaving a hole in the crevasse bridge through which he had fallen.

Peering into the depths Stokes called repeatedly and was greatly relieved to be answered. Lowering a rope almost a hundred feet, he told Bell to tie himself on. As he could not haul up the weight, he hitched his end of the rope to the team, the dogs took the strain and began to pull. Now it was easy and everything was going well. But Bell had tied the rope through his belt instead of round his body, perhaps because of the angle at which he lay in the crevasse. As he reached the top his body jammed against the lip, the belt broke, and down he went again. This time there was no reply to Stoke's calls. It was a particularly tragic fatality which one really felt should never have happened, and thus doubly grievous.

The following year saw the completion of the field work, and since it was considered that meteorology was sufficiently covered by the adjacent Argentine and Chilean stations at Greenwich and Half Moon Islands, Admiralty Bay was closed in January 1961.

1959/60 'Ice Cold Katy' had crashed in 1946. Her replacement never flew because the skis were not delivered. Thus the reintroduction of aircraft in 1959/60 was a major advance. The TAE planes, an Otter and a Beaver, had proved their worth in Antarctic operations, so with surprisingly little difficulty the Colonial Office was persuaded to allow the purchase of one of each type for FIDS. Deception Island was chosen as our operational base because it provided the only possible land surface suitable for a runway.

At last the airstrip surveyed by Mason in 1946 was going to be used, though it was possible to clear only 700 yards of the 800 he had proposed. Innumerable boulders of volcanic scoriae were removed and the remaining ash was rolled into a hard surface. Having no roller, the Fids ingeniously improvised one from a huge steel barrel filled with concrete, which served their purpose admirably.

We arrived with the crated planes on 26 January in the Danish *Kista Dan*, chartered from J. Lauritzen Lines and commanded by Captain K. Hindberg. Our first priority was to build a raft on which to tow the Otter's fuselage ashore. For this we had brought a number of Army bridge-building pontoons, on which a platform was now constructed. Once ashore the plane was man-hauled onto the beach and up to the airstrip. The wings came ashore the same way in immensely heavy crates.

Fitting them was a formidable task for there was no mechanical means of lifting them into position, but the operation was another triumph of Fid-power. An empty crate was hauled into position and sixteen stalwarts stood on it. A wing was then passed to them, and amid many a groan and grunt of 'Careful, for God's sake', they managed to raise it above their heads. Now came the strain, for tall men bore the weight on hunched shoulders, while short ones had their arms fully extended above their heads.

A comic situation developed when it was found that two volunteers were too short even to reach the underside of the wing, and a second tier of boxes had to be provided to enable them to play their part. Then, proud of their success, the Fids had to repeat the whole exercise on the other side. Fitting the propeller and the brake hydraulic system also gave the engineers trouble, but two days later the first test flight was made.

The small Beaver was built on board, fitted with floats, and lifted over the side into the water by derrick. On 7 February she also was test-flown, then reloaded and parked on the forward hatch ready for ice reconnaissance ahead of the ship.

Next day *Kista* sailed for the Argentine Islands. The Lemaire Channel was congested with floes and clearly it was going to be another difficult ice year. Our intention was to set up a new base on the southern end of Adelaide Island or, alternatively, at the Léonie Islands lying to the east of it in Marguerite Bay.

Before attempting the passage further south Flight Lieutenant 'Paddy' English RAF flew an ice reconnaissance from the open water around the Argentine Islands. His first sortie lasted less than an hour, for low cloud immediately drove in from the west and he hastily returned at 500 feet, to land in a different channel from where he had taken off. Once down among the many small islets, neither the occupants of the plane nor the crew of the motor boat which had been lowered to tow her in, could see each other. From the bridge of the ship we could see both, and watched with amusement as they chased each other round the bergs. The plane eventually came alongside under her own power, shortly followed by the tender belching angry clouds of black smoke which drifted across the peaceful scene.

Two days later the weather cleared and English took off again, this time with the First Officer and me as observers. Flying due west we reached open water after forty miles, then turning south to follow the ice edge, found ourselves being forced away from the coast west-southwest. This was ominous for the ship would have to enter ice long before she reached Marguerite Bay. Turning east towards Adelaide the usual coastal lead had not formed, there was no short cut in that direction. The only hopeful sign was a dark water-sky some fifty miles beyond the southern end of the island. If *Kista Dan* could force a way that far, we might find better conditions in the bay itself. A hundred and fifty miles to the south the high sunlit peaks of the Douglas Range on Alexander Island glistened in the clear air – surely, I thought, a beckoning sign from old friends.

We sailed as soon as the plane was back on board, trying to break out to the open sea through Bismarck Strait. Two hours of hard work accomplished nothing. Next the Captain tried the Schollaert Channel, which was relatively free of ice and soon we were in open water. But the air

Beaver at the Argentine Islands. (V. E. Fuchs)

reconnaissance had established that this would not last for long, and in latitude 66°32′S we turned southwest into the pack:

Gradually movement became more difficult but the ship keeps going with ice heaving from below, great lumps and plates rising out of the water and falling slowly back into the turbulence of the porridge-like brash. Ahead the floes struggle and rotate as they adjust themselves to the thrusting bows of the ship. If they cannot move they either split into many pieces or stop the ship. Then we go astern and charge again. Overall she keeps going remarkably well, making about half to three knots. *Author's Journal*

For three days the slow battle continued, then we found a small stretch of open water from which the Beaver could take off. Hurriedly she was put over the side carrying the First Officer and Alfred Stephenson (ex-British Graham Land Expedition and our guest for the season). English flew off to look at the ice in the direction of Cape Alexandra, Adelaide Island. Forty minutes later we lost radio contact.

Our pool was shrinking and the surface beginning to freeze. As we listened-out the Chilean ship *Piloto Pardo* called us, asking for an ice report as she too was trying to get into Marguerite Bay. I supplied it as quickly as possible and closed the contact so that we could resume radio watch for the Beaver. Suddenly she came up, reporting that they were returning, and in fifteen minutes landed alongside, sending a shimmering shower of thin ice plates slithering across the newly frozen water.

Apparently there was open water around the southern coasts of Adelaide, and a wide lead extended southward past the Dions and Faure Islands towards Alexander Island. But to the east the whole of Marguerite Bay was filled with unbroken fast ice. *Kista* lay in the heaviest and closest pack ice, but if we could force a passage south, then east and north, it should be possible to reach Adelaide.

So the battle started again. That day the ship covered twenty-eight miles before being halted by heavy pack, which closed up under a gale force wind, and driving snow which blotted out all visibility. Eventually a sixty-five-knot wind produced heavy pressure until ice tilted *Kista* eleven degrees to port – and at that very uncomfortable angle we lived for the next eight days.

Existence itself became an irritation, for everything, even pieces of paper, slid to the floor, cabin mats formed into piles about the doors and meals had to be eaten holding the plates level. The constant wind fluctuated between twenty and fifty knots, while the beset ship drifted helplessly southward in an icy grip. No water was visible, but movement within the ice was only too apparent. Floes split and buckled in every direction, from time to time huge ridges and pinnacles rose up to ten feet or more. Finally ice piled up to deck-level – but our luck held and there was no serious damage.

On 22 February we drifted thirty miles, and heard the *Piloto Pardo*, then in the vicinity of southwestern Adelaide Island, had turned back. The Argentine icebreaker *San Martín* was beset some thirty-five miles northeast of us, having drifted south at the same rate as *Kista Dan*. Two days later we made radio contact and I arranged with Capitán Boffi for twice daily 'scheds' to keep each other informed of our relative positions.

Our respective predicaments remained unchanged for four days, then Capitán Boffi told us that he had lost a blade from one of his propellers; he had asked the American icebreaker USS *Glacier* for assistance. This powerful, 8,000-ton ship, with ten engines developing 22,000 horse power, was then 600 miles away. Hearing that she was coming into the area, I also made radio contact with her captain, Commander Porter, who agreed to come to our aid after he had freed *San Martín*. But on 2 March, under the influence of a southeast wind, the ice suddenly began to move:

. . . from then on ice activity increased and soon the ship was heaving and twisting, sometimes returning to an even keel, sometimes heeling over as much as sixteen degrees. All around us the ice was buckling and rising in tumbling masses that here and there advanced across the floes like the slow moving, rolling front of a lava

MV Kista Dan *beset. (V. E. Fuchs)*

stream. From time to time she was squeezed tight, and huge plates of ice four feet thick would up-end and drive under her, only to re-emerge with a rush and a great swirling turbulence a few minutes later.

Meanwhile the ship's heading was constantly changing as she was pushed and nudged by the shifting, rotating floes. Now we are heading fifteen degrees east of north instead of sixty-eight degrees, as we have been doing during the past days. This evening things have quietened down with the easing of the wind, and the area around us looks like a battlefield, for the floes and brash are stained with great patches of red paint scraped from our hull. The rest appears in various shades of black or grey due to the churning of the waste pumped from the bilges during our long stay.

Everywhere cardboard cartons, beer cans, bottles and other rubbish has been scattered by the movement of the ice – really a disgrace to see. Unfortunately we can only throw rubbish over the stern, and it is nature's forces which have scattered it so widely.

Author's Journal

Despite all this movement it was two days before a small lead appeared and *Kista* was able to sail voluntarily for the first time in nearly a fortnight. Conditions had also eased for *San Martín*. With assistance from *Glacier* she had reached open water. Apart from the broken propeller blade, she had suffered enormous pressure which had buckled thirty frames in her hull.

Two days later *Glacier* arrived in our area. We had moved a few miles but were once more held fast in ice which even she found difficult to negotiate. On 9 March we followed in the channel she was painfully cutting and made twelve miles in twelve hours. Even this was difficult, for her wash constantly packed huge broken fragments into an almost impenetrable barrier behind her. Next day we in turn reached open water, and with an exchange of farewells and many expressions of our most heartfelt gratitude, *Glacier* left us. For the moment the struggle was over, but our carefully scheduled plans for the season were in total disarray.

Having failed to establish a base on Adelaide, I now planned to put that party ashore in our abandoned station on Anvers, under the command of Ted Clapp. But a flight over the area showed the narrow ramp of ice up to the piedmont to be dangerously crevassed. The only alternative was for them to winter in Wordie House, the unoccupied hut a mile from the Argentine Islands observatory. Stonington would have to remain closed, while Horseshoe could be relieved by air. There would be no access by ship to the southern bases.

With the Beaver on our foredeck we sailed into the confined waters around the Argentine Islands and thankfully anchored near *Biscoe*, already lying close inshore. That evening the wind suddenly increased to fifty knots, and Bill Johnston found his starboard anchor dragging; *Biscoe* was in serious danger of drifting onto a small rock astern. To compound our troubles *Kista*'s port anchor lay across *Biscoe*'s starboard one and it was now imperative that both ships should move – a tricky manoeuvre in the confined space, with so strong a wind and little steerage way. Despite the greatest care the vessels drifted so close together that the Beaver's port wing was torn off and fell over the side, where it promptly sank.

Now our only chance of relieving Horseshoe depended on the Otter which was at Deception. She was not equipped to fly with floats and the problem was to find a snow runway in our vicinity. There was nothing suitable on land, so it would have to be the sea ice if we could find a sufficiently stable area. I transferred to *Biscoe*, and our searches revealed a wide strip of unbroken fast ice two-and-a-half feet thick, south of the Argentine Islands and west of Beascochea Bay. After one abortive attempt foiled by bad weather, Flight Lieutenant Ron Lord RAF flew the plane down on 18 March.

Next day he flew to Horseshoe to evacuate the six men who had wintered, replacing them with Peter Forster, Peter Grimley and Charles Le Feuvre. The plan was for these three, together with Dr Tony Davies who joined them on a later flight, to winter at Horseshoe, then to sledge south to Stonington whence they would work in the spring and summer until, hopefully, the base could be relieved the following season.

Two more flights were needed to complete the relief but low cloud, snow and mist persisted for the next three days. Then the fast ice began to break up, reducing our runway to 500 yards. Soon large, heavy floes were arriving from the north, threatening to block the ships' route out. It was late in the season and the clear weather we so desperately needed for flying would assuredly bring with it a cold spell sufficient to freeze the leads and lock the floes together. Captain Hindberg was understandably anxious to get *Kista* clear of any more trouble, but she carried the only automatic radio beacon on which the Otter could 'home'. Bill Johnston, wonderfully phlegmatic as ever, was willing to remain in the area until 1 April.

Then at last we had some luck. The weather cleared enough for the final relief flights, after which Lord flew safely back to winter quarters at Deception on 27 March. The ships sailed, extricating themselves cautiously from their increasingly precarious position and struggled back to open water. *Kista* left for Deception and home, while *Biscoe* headed westward through the Schollaert Channel to continue her interrupted scientific programme, which included landing Professor David Griffiths and his team from Birmingham University at various points to make gravity observations.

Kista had on board *Biscoe*'s heavy cargo scow, containing four diesel generators which were to be delivered to Deception. On 1 April she reported that this had slid over the side in a heavy sea, and floated away in the driving blizzard. A search was in progress, and they asked for a radio 'sched' to speak to them again just before noon. In view of the date and time suggested we suspected a hoax, but alas it was true, and the scow was never seen again.

Some days later we in turn arrived at Deception, and unloaded some 450 tons of cargo, including 100 tons of steel for the erection of a hangar to be built on the airstrip. We also put down the hutting stores which had been intended for delivery to Adelaide and Stonington.

The wintering air party was already established in the old FIDASE hut close to the main base. As soon as *Biscoe* could get back to Stanley and bring out a new wing, they would fit it to the damaged Beaver.

So ended a disastrous season. We had suffered much from ice and weather, but human error too had added its quota to the sadness and frustrations we all felt.

The best laid schemes o' mice an' men,
Gang aft a-gley.
Robert Burns

10

The Troglodytes
1959–73

In the 1955/6 season when the Royal Society IGY Expedition built their base on the Brunt Ice Shelf it was intended to last for two years. However, the international decision to encourage further work in Antarctica through the IGC, and the discovery that Halley Bay lay under the belt of maximum auroral activity, made it desirable to keep the base open and continue the ionospheric, geomagnetic and auroral studies. On 10 January 1959 the station was handed over to FIDS. Already deeply buried in snow, access to the surface was by ladder and the occupants led a troglodyte existence, only rarely seeing the light of day.

David Dalgliesh (ex-Stonington), the Royal Society Base Leader, had been out taking the air in 1956 when he saw a dark spot appearing and disappearing over the eastern horizon. He concluded that this could only be some distant mountain, revealed by atmospheric refraction. When the TAE party passed through in 1957 he persuaded me to fly him inland to establish the truth. During this flight we passed over a great ice stream with chaotic tumbling ice falls which we intended to name after Dalgliesh. But later the feature was found to be the source of the glacier which in Shackleton's day extended its tongue far out into the Weddell Sea. He had named this the Stancomb-Wills, a name which had priority. After flying 250 miles we found ourselves over mountains 7,000 feet high and in Norwegian territory. Dalgliesh's theory was proved correct, and the mountains were named the Tottanfjella after the *Tottan* in which the IGY expedition had arrived.

1960   The Royal Society expedition had not been equipped for extensive travel, but after FIDS took over the base, attempts were made to find a route from the Brunt Ice Shelf up onto the inland ice. This was no easy matter, for a wide area of crevasses and chasms bounded the inland margin of the ice shelf where it met the land ice. It was not until two years later that the Base Leader, Colin Johnson, and Denis Ardus succeeded.

1961   During March and April 1961 David Easty and Alan Precious had begun systematically searching for a possible crossing point, but every attempt was frustrated by precipitous ice cliffs or chaotic crevassing. In October Ardus and Johnson renewed these efforts. After travelling seventy-five miles due east from base they were at last able to turn southward and succeeded in crossing the fracture zone. For another eighty miles they followed the edge of the inland ice, looking down on a confused and impenetrable maze of crevasses below them. From their height of 2,000 feet they could see the peaks of the distant Tottanfjella along the eastern horizon. Unable to resist this challenge they pushed on for another hundred miles, and on 14 November became the first men to set foot on these mountains.

Thus we learnt that from Halley Bay a detailed survey of the Tottanfjella and its geology could be mounted. It might even be possible to turn south and extend their studies to the distant Theron Mountains and the Shackleton Range, in both of which work had been started by TAE parties before the continental crossing began.

In February the next year a further reconnaissance made with Muskeg tractors found another, seemingly safer, route across the hinge zone almost due south of base. This became known as the 'Bob-Pi Crossing' and a depot was laid there, known for many years as Crossroads Depot. The same route was later used to establish Middle Dump, thirty-seven miles east of Bob-Pi, and the way was now open for future operations.

1962/3   In August 1963 Gordon Mallinson and Neville Mann took two dog teams and their cameras down to the sea ice on a training run, hoping to get some dramatic pictures of the ice cliffs. Quite unexpectedly a strong wind arose and they lost each other in the all-enveloping drift. For some time Mallinson searched without success and then, confident that Mann must be finding his own way home, he returned to base – where he was horrified to discover that his companion was not there.

Though a seemingly hopeless task in the blinding blizzard, search parties immediately set out, but finally they themselves were in danger of falling over the invisible edge of the high ice cliffs, and were forced to retreat to the hut. When the storm abated and visibility returned there was no sign of Mann or the missing team, all the sea ice had blown away and open water extended to the foot of the cliffs. There could be no hope at all.

The shocked base had to absorb this tragic misadventure right on their doorstep, and for Mallinson it must have been, a particularly grievous experience. Later a memorial cross was erected, and perhaps stood as a guardian, reminding those who came after about the dangers of sea ice.

1963/4   During 1963 and 1964 mapping and geology of the Heimefrontfjella, which includes the Tottanfjella, went on apace. Field parties used dog teams in the

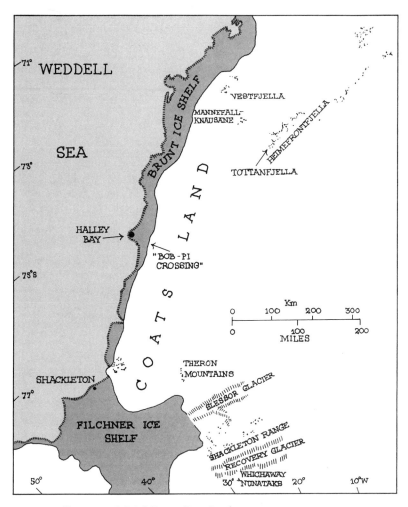

Map 7. Halley Bay and Caird Coast, Coats Land

mountains, and most were supported by Muskegs which sustained long periods of work. During the season Dick Worsfold, 'Sam' Samuel, Gordon Bowra the doctor, and Gordon Mallinson were away from base for 179 days. As they approached the Bob-Pi on their return, an entire dog team fell into a crevasse and eight of the nine animals dropped out of their harness, falling ninety feet on to a ledge. Mallinson was lowered on a rope and all the dogs were hauled safely to the surface, surprisingly enough unhurt.

Shortly after this episode Mallinson and Bowra with their sledge fell twenty feet into another crevasse, this time leaving all the team on the

The Tottonfjella. (P. I. Whiteman)

surface. They in turn were rescued by the other two drivers, and it then took them all another three hours to haul up the sledge and all their equipment. The final accounting showed the loss of only one ski, but taught everyone that the Bob-Pi certainly demanded respect.

1964/5   The following season Tony Baker, Lewis Juckes, Simon Russell and David Wild spent 206 days in the field, most of the time completing works in the Heimefrontfjella. They also visited what were then known as the Milorgknausane nunataks forty miles to the west to begin the survey and geology of this group. At various points they found much crevassing, and it was these bad areas which were later to be the scene of a tragic accident.

1965/6   In 1965/6 a new project was introduced, to sound the ice depth using radio-echo equipment recently developed by Dr Stan Evans at the Scott Polar Research Institute. It had been tested in the Arctic but this was its first use in the south, and Jeremy Bailey was the physicist in charge. He had already successfully installed and operated the equipment on a tractor, and made short journeys around base. It was then decided to attempt soundings during a major journey to the mountains.

In September ten men set out with three Muskegs and three dog teams. Despite constant mechanical troubles largely due to very heavy loads, they arrived at 'Pyramid Rock', the main depot in the Tottanfjella. One tractor with a broken propeller shaft had had to be towed over the last mile and it was obvious that there must be a pause for fairly lengthy repairs on two of the vehicles. Doug Beebe and Brian Porter, the mechanics, made camp and set about the overhauls.

On 12 October the remaining eight men split into two groups. Roddy Rhys Jones, Geoff Lovegrove, Paddy Haynes and Juckes began topograpical survey and geology in the mountains. Wild was in charge of the second unit – John Ross, Dr. John Wilson and Bailey. They travelled westwards with one Muskeg and a dog team, intending to lay a depot near the Milorgknausane nunataks for use by future parties visiting the Vestfjella, a mountain group 100 miles further on.

Wild believed that by following the route he had travelled the previous season, they would be able to reach a point thirty miles south of the nunataks without crossing any dangerous areas. On their first day they covered only twelve miles, held up by difficult terrain associated with an ice fall ten miles from 'Pyramid Rock'. Then the going was excellent, although low drifting snow obscured the surface, and it was agreed to travel late. At eight o'clock in the evening, having made thirty-eight miles, the accident happened.

Wild, Bailey and Wilson were in the Muskeg. The dog team, with Ross sitting on the sledge, was attached to the last of two tractor sledges, thus thirty yards behind his companions. While he happened to be glancing backwards his sledge suddenly stopped moving. He turned to see the leading sledge tilted up over a yawning hole, and there was no sign of the tractor which hauled it.

Anchoring himself with rope, he rushed forward and peered down to see the Muskeg jammed in a crevasse more than 100 feet below. There was no immediate response to his continual shouts, but twenty minutes later he heard Bailey's agonised voice crying out that both Wild and Wilson had been killed, while he himself was badly injured and could not survive. Poor Ross lowered a rope but Bailey ceased to answer his calls.

Darkness was falling, and even if Ross had attempted to go down into the crevasse, there was little hope that he could have got out again unaided. That nightmare of a night he camped alone at the scene quite distraught, trying frequently to make contact again but there was never any response. By morning he had to accept that his three companions had died.

Frantic attempts to make radio contact with base or the other field parties all failed, and at last Ross set off on the forty-five-mile journey back to 'Pyramid Rock' to rejoin Beebe and Porter. After the first shock of hearing the news, they managed to make radio contact with base, who immediately ordered Rhys Jones to take his party back to 'Pyramid Rock'.

By the 23rd they had all joined forces and set out together for the scene of the accident. On arrival Beebe was lowered down to the fallen Muskeg, where he discovered that the three occupants had been crushed by the cab as it fell between ever-narrowing walls in the crevasse. It was not even possible to attempt to recover their bodies. The overwhelmed and silent little party stood in mute prayer while Lovegrove conducted a short service. An improvised wooden crosss was erected to mark the spot.

It will not be without honour to have died at the very end of lands and nature.
Tacitus

Reluctant though one is to criticise when death has supervened, in the interests of those who will follow it is perhaps permissible to examine the causes of this accident. It was unwise to have continued travelling in drift conditions where crevasses might exist. The party believed they were on a route pioneered and proved the year before, but in fact they were off course and headed into a crevassed zone which the drift had prevented them from seeing. Furthermore, a technique had been developed whereby dog teams were helped to keep up with tractors by hitching them onto the last sledge towed by the vehicle. This was not recognised as a dangerous practice by eager young men understandably anxious to accomplish the maximum amount of field work in each short season.

If the dogs had been leading, the crevasse might well have been found without untoward results. Again, since dogs are always reluctant to move in drift conditions, the discipline of always running them in front would surely have brought the column to a timely halt. It is easy to say all this with hindsight, but perhaps worthwhile so that others may learn, and even be saved from similar tragedy.

The severe shock we all felt was particularly poignant for the twenty-nine Fids at Halley Bay, and it is a great credit to them that the summer work continued. Lovegrove and Haynes remained in the field to finish the survey while the others returned to base to reorganise. Then Samuel, Dave Brook, Beebe and Chris Gostick set out once more in a Muskeg to try and retrieve the broken tractor and other equipment which had been abandoned at 'Pyramid Rock'. This was not successful since there were now only a few hours of daylight, and they suffered high winds and drift. Of the forty-two days spent in the field, twenty-five were 'lie-ups' when it was impossible to leave the tent. Despondently they returned to base at the end of May.

1966/7   The geology and surveys in the Heimefrontfjella being finished, our scientific plans turned to the Theron Mountains and the Shackleton Range. At the beginning of the following season Haynes, Dick Cuthbertson, Brian Swift and Stuart Noble made a depot-laying journey to cache supplies for later parties trying to reach the Therons. They then travelled to 'Pyramid Rock' and recovered the Muskeg and all the material abandoned the previous year. An engraved memorial plaque had been made and sent south in the relief ship. Now this party climbed to the highest survey point and fixed it to the rock as a tribute to the three men who had lost their lives. It was the final act of the last party to visit the area from Halley Bay. In their memory the Norwegian authorities re-named the nunataks Mannefallknausane.

By this time the base was in a terrible state. Everywhere meltwater was dripping through the roofs of the distorted buildings, plastic sheets hung beneath the ceilings and drainage gutters festooned the walls. Even bits of string were hung about to direct the drips. All this water drained into numerous buckets strategically placed, which required emptying two or three times a day. Tunnels in the ice outside the buildings were wet with standing or trickling water. The cause was movement of the enveloping ice which had fractured the hut, allowing the internal heat to escape and melt the ice outside.

Quite apart from intense discomfort to the occupants, the depth of the lower buildings was a serious fire hazard, for the exits were now by ladders up fifty-foot vertical shafts. A new base was needed on a new site. In January 1967 *Biscoe* and *Perla Dan*, another Danish chartered ship, arrived with material for a new station. Paul Whiteman, the Base Commander, had had a truly difficult year. It was a credit to his leadership that despite the dreadful conditions under which they had lived, base morale was high.

That season I went south myself, accompanied by Monsieur Pierre Rolland, the Governor of Terre Australe Française, who was visiting the British stations as official French observer under the terms of the Antarctic Treaty. Halley Bay certainly provided him with a variety of incidents.

On our second day there 'Wee Georgie' McLeod, five feet two inches in his socks, developed acute appendicitis. He was *en route* to Stonington, and as we had not yet disembarked men to other bases, we had no fewer than three doctors, Ron Lloyd, John Brotherhood and Dick Williams, together with a visiting dentist, Robin Hubbard, on board.

Using an improvised base surgery, among all the drips, they took charge of the crisis and a prolonged operation began. It was complicated by the fact that they could not find an appendix for quite a long time. But McLeod was nothing if not tough, and three days later the medical team pronounced him fit enough to be moved back to the comparative comfort of the ship. Bound like a mummy to a stretcher, he was pushed and pulled up the shaft to the surface and strapped on to a sledge for the mile-and-a-half ride down to the shore.

I was only just in time to veto the proposal that this should be on a cargo sledge towed by a tractor, which would race him back on board over the rutted bumpy surface. Instead his nursing team were persuaded to man-haul him slowly and carefully over some very rough terrain, and he was happily put to bed in his bunk. However, my protective efforts were probably quite unnecessary, for nine days later when we reached Signy he went off to climb the local mountain – and I stopped worrying about his health.

While relief was going on, a large piece of the ice shelf calved, setting up a chain reaction which resulted in further collapses of the seventy- to ninety-foot cliffs of the ice front north and south of the base. In turn this caused a swell which broke off part of the ice slope onto which we had been unloading. Suddenly the ships were forced to cast-off and move hurriedly into open water, many square miles of which were now covered with loose fragments of brash ice. After a few hours we nosed our way cautiously back – but Halley *Bay* had vanished. (Some years later the station was officially renamed 'Halley'.)

Work started again but soon a seaman was struck by a sledge which was being unloaded, and he fell fifteen feet into the water between the ship and the ice cliff, luckily just where a tiny embayment protected him from being crushed. We fished him out with chattering teeth, a gash in his neck which required stitching, and severe bruising.

During the next few days fragments of the ice slope repeatedly broke away, forcing the ships to keep changing their moorings, but building still continued in shifts round the clock. Seven seventy-foot long huts had been specially designed by Colin Baldwin of the Crown Agents staff, and he came south with us to supervise their erection.

A main feature was the great strength of the steel arches set every ten feet throughout the length of each building. We hoped that these could prevent distortion as the huts became buried. The foundations too were immensely strong, the main beams weighing sixteen hundredweight each. These we laid on a grill of expanded metal, hoping to prevent differential sinking into the snow. This 'metal carpet' soon gave rise to the local name of 'Grillage Village', later contracted to 'the Village' for the new base. It was often to sound absurdly incongruous to many an untutored summer visitor.

When *Biscoe* sailed on 1 February four huts were finished and weatherproof, leaving only internal fitting-out to be done by eight wintering carpenters. *Perla Dan* stayed until the other three huts were built. In all thirty-eight men wintered under the command of Ricky Chinn, who had by now become

Emperor penguin rookery near Halley Bay. (R. V. Gill)

something of a 'professional' Base Commander. An apocryphal story relates that five years earlier he had appeared in our London office as a sales representative, trying to persuade Gipps to buy climbing ropes from his firm. Liking him immediately, and the time being around noon, Gipps and Green had taken him off to share a pub lunch, during which they decided to recruit him. By two o'clock he was brain-washed, and went back to explain to his employers that he would be leaving them in the autumn for Antarctica. Understandably chagrined, they told him he could leave at the end of the month.

The story goes that he arrived ruefully back at our office next day to report that he had got the sack, and had no means of support until we signed him on four months later. The ever-resourceful Gipps promptly phoned the firm to point out that there were several sources of good climbing ropes, and Chinn's valuable services were retained until sailing date. He went first to

Deception as Base Commander, an unusual appointment in a man's first year but amply justified in this case. The following season he took charge of the Argentine Islands, and now here he was, specially chosen to take over Halley Bay in particularly difficult circumstances, for apart from the actual building problems, the move and the transfer of all the scientific equipment had to be gradual in order to minimise interruption of the programmes, and he was virtually administering two bases two miles apart.

By June the Village was ready for occupation and the major task of transferring so much sophisticated equipment and heavy machinery began. The wiring was an electrician's nightmare, but we hoped to be able to look forward to at least ten trouble-free years when living conditions would be comfortable and operations more efficient. This proved over optimistic, for after seven years another new station had to be provided.

In 1956 TAE surveyors had drawn a preliminary map of the Theron Mountains, and it had been established that they are composed of Permo-Carboniferous sediments intruded by dolerite sills. Ten years later FIDS had the opportunity to complete the work in detail, provided that a land route from Halley Bay could be found.

On 4 October 1966 Lovegrove, Alan Johnston, Dave Brook, Colin Wornham, Dave McKerrow and Mike Shaw took three dog teams to break a trail towards this area. Four weeks later a support party consisting of Samuel, Haynes, Peter Blakeley and Andy Williams followed them in three Muskegs, establishing depots at fifty-mile intervals. Seventy-five miles from 'Bob-Pi Crossing' they were surprised to find themselves at over 4,700 feet but thereafter it was downhill all the way to the Therons.

On 15 November the tractors caught up the dogs and survey began, the teams working ahead to find crevassed areas which began to appear fifteen miles from the mountains. These caused the vehicles some trouble but no major recoveries were necessary. In a few weeks the mapping was finished and only a small part of the geology still remained to be done.

1967/8   The next step was to establish a safe route to the Shackleton Range on the south side of the great twenty-five-mile wide Slessor Glacier. For this a party of eight left base in two Muskegs on 28 October 1967 to lay a depot at the head of the Goldsmith Glacier in the Therons. To hasten their travel over known safe terrain, they adopted the original method of carrying two dog teams in kennels mounted on cargo sledges towed by the tractors. One team was to be used by Brook and Wornham to finish off the Theron geology, the other by Samuel and Nick Mathys to reconnoitre the new route to the Shackletons. This left Etchells, Noble, Chris Sykes and Mike Skidmore to bring home the empty Muskegs. They made the return journey of 546 miles

A Muskeg in trouble. (H. B. Rogers)

in the remarkable time of seventeen days. Ten days later they set off again with fresh supplies, this time in an attempt to reach the Shackleton Range itself.

Meanwhile the teams were busy. Samuel and Mathys sledged south for forty miles before reaching the northern margin of the Slessor Glacier which separates the two mountain ranges. Looking down they stared at two miles of chaotically rumpled ice along its northern margin, the central area broken by huge longitudinal crevasses. Twenty-five miles distant on the other side lay Mount Sheffield, part of the Shackleton Range.

It was a daunting sight. The way ahead was clearly impassable, even on foot – let alone with dogs or vehicles. So they turned east along its margin in the hope of rounding the head of the glacier, but were soon forced northeastward. In the next seven days they sledged eighty-four miles and still it trended northeast. By then they were seventy-five miles east of the Goldsmith Depot and heard by radio that the tractors were already on their way back from base. To save the vehicles fifty miles, they headed back to the depot to meet them and draw further supplies.

By this time the geologists had finished their immediate task and on 29

November the three groups met at the Goldsmith Depot. As one party they then began probing a cautious way along the glacier margin, always trying to move southward. The teams worked ahead, the tractors following when a route had been established. Twice they saw an American Hercules flying at about 30,000 feet, and fleeting thoughts of a nice warm cabin sailing so easily through the air contrasted sharply with their grim and always frustrating struggle to find a way onto the cold glacier surface.

On 21 December the tractor party entered an area of small crevasses which would take some days to negotiate. As they only carried fuel for another twenty miles before they would have to turn for home, it was decided to call it a day. The main depot for future use was established at 79°12′S, 15°00′W and they said goodbye to the sledgers. For the next week the Muskegs were driven throughout the twenty-four hours, covering the 432 miles back to 'Bob-Pi Crossing' – a remarkable achievement.

For another month the sledging party continued their search, by which time Peter Noble and Skidmore had extended the route another ninety miles and actually reached the Shackletons at 80°18′S, 17°05′W. Meanwhile Mathys and John Gallsworthy had reconnoitred the first eighty miles of a direct return route to Bob-Pi. The crossing point lay 230 miles from the depot which had been laid, and this would shorten future journeys by 200 miles. Finally both sledge teams joined up, to return via the Therons through the existing line of depots.

While these journeys were going on, short local trips for glaciological and physiological studies were being made from base. One of these was a man-hauling traverse by John Brotherhood, the doctor, and Jim Shirtcliffe. They were due home on 28 November but by seven o'clock that evening they had not arrived. Chinn himself and 'Big Al' Smith set off on a Skidoo motor toboggan to search for them, Smith's twenty stone plus Chinn's stocky frame adding up to quite a load. Travelling some miles along two known routes proved unfruitful, while falling snow reduced visibility until only occasionally could they see even half-a-mile ahead and were forced to return.

Next day several search parties scoured the area without success, but just before midnight the missing men were found, having fallen thirty feet over an ice cliff in a 'white out'. Both were injured. Shirtcliffe suffered a painfully damaged ankle, and Brotherhood was completely immobilised with a seriously injured spine and severe damage to his face and teeth. Fortunately the sledge had fallen with them so Shirtcliffe had been able to put up a tent over him until help arrived. He was the first to be brought back to base on a sledge, the rescuers then returning for his companion.

Chinn, Smith and Paul Wharton, the electrician, then set about trying to

Skidoo following a marked route through crevasses. (M. Pinnock)

figure out how the X-ray machine worked. After a number of misfires they achieved photographs which the patient had to interpret for himself. He had suffered compressed fractures of two vertebrae, his left maxilla was broken, and two teeth had been forced through his lips. Shirtcliffe's ankle was not broken.

It was Friday 1 December. In London we always said that all Fids' crises happened over weekends when it was difficult to contact the best people to advise or help us. Only on the Sunday did I learn the seriousness of Brotherhood's condition. Unless something could be done to get him hospital treatment quickly, it would be impossible to prevent permanent crippling or disfigurement. But no ship could get through to Halley Bay until January at the earliest.

The Americans had long-range, ski-equipped aircraft, but it was Monday morning before I could raise anyone in Washington. By nine o'clock I was calling Philip Smith, an old friend at the National Science Foundation and he took immediate action. How immediate I did not realise at the time, but that same evening Halley Bay received a message telling them that two L-C130 ski-equipped Hercules planes were already on their way, crossing the continent from McMurdo Sound.

There was a rush to dig out the pile of empty fuel drums to mark out a runway. In the two-and-a-half hours it took the aircraft to arrive overhead the base had laid out two lines of drums at fifty-yard intervals, marking a strip one-and-a-half miles long and 300 yards wide. At the approach end Geoff Smith and Chris Sykes spread the station's entire stock of cocoa on the snow across the strip, with an arrow pointing eastward along its length to indicate to the pilot where to land.

During this feverish activity the Halley Bay operator made radio contact, and found the American pilots already talking to our Stanley station where Ted Clapp had personally taken charge of communications. The drama was unexpectedly heightened when they were all suddenly interrupted by urgent and continuous SOS signals from Deception reporting that the 'extinct' volcano on the island was in eruption, the Chileans had already abandoned their stations and were now refugees at our base, and vast quantities of ash were falling out of the sky.

Unwilling to turn off his American contact, Clapp started up an automatic transmitter, sending out the unexplained but dramatic message 'Shackleton to go to Deception' over and over again. The ship soon picked it up and a very puzzled Captain Turnbull altered course, called for full steam ahead and raced to the scene. The story is told in Chapter 13.

As the American planes arrived at Halley Bay one began circling the base, thus avoiding committing both to landing on an unknown surface. The other came down, to be met by everyone save the nursing staff, including two chocolate-coated Fids, for by now Smith and Sykes were completely smothered in cocoa having spread it around in a high wind.

Commander Schneider USN and Dr Noll, the American medical officer, paid a quick visit to the Village, where Brotherhood's diagnosis of his own condition was confirmed, and he was immediately sledged out to the aircraft. It took off amid the combined roars of engines and JATO (jet assisted take-off) bottles and a rising cloud of billowing snow. Six hours later they landed 2,000 miles away at McMurdo Sound to refuel, and then flew a further 2,000 to New Zealand where Brotherhood was rushed to Christchurch Hospital.

With proper surgical treatment the patient made a complete recovery, and the whole Survey joined him in thankful appreciation of American generosity in a dangerous situation which could have led to severe handicap for the rest of his life. Ray Adie happened to be in Christchurch when Brotherhood was flown in and visited him in hospital; and in due course Brotherhood spent his convalescence with Bernard Stonehouse (ex-Stonington) and his family who were living there.

It was the longest rescue operation ever carried out in the Antarctic, and remarkable for the speed and efficiency with which it was mounted. One year later a small ceremony took place in Washington, when a hand-painted shield bearing the Survey's coat of arms was presented, in memory of the occasion, by Rear Admiral Le Bailly, the British naval attaché, to VX-6 Squadron USN, to which the two rescuing aircraft had belonged.

At home during 1967 arrangements had been made for the regular reception of United States photographs from the ESSA-3 satellite then in polar orbit, and it was interesting to observe in them the cloud of ash blowing northward from Deception to Livingston Island. However, the real reason for obtaining the pictures was so that we could monitor the break-up of sea ice in the Weddell Sea and around the Antarctic Peninsula as an aid to navigation.

1967/8 The 1967/8 season ws the first time it was possible to offer information to the captains of ships trying to reach Halley Bay. It was clear to me that this innovation might appear to them as an unwelcome form of back-seat driving from London, so the signals we sent were couched in terms of factual information without any implication of instruction.

Biscoe and Perla Dan were both going to Halley Bay and the latter left South Georgia four days ahead. Their daily position reports enabled me to judge the appropriate moment to send the first message. From the photographs I had identified an area of unbroken ice extending for 300 miles to the north of Cape Norvegia, the point where ships usually attempted to reach the strip of open water that normally develops along the east coast of the Weddell Sea. I could also see that unconnected areas of water had formed deep into the Weddell Sea along the approximate line of longitude 20°W, some 250 miles west of Cape Norvegia. I reported this situation to both captains, and sat back to see what they would do.

Perla held her course to the east and was clearly going in by the usual route to the land water, but Biscoe turned south and began working her way into the ice along longitude 20°W. Two days later Perla reported that she was battling through heavy close pack, and then that she was beset but endeavouring to free herself. By this time Biscoe was almost 100 miles inside the ice edge, but then she too had been brought to a halt. Tom Woodfield's message stated, 'No water visible in any direction. Any suggestions?'

Dogs' winter quarters at Halley Bay. (S. Valance)

The latest satellite pictures were now showing extensive open leads some twenty miles to the southwest of his position. I therefore encouraged him to work towards them and provided suggested directions which, if he succeeded, would enable him to reach Halley Bay without trouble. With creditable, if surprising confidence, he made the attempt and got through. He was totally astonished at actually finding the passage where I said it would be, and later told me, 'We imagined old Father Fuchs, up there in the sky, smoking his pipe and looking down on our every move'.

Meanwhile *Perla* reported that she had worked free and managed to turn north. This gave me the opportunity to send a firm sequence of courses which would enable her to follow the *Biscoe* in. This she successfully did, but as a result of her manoeuvres she had lost the four days she had had ahead of

Biscoe. Thus the value of satellite photographs had been demonstrated – so much so that in subsequent years the captains insisted on satellite reports before entering ice.

This is not to say that the pictures provide anything more than a strategic view of the prevailing situation. A captain still has to handle his ship through the detailed problems posed from moment to moment by the intricate jigsaw of shifting icebergs and floes. For this, his view from the bridge or crow's-nest is adequate, but his capability of assessing the situation ahead is limited to no more than six or seven miles, which is totally inadequate if his course leads through several hundred miles of ice. Small wonder that the broad view of the scene as seen by the satellite is now recognised as an invaluable aid to ice navigation.

The Shackleton Range reconnaissance journey had proved the feasibility of a surface party working in at least part of these mountains, but it was painfully clear that the distance there and back was uneconomical in effort. While in London we pondered this situation, it so happened that the Americans undertook a joint project with the Scott Polar Research Institute in which they were making long-range flights for radio-echo sounding over the continent. To extend their possible range they approached the Survey with a request to refuel at Halley Bay if the amount of fuel they required could be carried there in our relief ship.

This juxtaposition of events was most felicitous. We arranged to supply them with fifty-five tons in 1968, and in return they agreed to fly six of our men and three dog teams into the Shackletons, picking them up again after nine weeks' work. There was a further mutual spin-off – the Americans had already photographed the area from the air but lacked the necessary ground control for their mapping, and this our surveyors would be able to supply.

For a period there was uncertainty about these joint plans, so we authorised another ground journey from Halley Bay in the 1968/9 season. In the end both parties worked in the mountains at the same time.

1968/9 On 31 October 1968 Noble, Etchells, John Carter, Stuart MacQuarrie, Norris Riley and John Gallsworthy left base with two heavily modified International Harvester tractors and two Muskegs, towing between them twelve sledges with a total load of twenty-nine tons. Their main purpose was to lay depots in the mountains to support future work. The largest, with sixty days' supplies, was established at 80°30′S, 20°16′W, and a smaller one was laid twenty-four miles further west. This party also visited and collected specimens from nine separate rocky spurs on behalf of geologists who would later be working in the area. As no one had ever been to the eastern end of this range it was a valuable contribution. When they got back to base they had covered 1,000 miles and paved the way for substantial work.

The planned American airlift took place on 23 November, just a week before the ground party turned for home. We had sent two surveyors, Ken Blaiklock (ex-Stonington and TAE) and Tony True, to New Zealand whence the Americans flew them in to McMurdo Sound to join the aircraft coming over to Halley Bay. Here two base geologists, Peter Clarkson and Mike Skidmore, with Nick Mathys and Harry Wiggans as General Assistants, made up the air party. They expected to spend up to seventy-six days in the mountains, and for this the total load, including three dog teams but excluding the men, was 11,096 pounds.

Ever since the Survey had had aircraft, teams had been flown into the field to save travelling time. Usually the pilot turned the heat full on, the dogs became soporific and travelled quietly, even sleepily, enjoying the flight. But for the American authorities our request that their planes should carry dogs was a new and daunting idea. They have never used them, and had visions of quarrelling huskies at close quarters, fighting to the death with damage if not disaster resulting.

They were too nice to refuse, but stipulated that a separate kennel and a muzzle must be provided for each animal. Blaiklock took the muzzles out from England and kennels were built for us at Christchurch. On arrival at Halley Bay all these preparations caused endless amusement to the drivers, to whom the teams were gentle and well-loved friends. Even the pilots got the idea, and were quite happy for the dogs to be tethered individually, and the aircraft protected by tarpaulins. This saved a lot on the pay-load.

On reaching their destination low cloud obscured the mountains so the Fids were landed on Recovery Glacier, some thirty miles from the nearest rock. A main depot of 9,000 pounds was established nineteen miles nearer and the group split threeways, the two geologists working together, each surveyor with an assistant. This exercise proved to be eventful.

At the end of the first week Mathys broke his leg skiing and all their plans had to be reorganised. He was moved carefully back to the depot, where constant radio 'scheds' with Murray Roberts, the doctor at base, established that he had suffered a simple fracture. Under Roberts' long distance medical guidance the leg was set with plaster of Paris bandages, always carried by field parties, and True remained to nurse him. Blaiklock and Wiggans carried on the mapping with two teams.

The next complication occurred two weeks later. Skidmore slipped on a patch of bare ice, slid 150 feet down a snow slope and then bounced fifty feet down a rocky scree. Fortunately he suffered nothing more serious than severe bruising and a badly split lip. He joined the 'hospital' where 'Nurse'

Clarkson skillfully stitched his mouth, and those still fit continued to work.

For Mathys particularly, this was an unhappy experience, but his mending fracture was yet another proof of the ingenuity and resolution of Fids when things go wrong. On 26 January the Americans flew in to pick them up again, and were completely astounded to find two patients who had been well cared for in a tent for so long. They could not understand why they had not been called in to the rescue. Yet this field party's endurance not only ensured that the work got done, but also demonstrated that the Survey called for assistance only when it was absolutely necessary.

1969–72   It took two more seasons to complete the geological reconnaissance and ground control of this area. On both occasions the Americans flew in working parties. In 1969/70 Clarkson, now Base Commander, Wiggans and True returned to the mountains, with assistants Graham Wright, Allen Clayton and Malcolm Guyatt, and the survey was finished. At the end of the season Clarkson came home, but six months later he in turn travelled to New Zealand and flew back to Halley Bay with the Americans. This time he led a new party consisting of Bob Wyeth, Mike Warden and Graham Wright, with two dog teams, who were again air-lifted into the Shackletons. This completed the work.

Though during these years our major effort was concentrated in the mountain areas, many shorter journeys were mounted. In 1969, during one of these, a party of six, with four tractors and twelve sledges, were crossing the heavily crevassed zone where the Brunt Ice Shelf joins solid land ice, when one of the International Harvesters broke through a crevasse bridge and became lodged in a hole with the top of the cab two feet below the surface.

Five minutes later, while they were still considering what to do about it, the tractor suddenly dropped another six feet. So precariously was it now poised between the opposing walls, which widened rather than narrowed below, that they felt recovery was not only risky but impossible. It was abandoned, together with one partly sunken sledge loaded with six 420-pound barrels of fuel which it had been towing. At home we saw this as a write-off, and another vehicle went out in the relief ship.

Three years later, in 1972, another Halley Bay party came upon the rear end of the sledge still standing above a smooth snow surface which treacherously hid all the crevasses. There and then Bruce Blackwell, the tractor mechanic, was inspired to start thinking about ways and means of recovering the vehicle which lay underneath.

Soon he was thinking of little else – the challenge had become a dream. Back at base he worked on a carefully thought out plan and began to assemble a multitude of paraphernalia – heavy cables, pulley blocks, a winch, shackles, thimbles, railway sleepers to act as deadmen, and much else. On 19 October he was ready and set out to make the attack, taking with him Ian Bury, Dave Fletcher and Gordon Ramage. On arrival at the scene the ground was very carefully probed every yard of the last four miles, by men on skis. The next step was to lay out the pulley system and clear ice and snow from above the fallen tractor. Its roof was now nine feet below the surface. Then they cut a steep ramp down to a point about five feet above the tracks, and strops were attached linking the vehicle with the pulley system. This consisted of two fourteen-ton blocks attached to deadmen and the hand winch.

The tractor itself weighed five tons. At their first attempt it was hauled up inch by inch, its tracks against the vertical wall of the crevasse, until it was a third of the way out. Just as success seemed certain a cable broke, and it fell back to a point two feet below its original position. Preparations for retrieval had to begin all over again.

Two days later they were ready once more and had another try, this time it worked and presently the Harvester stood on the surface. When the engine compartment had been cleared of snow and new starter batteries were fitted they pressed the switch. To their gratified astonishment the motor fired immediately. No other mechanical work was necessary. Even the anti-freeze in the radiator did not need topping up. Though jubilant at their success, they still had to drive the tractor out of the crevasse field and coax it 100 feet up a snow slope, part of which lay at an angle of seventy degrees – too great for it to be driven. Blackwell attached the steel cable from the tractor's winch to a deadman at the top of the slope. Thus when the engine was started, it slowly hauled itself to the top.

Twenty-four hours later, just three years and one day after the original accident, they drove it triumphantly into base. As the result of a remarkable piece of ingenuity Blackwell had fulfilled his dream, and the Survey had benefited to the tune of £7,000. Five years later it was ordered home for overhaul. On the way out to the ship it broke through the sea ice and sank. As Pete Witty, who was driving it, surfaced in his ballooning anorak his first comment was, 'Damn – got me blooming fags wet'. True Fids phlegm, but sadly no epitaph for a tractor which had served us well.

By 1971 the roofs and walls of the second Halley Bay were badly distorted, some even caving in despite the intervening strengthening of steel arches. Once more a new station was needed. This time we were determined somehow to overcome the destructive ice pressure, and Gipps investigated the possibilities of putting up a base inside steel culverting.

Armco tubing was used, composed of curved corrugated steel plates,

Building the Armco tubing for the third Halley Bay, 1971. (V. E. Fuchs)

bolted together to form an egg-shaped tunnel twenty feet high. Since this was intended to bear all the exterior stresses, the huts themselves could be lightly constructed. It would have been possible to build one long tunnel but various factors mitigated against this. The generators at least had to be separately housed so that their noise did not resonate throughout the base. Also, the known differential movement of the ice indicated that one end of such a long tunnel was likely to move more quickly than the other.

1972/3   The final decision was to construct five separate tunnels in line, linked by small diameter Armco passages, and to build escape shafts at either end of these. In January 1973 *Bransfield* arrived, the normal relief stores plus materials for the new base totalling some 650 tons to be unloaded. A suitable landing site selected by the resident Fids between high ice cliffs was indicated by billowing clouds of black marker smoke rising into the clear air from a gleaming icy headland. At the head of the crack the ice slope which had once reached down to the water had broken back so far that the ship had to lie alongside an ice cliff thirty-one feet high, the deck below the bridge being almost level with the surface.

Our available work force was fairly large. Forty-five new Fids on board, twenty-two more from the base, plus twelve Royal Marines from Stanley who had volunteered to come with us, and about a dozen crew members whenever they could be spared from ship's duties.

The base members continued their scientific programmes and handled all the new supplies. The rest were divided into two twelve-hour shifts, a few unloading the holds with the crew, the remainder ferrying building materials up to the new site, or engaged in the actual construction work under the gimlet eye of 'Big Al' Smith, the senior builder. Shirtcliffe, who had helped to build the existing station, and many another too, was on his ninth visit south, having taken time off from university to re-engage for the season. This time he found himself with the dubious privilege of being in charge of the night shift.

During the days which followed the ship often had to move, either because of the threatening ice or actual collapses which forced her from her moorings. One day as a seaman and our vetinerary officer, Bob Bostelman were loading a cargo sledge, the entire ice edge collapsed, tearing out *Bransfield*'s forward mooring. With skill and a good deal of luck they retained their hold on separate blocks of fallen ice now floating in the sea. By careful manoeuvring the Captain managed to recover them from their precarious positions with the ship's crane. Surprisingly, they did not even get their feet wet.

On the 29th we decided that it was no longer necessary for the night shift to continue unloading. It was a very fateful decision, for just before midnight there was a catastrophic collapse of the entire loading ramp. The first piece of ice to calve off once more nudged the ship away, breaking the ropes which held her. Then followed a spectacular collapse of several hundred yards of the slope up which the tractors had been hauling loads all day. Huge ice blocks rose and fell as the cracks spread from one side of the ramp to the other. Stray timbers, then three cargo sledges lying on the surface, slid down into the mêlée of churning ice, never to be seen again. Had they been working, we would have lost the night shift.

The ship had to search for an alternative unloading site up and down the coast. At one point we saw two old barrels in the face of the ice cliff thirty to forty feet below the surface. Associated with them was an horizon of dirty ice extending for thirty yards along the cliff face. These represented the remains of Mike Thurston's camp, occupied when he was studying the emperor penguins in 1961. At that time it had been built nearly half-a-mile from the cliff edge. Its position twelve years later revealed not only the accumulation but also the rate at which the cliff face was retreating. Unable to find a convenient slope we perforce secured alongside the lowest point of the ice cliffs we could find. This was forty-five feet high, and it was only just possible to use the ship's crane to unload onto it the last few hundred drums of fuel. Meanwhile building operations had been going apace. The engine room was complete and the other five Armco tubes were almost finished.

One week later our two de Havilland Otters made the first ever flight of 1,000 miles across the Weddell Sea, from Adelaide to Halley Bay, to pick up and fly some of us back to the peninsula. Their point of no return had been some 750 miles out from Adelaide. As this was reached we had assured the pilots that conditions at our end were perfect, clear skies, little wind and no drift. Forty minutes before the planes were expected to land I was hastily called from my cabin to find that low mist shrouded the ice shelf and was pouring down over the cliffs to the sea ice.

This was serious indeed. The pilots, who could not now turn back, would not be able to see the surface. Guessing that it was probably a local phenomenon, I rushed up to base to organise a tractor with radio facilities to drive eastwards, hoping to find clear conditions a few miles inland, while the operator monitoring the flight kept the pilots informed of our situation.

But only half-an-hour later, even before the tractor had left, the mist cleared as quickly as it had formed and the panic was over. Within fifteen minutes both planes landed, and despite their very long flight, they still had enough fuel for another four hours' flying. Thus it was a relief to know that, had it been necessary, we could have diverted them to Belgrano, the Argentine station 200 miles further south.

Next day bad weather at Adelaide precluded the return flight, so we took the opportunity to fly a short 'recce' both north and south, looking for a new site where the ship could unload the following season. Nowhere very suitable was found, but following high ice cliffs thirty miles to the south we saw an area of low shelf where a vessel could probably lie alongside, although she would be exposed to swell and drifting 'bergs. Inland, too, lay the problems of numerous crevasses which would have to be negotiated before tractors could reach the top of the higher ice shelf.

(As things turned out, this area had to be used in 1974, and owing to the swell the ship did have to leave her moorings on several occasions. Although a route through the crevasses was established, it proved to be a forty-mile journey to the base – much too far for an efficient relief of the station.)

The following morning Adelaide reported reasonable weather, but now the problem was for the planes to take off from the soft surface of newly fallen snow when each carried a load of nearly three tons of fuel. Dave Rowley, with whom I flew, made the first attempts. Three times he roared down the marked runway but we always failed to gain flying speed. Then Flight Lieutenant Bert Conchie had a go carrying his mechanic, Dave Brown, with Gipps and Barry Peters as passengers. His third try found the plane staggering into the air at only forty-five knots while we all held our

The base after seven years; tunnel leads down to the garage/workshop. (G. J. Gilbert)

breath. By then the new snow was becoming more compacted, but even so Rowley's fourth attempt failed. After we had moved more weight into the tail, his fifth try saw us all thankfully airborne.

Flying west at 7,000 feet, we were over open water for the first 200 miles, with not even a 'berg in sight after leaving the coast. Then came intermittent clusters of small floes, which gradually became more numerous until they gave way to huge heavy floes one to two miles across. At this point we entered cloud, which rapidly built up ice on the leading edges of the wings until Rowley took us up to 13,000 feet. There he remained, flying on instruments until the mountains of the Antarctic Peninsula were suddenly clear below. Dead on course, we passed the well-know landmarks of Cape Berteaux and the Terra Firmas, and landed at Adelaide after just over six hours in the air.

Shortly after our arrival, Halley Bay reported by radio that the ice had made yet another attack on *Bransfield*. Work over for the day shift, those on board were resting or watching a film when there was a monstrous crash and the ship heeled over on her beam ends. Three hundred feet of the ice cliff

The front door; the Underground *sign is on the shaft entrance. (G. J. Gilbert)*

against which she was lying had fallen, crushing flat 150 feet of the bulwarks, and leaving a pile of ice blocks fifteen feet high on the foredeck. A hasty visual check showed one man missing, presumably somewhere underneath the grotesque ice pile.

Frantically everyone seized an implement, rushed out and started chopping, heaving, digging their hearts out, praying that somehow he had escaped serious injury. It was a long time before a more thorough count revealed that the victim they sought so strenuously had apparently changed his clothes and unrecognised, he too was busily digging for all he was worth, searching for himself.

As soon as the new base was fully weatherproof, with much of the internal construction finished, *Bransfield* sailed for the peninsula stations. Six builders and an electrician remained to winter and complete the complex.

We knew that only time would tell how successfully the steel shells would resist ice pressure. If it succeeded, the base could be used until it became too deeply buried under the ever-accumulating snow. To this last problem there is as yet no answer.

I I

The Banana Belt
1953–73

Two of the FIDS stations are amiably, if unjustly, spoken of as being in the 'Banana Belt'. Signy Island, in the South Orkney Islands, is only just south of latitude 60°S; while the position of South Georgia between 54°S and 55°S is equivalent to York and Newcastle in the northern hemisphere. Yet both have a rigorous climate, both are largely snow-covered, and present a climatic challenge to those who work there.

The South Orkneys can experience very severe weather, with winds up to 100 knots and temperatures as low as −40°C. These extremes are unusual, but even in summer freezing mist and strong winds can make travelling difficult and hazardous. In winter, when the sea freezes, it is possible to move between the islands, but the ice is unstable and liable to break up unexpectedly.

In the early years when only a handful of men occupied the Signy station, work was almost wholly confined to the island itself; but even then it was recognised that an attempt should be made to map the whole group and initiate geological work. This would require more men and a larger base, which perforce had to wait until more money was available, and for four years after Dick Laws' party left in 1950 work was reduced to meteorological reporting only.

Nevertheless, the Fids always willingly undertook numerous *ad hoc* tasks quite outside their official duties. For example, when Alan Tritton was Base Leader in 1953, at the request of the Scientific Bureau he and his four companions measured a series of Weddell seals and collected skulls from those killed for dog food. They also continued the bird-ringing programme in order to provide a marked population for future studies.

None of them were surveyors or geologists, yet Tritton felt frustrated at being unable to make any contribution to the knowledge of the then almost unknown mountains of Coronation Island, only a few miles across Normanna Strait. Though unequipped to travel, he and his companions initiated a number of useful journeys when the sea froze over using their small team of five dogs. These ventures led to a number of 'first ascents', and Tritton brought back a collection of rock specimens which, at that time, were valuable in demonstrating the general geological nature of Coronation Island.

1954/55   By 1954 the base hut, known locally as Clifford House, was seven years old, and owing to differential sinking of the foundations it had deteriorated so much that a new building was essential. This gave us the opportunity to put up a larger station with improved facilities. In February 1955 *Biscoe* arrived with materials to build anew, this time at a lower site near the old whaling 'plan' where once the huge carcasses had been hauled up for flensing.

First the old rusted steam winches and large digesters used to extract the whale oil had to be cleared, but by the end of April Tonsberg House, named after the old whaling company, was occupied. The original hut on the hill above was demolished and the materials used to construct a combined sledging and boat shed. A concrete slipway on which boats could be hauled up was added.

1955/6   Thus equipped with a fine new station we turned our attention to the survey and geology of Coronation Island. In 1956 Norman Leppard (ex-Hope Bay) and Doug Bridger greatly extended the mapping, while Drummond Matthews made a considerable geological contribution. The

1957   following year the survey was completed, and six weeks were devoted to extending it to Powell, Michelsen, Fredriksen and Christoffersen Islands. Mount Nivea (4,180 feet), the highest peak on Coronation, had always been seen as a challenge, and Lance Tickell, the Base Leader, with Alan Grant made the first ascent.

1958–60   During the next three years the formal work was again confined to meteorology, but everyone also took part in extensive bird-ringing and seal-tagging, programmes. Many giant petrels ringed as fledglings at Signy were later recovered in Australia or New Zealand, while at least two cape pigeons ringed in New Zealand were captured at Signy.

1960/1   Although appointed as a meteorologist, Roger Filer became keenly interested in the bird-ringing; hardly a day passed without him setting out from base to further the programme. At twenty-two years old he was already an experienced climber. On 13 February 1961 he left to visit the Gourlay Peninsula some two miles away but failed to return that evening. Russell Thompson (ex-Admiralty Bay) and Phil Mander immediately set out to search for him, but finding nothing they concluded that he must have gone on to spend a night with Derek Clarke and Ron Pinder who were camped at Foca Point. Returning to base they were not unduly worried until the next radio 'sched' with Foca revealed that Filer had never arrived.

Clarke and Pinder hurried home and at first light all four men set out for

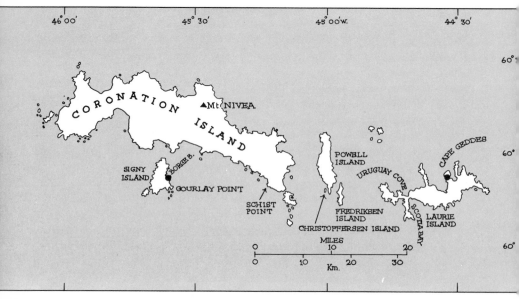

Map 8. South Orkney Islands

Gourlay. Combing the ground for three hours they at last saw him, lying on the rocks at the foot of a ravine near Pantomine Point. Climbing down by rope they found him dead. He had fallen fifty feet and been killed instantly, and just below a steep overhang at the top of the cliff was the sheathbill's nest which he had obviously been trying to reach.

Gourlay Point was Roger's favourite part of the island, a place where he had spent many happy solitary hours with the birds. Now in this tragic ending his stunned companions all felt he would see it as a fitting last resting place. Four days later they held a brief service and buried him near the spot where he died. He was a very popular young man and not only the base but the whole Survey shared his family's sense of loss.

Later in the year when HMS *Protector* visited Signy, her padre held a full memorial service at which the ship's company supported the Fids in paying a final tribute to a friend who had for more than a year shown such enthusiasm for the life they led together. Eventually there was a happy sequel when Roger's sister married Derek Clarke, one of his Antarctic companions.

During the IGY very little serious biological work had been done in Antarctica by any of the participating nations. On my return from the TAE I felt that, in keeping with the proposals of other national agencies, we should embark upon a regular long-term biological programme. Many years of deep-sea work had been done by Discovery Investigations, and it seemed

Signy Island huts, 1953; Coronation Island in background. (R. J. Tanton)

appropriate for FIDS to complement this by undertaking coastal-marine, terrestrial and freshwater studies.

There were two obvious sites – Signy and South Georgia. The latter's sub-Antarctic climate is intermediate between polar and temperate conditions, so could be expected to provide biological links between the two. It therefore seemed better to establish some knowledge of the polar biological processes first, leaving work on South Georgia to a later date.

In the South Orkneys there are relatively quiet coastal waters, freshwater lakes, and extensive moss carpets and peat deposits, but was Signy really the best place at which to build up a substantial biological facility? With these considerations in mind, Professor Jim Cragg of Durham University agreed to go south and report on the various possibilities. He spent a season touring the stations, and on his return the decision was made – Signy it would be.

1961   Peter Tilbrook and Barry Heywood were recruited to initiate terrestrial and freshwater zoological studies. As it would take time to design and build laboratories, as an interim measure the generators were moved from Tonsberg House to the boat shed and the engine room was turned into a laboratory.

1961/2   Martin Holdgate, the first Head of our newly formed Zoological Section, spent the summer on the island supervising the early work. When he left for home in HMS *Protector*, he took with him two breeding sheathbills caught by Neville Jones. He relates the following story:

The Sheathbill is a small, and most unseamanlike bird, with its dumpy body and lack of webs on the feet, yet in winter its numbers decline at Signy and increase in the Falklands. Was there a northward migration? Could these small birds cross the open waters of the Drake Passage? I promised to release Nev's victims a day before arrival in Stanley. The Navy entered into the spirit of the thing. '0930', said the ship's Orders of the Day, 'Fly off sheathbills'.

I explained that, unlike helicopters, sheathbill flights did not demand that the ship came head to wind. At the due time, feeling distinctly ridiculous under the watching eyes of half a dozen matelots, I humped the two wooden boxes onto the open flight deck, checked that the occupants were fit for duty, and opened up. For a while they scurried about on the deck, stretching their limbs maybe, and then they were off – one, clearly what the Americans term 'motivated', strongly circling the ship and heading to sea, and the other weakly fluttering in the direction of the Falklands. The determined character took five days to get back to Signy, home and offspring.

1962/3   December 1962 saw the introduction of diving, initiated by Peter Redfearn and Charlie Le Feuvre. This was a considerable advance on the time-honoured use of grabs and dredges, for it enabled the ecological relationships of bottom-living organisms to be observed and studied. It was to become an important tool in both marine and freshwater programmes.

1963   At this time there were still dog teams at Signy, and the occasion was long remembered when 'Mutt' lived up to his name by falling into the sea. He managed to swim ashore, and was found some time later waterlogged and exhausted. After a rub down he was shut up in a box in the workshop to dry off, but huskies do not take kindly to this sort of incarceration. Inevitably he gnawed his way out, and in doing so succeeded in falling into and upsetting a large bucket of bright green paint, in which he then rolled. When the men came back to see how he was getting on, they found themselves fending off the boisterous but unwelcome attentions of a strange green monster.

As a first step he was bathed several times with petrol, then washed repeatedly with hot water and detergent. This removed the worst of the paint but left him 'looking decidedly seasick'. After two more days in the loft he at last accepted food, and a week later, still green, he rejoined his companions on the span – much to their suspicious astonishment.

1963-4   In December the dogs were finally removed, most of them being transferred to Stonington. Sad though it was for the base to lose this source of constant interest and excitement, their presence at a biological research station was hardly compatible with the scientific programmes.

This was the season in which the building of the new biological laboratory was to begin, and the materials for it had been loaded into both *Biscoe* and *Shackleton*. It was intended that *Biscoe* would unload first, while *Shackleton* and *Protector* spent some weeks on a seismic shooting programme directed by Professor Griffiths for his long-term geophysics project begun in 1959–60. This was aimed at determining the submarine structure of the Scotia island arc and had been in progress for several years. The practice was for *Protector* to tow large explosive charges which were fired from the ship, the reflected shock waves from the rocks beneath being recorded by equipment in *Shackleton* at a distance of some miles. Thus a picture was gradually built up.

That season one of *Protector*'s charges was accidently exploded on deck near the stern, killing two sailors and seriously injuring a third. Had it not been for a potato store which absorbed much of the shock, the damage and loss of life could have been far greater. It was a most distressing incident. Seismic shooting was cancelled and *Protector* sailed back to Stanley where there were hospital facilities.

Thus *Biscoe* and *Shackleton* arrived at Signy together early in December, and unloading both ships simultaneously placed a heavy strain on the base. Dick Stocks, already a very experienced FIDS builder, was in charge of the construction work, which included a circular, open-topped 10,000-gallon water tank as well as laboratories. This had become necessary because the annual local snowfall was sometimes insufficient to provide a constant supply of melt water in summer. In 1961 the base had even been reduced to the time consuming occupation of capturing bergy bits in the bay for drinking water.

To assist and hasten the unloading the Fids set-to to build a light railway along the jetty they had earlier constructed and up to the new site. This they proudly believed to be the most southerly track in the world and it was a great success.

The new base was a two-storey building consisting of a steel framework clad with precast yellow plastic-bonded glass fibre panels. The problem was to establish firm foundations on which to build. This was done by erecting concrete pillars extending through the sloping ground to bedrock.

The Fids were justly proud of their ingenuity and hard work, and decided that there ought to be a ceremony. I arrived while the pillars were still going up, and was invited to lay a token foundation stone – an immense inscribed concrete block they had cast for the occasion. True to style, everyone produced his camera, and suddenly I was alone in the Antarctic performing my appointed task – it was hardly photogenic without the 'cheering crowd'. A hastily called conference agreed that one man should click all the cameras in turn, while I did my piece over and over again with everyone else playing the extras for the crowd scene.

As the season progressed anxieties began to arise. For some weeks *Biscoe* had been beset in the ice off Adelaide Island, and in consequence one of the Otters was grounded for lack of spares which the ship could not deliver. Having relieved Halley Bay, *Kista Dan* was having difficulty in extricating herself from the Weddell Sea ice.

Then suddenly things got better. *Biscoe* got into Adelaide, *Kista* reported that she was clear and on her way to South Georgia, and we who were at Admiralty Bay in *Shackleton* met HMS *Protector*, whose Captain offered to carry the essential Otter spares south and lift them in by helicopter. Happy at this change in our fortunes, *Shackleton* sailed for Signy to deliver new generators and the material for a new building, and to rendezvous with *Kista*.

However, the weather became so bad that *Kista* took six days instead of the normal three to reach South Georgia. When she finally arrived at Signy, winds gusting to sixty knots made it impossible to transfer cargo, and both ships were forced to seek shelter behind the high ice cliffs of a twelve-mile long iceberg grounded on the island.

As *Shackleton* slowly steamed up and down a mile from the 'berg, we watched it begin to break up. First small pieces fell from the edge, then enormous blocks plunged into the water and surged to the surface, tilting and rolling until it seemed as though an earthquake was upheaving the whole iceberg. Soon these large fragments, which themselves formed fair-sized 'bergs, separated from the main mass and, together with a huge quantity of brash and growlers, they spread out over about two square miles of sea.

As all this began we saw *Kista* disappearing behind an angle of the iceberg. The next moment she was calling by radio to know if we were all right. From her Captain's vantage point it had looked as if the ice blocks were falling on to our decks. In fact we were only being thrown about by the surges of water displaced by falling ice. Thereafter both ships stayed in company for the remainder of the night, but at a more discreet distance from the iceberg. By morning the wind had dropped and the relief of Signy proceeded.

The new hut was finished by mid-January and occupied in May. It looked incongruously like a yellow double-decker bus, with laboratories on the ground floor and living accommodation above. It was heated electrically, and since the laboratories also required power, larger generators had been installed. This in turn led to increased consumption – a problem to be faced the following season.

1964/5   The 1964/5 season was enlivened by visits from two Russian fishery vessels, *Gnevny* and *Obdorsk*, to take on water. For some undivulged reason the former carried an alleged Russian film star, Svetlana, who caused a tremendous stir at the base when she arrived appropriately dressed for an evening visit. There were those who had even shaved, and the love-lorn had a talking point which lasted them many weeks.

Later *Protector* came in, and her helicopters made a series of photographic flights for survey purposes. She also carried a hydrographic survey party who were established ashore to begin charting Borge Bay.

For Fids the chief preoccupation was the construction of a large 450-gallon fuel tank to supply the larger base. This was more than their actual requirement, but we also saw it as a useful reserve for ships, especially those returning from Halley Bay. It took nearly three weeks to level and build up the sand foundations on the irregular rocky terrain. Welding lasted nearly two months, and this was followed by the construction of the pipeline and pump house situated near the shore. When everything was ready *Shackleton* arrived with fuel and anchored close in to begin filling the tank.

All seemed to be going smoothly and the ship departed, but on 10 April there was consternation when oil was found seeping out from the foundations. There was a leak in the bottom, the least accessible place. It all had to be drained out into barrels. Fortunately *Shackleton* had delivered only about 20 tons and most of this was saved. The welders had gone home so repairs would have to wait for next season. A problem would be blowing the tank clear of noxious and dangerous fumes before any welding could begin.

1965/6   Signy was becoming a busy harbour. During the season there were two visits from USS *Eastwind* making oceanographic studies, HMS *Protector* called twice to put down and pick up another hydrographic survey team, and our own ships made thirteen calls. *Kista Dan*, on her way to relieve Halley Bay, arrived with a Danish steward suffering from acute appendicitis. Luckily John Brotherhood, the Base Leader, was a doctor and Ron Lloyd the new medical officer for Halley Bay was on board. Having tossed for which of them would give the anaesthetic or perform the surgery, they set about scrubbing out the chemistry laboratory, transforming it into an operating theatre. As the operation proceeded Bob Ralph, peering through the window, provided frequent bulletins for the base, until at 11 pm the patient was declared out of danger, and the offending organ publicly displayed. The following year Brotherhood himself was to transfer to Halley Bay and become the victim of a much more serious incident without such a happy result.

1966/7   The annual damage to successive jetties led to a decision to build a really solid one which we hoped the ice could not destroy. An old whaling barge lay submerged at the seaward end, so a start was made from the shore, banking on the possibility that by the next season someone would have thought of a way to remove it. The best idea was a proposal that *Biscoe* should haul it into deeper water. By this time Tom Woodfield had succeeded Bill Johnston as Master, and twice in December 1966 he attempted this but only managed to move it a few yards. The base were left to think again.

Refusing to be beaten, Ernie Thornley, the diesel mechanic, began welding forty-five-gallon drums together to form pontoons. The idea was to attach these to the barge at low tide and allow the rising water to float her off. His first guess at the number required for success proved over optimistic, but having added a few more, his second attempt brought her gently up until she could be towed away across the cove. Then they completed their jetty.

1967–73   The numbers of biologists were gradually increased, and we also tried to maintain meteorological observations as part-time occupation for some of them, but this was not a success. Regular synoptic work was abandoned, though autographic records were continued to provide essential background for the biology.

Another advance was the provision of a number of small field huts. One of these was an aluminium Rollalong cabin, put down beside a freshwater lake. This weighed half a ton and, with considerable trepidation, was lifted into position by a helicopter from HMS *Endurance*, which replaced *Protector* in 1969. It was an awkward operation, full of dangerous moments when wind gusts forced the pilot to jettison his load.

Unfortunately the ground party did not ensure that the retaining cables holding it down were sufficiently taut. Later, after a three-day gale, with gusts reaching eighty-six knots, it was found completely wrecked, little more than a heap of twisted metal. Slack cables had allowed the wind to straighten out the attachment hooks, after which it had lived up to its name and rolled over three times before 'exploding' into a tangled mass. The following season a replacement was firmly anchored and has survived ever since.

As the biological programmes expanded the number of dives increased from less than fifty to over two hundred a year. This expansion demanded better equipment, including a decompression chamber and better boats. Water temperatures restricted dives to a maximum of thirty minutes, and there was also the problem of occasional sudden appearances of leopard seals. They were unwelcome as a potential hazard, though none of them ever showed more than a temporary curiosity by circling uncomfortably near the strange creatures in wet suits crawling about the sea bed. Ian Rabarts and Ray Townley-Malyon were once carefully inspected by a seal from a distance of only three feet, which they found distinctly disconcerting. During winter divers went down through holes cut in the ice, always roped to ensure they would not miss the exit when surfacing.

Crabeater seal as seen by the diver. (D. G. Allan)

In October 1970 Owen Darling, Adrian Gilmour and Rabarts sailed a boat to Schist Point, near the east end of Coronation Island, to re-site a depot previously laid by a sledge party. There they were half way to Orcadas, the Argentine station on Laurie Island, and the idea developed that in good conditions a visit should be possible. They had seen the rest of the route from *Biscoe* the previous March and determined to have a go.

Rightly suspecting that London would not sanction such an adventure in a small boat, they were careful not to ask permission but, to the their credit, took great care in their preparations. The sixteen-foot dinghy *Desmerestia* was decked over at the bows and a high splash board fitted, together with buoyancy chambers fore and aft. Having assembled two outboard motors, camping gear, wet suits, rifle, radio, compasses and food, they waited patiently for suitable conditions.

The Argentines never expected them to arrive but sportingly cooperated with weather forecasts, and at 4 am on 23 October on a clear sunny morning the mariners set out. Eight hours later they landed, to a disbelieving but most cordial welcome. It was a satisfactory 'first' between stations.

Next day three Argentines joined them in *Desmerestia* to visit the old FIDS hut at Cape Geddes which had been abandoned in 1947, and reported that the building had withstood the intervening twenty-three years remarkably

Elephant seals fighting, South Georgia. (A. K. Donnelly)

well. Returning to Orcadas they remained there for five days, making merry in a few words of both languages while waiting for another propitious weather forecast. They then made a fast run back to Signy enjoying a pleasant sense of achievement – and confessed to London where they had been. I was delighted for them, and relieved not to have known about it in advance!

In 1971 Laws, newly in charge of biological programmes, returned to his old stamping ground after nineteen years to acquaint himself with the current field work. He immediately noticed a marked reduction of the permanent snow and ice cover over the island, and this was in keeping with my own observations in the Stonington areas after a similar lapse of twenty years. We must assume that there had been a considerable decrease of snow accumulation over a wide area in this part of Antarctica. The apparent amelioration of climate was supported by Laws' comment that the small isolated clumps of the grass *Deschampsia* which he had known in 1948 had developed into extensive swards.

As the pressure of biological research increased, the opportunities for local journeys on Coronation Island were reduced. Yet young men who volunteer for work in wild parts of the world demand a degree of 'adventure' in addition to their more studious activities. To some extent diving replaced the action previously provided by sledging or climbing. There were always eager volunteers to play some part in it regardless of whether or not this contributed to their particular research.

Since they all lived a life closely associated with boats, diving and sea ice, it was scarcely surprising that in 1971 they developed a ridiculous competition known as the Signy Thin Ice Race, which became an annual event.

At the beginning of winter when the sea in the little cove begins to freeze, the Base Commander has the honour of deciding when the ice is fit for the event. Clad in a wet suit, he ventures carefully onto the course and tests the thickness with a long-handled ice chisel. If it is still too thin the race is impossible, if too thick it is too easy and no fun. Perhaps two inches is about right, because there are always unseen thicker and thinner patches. The route is across the cove and back, a total of 250 yards, and the rules are unusual and elastic.

Once the ice has the Base Commander's blessing, everyone hurries away to dress in wet suits and make their private, if unworthy preparations. They may wear what they please and national pride often influences choice, as when a sturdy Welsh competitor bedecked himself in a long home made shroud emblazoned with a red dragon. This proved a serious embarrassment when every time he tripped over it he disappeared through the ice. Other gimmicks may be employed to favour the athlete or distract his opponents. Pyjamas, overcoats, singlets and drawers, beach balls, balloons and umbrellas are all considered fair.

When this motley crew is lined up the firing of a flare signals the start. Snowshoes or skis are, of course, forbidden so the favourites are the lightest men with the largest feet. Skipping across the first few pans of ice broken up by the tide along the shore, they quickly take the lead. For them the hazards are the unseen thinner patches along the route, and breaking through these they provide warning for the heavier contestants behind.

Soon the ice is dotted with floundering figures struggling to elbow themselves out of pools of water onto ice strong enough to bear them. No holds are barred, especially to those still on the outward leg as they meet the more successful on the return run. Then the laggards join forces to converge on any potential winner, their combined weight precipitating him, and incidentally them, into the water. It has even been known for one man to jump onto the back of another, thus providing the weight to delay his progress.

Seldom are the last men home in less than an exhausting hour, many having to ice-break their return to shore. Throughout the event outraged

Signy Island in winter showing the modern two-storey hut. (I. B. Collinge)

curses and shouts of triumph mingle with wild laughter, driving astounded seals and indignant birds to leave the once peaceful scene to the mad antics of these strange interlopers.

Lest any reader should fear that this curious practice is dangerous, wet suits provide a lengthy survival time in water down to −2°C and many men are involved, all able to help each other as efficiently as they destroy the opposition. Boats and ropes are always available though neither have yet been needed.

In Fids' parlance South Georgia certainly qualifies for the 'Banana Belt' – there it actually rains. A sub-Antarctic island some 100 miles long and thirty wide, it has a central spine of mountains rising to over 9,000 feet. Perpetually mantled in snow, innumerable glaciers descend to the sea, and sudden katabatic winds of great force menace all who travel by land or sea. The

Signy Island in Summer – scene of the Thin Ice Race. (B.A.S.)

coastal regions are vegetated but without trees, and apart from reindeer which were introduced by whalers in 1907, there are no land animals except rats and mice, also introduced, though accidentally, by whalers.

It is a dependency of the Falkland Islands and being north of latitude 60°S, is not covered by Articles of the Antarctic Treaty. At one time its shores teemed with vast numbers of fur seals but by 1830 the horrendous demands of fashion for women's fur coats, and the large fortunes to be made supplying them, had resulted in the populations being all but exterminated.

The sealers, however, never established themselves ashore. It was left to the whalers to set up the first settlement at Grytviken in 1904. Two years later the Falkland Islands Government wisely introduced a licensing system to control the taking of whales, at the same time leasing land to the whaling companies for the building of shore installations. Later a Government administrative station was established at King Edward Point and regulations

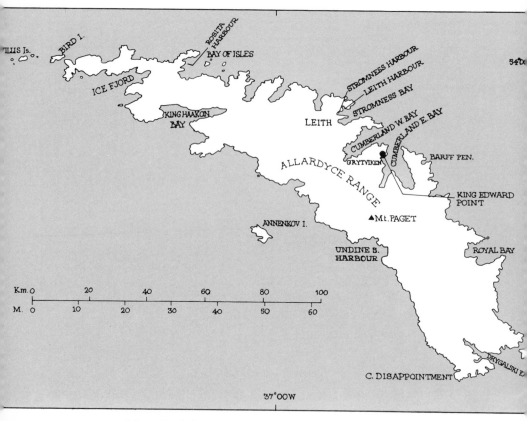

Map 9. South Georgia

were imposed for the preservation of the fauna, particularly the few remaining fur seals.

The arrival of Government personnel to live on the island included families, and South Georgia became one of the most isolated colonies in the Empire, a place where women lived and brought up their babies, dependent on the Falkland Islands and the whaling communities for their housekeeping.

FIDS interest began in 1950 when Sir Miles Clifford decided that the Survey should open a meteorological station to provide a forecasting service for the whalers. This base did not last long for in 1952 the forecasting responsibilities were taken over by Government, the station being manned by staff seconded from the Meteorological Office in England.

The most important scientific advance during the short FIDS tenure was in 1951 when Laws was Base Leader. He developed a means of 'ageing' the elephant seal population which at that time was being exploited under licence by the whalers, some 6,000 bulls being taken annually. By sectioning a canine tooth from every twentieth seal killed, it was possible to establish the mean age of the annual take. Thus a reduction of the mean in a given year would indicate over-killing. In fact over a number of years no significant change occurred, thus demonstrating that no damage was being done to the total population.

During the 1950s the winter population usually numbered some 250 people, of whom about twelve were British. The remainder were mainly Norwegian maintenance staff at four whaling stations. The one at Stromness provided ship repair facilities, even a small floating dock for the whale catchers. The other three, at Grytviken, Leith Harbour and Husvik, received whole carcasses brought in by the catchers, which were hauled up onto a 'plan' to be flensed and butchered. The oil was obtained from blubber boiled down in huge digesters, the meat and bone were ground down and dried to become bone-meal fertilizer.

In 1954 Stonehouse (ex-Stonington) and Niger Bonner built a small hut at the Bay of Isles where they spent a year studying king penguins. This was a private expedition organised by Stonehouse, but it went with our blessing and received some FIDS assistance.

In 1956 I passed through South Georgia in *Magga Dan*, taking the TAE party to Shackleton Base at the head of the Weddell Sea. Bob Spivey (ex-Stonington) was the Government Administrative Officer and he had a big problem. Two days before we arrived one of his meteorologists and a radio operator had dined unwisely, and in the middle of the night had felt it appropriate to shoot out the light on the roof of the Meteorological Office. They were now under arrest, awaiting trial and incarcerated in the small gaol guarded by the one policeman. When Base Leader at Stonington I had been sworn in as a magistrate and, as far as I knew, I still held that authority. As I had no involvement with the small local community, Spivey asked me most fervently to preside over the trial.

Magga Dan was also carrying the Royal Society IGY party going to Halley Bay. I hastily co-opted their leader, Colonel Robin Smart, and swore him in as a magistrate. We both put on our best clothes and prepared to sit on the Bench, with every intention of upholding the highest traditions of the British Judiciary.

It transpired that most of the community had been awakened by a fusilade of shots from a .303 rifle, interspersed with gleeful laughter. The assistant radio operator, Henry, was a crack shot, but since on this occasion his condition had precluded him from steadying his rifle, his buddy, John, had obligingly offered his shoulder as a rest, the muzzle thus lying a few inches from his head. However Spivey and Basil Biggs, the local policeman, soon arrived on the scene and the cheerful miscreants were led off to the small gaol block to sleep it off.

When at last quiet prevailed, the pale faced figure of Lofty, the duty meteorologist, emerged gingerly from the building, where he had been lying low as bullets whizzed through the walls in his vicinity, firmly convinced that someone was out to get him. He had been too terrified to shout less he pin-point his position.

The following morning the prisoners, now sober but irrepressible to the end, entertained the locals who had come to watch developments, by brandishing a rifle through the barred window. In the confusion of the night they had inadvertently been locked up in a cell used as a magazine – full of guns and thousands of rounds of ammunition!

Nan Brown, wife of the senior radio operator, has given a racy account of this Gilbertian episode in *Antarctic Housewife* (Hutchinson & Co, 1971).

The trial, held in the main office building, was simple but dignified. The defendents, chastened and apprehensive, were arranged before Dr Fuchs and, against a backdrop of the Union Jack, Basil Biggs, in Constable's uniform, read out the charge – 'Releasing a firearm in a public place and disturbing the peace'.

The impression given was that Henry had been shooting in the vicinity of the beacon, and only stray shots had actually hit the building. Both pleaded guilty, and were fined £20 and given a good dressing down. Everyone was happy with the outcome. The miscreants were again shouldering their responsibilities with a will, and extremely grateful for Dr Fuchs' understanding attitude; and the geometrically precise row of bullet holes up the Meteorological Office wall disappeared with a bit of carpentry and paint.

Lofty, mollified by John's return to duty and the knowledge that he was not really a marked man, magnanimously overlooked the incident.

In 1963/64 I was south touring the bases and again visited South Georgia in *Kista Dan*. Captain Denis Coleman, who was then the Administrative Officer, introduced me to Captain Nyatta, head of a Japanese whaling company which had rented the Leith whaling factory from the Salvesan Company.

Later we put into Leith to take on additional fuel, and had the opportunity of seeing the Japanese operations. Contrary to British and Norwegian practice, they did not allow their catcher captains to work independently. Furthermore, they were not 'gunners'. Specialists who had no other function were employed for this crucial task.

Detailed instructions from the shore station were issued daily to the catchers. These were based on reported sea temperatures which indicated the position of the Antarctic Convergence, where the upwelling nutrient-filled cold waters meet warmer waters from the north. There they believed the

Vegetation on lower slopes of Cumberland East Bay, S Georgia. (R. I. L. Smith)

best whale feeding grounds existed, and this method had proved highly successful.

They were also investigating the possibility of developing a fishing industry. The first ideas had not worked out, but they had high hopes of the inshore fishing and intended to try the deep water later on. As *Kista* sailed away the Japs made an astonishing gesture. Across the calm waters of the harbour, loudspeakers were blaring out *Auld Lang Syne*.

As whales became scarce the shore-based industry became less profitable, and by 1967 all whaling and sealing from the island ceased. As this had been unforseen, the Government had just finished putting up a large new two-storey administrative building named Shackleton House, which even included hospital facilities for the whalers. Suddenly it became a white elephant, while the small Government staff were left with nothing to do but act as an official, but expensive, presence on the island.

Grytviken whaling station in operation. (G. B. Davies)

By this time the developing FIDS biological programmes at Signy had given impetus to the idea of extending the studies to South Georgia. It was also apparent that there could be a future potential in fishing and in the use of krill. It was therefore decided that the Government should hand over the station and its equipment at King Edward Point to the Survey for a scientific base. In return the Survey would perform any necessary administrative functions, particularly in regard to visiting foreign ships, of which by now there were a considerable number each season.

Accordingly in 1968 a summer party of builders was sent out to modify Shackleton House and install laboratories. On 11 November 1969 a party of ten under Ricky Chinn arrived in *Biscoe* to take over the base. Chinn had accepted a five-year contract as Base Commander of South Georgia. The arrangement was that he would spend the first winter there, but subsequently a wintering deputy would run the base while he returned home to help organise the requirements for the following season, when he would go back to control the station during each busy summer.

So began the continuous occupation of this somewhat unusual base. Chinn's party quickly acquainted themselves with the complexities of the station. Besides the very large modern Shackleton House which formed their living quarters and work place, and was capable of accommodating thirty men, there were many other buildings. Near the old Discovery House of the 1920s, once the laboratories of Discovery Investigations, there was a newly built Administrative Officer's house, four bungalows, the Post Office and administrative buildings, a large power house, a building containing refrigerated store rooms, a meteorological office and a 325-ton fuel tank.

Even if the bungalows were unoccupied, the task of maintaining all these buildings would be formidable, and the scientific programmes would require extensive modifications to Discovery House itself. Besides all this, each summer brought a constant stream of visitors, including numbers of Russian fishing vessels with their attendant tankers, many of which came to take on water and give their crews a spell ashore.

As well as Base Commander Chinn was also Magistrate, Harbour Master and Postmaster. For all these tasks he was responsible to the Governor in Stanley, now Sir Cosmo Haskard who had succeeded Sir Edwin Arrowsmith in 1964. Chinn was required to clear every ship for customs on arrival and departure, to levy the harbour dues, and to charge for water taken on board. He was a very busy man.

So also were his companions. Two were botanists, two ionosphericists and one a meteorologist, each with their own scientific problems and programmes. There was also a diesel electric mechanic, a radio operator and two builders. They all shared the cooking and domestic chores which, with the need for everyone to help with other people's projects, made excessive demands on the available manpower. Alan ('Dad') Etchells, the engineer, soon found he had to replace old wiring in the main building, then one of the refrigerator motors broke down, and the fire pump would not work until he discovered that the fuel tank had been filled with water.

All had problems: the botanists, David Walton and Clive Stephenson, with the weather and their experimental sowings; the ionosphericists, Steve Chellingsworth and Terry Chamberlain, with the tall aerial mast they had to erect. Indeed, on their first attempt the three-ton base of cement they had constructed tilted in the soft boggy soil, and they had to begin all over again.

Minor chores included caring for the chickens from which they hoped to maintain an egg supply. One day Chellingsworth arrived with his bucket to feed them and collect the eggs, to find a skua actually in the hen-house. While his back was turned it stole an egg out of his bucket and swallowed it whole. During the next few weeks the Fids successfully developed anti-skua precautions, but when eggs began to be eaten again, suspicion fell on the chickens themselves. By leaving a decoy egg behind and watching through a window, two culprits were identified – and removed to an avian gaol to await execution for the midwinter feasting.

HMS *Endurance* arrived on Christmas Eve 1970. Suddenly life was enlivened by films on board, parties for the crew ashore and, of course, a football match against the ship's company. Gear for this game was unorthodox and varied, soon the rules were ignored and a number of stars ended up in the chilly waters of the local stream. The result was never determined.

But on Christmas morning decorum prevailed. The ship held a Carol Service in the little white Norwegian church formerly used by the whalers, and now specially opened by Ragnar Thorsen, who had spent twenty-five years in the service of the Company and was living in solitary state at the old whaling station as caretaker. All the Fids attended, in full voice, feeling it a fitting start to their Christmas festivities.

Later a number of trawlers from the Soviet fishing fleet visited the island, including the *Akademic Knipovich* which stayed three days. She was a research vessel, using gamma rays from Caesium 174 to irradiate fish immediately after they were caught. This preserved them for up to one month without the need for freezing. Trawling was carried out to a depth of as much as 500 metres, and sometimes one haul would bring in twenty tons of fish. The Russians were also technically advanced in the catching, preservation and preparation of krill, so prolific in the Southern Ocean. It was presented as a paste which tasted like prawn and was considered very palatable. Krill was once food for many species of the vast whale population, and has long been known as a potentially enormous food resource (30 per cent protein) for man. Perhaps fifty to a hundred million tons could be taken as an acceptable annual yield.

Another quite different sort of visitor was the *Lindblad Explorer*. Built in Finland and specially strengthened for work in ice, she was operated by an American company and brought regular tourism to the Antarctic. Each season she made a number of two-week cruises, penetrating as far south as the Argentine Islands. On this first visit to South Georgia in 1970, fifty passengers came ashore to scramble round the beaches, visit Shackleton's grave and buy stamps at the Post Office.

Fids were invited on board where they enjoyed warm hospitality, and in turn were happy to guide the tourists round various shore installations. Nevertheless, it had become apparent in earlier seasons at other stations that successive visits were disruptive to base routine and a hindrance to scientific programmes. Therefore, however popular such social contacts are to the men, they cannot expect to commend themselves to authorities responsible for producing results if they occur too often. On this occasion, though, everyone was very pleased to welcome Sir Raynor Arthur; now retired, he had happily accepted Linblad's invitation to join the ship to lecture to the tourists on Antarctica.

FIDS ships of course paid a number of visits, bringing out relief personnel and inter-changing men between bases. But by the end of April the 'silly season' ended, the inshore waters froze, deep snow covered the ground, and constant high winds confined activities to the base area. Those wintering were at last able to settle down to another six months of uninterrupted work. Even so there were a few 'occasions', as when the Russian tanker *Argon* paid a late visit in May 1971. After being entertained to a film show on board, the base invited the Captain and officers to an evening at Shackleton House. This turned into a hilarious party as each side battled with the language problems, and ended up with Dave Hill, one of the builders, finding himself 'engaged' to the Chief Engineer's daughter who was on board for the trip.

In June their midwinter celebrations included a six-course dinner in the lounge, decorated to resemble a Wild West saloon, including large posters depicting penguins as cowboys and Indians. A huge cake, iced as a skiing scene, topped the scales at seventy pounds. (By August this had been reduced to twenty pounds.) Next day a cold buffet was provided for any still hungry. Over the 'holiday period' eighty pounds of pork, venison (reindeer), beef and turkey were consumed. Even the chickens perked up and began to lay – perhaps as a result of the sherry trifle left over from the feasting. Despite the tall stories Fids delight to tell, Antarctic life is not all 'rugged'.

The 1970/1 season was full of difficulties and alterations to programmes. The new *Bransfield* should have been completed in time to sail in October but strikes and other delays had kept her at home until January. *Biscoe* left Southampton on time, but in mid-Atlantic one of her electric armature windings burnt out and she had to spend three weeks in Rio de Janeiro while it was repaired. She finally reached South Georgia on 1 December, the relief supplies including teleprinter equipment to bring the station into line with communication systems at the other bases. She also delivered a pile driver and steel piles for protecting the shoreline from further erosion which was undermining the jetty. Small parties of geologists and botanists were then landed at selected localities round the island to carry out their summer projects.

The 'great day' arrived at last on 3 February. Bunting was strung along the jetty reading WELCOME, as Tom Woodfield, now Master of the RRS

Bransfield, dressed overall, brought her gingerly and with great precision alongside the rather aged landing stage. It was her first 'Antarctic' port of call, and the occasion was suitably celebrated. The base Fids were amazed at the facilities on board, and the comfort in which the new boys had travelled out. Times had changed indeed – it was a far cry from the maiden voyage of the *Biscoe* twenty-four years earlier.

An even more dramatic occasion occurred two months later. On 5 April a small boat was seen entering the bay, sailing under jury rig. Chinn with two companions immediately set out in the motor boat to find that she was the *Damien*, out of La Rochelle, flying the French ensign and an English flag of courtesy. Aboard were Jérôme Poncet, Master, and Gérard Janichon – both in bad shape. Ten days earlier, when fifty miles south of Cape Disappointment, they had capsized three times in heavy seas and were fortunate to have survived.

They had left La Rochelle in 1969, sailed north to Spitzbergen, then via Jan Mayen Island, Iceland, Cape Farewell, Greenland to Newfoundland, and south along the American coast to the West Indies. There Poncet had a kidney removed and they had to rest for three months. They set off again for Panama, then 1,000 miles up the Amazon to Manaos before moving from port to port along the South American coast, finally reaching Ushuaia, the most southerly city in the world. While sailing through the Beagle Channel they were arrested by a Chilean gunboat and held in the Puerto Williams gaol for five days. Released early in March, they set course for South Georgia.

Fifty miles south of the eastern end of the island they capsized three times, pitchpoling (stern over bow) on one occasion, and on another remaining upside down for four minutes. This, they thought, was surely the end, but a lucky wave lifted and righted them again. They were now dismasted. Exhausted, wet through and bitterly cold, for two days they could not summon sufficient strength to pull the mast and rigging aboard. When at last they managed this, they rigged a jury mast from a genoa pole, and using an inverted stay sail, steered for Grytviken, 100 miles away.

Here they only hoped for shelter, believing that the whaling station was abandoned. The weather eased but prevailing winds slowed them considerably, and it was ten days later that they sailed into Cumberland Bay. To their astonishment and thankful relief, they found themselves being met and warmly welcomed by the British party.

The Frenchmen stayed at base for three weeks to rest, recuperate, and carry out urgent maintenance on their boat. Everyone helped with the problems. A shortened mast was stepped and the engine completely overhauled in the workshop. The Fids were amazed at their voyage, and delighted to assist them in continuing it. On their last evening a party was held in their honour, and next morning *Damien* sailed for Cape Town, 3,000 miles away, while every camera on base clicked away recording her departure.

This was not the end of the Jérôme Poncet story. He returned south in 1972/3 and again in 1977/8 with a new *Damien II* and his wife Sally. They wintered by themselves in Marguerite Bay, before calling once more on our base at Grytviken in March 1979. Then they moved on to the deserted whaling station at Leith Harbour where Sally gave birth to a son. So it fell to the lot of Mick Pawley, Base Commander and Magistrate, to enter the first record of a birth in the 204 years since Captain Cook had made the first landing on South Georgia.

Brian Jones was the wintering Base Commander in 1971. The scientific programmes had already been extended by the introduction of geomagnetic, seismological and ozone recordings, and marine zoological studies had begun. Since these were additional to the existing meteorological, botanical and ionospheric work, the seven scientists were hard pressed to keep all the disciplines going.

There were more to come. When *Bransfield* returned in November a three-man summer biological team, Mike Payne, Bob Burton and Peter Prince, were landed on Bird Island to study the rapidly increasing population of fur seals, and the albatrosses, mollymauks and diving petrels.

Fur seals at Bird Island. (J. Croxall)

These men occupied a small hut which had been built by Lance Tickell and Harry Dollman in 1962 when they had been working on albatrosses under American auspices. Their only predecessors had been Stonehouse and Tickell, who had built an even smaller hut during a private expedition to South Georgia in 1958. Now the arrival of Fids heralded annual studies which have continued ever since.

Bransfield also brought to King Edward Point two glaciologists, Ian Hogg and Andrew Jamieson, and a surveyor, Bob Hayward, to begin a glaciological/hydrological study of the Hodges glacier. This was a joint project with the Hydrological Institute whose representative was Tony Edwards, himself an ex-Fid from Hope Bay. He had come out for the summer to set it up.

Their object was to study the heat, ice and water balance of the glacier, as a contribution to the International Hydrological Decade which already had associated work in progress at a chain of stations in the Arctic and southwards through the Americas. The Survey's work at South Georgia would be in a key area where glacier regime is sensitive to even small changes in meteorological conditions. We also began similar work in a true polar environment on the Spartan Glacier at 70°S on Alexander Island, which became the most southerly station in the international chain.

The erection of a field hut and four automatic weather stations on Hodges Glacier, and the building of a concrete stream gauge, had to wait until *Endurance* arrived in December, for all the cement and other materials could only be lifted up onto the glacier by her helicopters.

Two geologists, Phil Stone and Roger Crews, had also come for the summer and, with their field assistants, were established at Royal Bay and on the Barff Peninsula respectively. During winter three new zoologists – Garrey Maxwell, Andrew Clarke and Payne – were at work at base, but before they could be fully operational a large wet laboratory had to be built between the piles upon which Shackleton House had been erected. This, together with aquaria and a pump house to provide a continuous flow of sea water, was completed by the end of March.

The steel piling and concrete sea defences begun the previous year were extended to protect the power house. The exterior of Shackleton House, including 110 windows, was repainted, and two one-time medical wards were converted into two-man laboratories. Two new 120kw generators were installed to provide more power, and finally a wooden field hut was erected on Barff Peninsula. By the end of this hectic season during which the base population fluctuated around thirty men, provision had been made for the future needs of the various programmes in Earth, Life and Atmospheric Sciences. That winter twenty-two men occupied Shackleton House, fourteen of them scientists.

12 *Heavy tractor in crevasse, 1969. (M. Macrae)*
13 *Recovering tractor, 1973. (G. Ramage)*
14 *Tractor winching itself up a 45° slope. (G. Ramage)*

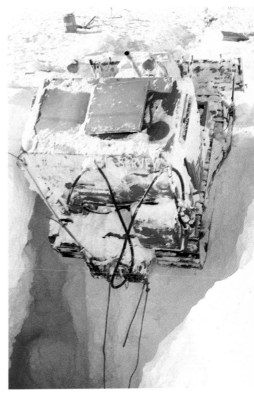

15 *Descent into crevasse. (A. Moyes)*

Reindeer in August: males have cast their antlers. (N. Leader-Williams)

Nineteen seventy-three was my last year as Director and I made my last tour. Arriving at King Edward Point in *Bransfield* we found the station in the throes of another busy season. Forty-five men were working at or from the base, geological parties having been landed from *Biscoe* on Annenkov Island, at the Bay of Whales and Rosita Harbour. Three biologists were again on Bird Island.

A field hut was being built at Hound Bay and a depot placed at Stromness, both to support future work on the reindeer herds. A combined zoological/botanical party was landed at Moltke Harbour, and with the help of *Endurance*'s helicopters geologists were placed on the otherwise inaccessible Clerke Rocks and at Royal Bay. The 'choppers' also flew vertical photographic runs over Drygalski Fjord, besides taking pictures of the Barff Peninsula and the Husvik area for reindeer counts.

We had brought with us Dr Hoshiai of the National Science Museum, Tokyo, who wanted to make marine biological studies at Signy. Unhappily the island was still surrounded by thirty miles of sea ice and ships could not yet get in. We necessarily postponed our visit, and 'the Professor' perforce transferred his interests to South Georgia, where he took up residence in Shackleton House. The night before we sailed to relieve Halley Bay the base gave a dinner in his honour. Wearing our best clothes, we entered the dining-hall to find a pair of locally made chop-sticks beside each plate in lieu of forks. Since the main course was based on vermicelli, chaotic scenes developed as thirty newly initiated chop-stick handlers twirled and dangled their elusive meal. The Professor was delighted at our struggles.

On reaching Halley Bay Derek Gipps and I were picked up by the Otter and flown across to Adelaide, while *Bransfield* spent the next six weeks relieving other bases. She then returned to South Georgia to move various field parties to different locations around the island, and in April made a final visit to bring them all back to base and so home, including our Japanese guest who had had a profitable stay. The wintering party of twenty-two were perhaps thankful that the 'silly season' was over once more.

So it was that a new chapter opened in the history of South Georgia, and in three years a broad spectrum of scientific studies had been established. Originally claimed for the British Crown by Captain Cook in 1775, the island had became a happy hunting ground for sealers in the first quarter of the nineteenth century. In 1821 no fewer than ninety-one ships were sealing around the coast. Men were greedy for profits and callous in their lack of thought for the future, until the fur seals were almost exterminated. In 1904 came the whalers whose activities finally ceased in 1967. By then pelagic whaling from factory ships had resulted in a disastrous decline in the whale population and this made shore-based whaling unprofitable.

Now science has taken over in South Georgia. Studies of fish and krill are being made with a view to acquiring sufficient knowledge to prevent a similar destruction of stocks. We can only hope that it is not already too late, for in 1970 Russian trawlers took 240,000 tons of fish in South Georgian waters, and the following year the grounds were found to be unprofitable. With increasing concern about conservation and excessive exploitation of resources, we may hope that science will produce the knowledge necessary for the proper control of future fishing in the Southern Ocean.

I 2

The web of our life . . .
1960–7

The web of our life is of mingled yarn, good and ill together.
Shakespeare

It had always been apparent that work in the southern areas of the Antarctic Peninsula, on Alexander Island and in George VI Sound, was restricted by the distances which had to be travelled. In addition there was uncertainty about the stability of the sea ice route south of Stonington. With the advent of aircraft we had the opportunity to operate much more freely and efficiently; but in 1960 Stonington was closed, and no suitable site for an airstrip had yet been found so far south. The years 1960–6 brought changes which were to lay the ground for the future.

Antarctic flying is always risky and often dangerous. Pilots arriving on the continent for the first time are faced with a whole series of problems they have not met before. The weather, is highly capricious and forecasting is, to say the least, primitive, navigational aids are minimal, and landings have to be made on skis on unprepared surfaces, which constantly vary with snowfall and wind. Low or deep drifting snow can completely obscure the airstrip, while whiteout removes all perspective and precludes a proper judgement of surface conditions.

Even in clear weather, which can so quickly deteriorate, the unalleviated whiteness of the ground makes it difficult to assess height and distance when bringing a plane in to land. And there are crevasses. These are usually covered by snow bridges (lids), and are difficult to identify from the air – yet woe betide an aircraft which lands in such an area!

The Survey owes an enormous debt to its pilots and their air mechanics. They have come from the Royal Air Force, the Army and civilian life, and some have flown with us for four and even five consecutive seasons – always with courageous determination to ensure that the field parties who rely on them are never let down.

On my retirement Fids were kind enough to institute a Fuchs Medal, to be awarded annually to those considered to have made a contribution far in excess of the normal call of duty. This is a grass roots honour. Recipients are not chosen by the hierarchy but nominated, for specific reasons, by the Fids themselves – and who can judge better the worth of a man than the companions who have shared his Antarctic life? Some of our RAF pilots have received appropriate decorations for their Antarctic flying from their own Service, and it gave me very great pleasure to be invited to present the first Fuchs Medal to our first civilian pilot, Dave Rowley, who was nominated jointly by the field men from the southern bases. He would be the first to agree that not only was this a personal tribute, but also a recognition of the vital role which the air crews have played so superbly.

1960/1   During the winter of 1960 the Beaver had been fitted with a new wing at Deception, and once more two aircraft were operational. The RAF pilots flew them south, intending to support field parties working out of Horseshoe Island. *En route* they landed at the Argentine Islands where sea ice still provided a stable runway, but because local currents and upwellings had produced thin patches the base had marked out a safe strip.

Ron Lord, flying the Beaver, came down on this and taxied out of the way of the incoming Otter. When Paddy English had landed safely, Lord turned to follow him to the shore. In leaving the runway he unknowingly motored over a thin patch and, to everyone's horror, first a ski and then the whole undercarriage broke through the ice.

Nothing could be done until the weight was greatly reduced, so most of the fittings and both wings were removed. Even then the efforts of twenty Fids and two dog teams were insufficient to pull the plane clear. Because the surrounding ice was so thin, it was impossible to rig lifting gear, and any further attempt at recovery had to be abandoned. Ironically, the accident took place just a hundred yards from where the wing had been torn off six months previously. It was a bad start to the season, but at least no one had been hurt.

After two seasons of bad ice conditions, it was encouraging to find the west coast of Graham Land and Marguerite Bay clear enough for ships to work with comparative ease, and in late January *Biscoe* embarked Ted Clapp's party, which had wintered in Wordie House, Argentine Islands, and at last established them at the southern end of Adelaide Island. There had been a suggestion that the new station might be built at Rothera Point on the east coast, but there the sea ice was still unbroken. John Green, SECFIDS, decided it was too late in the season to wait for it to go out, and furthermore, that a similar problem arising in later years could make relief difficult or even impossible.

While the hut was being erected at Adelaide, *Biscoe* put ashore a new party

Single-Otter at the Argentine Islands. (J. C. A. Stokes)

of eleven, under John Cunningham, to re-open Stonington. She then returned to Adelaide and landed building materials and stores for a small advance base, to be known as Fossil Bluff, which was to be put in by air 250 miles south, on Alexander Island, George VI Sound. (Adie and I had identified this site in 1949, but before the advent of aircraft it was impossible to take in building materials.)

At Adelaide everything had to be landed on the rocky coast and carried up a narrow gully, past the builders working on the new hut, so there was considerable congestion. Furthermore, all the paraphernalia to be taken to Fossil Bluff had to be dumped at the foot of a very steep ice slope which led to the airstrip 300 feet above. While a tractor, landed from *Biscoe*, repeatedly clawed its way up with load after load, flying also began.

The first flight to the Bluff was on 20 February, already late in the season to begin building so far south; but the shuttle went on, everyone working hard for long hours until the four-man hut was completed. The wintering party, Clifford Pearce, John Smith and Brian Taylor, were flown in during March. It was frustrating to have arrived so late, especially for Taylor, for after only five weeks of field work, fading light and increasing snow cover brought his geological studies to an end for the winter.

It was planned to provide Muskeg tractors for the use of summer field parties which would later be working from Fossil Bluff, but as these were too large to be flown in, two had been landed at Stonington, to be driven the 250 miles, partly over sea ice, in the following spring.

1961   In July a reconnaissance journey made with dog teams revealed that the direct route via the Terra Firma Islands was impracticable for tractors, because the surface consisted of consolidated brash and bergy bits from the previous year's break-up. However, travelling westward to Compass Island, the party found smoother ice, and felt that a satisfactory route had been proved thus far.

1961/2   On 24 August Brian Bowler, Howard Chapman, Bob Metcalfe and Arthur Fraser set out with the Muskegs, on a preparatory depot-laying journey to provide a fuel dump at Mushroom Island, south of the Terra Firmas. This was laid, but on their way back they were caught by an easterly blow when camped beside Compass Island. The storm lasted thirty-six hours, during which the ice broke up, and they were dismayed to find themselves isolated on a floe seventy yards wide. Very fortunately this drifted towards the island and twenty feet of it pressed against the rocks, which enabled them to scramble ashore with their camping gear. The tractors had to be abandoned on the ice, but later they managed to hack a deep cutting into the low ice cliff bounding the island, and with the help of planks they brought them both ashore. During the evening radio 'sched' with base they learnt that all the ice to the north of them had broken up, making it impossible for them to return.

They decided to sit it out and wait for the sea to refreeze, and then to push on towards Fossil Bluff. It took sixteen days for the ice to consolidate sufficiently for them to drive back to Mushroom Island, where they waited another four weeks before it was possible for dog teams from Stonington to bring them the additional stores, spares and equipment needed to get to the Bluff.

At last on the move again, in company with the teams which had resupplied them they reached Cape Jeremy. There they found a series of depressions which represented snow-covered refrozen leads in the older sea ice. Two of these were safely negotiated, but as the leading tractor climbed the slope out of a third, it quietly sank two feet into the snow. This appeared to be just another case of 'bogging down' and, disconnecting the sledges, they prepared to pull it out backwards with the second Muskeg.

The plan worked well until it suddenly slumped back and water began spurting through holes in the steel flooring. Bowler leapt out, to find himself standing in deep slush which had not been there only moments before. The Muskeg had broken through new ice forming the bottom of the depression.

Muskeg tractor. (BAS)

Quickly it filled with water, sinking slowly but inexorably deeper and deeper. Fearing for the second tractor and the sledges, they hastily cut the tow-rope – and it disappeared from sight, leaving only a sodden patch of watery slush to mark its grave.

The one remaining vehicle was thus committed to towing three heavily laden cargo sledges, the last of which carried all their camping gear and food. This was wisely protected by a rope link inserted in the towing system, which could be cut quickly if the tractor should break through, but there were no further disasters. The surface held, and having spent thirteen weeks in the field, during which they had travelled 350 miles, the party at last reached Fossil Bluff. The following year two more Muskegs were driven to the Bluff without incident, and these three tractors have remained in operation ever since.

It had been mid-September before Taylor was able to start field work again. Five idle winter months must have seemed a high price to pay for an early start in the new season. But as things turned out, his early presence there had been an advantage, for had he arrived at the Bluff with the delayed tractor party, two months' work would have been lost.

Later in the summer Metcalfe and Chapman began to establish a ground control scheme for George VI Sound with tellurometers. These were then relatively new instruments, based on radar, which enabled distances of thirty to forty miles to be measured with great accuracy. Thus survey control could be provided, only occasional angles having to be measured by theodolite as checks to the scheme. Although two stations had to be occupied at the same time, measurements could be made through mist or cloud without the need to wait for clear weather. In subsequent seasons this control network was extended throughout George VI Sound into Palmer Land to the east, and northward until the entire length of the Antarctic Peninsula had been covered.

1962/3   The original reason for a base at Adelaide Island was to study the rocks and map the topography. In the first year Graham Dewar completed a geological reconnaissance of most of the eastern and northern areas. Alan Wright, aided by Alan Crouch and Gordon McCallum, established a survey scheme for the east coast which was linked with the Horseshoe Island survey, while Frank Preston, the Base Leader, worked northwards. By the end of the season ground control for the existing FIDASE air photography was well advanced, and numerous routes giving access to the interior or crossing the island had been proved.

By the time all the scientific work had been completed we had realised that the surface of the Fuchs Ice Piedmont above the base provided a good advance airstrip, and it was decided to maintain, and even enlarge, the station as the support centre for all field parties operating in the region. Such a staging post opened the way for more extensive work in regions further south.

The following season both Stonington and Adelaide were provided with Eliason motor-toboggans. These were each approximately the size of a Nansen sledge, powered by a nine-horse power air-cooled engine driving a belt track between two solid runners. They were capable of hauling one or two Nansens, with a maximum total load of 2,000 pounds on a good level surface. They were, in fact, 'mechanical dog-teams' but, unhappily, not so reliable as dogs. However, they ushered in a new era which represented a threat to the dog men, although it was to be many years, and the trial of many different types of toboggan, before machines superseded the dogs.

One of the early journeys with machines working alongside dogs was a depot-laying and geophysical run from Stonington to Three Slice Nunatak, on the east side of the Antarctic Peninsula. This entailed climbing the steep slopes of 'Sodabread'. At first the surface was soft snow, and the Eliasons could not haul a load at all, while the dogs managed with difficulty. Then came a blow which hardened the surface and, to everyone's surprise, the

16 *View over Alexander Island (C. Swithinbank)*
17 *Eureka Glacier, northern Palmer Land. (C. Swithinbank)*
18 *(Overleaf) Argentine Islands and Lemaire Channel. (C. J. Gilbert)*

19 *Twin-Otter flying over southern Marguerite Bay: Alexander Island in distance. (R. M. Laws)*
20 *Fossil Bluff field station. (M. P. Landy)*

toboggans climbed the slope carrying a man and 120 pounds. The dogs managed 260 pounds but took twice as long. Advantage lay with the machines, for they could repeat the trip without tiring the driver, whereas the dogs and their drivers were exhausted after one climb.

Comparisons did not end there. Dogs may be recalcitrant, but they do not have clutches and chains and oil pipes, all of which caused constant trouble. Nor would the Eliasons start easily in temperatures below −20°F. In one respect though, these motor monsters showed that they could emulate dogs. Once when Peter Kennett was warming up his machine by driving round his camp, he was thrown off by a bump. Joyfully the toboggan set off towards the horizon at full throttle. Mike Fleet immediately gave chase on his machine, but made no headway and had to return for fuel. Setting off a second time he finally caught up with the runaway only when it ran out of petrol, and three hours later he returned to camp with both toboggans. The dog men may be forgiven a sardonic smile.

1963/4   At the beginning of 1964 Cunningham returned for a second tour, this time as Base Leader of Adelaide, with the additional responsibility for coordinating all field operations in Marguerite Bay and further south. Once more we were hampered by difficult ice conditions, and by the third week in February *Biscoe* had still failed to relieve the base. In desperation it was decided to unload the stores over the high cliffs of the Fuchs Ice Piedmont, thirty miles to the north, and from there men began to sledge them to the station. A few days later the ship fought her way through to Adelaide, but it was still not possible to use the normal landing site. Hundreds of cases had to be unloaded onto rocks below the ice sliff, and due to their very awkward position, the shore party then had difficulty in moving the material.

The stores were coming ashore very rapidly, for Captain Johnston feared besetment and wanted to get away into safer waters. After the ship had left there was still a great quantity to be moved when a freak thaw and high winds made further work impossible. When the storm eased the men found that drift pouring over the cliff had buried everything under thirty feet of snow. They worked their hardest, but the task of digging up material from this depth finally proved too great and it had to be abandoned. Thus a spare Otter propeller, an aircraft ski, a radio mast, one ton of anthracite and eighty drums of aviation fuel were lost.

This episode emphasized the need for a small wharf onto which a ship's scow could unload. Indeed, the first preparations for this had begun the previous season. The scheme was to block off a small gully between the rocks with a concrete wall, back-fill this with rock and cap the whole with cement to form a platform. This entailed considerable blasting, which was carried out by Ken Doyle who promptly became known as 'Bangs'. One day he was crowned by a falling rock while admiring his explosive handiwork, but happily, when Dr Tom Davies had stitched and bandaged him up, he lived to blast another day.

1964   Arrangements had been made through the Royal Society for an exchange of scientists between Britain and the Soviet Union, to work in Antarctica. Since they were to winter, each nation was doubly careful to choose a worthy representative. Charles Swithinbank went to the Russian Mirny Station as glaciologist, where his aptitude for languages enabled him quickly to learn sufficient Russian to make friends. Previously he had been a member of the Norwegian-British-Swedish Expedition, 1949–52, and had later served for two years with the Americans at McMurdo Sound, so he was an excellent ambassador for Britain and greatly enjoyed his Russian year.

The Soviet Union sent us Garrik Grikurov. Aged twenty-eight, he had already spent seven years working in the Arctic and, posted to Stonington, he proved to be a very competent geologist who quickly became acceptable to his companions. He had a wry sense of humour, and while always retaining his own values, he never put a foot wrong in discussion or argument.

1964/5   On the voyage out I remember him watching his first game of Monopoly, immediately recognising that its theme is the buying and selling of property. 'Ah', he said in his still hesitant English but with a broad grin, 'You are all bloody capitalists – you should be put in prison.' Another new experience was the then popular James Bond films shown in the ship. Although no more than good thrillers, they all had an anti-Soviet flavour. Some weeks later we reached Deception, where it was customary to invite visitors to sign their names on the wall. With a flourish he wrote his name, then added wickedly, '007 – SMERSH' (a combination of the British agent and the opposing Russian organisation in the films).

This ability to express his views with a light touch was a great asset in his personal relationships at base, and in the field he was indefatigable, making a substantial contribution to the geology of Alexander Island. In every sense Grikurov was a good Fid – the highest accolade. We were delighted to have him and genuinely sorry when his tour ended. Great efforts were made to arrange for him to work up his geology at our Section in Birmingham, which he himself wanted to do, but permission for this was never forthcoming.

The depot laid at Three Slice Nunatak was used in 1964 by parties working on the east coast of the Antarctic Peninsula. This included geological mapping by Guy Stubbs and Tony Marsh, and gravity and magnetic traverses made by Geoff Renner. It was not then recognised that for flying the peninsula formed a meteorological dividing line, which led to low cloud appearing on one side or the other, usually on the east. Consequently there were very few days when conditions were sufficiently clear over the whole area to permit air support for field parties on the east coast. Either aircraft could not take-off from Adelaide, or they could not land at their destination.

This caused considerable frustration and sometimes occasioned anxiety. When Noel Downham, the Base Leader, was working on the east coast and found his supplies dwindling, he was sufficiently resourceful to use old depots laid south from Hope Bay in previous years. These were not completely cleared, but nearly five tons of man food, dog food and fuel were used, and a good season's work accomplished.

The loss of eighty drums of aviation fuel in the previous season meant that by December air operations had to be restricted when the station was down to its last twenty barrels. *Biscoe* therefore attempted an early relief and managed to get in to Adelaide on the 28th. But with better ice conditions a different problem arose. Days of unusually warm weather reduced the steep snow slope up to the airstrip on the piedmont to slippery ice and slush, which precluded the Muskeg from towing fuel barrels landed from the ship to the top.

Flight Lieutenant Edward Skinner suggested that she should move out to the edge of the unbroken sea ice about thirty miles away, where the plane could pick up the drums and fly them directly to the dump on the piedmont. It all worked according to plan until there seems to have been some delay in maoeuvring the aircraft to the unloading point, and for convenience Skinner decided to land from a different direction. From the air it was not apparent that there were undulations on the surface. Just as he was about to touch-down this fell away and the plane dropped heavily some thirty feet, driving the struts of the undercarriage up through the fuselage. The pilot came out unscathed, but the Otter was a write-off.

This was a serious loss, for Grikurov's geological group was working on Alexander Island, and two survey parties had been flown into Palmer Land. The second Otter had already been damaged taking them in, when its tail assembly had been trapped in a small crevasse at Keystone Cliffs. Although still capable of flight, it was being used as little as possible. Now it came back into action to recover the field parties, and was then flown back to Deception, to be overhauled during the coming winter.

By February all the ice in Marguerite Bay had broken up, and *Biscoe* came back comparatively easily to make last calls at Adelaide, Stonington and the unoccupied base at Horseshoe Island. Len Mole, who had wintered as Base Leader at Deception, arrived to take over Adelaide. The field work had been finished, and the complement was reduced from twenty-one to nine men, but meteorological observations continued, and Dr Davies began a physiological project.

His purpose was to study the influence of the unusual physical and mental factors of the Antarctic on the blood pressure level in healthy young men. This entailed considerable cooperation from his guinea-pigs. At frequent intervals their pulse rates were recorded during their various and varied activities, and every two hours throughout the day they were required to answer questionnaires revealing their transient moods. The excretion of particular metabolites was measured every four hours, and at intervals they were put through a 'step test', which involved stepping on and off a twenty-four centimetre block at twenty steps a minute for differing periods up to an hour-and-a-half at a time.

During the season there had been a number of incidents at Stonington which could have had serious consequences. Out sledging, John Tait and Neil Marsden were camped at the foot of 'Sodabread', and as darkness fell increasing wind, which blew all night, raised heavy drift. Suddenly the guy at the back of their pyramid tent loosened and two of the poles bent. First thing in the morning they strengthened the guys using climbing ropes and placed 480 pounds of boxes and gear, all buried in snow, on the skirt to hold it down.

During a second sleepless night tremendous gusts again buffeted the tent, the poles bent almost to right-angles trapping their legs and finally snapped. Then the tent seams began to tear. They had no choice but to abandon it, and prepared to take up life in the smaller, auxilliary, ridged 'pup' tent. While they were packing up, the outer cover of the pyramid tent ripped completely – in a few minutes all that was left were a few shreds of canvas. At this point they discovered that all the boxes on the skirt, and the 'pup' tent itself had blown away.

They then tried to get into protective windproof bags known as Zordski Sacks, but the wind was so violent that they were blown along the ground, ripping the sacks in two. So went their last shelter. Now desperate for protection, they contrived to build something from the sledges and a few remaining boxes, behind which they crawled into sleeping bags and hoped to ride out the blizzard. But drift penetrated the small breathing holes and filled the bags, where it melted against their warm bodies and soaked them. It could not go on.

Somewhere a short distance to the east they knew there was a crevasse which might offer protection:

Both of us climbed out of our bags, placing boxes on them. Then we were blown off our feet. Marsden held onto a sledge, I caught hold of one of the dogs and his trace.

Getting back to the sledge we found that Marsden's sleeping bag had gone. Leaving him with the gear, I tied two 200-foot climbing ropes together and set off in visibility of less than ten yards to find the crevasse. Eventually we established ourselves about thirty feet down in a small cavern, together with what was left of our equipment. A cold, wet and miserable night ensued.
Official Report

By morning visibility improved despite the strong wind still blowing. After feeding the dogs they harnessed up and fought their way home to base. The strength of the wind may be inferred from the fact that a steel-hafted ice axe used to hold in the back guy of their tent had been bent an inch out of true.

1965   At the end of July Tony Rider, James Gardner and Tait left on a survey journey intended to link the triangulation schemes already established from Stonington, Horseshoe and Detaille Island to the north. In seventeen days they were on the shores of Lallemand Fjord, where the sea ice appeared to be very solid. They therefore decided to visit Detaille to check the condition of the abandoned hut. They found that tins of food stored in the loft had burst and dripped through to the floor below, so spent two days clearing up the mess and checking the remaining stores. Then a southwest gale blew up and the accompanying drift obscured everything. When good visibility returned, there was open water to the north and loose pack ice to the south. They were isolated, and would have to wait for a refreeze, or for a ship to rescue them – perhaps five months later.

1965/6   As soon as flying recommenced Flight Lieutenant Julian Brett dropped food and coal to augment the supplies at base, but could not land on the island itself and there was no available sea ice to use as a runway. Out of the many free-drops he made, the only loss, unhappy though it must have been, was the present of a bottle of whisky. *Shackleton* reached them at last on 23 January, which was six months later.

While the Stonington summer field parties were out sledging, only four men were left to keep the base running. Two of them, David Todd and David Vaughan, once sledged a short distance over the sea ice to collect some seals for dog food. To reach these Vaughan, who was some way ahead of Todd's team, drove round a dark patch of ice which looked thin, and had shot the number required by the time his companion arrived. Seeing the carcasses, the second team headed straight for them despite their driver's frantic efforts to steer them round the thin ice. Horrified, Vaughan watched it 'rippling like the sea under water skis', and in a trice Todd and the sledge broke through, leaving five dogs still standing on the thin ice. But not for long, for as soon as they moved they too fell into the water. Todd could not swim. Frightened dogs began to clamber onto him, entagling him in their traces and repeatedly pushing him under water – and time was very short.

From where he stood there was no hope of Vaughan reaching the débâcle, so he rushed his team round to the other side, where he tried to throw the lash line of his sledge to Todd. It was too short. Then he, in turn, broke through the ice, but managed to retain a hold on his team's main trace and pull himself out. Next he tried throwing out the handle end of his long dog-whip, which Todd managed to grasp, but tangled up as he was with his own dogs' traces, the strain was too great and the whip broke.

Undaunted, but desperately anxious, Vaughan made another effort, with the lash line tied to the end of his team's centre trace. At the third attempt Todd just managed to reach this with one outstretched hand. The haul to safety seemed an eternity as he was dragged across the ice like a dead seal, for by now he had been in the water twenty minutes and could not use his legs. Vaughan lifted him onto the sledge, wrapped his own pullover round his hands, his shirt round Todd's neck and, stripped to the waist, he drove furiously back to base shouting for help.

Mike Thomson and Don Parnell heard the noise, but assumed that he was just encouraging his team to arrive back with a flourish; as they approached, Todd's body on the sledge looked to them to be a seal carcass. It was some time before they appreciated the situation and rushed out to help.

As soon as the patient had been carried into the hut his clothes were cut off, and they wrapped him in blankets before a fire. An hour later hot tea, brandy and massage had brought him almost back to normal. It had been a close shave, for his whole torso was deep chilled, and large blue patches covered the upper part of his body. The saddest thing was the loss of five dogs which Vaughan had been unable to save.

Work had been concentrated in northern Marguerite Bay and the area round Mobiloil Inlet on the east coast. Topographical survey had been largely frustrated by the surveyors being marooned on Detaille Island. Indeed all activities had been restricted by generally higher temperatures which caused melt, and exceptional winds gusting to a hundred knots. In such conditions the sea ice was unreliable and constantly breaking up. It was fortunate that operations in George VI Sound had been temporarily suspended, but even so all this meant that Mike Cousins, the Base Leader, had had to contend with a difficult year.

Despite many frustrations the geologists did a considerable amount of work; Marsden and Thomson on the east coast, and Dave Matthews on Horseshoe and Pourquoi Pas Islands. The latter, accompanied by Jim Steen, was away from base for 181 days, during which they spent eighty-three days lying-up – a measure of the bad conditions. After three months' work in

Marguerite Bay they travelled up the Forel and Finsterwalder Glaciers, returning to Stonington via the plateau. Bad weather prevented the promised air support, forcing them to relay very heavy loads up to the plateau, but on their final run into base they suddenly found good surfaces, covering fifty-six miles on the last day – and creating a new Fids record.

1966   It had long been the custom after a season's hard work for those whose duties had kept them slogging at base to be given the opportunity of making short sledging trips away from normal routine, and these 'jollies' were greatly prized by the static staff. Thus on 24 May Tom Allan and John Noël, diesel mechanic and radio operator respectively, left on a ten-day traverse with two dog teams, heading up the Northeast Glacier then northward past Butson Ridge. Twenty-four hours later they reported that they had reached Butson and were still moving, but in deteriorating weather.

At Stonington the wind was thirty knots and by next morning it was gusting to between eighty and a hundred knots. The whole hut shook and everything was falling off the shelves. These conditions continued for the next two days, so no one was surprised when nothing was heard from the sledgers – anyway, radio contact often broke down for mechanical reasons. But after a week of fine weather, and still no news, obviously something had gone wrong.

Marsden and Keith Holmes immediately set out to follow their route. On the second day they were beginning the descent of a glacier towards Square Bay when Holmes noticed some small black dots and steered towards them. These proved to be the two missing men and several dead dogs, lying on a slope beneath a rocky bluff. Allan lay on the surface, with a shovel near him, and fifty yards away Noël was apparently standing buried in the snow, his head and arms above the surface.

Without disturbing anything the shocked search party returned twenty miles to base to report the tragedy and get help. They went back accompanied by John Ross and Ken Doyle to help in the sad obsequies. First Allan and Noël were laid on specially prepared sledges, then further excavation revealed their tent, sledges and dogs which had been buried by drift, and evidence of what had happened began to appear.

Noël had been standing in a dug pit leading down into a snow hole, where two sleeping bags were laid out, together with the Primus, food, and pots and pans – which showed that they had spent some time in the hole. It was obvious that, quite rightly, when caught by bad weather the two men had dug-in. The dogs were correctly spanned a short distance away.

We shall never know for sure why Allan left the snow hole, but the teams had to be fed, probably their picket line needed to be raised above the rapidly accumulating drift; or perhaps he went out to fetch more paraffin, for the

272 THE WEB OF OUR LIFE

can in the hole was empty. Whatever the reason, he did not expect to be out long, for he was wearing two left-footed mukluks, and his windproof trousers were not tied at the ankles. Once out in the dark and the tearing drift, he must have lost his sense of direction and failed to find the way back.

When he failed to return one can imagine Noël becoming more and more anxious, going to the entrance and calling over and over again, his voice carried away by the wind. It was apparent that he had no intention of going out, for he was not properly dressed below the waist, nor did he wear mukluks. Indeed, he must have realised that there was absolutely nothing he could do outside. If Allan was lost, his only hope was for Noël to remain at the entrance to their shelter, shouting and shouting in an effort to guide him back to safety. Had he left his post, the entrance to the hole would have immediately filled up.

Becoming colder and colder, and more and more tired as he called continuously, Noël must at last have fallen asleep with exhaustion – and he never woke up. It was a tremendous example of courage that he remained to the last, and most assuredly he gave his life for his friend. – 'greater love hath no man. . . .'

The two men were brought back to base, and buried by their comrades on a rocky point of Stonington Island, beneath two great piles of stones surmounted by commemorative crosses.

1966/7   The following season's early operations in Marguerite Bay were supported by the one remaining Otter, flown by Flight Lieutenant Bob Burgess. But on 7 January 1967 a new light aircraft, the Pilatus Porter, was landed from *Perla Dan* at Deception. It took six days to assemble the plane, after which our new pilot, Flight Lieutenant John Ayers, made a series of test flights before taking off for Adelaide to start work. *Biscoe* had not yet succeeded in getting through to the station, and since this was the first turbo-engined aircraft we had used, no aviation paraffin was held there. Fortunately the Pratt and Whitney engine was reasonably omnivorous and it was safely fed a mixture of eight-year-old tractor petrol and contaminated aviation petrol which could not be burnt by the Otter.

From this season regular airborne radio-echo sounding of the ice depth became a feature of our summer programmes. The early tractor-towed equipment developed at the Scott Polar Research Institute had been tested at Halley Bay in 1965. Then a Mark II sounder was produced, fitted into an aircraft, and tried out by Gordon Robin and Stan Evans over Ellesmere Island in the Arctic. This had proved so successful that similar equipment was acquired by the Survey.

In January 1967 Swithinbank, with David Petrie as the electronics engineer, began the radio-echo sounding programme using the Otter,

21 HMS Endurance. *(BAS)*
22 RRS Bransfield. *(C. J. Gilbert)*

Pilatus Porter at Succession Cliffs, George VI Sound. (J. R. Ayres)

usually flown by Bob Burgess. They made flights over the Wordie and Larsen Ice Shelves, along the length of George VI Sound, and across Wilkins Sound in southwest Alexander Island. Towards the end of the season further soundings were flown northward along the Antarctic Peninsula and around the American Palmer Station on Anvers Island, the latter to aid glaciological studies by Dr Honkala of the United States Antarctic Research Program.

During February the equipment was transferred to the Pilatus Porter, and successfully used for sounding the Larsen and Wordie Ice Shelves from altitudes of 10,000 feet down to as little as fifteen feet. Since the recordings produced traces of both the bottom and the surface of the ice, here was a rapid means of sufficient accuracy to determine surface elevation, and so obviate the need for laborious heighting by surveyors.

When the programme was completed, the Pilatus flew south again and joined the Otter in pulling out the various geological and geophysical field parties which had spent the summer working in George VI Sound and on Alexander Island. The latter was ageing and showed signs of extensive damage to the fuselage. When it finally returned to Deception in March, it was grounded. Once again we had only one serviceable aeroplane. Nevertheless, it had been shown that the development of Adelaide as a summer airbase had opened the way to extensive operations to the south of Marguerite Bay. We would not look back.

13

Alarms and eruptions
1960–70

The bases at Deception and the Argentine Islands have figured frequently throughout this story. Both were key stations, and played an important part in our annual operations, though neither of them lies in a position from which deeds of derring-do could be mounted. However, each made its mark – Deception as a staging post for the ships, and as an air facility in the early days of flying; the Argentine Islands as a geophysical observatory producing scientific data which are internationally recognised as of exceptional quality. The IGY had overcome the causes of international friction, and the last manifestation of political rivalry had held a large element of farce.

It had occurred when the Argentines on Deception Island quite gratuitously decided to put up a small concrete block-house about two hundred yards from our base, although their own station was on the other side of Port Foster. They built it right in the middle of a flat area which the Fids habitually used as a football pitch. To say the least, this was tactless, producing a strong local reaction, and an official response in Stanley.

It was not long before Sir Miles Clifford arrived in HMS *Veryan Bay*, bringing with him the only Spanish-speaking policeman in the colony. With a section of Marines from the ship lined up outside, the representative of the civil law knocked politely on the door of the offending edifice. The occupants proved to be two Argentine seamen, who were informed that they were about to be arrested and removed to South Georgia, for later deportation to Buenos Aires in a whaling ship. They were genuinely disconcerted at the timing. 'But please – not now', they pleaded. 'Our officer is away, and he will be very sorry to miss this.'

However, they were relentlessly marched off, and when last seen were happily learning the time-honoured game of 'Uckers' in a seamen's mess on board *Veryan Bay*. The block-house was blown up – football resumed.

About 175 miles southwest of Deception, the Argentine Islands lie a few miles off the west coast of the Antarctic Peninsula. The intervening Penola

Strait is normally frozen for many months of the year, and then it is possible to reach the mainland. Generations of Fids have taken advantage of this to get away from the confines of the islands, and there have been many 'first ascents' in the coastal mountains. In seasons when the freeze-up is insufficient to provide a safe crossing, holiday 'jollies' have to be restricted to local island visits and short boat trips. Even kayaks have been introduced, but for safety reasons these have only been put in the water when a boat was in attendance.

Through the years many attempts were made to find a route from the coast to the plateau above, which lies at some 5,600 feet. None was successful until 1965 when Frank Stacey, Tony Bushell and Terry Tallis made the first ascent of Mount Peary. This proved to be flat-topped, and in fact forms a spur from the edge of the plateau. They drove a dog team up to 2,500 feet, at which point they were two miles from the summit. Leaving their camp the following day, they skied, then walked, and finally took to crampons and step-cutting to reach the top.

At last the plateau had been achieved; but triumphant as they were, it was a hollow victory, for clearly it was not a possible sledging route and their dreams of distant travel remained unrealised. However, before returning to base they claimed another 'first' by climbing the prominent cone of Lumière Peak (3,100 feet) which stands above the Bussey Glacier.

During the mid-sixties the Argentines began sending tourist ships into this very picturesque area, but confined their visits to their own stations. Then in 1968, when John Dudeney was the senior ionosphericist and Base Commander, the Chilean *Navarino*, on charter to an American tour operator, Lindblad Incorporated, put ashore the first party of British and American tourists to visit our bases. Dudeney, then twenty-three years old, was lightly built, clean shaven and looked absurdly young. The group he found himself welcoming included some charming, elderly blue-rinsed American matrons eager to be shown over every inch of the hut. Thrilled with everything, to his mortification one of them patted him kindly on the head and, intent of making him feel comfortable, asked 'And what do you do, sonny? Make the tea?'

Brushing aside the indignity, he began the guided tour down the narrow passage running through the hut. Richy Hesbrook was a very tall and handsome young man who had been on night met. duty. He had retired to the peace and privacy of the loft to catch up with some sleep, knowing nothing of the unusual visitation. Suddenly a trap-door in the ceiling opened and Adonis, naked except for his Y-fronts, dropped unsuspectingly right into the midst of the tour. There were startled gasps, some smothered screams, and the god-like apparition, scarlet with embarrassment, fled ignominiously to the sleeping quarters without a word. It all took a little getting used to.

A few weeks later poor Dudeney's ego took another bruising when the Captain of *Piloto Pardo* and his senior officers came ashore to make their official call. On being greeted by a lad sweeping out the passage, the Captain said somewhat briskly, 'Good morning – please take us to your Leader'. With modest diffidence Dudeney replied, 'I am the leader here, and I am so glad to welcome you', which the Chileans took as a rather feeble joke and the visit began to turn sour. To their confused astonishment he finally assembled the whole base, most of them very large, bearded men, and asked them collectively, 'Who is your Leader?' 'You are' they chorused gleefully – and the drinks were produced.

These early tourists were the forerunners of regular cruises in the years to come. Lars Eric Lindblad commissioned a specially ice-strengthened ship in Finland, and *Linblad Explorer* became an annual visitor to the northern bases, sometimes making as many as four or five cruises from South America in one season.

Linblad made every effort to ensure the safety of the tourists he put ashore, and briefed them on behaviour compatible with wild life conservation, but even so the visits posed problems. It soon transpired that although the passengers had come to view the beauties of the Antarctic scene, they also expected to visit the strange voluntary exiles who live and work there. It is not always realised that a group of men living for two years in isolation develops its own unique dedication, morale, and hard-core resistance to that isolation. Repeated exposure to strangers, let alone luxuries from the outside world, are in this sense disruptive – however much they may be welcomed at the time.

As a break from routine they are indeed welcome. The men see new faces, are generously entertained in the ships, and can show off their activities. They also enjoy feminine company, even though this is perhaps rather like a visitation from a batch of favourite aunts, for usually it is only the elderly and retired who can afford the time and the very high cost of the cruises. Nevertheless, there have been a few occasions when the *rara avis* has caused a flutter in the dovecots.

The visitors all have to be guided, looked after, and not allowed to wander in dangerous areas, for the inexperienced can get into difficulties – tide-cracks, cliffs, ice slopes, screes and crevasses all present dangers. These things place responsibility on the members of a base, which are difficult to fulfil without a great deal of time-wasting. A story is told of one eighty-year-old American lady who, being escorted by a Fid along the beach at Deception, saw a gigantic whale vertebra and asked what it was. 'A whale's knee-cap, ma'am' was the jocular reply, to which he got, 'Oh! – left or right leg?', which perhaps served him right.

Surveyors at work. (J. C. A. Stokes)

When visits become too frequent the Base Commander has problems, for besides extending the normal courtesies and showing visitors around his station, he still has somehow to maintain the scientific programmes. Without the manpower to handle large groups, he is often reluctant to allow so many people to stroll unattended around the installations. National government agencies will probably continue for some time to look upon tourists in terms of Thomas Campbells' *Pleasures of Hope*, 'Like Angel visits – few and far between'.

The Argentine Islands were also frequently visited by both British and foreign operational ships and helicopters. Sometimes these too caused interest and amusement, as when a platoon of Royal Marines from HMS *Endurance* was put ashore to practice the art of skiing. With some difficulty their officer was dissuaded from taking them on a skiing exercise down a steep, heavily crevassed slope, ending in an ice cliff with a drop of eighty feet. When asked respectfully whether it wasn't a bit hard on his inexperienced men to tackle such a slope, although he himself must, of course, be a skier of some note, he fished out a small booklet and said, 'Actually I haven't done much, but it tells you all about it here'.

He then turned his attention to mounting a landing exercise. With his men crouched in a launch, their commander stood in the bows, one foot forward in the approved manner, and watched by the inevitable row of expectant Fids with cameras at the ready. A few feet from shore, and overcome by the drama of the scene, he cried 'Follow me, men' and leapt over the side, disappearing through the thin ice with a huge splash into twenty fathoms of very cold water.

1968 That winter the jokes ceased and Dudeney's party faced one of the most stressful and protracted situations a base has ever experienced. Ken Portwine was the cook, and during the medical he had undergone before being recruited, he had not been completely open about his health record in India some years previously. Now he developed ulcerative colitis, but largely because he refused to admit he was ill, this was not at first recognised.

They had no doctor at base but as Portwine progressively deteriorated, their radio reports to Mike Holmes at Stonington finally resulted in the true diagnosis. It was a condition which required not only very skilled nursing but also laboratory techniques of a high order. The base reorganised their lives to meet the new demands. Every man now cooked for one day in turn, while Bob Davidson undertook all the baking, and a nursing rota was instituted. They looked to Holmes for guidance.

Dick Kressman had learnt some physiology and found a book in the library which described the techniques of making blood counts. Having next discovered how to obtain the blood, and persuaded an obstinate and very reluctant patient to submit to the needle, he and Dudeney then taught themselves to count the red cells. Very soon they embarked on the more complicated processes of white cell counts, and were at last ready to make their first report. Medical 'scheds' with Stonington had already been set up throughout the day, and Holmes was waiting anxiously to hear their results. As Dudeney called out the figures there was a stunned and prolonged silence at the other end. Finally the doctor said succinctly, 'Then he's dead'. Hastily they went back to their books.

Four men formed the day nursing team, each one responsible for the different treatments, which included injections, ordered by Holmes. The night met-man looked after the patient while he slept. Detailed bulletins on temperature, blood pressure, blood counts, liquid intake and output, excreta content, weight, and mental condition were reported to Stonington at least once daily. Holmes was also in frequent consultation with the Chief Medical Officer in Stanley, and they supervised every detail of the nursing, but despite the most devoted care Portwine remained a very sick man.

Holmes was a strength to everybody. Psychologically wise, he realised the tensions that must be building up, and had the knack of giving acceptable personal encouragement and comfort quite apart from the much needed medical advice. Later he was to speak in the highest possible terms of the quality of nursing care which the patient received, while those involved all recognised his great supportive role in their communally distressing situation. They were all determined not to be beaten by circumstances, and despite all their worries and problems the scientific programmes were all fully maintained without interruption.

The weeks passed, but Portwine's condition continued to worsen. In the light of specialist medical advice which we obtained in London it became clear that somehow he must be evacuated to hospital at the earliest moment possible. It was still winter, the sea was frozen, there were no ships in the area, and no long-range aircraft could land in the limited space available at the station.

I felt it necessary to ask the Argentines for help. Could a plane be flown over the islands to drop some much needed drugs which would be sent out from England? Without hesitation they agreed to do this, and furthermore they accelerated the refitting of their icebreaker, San Martin, so that she would be ready to sail immediately it became possible to force a passage through the ice.

When their aircraft left Rio Gallagos the weather at the Argentine Islands 1,000 miles to the south was fine and clear, but just before it arrived snow began to fall, reducing visibility dangerously. Undeterred by the nearby mountains the pilot made nine separate runs through the murk, successfully delivering numerous parcels to the dropping zone, and returned home safely. It was a very skilful feat.

A few weeks later, with Portwine still getting weaker, the base suddenly heard a plane passing over, and then watched a de Havilland Beaver land on nearby Skua Island – something which had never before been attempted. It was an Argentine Air Force machine from Matienzo Station on the other side of the peninsula, carrying five men and a doctor. They announced that San Martin hoped to reach their northern station, Esperanza, shortly and proposed to take Portwine there to await her arrival.

Bad weather prevented any flying for eleven days and during this time the Argentine doctor gave the patient a number of blood transfusions from appropriately selected members of the base. He also confessed amazement at the standard of nursing which had been maintained.

On the first clear day the plane took off carrying two pilots, the doctor, Portwine, and Dudeney who felt he should stay with him until he was safely delivered to the ship's medical team. Scarcely were they airborne than the pilot had to bank steeply, and in doing so his wing-tip touched an iceberg.

The inevitable crash was not as serious as it might have been, for instead of careering into the rocks, the wildly spinning plane was brought to a standstill by hummocked ice.

No one was injured though the unfortunate patient was badly shocked. He was sledged back to his bed and put on an intravenous drip. Meanwhile Posé, the pilot flying the aircraft, was soaked, shocked and in a state of despair. The senior pilot, Lehan, on being told of this while he himself was wading up to his knees in very cold water remarked philosophically, 'Not worry, not worry – this only his third crash – my seventh – real bush flying – yes'.

Early in September *San Martin* reached the ice edge west of our base and at long last Portwine was lifted out by one of her helicopters. As the 'chopper' came in to land, Posé was directing its descent most efficiently, making all the right hand signals while walking backwards, Suddenly he was enveloped in the cloud of snow thrown up by the rotor, and when this cleared was nowhere to be seen. He had disappeared over an ice cliff and fallen thirty feet, fortunately into a snow drift.

After that the evacuation proceeded as planned, and soon Portwine was safely in the English hospital in Buenos Aires where he underwent two serious operations. After a few days the base was shocked to learn that he had died of peritonitis. It was a particularly sad ending after the tremendous fight his companions had put up to save him.

John Killingbeck was Base Leader at Deception when the hangar was put up. Our original intention, in 1958, had been to build it at Stonington, but that season the ice in Marguerite Bay defeated the relief ships, and the steel work had to be taken back to Stanley for storage. A second attempt the following year was equally unsuccessful, for the same reason, and we then decided that the main air facility must be established where it was annually accessible to ships, so the materials were landed at Deception.

1960/1   Building began in December 1960 and the heavy framework was completed by the end of the season. The flooring and cladding were finished during the 1961/2 season, by which time Ricky Chinn had become Base Leader, and for the first time the two aircraft wintered under cover.

One of the meteorologists, Graham Kyte, often discussed with Chinn his theory that freshwater lay deep in the volcanic ash under their hut, but it was not until the following summer, after Chinn had left to take charge of the Argentine Islands, that serious digging began. At a depth of just over twenty-two feet they reached water, and Kyte's hunch was confirmed.

1962/3   He at once installed an electric pump, which thereafter maintained a constant water supply to the roof tanks. Since volcanic heat in the ground

Whalers' cemetery, Deception Island. (E. D. Stroud)

kept the water temperature constant at 58°F throughout the year, there was no supply problem, even in winter. This was a very great boon, for it was no longer necessary to collect snow or visit the shallow well on the foreshore beyond the old whaling station.

During the early sixties the Deception ghost manifested itself at intervals, not least perhaps because of the fortunate proximity of the old whalers' graveyard. First seen as a white-draped figure, it appeared and disappeared only in the cemetery. Chinn related how, late one night when a visiting Argentine Station Commander was present, he and Bob Bond, the pilot, began swapping ghost stories. Gradually the little group edged even closer round the fire, the developing atmosphere prompting them to seek mutual support.

Suddenly a slow measured tread was clearly heard in the loft above. After a moment's startled pause they all shot out of the room and up the two stairways – but there was no one to be seen. Back they rushed to the dormitory below, but everyone who should have been there was in bed and asleep. They never did discover who did what, but the shaken visitor was very glad to get back to his own station.

On another occasion the Chileans kindly brought over a present of the head of a sheep which they had killed and butchered. Seizing his opportunity the carpenter, Joe Sutherland, removed its eyes, fixed a light inside the skull, and placed it in the meteorological screen with the mouth wide open. Soon success was heralded by a wild scream from the unsuspecting night met. man who, opening the screen was faced with a gruesome sight. It was two weeks before he could be persuaded to undertake night observations again.

1963/4   When I called at Deception in January 1964 in *Shackleton*, we were astonished to see many thousands of birds – cape pigeons, chinstrap penguins, gulls and skuas – congregated along the shore. The attraction proved to be a vast quanitity of krill which had drifted into the bay. The masses were so dense that each wavelet appeared pink as it broke on the beach, where solid strand-lines of krill were left piled up by the receding tide. We wondered if their natural colour had been enhanced through parboiling by the hot volcanic springs along the shore They seemed to drift towards the beach as a semi-cooked meal for the eager multitudes.

uss *East Wind* arrived soon after us, carrying an inspection group of four in accordance with the terms of the Antarctic Treaty. They had investigated the Argentine Islands, now it was Deception's turn to show them round and explain the work being done. Once their official duties had been completed, their visit turned into happy social contacts, only marred when the icebreaker swung at anchor and went aground on the rocky underwater shelf by Kroner Lake. However, the next high tide, and a little manoeuvring, brought her safely off.

Our next scheduled task was the relief of the Argentine Islands, but *en route* we paid an impromptu visit to Gabriel González Videla, the Chilean station at Paradise Harbour. This had been built in the middle of a penguin rookery, which was not conducive to a clean and orderly life style, the stench alone took some getting used to. In addition the men kept chickens, sheep and pigs, all wandering around as they liked – an incongruous scene in the Antarctic environment.

While I took care of the international courtesies, Peter Tilbrook, Garrik Grikurov and Dr (now Professor) George Dunnet, a senior scientist from Aberdeen University on a summer visit, all rushed enthusiastically ashore to collect geological and biological specimens. It transpired that we had arrived at a Chilean Air Force station, with a winter programme confined to surface meteorology and seismology, but two ecologists and two physiologists were spending the summer there, the latter working on the thermal regulation of penguins.

Our voyage continued through the always spectacular Lemaire Channel. It was still filled with pack ice and Captain Turnbull never left the bridge as *Shackleton* slowly ploughed her way deviously through to the Argentine Islands. The relief occupied nearly a week, and in view of the ice situation

Adélie penguins – 'Here we go!' (H. Simpson)

Turnbull chose to return outside the islands, planning to rejoin the normal route by passing between Hovgaard and Petermann Islands.

Not only did sailing in these uncharted waters require great skill, but we found a huge floe many miles wide extending right across our proposed course. This was under considerable pressure from ice banked up behind it by a southerly wind and the set of the tide. Since there was no alternative, Turnbull started trying to cut through about a quarter of a mile of its western end, but the approach to the floe was between rocky islets which allowed only a minimum of manoeuvring space. The operations went well until the moment when the bows gently rode up onto a submerged reef and, very carefully, the Captain had to alter the direction of the cut. The ship then became jammed fast by pressure. ˙

When after an hour this did not ease, to my surprise (for I knew his aversion to using explosives) Turnbull asked what I thought about the idea of blasting her free. We discussed the methods used on TAE to free the *Theron*, which had been beset for thirty-one days, and I suggested a charge of four pounds placed ten feet from the ship's stem at a depth of ten feet. More talking reduced this to fourteen ounces at a distance of eighteen feet and a depth of five feet.

While the preparations for this were being made, all the Fids and most of the crew assembled on deck armed with cameras to watch and record the big bang. It was a cruel anti-climax. As the charge was fired there was a small spurt of ice, a sound like a squib, and not the slightest vibration in the ship. Even Turnbull burst out laughing.

He was convinced, and now ready to agree to a larger charge, but such are the perversities of ice that two minutes later *Shackleton* quietly slid free without any help from us. After that constant persistence gradually won the day, and although later we once more slid gently up a round rock, we reached open water in Lemaire Channel without any damage to the hull.

Next day when we were only eighteen miles from Deception a nasty vibration shook the ship and the main engines were hastily stopped. We were in an unhappy situation, for there was a high wind, a heavy swell, and the ship was surrounded by icebergs. For four-and-a-half hours the engineers worked furiously to overcome the trouble, while Turnbull paced his bridge checking the relative drift of the 'bergs and the vessel.

The problem was diagnosed as excessive clearance on a main shaft bearing, and this could not be properly repaired at sea. Just as the Captain was about to lower a motor boat in the forlorn hope of towing us clear of a dangerously close iceberg, the engines started up. Making slow headway, we gingerly crept into harbour and safety at Deception.

We put ashore Grikurov and Dr 'Sandy' Muir, both destined for Stonington, and Dr Michael Rice who was to winter at Adelaide, to be taken south later in *Biscoe*; for our first priority now was to get to Punta Arenas where *Shackleton* could be repaired. The Chilean ship, *Angamos*, lay in the harbour and Capitán Rotha invited Turnbull and me to lunch. He advised that in our damaged condition we should sail through the Beagle Channel, instead of risking the stormy waters of the open sea. This was to have repercussions.

We sailed that evening and two days later, after an easy passage, we were three miles off Cape Horn, steaming across an oily sea with not a breath of wind to ruffle the surface. Passing northward through the Murray Channel west of Navarino Island, the bare rocky coast gradually became clothed with mosses, grasses and then stunted trees cowering in sheltered hollows. Presently these grew more luxuriously until at about 2,000 feet a tree-line became apparent.

Soon were were entering the Beagle Channel where away across the water we could see Ushuaia, the most southerly city in the world. Above it towered high mountains, the most spectacular of them the pointed spear of Mount Pyramid. Turning west along the Beagle Channel, we passed numerous glaciers stretching down through the trees from the bare rock and snow-covered peaks and ridges above. A few even reached the water where ducks, geese, skuas and terns paddled among the fragments of floating ice drifting with the wind.

Next day *Shackleton* was docked in Punta Arenas, by happy coincidence alongside *Pilato Pardo*. The Navy Yard immediately began repairs, work continuing throughout the twenty-four hours for four days. By now the Chilean authorities in Santiago had learnt of our passage through the Beagle Channel and were demanding an explanation of our presence in territorial waters without permission. This greatly upset the British Consul, Sven Robson, but fortunately Capitán Rotha's advice in Deception was accepted as a reasonable excuse.

Seaworthy once more, we sailed east through the Magellan Straits, and helped by the tide which runs at seven to nine knots in the narrowest stretch, the ship was soon making fifteen knots. Compared with the Beagle, it was an uninteresting scene, with low sandy shores bounding the wide strait, and an occasional flare of burning gas from some distant oil well.

By 10 February we were back at Deception, where three Chilean Air Force officers from Presidente Aguirre Cerda Station were paying a visit. The senior officer explained that he was in charge of Chilean Antarctic communications and, to my surprise, asked if we would accept the collective meteorological observations from the four Chilean stations and transmit them from Stanley to the American Weather Centre at McMurdo Sound. From there they could be passed to the Melbourne Meteorological Centre.

This was an interesting and hopeful development towards mutual cooperation, for even during the IGY no Chilean or Argentine station had been permitted to feed into the British network. Arrangements were made for trial communications to begin.

During the late fifties and early sixties it was annually reported that the Deception hut was deteriorating and would sooner or later have to be replaced. Since the original FIDS building had been burnt down in 1946 one of the old whaler's huts had been occupied. This was large and spacious, but after more than forty years the foundations were sinking and the north wall was showing signs of rotting. In 1965, following the success of the fibreglass and plastic laboratory-cum-living quarters we had put up at Signy, it was decided to build a similar single-storey hut at Deception.

1965/6   At the time 'Twiggy' Walter was the energetic and inventive Base Leader. In the old hut he had already improvised a 250-gallon water tank in the loft by linking five empty oil drums, keeping them from freezing by ducting warm air from the bathroom below. When the new building arrived he found that the plans made no provision for drainage. This was normal practice for Antarctic huts, since any outside piping would quickly freeze in the low temperatures. But Walter realised that the situation at Deception is different – the ground is warmed by volcanic heat.

Therefore, before laying the foundations his men dug trenches six feet through the surface permafrost, in which drain pipes were laid. He planned an unheard of innovation – a flush lavatory. The drains for this led to a twelve-foot deep cesspit which overflowed into a soakaway. The bathroom and kitchen waste pipes led straight into this soakaway.

His ideas were put to the test when the building was completed and occupied in May, and everything worked beautifully. By then a cold-room had also been built to preserve supplies of fresh meat during the relatively warm summer months.

Walter then turned his energies to another project – the ships badly needed proper unloading facilities, and he determined to devise some kind of a landing-stage. At low tide some thirty yards of mud was exposed and to overcome this a jetty made out of scaffold poling had been used onto which stores were unloaded. But every winter this had to be dismantled to avoid its destruction by ice.

The party now set out to make two enormous concrete blocks which would withstand the ice and allow a platform to remain in place throughout the year. While it was in use during the season, supports had to be placed at intervals below the decking, but it was relatively simple to remove these before the winter freeze-up. At the end of the jetty they built a ramp, rather like a draw-bridge, which could be conveniently lowered to the landing barge whatever the tide level. This too was a success, and justifiably proud of their handiwork Walter reported: 'Deception Island Base is now the most comfortable and highly civilised in the Survey, no mean achievement when two years ago it was considered to be the worst posting one could receive.' Little did we think that one year later it would all be destroyed.

Before his tour ended Walter faced an unusual problem. We first heard of Bill Tilman's forty-five-foot cutter *Mischief* on 6 December 1966. Tilman was a well-known climber whose major achievement, in 1936, had been the first ascent of Nanda Devi (25,645 feet) in the Himalayas with Noel Odell.

This remained the highest mountain climbed until Everest was conquered in 1953.

Always independent, it was in keeping with his character that he did not announce his intention of sailing south to go climbing on Smith Island. This was unfortunate, not only because under the terms of the Treaty it is incumbent upon the Foreign Office to report any British expedition leaving for Antarctica, but also because none of the ships or bases could be warned of his possible arrival – much less his possible need for supplies or support. So it came as a complete surprise to hear from Stanley that the Americans had reported that *Mischief* had left Punta Arenas for the South Shetlands.

1966/7 Ten days later she reached Deception, her crew consisting of an Englishman, an Irishman, a German, a Canadian, and an Uruguayan who had replaced the only professional seaman and navigator, David Shaw, when he was lost overboard somewhere south of Las Palmas. Tilman was now the only navigator on board, there was no transmitter in the boat, and they were already short of food, fuel and water.

It quickly transpired that there was a lot of dissent among the polyglot crew, two of whom were seriously talking of jumping ship. This led the wary Walter to refuse them permission to come ashore. Tilman was demanding food and fuel, for which he was reluctant to pay, and when later *Shackleton* arrived to anchor in the bay, relations were understandably strained. Turnbull allowed *Mischief* to secure alongside his ship, but before he sailed again he took the precaution of having her searched from stem to stern to make sure he was not carrying stowaways.

Having been provisioned, Tilman left to visit Livingston Island and then called at South Georgia, from where Denis Coleman, the Administrative Officer, sent the following radio report:

Tuesday night Uruguayan crew member reported drunk and armed with knife creating disturbance on board [*Mischief*]. Took him in charge and put him in cell, searched him but found no weapon . . . Released next morning and on questioning found he was afraid to go [on] to Cape Town because of colour bar. His passport described features as negroid. Other crew members did not want to sail with him and Tilman anxious to get rid of him in South Georgia. Told Tilman I was not prepared to keep Uruguayan. Tilman decided to return to Montevideo.

Then German crew member asked for political asylum as he is afraid of being killed in Montevideo by Nazi agents. Finally Tilman decided to go to Buenos Aires, land the German, then Montevideo and dry-dock the vessel. Tilman tired and glad to call off voyage to Cape Town . . . supplied with oil and paraffin . . . bought food from Albion Star whaling station.

So ended the unhappy story of the first private expedition to visit our stations, demonstrating that even Antarctica is not without its potential political refugees.

At the end of his tour Walter handed over to Phil Myers, whose year in command passed uneventfully until shortly before he was expecting to go home. The first, unrecognised, warnings of trouble to come occurred in April 1967, when a number of minor earth tremors were noticed. In November they began again, increasing in severity throughout the month. Then,

> . . . it was noticed that the seals that usually frequent Whalers Bay had moved away. Also, the sheathbills that are normally present in large numbers were absent. We later learned that many had gone out to the RRS *Shackleton*, and sat under a life boat for two days . . . there were exceptionally low tides, with no corresponding high tides.
>
> On Sunday some of us went over to the Chilean base to say goodbye to the outgoing men who had wintered there. They returned with reassurances from the seismologist, who stated that as long as the tremors continued there was nothing to worry about. He also said that he would come across the following day to explain to us what was happening.
>
> All day on Monday there was a general impression of movement in the ground rather like being in a bus that has its engine just ticking over. From about three o'clock the general movement was greater, punctuated every few minutes by more violent tremors. Crockery on the shelves was rattling with the vibrations.
>
> One school of thought was that, as all Antarctic work was covered by international agreement, and information freely exchanged, London would already have the seismic records from the Chilean station, and if London was not worried, what right had we to be? There was [also] the suggestion, not to be taken seriously, that London was well aware of what was going on, and this was a psychological experiment to see how long it would be before we shouted for help!
>
> Some members of the base now began to make discreet preparations, checking emergency kit, survival packs, etc. We laughingly discussed the best way to avoid falling down a fissure should one open under us. It was first suggested that we should always stand with our feet wide apart. The answer was to wear skis all the time. This idea was improved upon by a suggestion that one ski should be worn the normal way, the other always put down at right-angles. So the discussion went on, amidst nervous laughter and the occasional rumble that came with some of the tremors. Then someone decided we needed cheering up, so they put on Tom Lehrer singing 'We'll all go together when we go'. Funny how that song caught on, before the night was over we were all singing it.
>
> *Base Report*

It was 10.40 GMT on 4 December when a column of black ash and vapour burst upward through the sea ice in Telefon Bay near the Chilean station. Ash from an even closer centre on the land blew 8,000 feet into the air, later reaching 30,000 feet, Nearby the sea began to boil, and the water level rose and fell every two or three minutes while the smell of sulphur filled the air. All the time ash and rocks up to four inches in diameter were falling on the Chilean hut. Within half an hour there was almost total darkness.

It was six minutes before Fids at the British base, some four miles away,

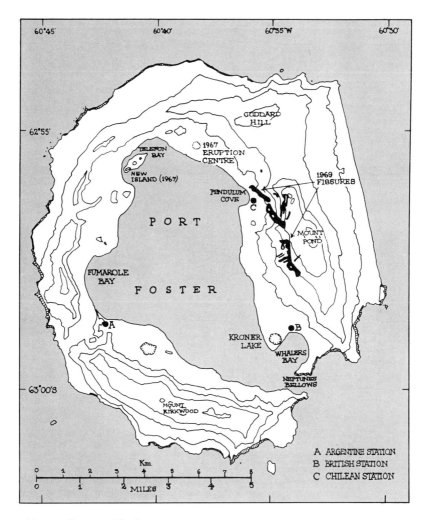

Map 10. Deception Island

noticed the eruption. Suddenly Henry Blakley rushed into the hut announcing that there was 'a funny-looking cloud near the Chilean station – sort of atom-bomb shaped'. By then cups were swinging on their hooks, pans were falling off shelves, and a tractor moved quietly off on its own.

Our first actions were quick and decisive. As a man we ran into the base hut, grabbed our cameras and rushed out again to take pictures. Having done the most important thing, we set about the secondary things like saving our skins – and our films! The Base Commander had already noted the occurrence in the log, and the radio operator was sending out SOS messages in an attempt to contact anyone within range. [These were

Main centre of eruption, Deception Island, 1967. (M. J. Cole)

the messages which had interrupted Ted Clapp when he was monitoring the American rescue flight to Halley Bay to pick up John Brotherhood – see Chapter 10, p. 218–21]

Elsewhere was organised bustle. We changed into our warmest clothing, collected goggles and silk scarves as protection against falling ash, and went out to launch two rowing boats. These were launched firstly with the idea of going to the aid of the Chileans, secondly with a view to saving ourselves should this be necessary. Since the eruption we had tried to contact the Chileans without success.

The boats were filled with the survival packs already prepared, water, sleeping bags and outboard motors. There were also rubber dinghies as we could not all have got into the boats. We had just completed these preparations when the ash started to fall. This was black, and like coarse sand, and fell for some minutes while we took shelter in a small hut. Walking became difficult because the snow was melting from below from the warmth of the ground, and because the ash and hail had fallen on top to a depth of some inches. All the time it was getting darker and darker, even though in summer the night was normally never more than twilight.

When the storm broke we made a dash for the base unit amid continuous thunder and lightning crashing round the hills. There were little flashes of fork lightning in the air at eye level and about three feet in length, looking for all the world like tinsel from a Christmas tree in mid air. About this time I saw a chinstrap penguin stagger from the sea with his 'shirt front' grubby and looking slightly dazed; he was the image of an evening-suited reveller on the morning after the night before.

Two of us climbed the hill behind base to see if they could see anything of the Chilean base, as we were worried about them since the eruption had been in their vicinity . . . later we heard that they were safe and on their way to us on foot, and that the *Piloto Pardo* was going to attempt to rescue us all from our base.

Midnight, and to our relief the twenty-seven Chileans arrived, frightened, weary, poorly dressed and shod, dirty, but still alive. They had good reason to be shocked for we discovered from them that a fissure was coming straight towards their base, and the walls of the cellar in which they had taken refuge were cracking, so they fled just as they were. They had ash in their shoes so tight it was almost impossible to get them off. Ash was down their shirts, in their hair, everywhere it could be. After a wash they were fed and clothed from our kit, and then we all settled down to a sing-song.

Piloto Pardo informed us at about one o'clock that she was coming through Neptune's Bellows, so the Chileans went down to the beach, and we set about tidying up the base. Then the weather changed, hail began to fall, and although there were no waves, the water in the bay was rising and falling up to five feet every minute or two. So the plan was changed and we were told to await daylight when the helicopter from the ship would lift us out. [If the cliffs of Neptune's Bellows had collapsed the ship would have been permanently trapped.] By 8.20 am the first helicopter arrived and then the second. Each took off two Chileans, then two more, time after time, until by 10 o'clock we were all on board ship.
Base Report

By this time four ships were lying off the island. *Piloto Pardo* had been joined by *Shackleton* and the Chilean *Yelcho*. The Argentine *Bahía Aguirre* was also evacuating the men from their station. They had been luckier, for despite being only a few miles from the nearest eruptive centre, the high winds had prevented their buildings from being engulfed by falling ash.

When it was certain that everyone was safe, *Piloto Pardo* and *Shackleton* moved to Discovery Bay, Greenwich Island, where the Fids were transferred. Two days later Turnbull rather daringly took *Shackleton* back to Deception to see whether it was possible to enter the harbour and salvage belongings and equipment. The weather was brighter, and as they approached fresh eruptions could be seen from a great distance. But now the billowing clouds rising into the sky seemed to be mostly steam, although one blast showered the ship with ash when she was still four miles from the island.

The wind blowing from the south was keeping Neptune's Bellows clear of falling debris, and *Shackleton* made a cautious entry, landing ten men at the base.

On shore the ground had frozen again and there were no tremors – the silence was strange. I think it was only now that we realised how much movement there had been in the ground all the time. In the base hut there was a smell of sulphur, and we quickly collected the things we had had the foresight to pack on the night of the eruption.
Base Report

Before leaving Turnbull sailed right into Port Foster, whence it was possible to see exactly where the eruption had occurred. As they watched, two more distant eruptions took place causing ash to rise to 17,000 feet.

So ended an event which might have had much more serious consequences. When it was all over a new island, 200 feet high and over half a mile long, had appeared in Telefon Bay, while nearly two miles to the east lay a deep isolated crater.

At the time we believed that this had been a minor, sporadic event in the life of a quiescent volcano, which was unlikely to be repeated for perhaps the next hundred years. It was therefore with optimism that a party of five reoccupied the base the following summer to complete an extension to the hangar so that it would accommodate larger aircraft.

1968/9   Early in February earth tremors recurred, and this led David Snell, the radio operator, to build a simple seismograph from a weighted boom attached to a barograph pen-recorder. It recorded tremors from the 7th to the 21st, then at half-past-three in the morning, local time, everyone was woken by a strong 'quake.

In a few hours the movements reached their peak, the steel roof of the hangar swung three feet out of line, and a large quantity of water spilled from the tank. The Base Commander, Dick Stocks, decided to evacuate his men, and asked *Shackleton* to pick them up from the South East Point on the outside of the island. *Piloto Pardo*, once again the nearest ship, was also warned of their predicament.

Just before ten o'clock, as they headed towards their rendezvous, a large white eruptive column rose up from Pendulum Cove. The sky darkened, and a deep rumbling heralded a second column to the east. The two merged and an intense electrical storm began, the lightning discharging onto the high points of Mount Pond Ridge.

Snow began to fall while volcanic material rained down, knocking one of the men to the ground and damaging the radio he carried. Sheltering precariously under their rucksacks, they moved to the protection of some rocks as soon as possible, and then down to an old corrugated iron shed in Whalers Bay. In the poor visibility the splash of falling debris made it seem as if the bay was boiling, and birds could be seen flying desperately about seeking shelter.

Ripping sheets of corrugated iron from the walls of the hut, the men

Their home was a shambles. (M. R. Sumner)

carried them over their heads, cautiously making their way along the beach towards base, where they hoped to use the transmitter to report their dire situation. Much of the old whaling station had been carried away by the melt water, which had deposited a vast quantity of ash and large blocks of ice. The shore line had been extended ninety yards to seaward, the jetty had disappeared, and the old whalers' cemetery had vanished.

A hole twenty feet wide had been cut right through the old wooden base hut. Inside was a chaotic scene of mud and ice blocks which had flowed into the rooms and down the passage into the new glass fibre living quarters, where later they were to fuse into a solid frozen mass. The generators were almost buried in debris, while the tractors parked outside had been swept away to sea.

Their home was a shambles, and their earlier decision to evacuate it had saved their lives. Now they collected what food they could and took refuge in the still standing hangar to await rescue. As a guide to their whereabouts they lit a beacon made from rag wicks in a drum of aircraft kerosene. All the time the storm raged on, ash continued to fall, and distant rumbling explosions were heard.

After three hours conditions eased, and with returning visibility *Piloto Pardo's* helicopters once more arrived first and picked them up. This was a courageous effort by the Chilean pilots, who took considerable risks in flying through thick snow and still falling ash. Landing on the deck was extremely difficult as the helicopter domes were completely obscured and there was a thirty-knot wind with a heavy sea.

The eruption was still continuing as the ship left Deception to rendezvous with *Shackleton* at Discovery Bay, Livingston Island. To quote Turnbull, 'The evacuation was a superb example of skilful seamanship and flying, carried out in appalling conditions.' That evening the Chilean Captain commenting with some justification on his successive rescues, was heard to mutter, 'One time – yes. Two time – yes. Three time – by God – not at all'.

Two days later when the eruption had ceased, Turnbull took *Shackleton* back to Deception to enable the men to salvage their belongings from the derelict base. They found that the runway had been destroyed by a six-foot-deep gully cut across it leading into Kroner Lake, which in turn had been breached and was now open to Port Foster. *Shackleton* also steamed round to the abandoned Chilean station, to find that it had been completely burnt out. Only some twisted bits of metal marked the site where it had stood.

In order to study the effect of this second series of eruptions before winter snow covered the evidence, the Royal Society and the Survey immediately sent out two vulcanologists, Peter Baker and Mike Roobol, who reached the island by 10 March. They found that the centres had been far more extensive than had been realised by the parties experiencing the events. A three-mile long chasm up to 600 feet deep had opened along the inner slopes of Mount Pond, and in the bottom of this were numerous craters and fumaroles. Separate craters lay beyond both its northern and southern ends. Volcanic activity had extended over more than seven miles to east and south of the new island which had appeared the previous year.

Clearly we had had a second warning. Deception Island had to be permanently abandoned. Six months after this the Chilean station Arturo Prat on Greenwich Island, and the Soviet station Bellingshausen on King George Island, both reported falls of ash on 13 August 1970. The day before our seismograph at the Argentine Islands had recorded an earthquake, probably in the vicinity of Deception. It seemed clear that a third episode had occurred, and this was later confirmed when an Argentine Air Force plane photographed the island, finding that considerable changes had taken place.

In December a summer party again went back to investigate and discovered seven closely clustered craters near the foot of Goddard Hill, while five new craters had appeared around the new island, half of which had been destroyed. A mile to the southwest a large area was covered by volcanic bombs which appeared to have come from a vent beneath the waters of Port Foster, less than three miles from the Argentine station. So ended an unwelcome natural phenomenon which denied us the use of the finest harbour in all Antarctica.

It also inspired an anonymous young man to the following irreverent thoughts on The Management; by this time the title FIDS had given way to BAS (British Antarctic Survey).

'Now have a good year', said Sir Vivian
As the ship sailed from Southampton quay.
'And always remember the motto,
'Whether on base or at sea'.

> BAS always knows best.
> There's really nothing to fear.
> Confusion may reign on the bases
> But it doesn't affect us back here.

Now the first time that I saw Deception
There was steam rising out of the sand,
But Sir Vivian had told us its history.
It's as safe as our own native land.

> And BAS always knows best,
> There really is nothing to fear.
> But I come from Tristan da Cunha,
> And its meaning is perfectly clear.

It's not very pleasant to look at,
The edge of the crater is round,
There's a ruddy great cloud hanging o'er it
That seems to come out of the ground.

> But BAS always knows best,
> There really is no need for fears.
> It's safe to stay here for the winter,
> It's safe for a thousand more years.

There are earthquakes which wake us for breakfast,
The tremors go on through the day,
But they say that volcanoes are harmless
As long as they grumble away.

> And BAS always knows best,
> There really is nothing to fear.
> But I'm not a bloody seismologist
> And I'm glad that the *Pardo* is near.

When the ash and the boulders start falling,
If things are as bad as it looks,
I'd rather a good air-raid shelter
Than these words from Sir Vivian Fuchs.

> But BAS always knows best,
> Tho' the truth be writ clear on the wall.
> Yet we know we can trust old Sir Vivian,
> *So it can't have erupted at all!*

14

We bring our years to an end
1967–73

... we bring our years to an end,
as it were a tale that is told.
Psalm XC v.9

De Havillands had ceased making Otter aircraft, and we had been unable to replace the machine which had been grounded at Deception, until Gipps' searches finally flushed out a secondhand one from the Norwegian Air Force. We bought this, crated it and sent it south in *Perla Dan,* but it did not arrive until shortly after the first volcanic eruption at Deception, when both the base and the air strip had been abandoned. Consequently the crates were landed at South Georgia, where they perforce remained for the ensuing year. Fortunately, after wintering at Deception, Ayers had flown the Pilatus Porter down to Adelaide before the eruption occurred, so there was at least one plane to support field parties from the southern bases.

1967   Alistair McArthur became Base Commander of Stonington in 1967. A lively man, he soon entered into the spirit of things, and as winter approached he pioneered a modified sauna technique, demonstrating it to his minions as a serious keep-fit exercise. First he sat in a bath, which acolytes made progressively hotter until he resembled a boiled prawn. Then leaping up, he tore naked through the hut in a cloud of steam, and so out into a snowdrift where the temperature was −20°F.

While he was thrashing about shouting encouragement to his stupefied admirers, half of whom were running for cameras, one of them quietly shut and bolted the door of the hut. After ten minutes of complete silence tension had grown and the door was opened, but McArthur was nowhere to be seen. Now thoroughly alarmed, everyone threw on outdoor clothing and began tearing the snowdrift apart before extending the search further afield.

But the Base Commander had the last laugh. He had crept quietly up the snowdrift and onto the roof, then down into the bunk-room where he was comfortably curled up in his sleeping bag.

When McArthur and his party were planning their summer programmes, they did so expecting the arrival of a replacement Otter, but wisely they also prepared alternatives on the basis that only one plane might be available. Even so, when this eventually became a fact, there were necessarily delays in starting some of their projects.

They felt it essential to use the Pilatus Porter first to establish sufficient depots to ensure a safe overland line of retreat late in the season in case air evacuation was impossible. Existing depots on islands along the sea ice route were useful only for as long as the ice remained stable. The critical factor was the possibility that something might happen to the aircraft after parties had been placed in their work areas, but before the pilot had augmented the main stock of dog food held at Fossil Bluff. If that happened, twelve men and eight teams would not be able to get back to base unless the new Otter arrived south before the end of the season, and this was uncertain.

1967/8 The task of augmenting existing depots in Palmer Land, and of putting in at least one new one, was assigned to Dennis Horley who knew the area. He made the necessary dispositions, and piloted by John Ayers, between 20 September and 9 October they restocked or established five depots between Fossil Bluff and Stonington.

This intelligent anticipation of possible difficulties could have been a vital factor in their safety, but in fact no mishaps occurred to the Porter until all field parties had been picked up and flown back to base at the end of January, except for Rod Ledingham and Charles Smith who were to winter at the Bluff.

On 26 February these two, and their dogs, were waiting to be picked up at the junction of the Millet and Meiklejohn Glaciers in Palmer Land, when disaster overtook the aircraft. Coming in for them, Ayers landed safely on a hard surface of three-inch *sastrugi* and embarked his passengers. Taking off again, just as he reached flying speed the port main ski suddenly turned outward and the plane slewed violently to starboard. Struggling with the controls and using partial reverse pitch, he brought it to rest – and everyone sighed with relief, happy that nothing worse had happened to them.

Inspection showed that a weld in the undercarriage had failed, allowing the ski to turn then, as the plane careered sideways, the tail ski had been torn off. Clearly the damage could not be repaired in the field, and Ayers courageously decided to attempt the flight back to Adelaide.

On the existing surface he thought it would be possible to remove the skis and take off on wheels. The main problem would be directional control because of the lost tail ski, and the rudder would only be fully effective at twenty-five to thirty knots. He had therefore to wait for a windspeed of this strength before he could try to get airborne.

When his opportunity came, the ski-less tail lifted clear after travelling only six feet, directional control of the rudder was excellent, and his speed rose rapidly to forty knots. Then a wheel broke through the windcrust, the aircraft tipped onto its nose and fell back with a horrible crunching noise as the tail hit the surface. The pilot was not injured, but all three blades of the propeller were bent, and the distorted fuselage made the rudder controls useless. All they could do was to secure the plane where it stood, and hope to recover the engine, radio and other parts in the following summer.

The three men began a sledge journey of 130 miles to Fossil Bluff. For Ayers this was a new experience, and the ten days it took can hardly have been pleasant when it came to crossing areas of the Sound still flooded with summer melt water. That winter of 1968 the small four-man hut at the Bluff sheltered five, and there were eight extra dogs to look after and feed.

1968/9   McArthur now realised that despite an extensive programme of survey, geology and geophysics planned for the following summer, no aircraft would be available in the early part of the season. It would also be desirable to reach the men isolated at Fossil Bluff as soon as possible, so he planned to start south himself in the early southern spring. He left on 19 September, with Ian Flavell Smith, Lawrence Willey, Shaun Norman and three dog teams. Once past the Terra Firma Islands the party was beset by foul weather, bad surfaces and open tide cracks. High temperatures just around freezing point meant soft snow, melting drift in the high winds, and perpetually wet clothing – surely there is nothing more miserable than a wet polar explorer.

These conditions persisted for the next twelve days, deep soft snow in which the sledges overturned, heavy snowfall reducing visibility to zero, and at one point they found themselves on what they described as 'uphill sea ice'. This turned out to be a large, sloping iceberg with a fifteen-foot drop on the far side.

Nearing Mushroom Island the snow turned to sleet, and it took all four men to pitch each tent in the fifty-knot wind. Every morning they spent two hours digging out tents and sledges, while the constant wet conditions caused them to eat into their fuel supplies to dry their sodden clothing. On they pressed, past the Puffball Islands with snow, wind and drift persisting.

Then they were in an area of pressure ice, where sledges regularly stuck in slush below two or three feet of fresh snow. Each time it needed three men to extract a sledge, sinking up to their waists in sodden snow. On their seventeenth day out they were only ten miles south of the Puffballs among a maze of leads in the sea ice, the largest one forty feet wide and extending out of sight in both directions. While trying to find a way through Willey involuntarily joined the 'Antarctic Swimming Club', falling through a concealed crack.

By now they were concerned about the general state of the ice, for it seemed only to need a strong east wind to blow it – and them – out to sea. They had three full days of fuel left, and it was still ninety miles to the depot just north of Moore Point in George VI Sound. However, it seemed better to go on than to turn back over the broken area they had just crossed. So they cut-in on a Fossil Bluff/Adelaide radio 'sched' and reported their situation, asking the Bluff to send a party north to meet them with supplies.

Resuming their efforts, they finally managed to cross the wide lead on slushy ice three to four inches thick. The dogs were cautiously led over, then stores were relayed across on one sledge which was pulled gently to and fro with ropes. This took one-and-a-half hours while the weather worsened.

Norman and Willey pitched camp, while McArthur and Flavell Smith recrossed the lead to kill a large seal which had appeared – an important addition to their dwindling larder. It was snowing heavily, and blowing at thirty knots from the south. Unable to manhandle the whole seal carcass onto the sledge, they started cutting it in half. While this was going on the sea ice suddenly parted ten feet from where they stood, to form a lead four feet wide. Thoroughly alarmed, they speculated on what might be happening to the ice between them and the camp site half a mile away. Were they going to be cut off?

As they made their way gingerly back, three times the sledge jammed in the pressure, until finally they were unable to move it. Loath to abandon the precious seal, McArthur skied back to camp to get more help, finding to his amazement that the wide lead had now completely closed up, a pressure ridge six feet high marking the spot where it had been. In the end the seal had to be left behind, the men returning to camp without their supper.

All that night the ice heaved and shuddered beneath them, and thoughts of a crack opening under the tents were not conducive to sound sleep. Next day they travelled five miles crossing many leads, some frozen over.

That evening they signalled London, giving essential details of their predicament and asking for any advice I could give from past experience in the same area. Desperately worried though they must have felt, their message ended: 'Feel situation not desperate but could become so . . . all in good spirits'. A quote from their journal for the next day, 7 October, gives some idea of what they were up against:

Shortage of paraffin forcing us to wear wet boots and gloves as now unable to dry them. However, attempts made by putting them beside the Primus in turns, and heat deflected from bottom of the cooking pot does help during the cooking period. Norman led the way to investigate large lead to south. No hope of crossing so we travelled west again. Continued west and north of huge tabular 'berg. Mist came down again and sledges became badly stuck in slush . . . Picketed dogs and McArthur and Willey reconnoitred 'interesting' route over cracks radiating to all points of the compass from the tabular 'berg . . . Started to snow. Dogs attacked a large crabeater

seal which appeared out of a crack, causing dog fights in all teams as they had been on
short rations for some time. Shot seal and cut it in half; each team then brought
forward to feed together on the carcass while the driver cut off selected portions for
us.

After this turned to cross the tide crack and found that it had widened from three to
sixty feet during the last hour. Consequently our route was now cut off except for the
way we had come. Therefore turned eastward along our tracks. More dog problems
when 'Randy Komet' fainted from loss of blood from nose wound received in fight,
and had to be placed on sledge. All sledges again stuck badly in slush so turned north.
Now appeared we had no way off the floe we were on, and in fact made no progress
all day. Snowing heavily with gale force winds, so pitched camp.

Next day they received my reply to their message which read:

Forecast for barrier difficult to assess but it must be under stress from glaciers entering
Sound and movement may be causing fracture of sea ice in your position. In past
years tide cracks have radiated west and northwest from Cape Jeremy. If continuing,
suggest approach Sound from Mica Islands close around Jeremy which seems safest
bet. Cracks may be local but could multiply. Hope you have depot on Mushroom
Island. Perhaps you could climb up on coast for view of area. It sounds that food
shortage will compel your return. The Bluff party cannot expect to make a quick
tractor run towards you and it may be risky if cracks extend.

My message when it left London had also included the comment that so
early in the season it was inconceivable that the warm conditions would
continue, and that they could confidently expect a refreeze. This was
intended as a small boost to their morale and to provide some
encouragement, but the Stanley office, on the advice of the meteorologists,
saw fit to delete this sentence when transmitting, on the grounds that in
London it must be impossible for me to forecast weather. Possibly true from
a scientific viewpoint, but in the Antarctic experience also counts for a lot,
and there had never been a year when high temperatures continued without
cessation from October onwards. I was not very pleased when I discovered
this.

Two days later I sent another message:

Your report indicates little advantage in pressing south, and for safety you should
endeavour to move away from tide cracks soonest to meet Stonington relief party
and return with them. Sounds that 'bergs may be breaking up ice which is being
flooded due to snow burden . . . Doubt that there is danger of ice going out, but take
no risks and return. Reorientation of programmes can be considered when you are in
the clear. Good luck.

By then men and dogs were living on half rations from the food saved
during the previous twelve days. Meanwhile parties from Fossil Bluff and
Stonington were heading towards them. For five days they were forced to

remain in camp, drifting slowly with the ice, but fortunately eastwards – not westwards towards the open sea. On the fifth day the temperature rose to + 3°C, and everything in the tents lay in three inches of water. They had to bring in boxes on which to sleep.

Then the temperature dropped, as I had expected, and a dramatic change in surface conditions at last allowed them to set off north towards the Puffball Islands where, after a further two days, they thankfully met the relief party. Ken Doyle, Derek Postlethwaite and Ian Sykes had made a rapid run from Stonington in only six days. Their return was relatively uneventful, though the final run into base across Neny Fjord took place in winds gusting to seventy knots, with sledges blowing sideways on the bare sea ice.

This episode had been another example of the unexpected conditions which sea ice travel can bring if high temperatures and wind combine to make the most solid-looking ice unstable.

With the return of the ships in October the crated Otter was picked up from South Georgia and landed at Deception, where it was assembled, tested and flown south to Adelaide by Flight Sergeant Mike Green. We also brought into service our first twin-engined aeroplane, a de Havilland Series 200 Twin-Otter, built on the same sturdy lines as its single-engined forerunner. Since it was not practical to ship so large a plane to Deception, Squadron Leader Derek Smith flew it from Toronto down the length of the Americas, and finally across the Drake Passage to Adelaide.

His first task on arrival was to carry eight men and a cargo of rations to Fossil Bluff. He was newly arrived, unacquainted with the terrain, and with no experience of the rapid weather changes which are such a feature of the area. When almost at his destination he received a report that the local conditions there were deteriorating and landing would be hazardous. He decided to return to Adelaide.

By now the plane was flying above a blanket of cloud through which only one or two mountains stood clear. Smith misidentified one of these as Mount Edgell near Cape Jeremy, which led him to believe that he was off course. Since he was not receiving the homing beacon at Adelaide, he adjusted course in relation to the mountains he thought he had recognised.

Time passed and still he flew above impenetrable cloud, until there was only half-an-hour's fuel left. He radioed base saying that he must land to await clearer conditions. Coming down the plane broke cloud at 400 feet and Smith reported crossing a wide chasm in the ice below, but he still thought he was over sea ice on the west side of the peninsula. A few minutes later he landed, but in the poor visibility no features could be seen.

Assessing their resources, they had thirty days' food, but by an oversight there was no stove, and the only fuel was in the aircraft's tanks – which the

302   WE BRING OUR YEARS TO AN END . . .

pilot rightly decreed must be reserved for the flight out. There were only two sleeping bags between nine men. The outlook, while not dangerous, was distinctly bleak and uncomfortable. The party settled down to a routine which included a few hours each in a sleeping bag, cold uncooked food and ice cold water to drink. This they obtained by hanging plastic bags filled with snow inside the plane, where it melted under the sun's radiant warmth through the glass ports.

Meanwhile we were all trying to decide exactly where the plane was. It was three days before the weather cleared sufficiently for Smith to report that he could see mountains to the northwest, perhaps seventy miles away. Meanwhile *Biscoe* and HMS *Endurance* had been alerted, and both were sailing south while taking bearings on Smith's periodical radio transmissions. These indicated a rough position in the vicinity of Joerg Peninsula on the *east* side of the Antarctic Peninsula, and therefore too far for the plane to fly back to Adelaide on the available fuel. They had indeed been lucky not to be over the high mountainous peninsula when descending through the cloud cover.

A search of the records at home revealed that there was an old depot containing food and some fuel at Three Slice Nunatak, some twenty miles from where they had landed. Hearing this Smith used some of his precious fuel to fly there but failed to find the depot, presumably now buried by several years of snow accumulation.

Somehow fuel had to be got to the marooned party, over the intervening 5,000-foot peninsula. To do this with the dog teams would have taken several weeks, so naval helicopters were an obvious answer – but *Endurance* could not penetrate the ice lying to the west of Adelaide. Captain Peter Buchanan agreed to fly both his helicopters to Adelaide and from there to Stonington, whence they would try to cross over the mountains to the east coast.

Such a flight would be hazardous because of the unlikelihood of good weather on both sides of the peninsula at the same time and, anyway, helicopters have their limitations. When heavily loaded their ceiling was barely sufficient to clear the mountains, and their rotors were very liable to ice-up in cold cloud. Four times they took-off from Stonington, and four times were forced to return.

On the thirteenth day after the Twin-Otter had force-landed they at last managed to bring in a load of extra fuel – just as the weather was once more deteriorating. As quickly as men could move it was transferred, Smith took off with all speed, and the three aircraft returned safely to Adelaide. Owing to the determination and skill of the naval pilots, no one was any the worse for their ordeal – just a little thinner, and with memories of cold uncomfortable days sufficient to prevent any future forgetfulness in stocking a plane with emergency supplies.

Twin-Otter re-supplying a field party in Alexander Island. (R. G. B. Renner)

Spartan Glacier, twenty-five miles north of Fossil Bluff, was chosen for heat-mass-water balance studies during the International Hydrological Decade, as one of a chain of stations extending from the Arctic, through the Americas, to the South Pole. The first steps were to make a detailed map of the glacier, to establish a stake pattern for the balance studies, and to obtain an ice-depth profile by radio-echo sounding.

Two years later the first air landing was made by Rowley, with Swithinbank and Martin Pearson as passengers, and carrying a small hut with provisions to maintain wintering parties. After four years, work at the station ceased, as it was found that local conditions made it impracticable to acquire sufficiently accurate information about the long-term behaviour of the glacier. However, it was of interest to discover that it was decreasing in size each year by one-five-hundredth of its mass.

1969/70   Weather in Marguerite Bay was exceptionally good during the 1969/70 season. Shaun Norman, now Base Commander at Stonington, reported clear skies, little snow, and unusually little wind throughout the summer. The result was a very active year during which ten dog teams, two of them from Adelaide, travelled 20,000 miles. Extensive geological and geophysical surveys were made north of Stonington in the Square Bay area, a new route onto the Wordie Ice Shelf and into the interior was established, and

Taking a gravity reading in central Alexander Island. (M. McArthur)

geophysical traverses were extended over Alexander Island and to the southern end of George VI Sound.

In the course of one of these Norman and Mike Burns, both geophysicists, reached Eklund Island, which they climbed on 23 November – just twenty years and two days after Adie and I had reached the top in 1949. We had brought back a message left there by Ronne and Eklund, leaving behind a copy together with our own record. Norman and Burns made it a tradition by substituting their own message for ours, and wondered whether another twenty years would elapse before a fourth group reached the peak.

I made a quick visit to the peninsula area in February, accompanied by Rear-Admiral Sir Edmund Irving who had recently been Hydrographer to the Navy and was now representing the Survey's interests on the Natural Environment Research Council. We sailed from Stanley in *Endurance*, where we found General Sir Gerald Lathbury, Captain Buchanan's personal guest for the season. We soon ran into a heavy swell, the ship rolling steadily through sixty degrees, periodically increasing to forty-five degrees each way. This would not have been so bad if the bunks had not been built athwart ship. The difficulty was to prevent oneself sliding from one end to the other with each roll. Suitably placed kit bags at top and bottom ameliorated the discomfort, but the feeling that one's stomach was alternately trying to join head and feet remained. Peter Buchanan told us that when *Anita Dan* had been refitted as a naval ship to become HMS *Endurance*, the yard had removed the bilge keels, and this was the unhappy consequence. It was with some relief that we entered the quieter waters off the Antarctic Peninsula.

Endurance's first assignment was to establish two Decca Hi-Fix radio stations on Winter Island and Laggard Island. These were to control the hydrographic survey the ship was to carry out. We then called at Palmer Station, where we were surprised to find that the Americans had no boat. The Station Commander, Lieutenant Don McLaughlin, was brought on board by helicopter.

Earlier I had sent him a message asking if he could arrange for a reconnaissance of the air strip and fuel dump we had established on the piedmont above the station the previous season. At the time I had had no idea of the problem I was setting him, for I now learnt that this party were not provided with skis or crampons in case they should break their legs. Similarly, the absence of a boat was designed to prevent an accident through foolhardiness.

With a justifiable sense of satisfaction McLaughlin reported that they had succeeded in finding and flagging a devious route through the crevasse zones, and had found our depot intact. He was a constructional engineer, serving fourteen months of his three years in the US Navy at Palmer Station. Neither he nor any of his men had any previous experience of snow and ice, and had remained confined to the few hundred yards around their station on Bonaparte Point. He told me that it was only when they started out, at our instigation, over the snow slopes towards the airstrip and Palmer was lost to view below, that he 'suddenly realised what the Antarctic was all about'.

I had a lot of time for that young man who, without experience or proper equipment, made a determined and successful effort to overcome what must have seemed to him a difficult and dangerous challenge. He even presented me with a meticulous route map. I thought he would have made a good Fid, which is praise indeed, and would never have asked him to leave his hut had I realised the circumstances.

After his visit we returned to the Argentine Islands in weather so thick that it was impossible to calibrate the ship's Hi-Fix equipment. We therefore spent time on a visit to Gedges Rocks, where tellurometer measurements were taken to aid the survey, landings being made by helicopter during bright intervals.

While all this was going on, a very old Austin motor car was suddenly raised from below and, to our astonishment, swung over the side and neatly landed on an ice floe, where it stood heaving gently as it awaited its final end. It was one way of dumping one's rubbish. Everyone hoped it would drift westward into the path of the *Biscoe*, which was then daily expecting to free herself from the restraining ice near the southern end of Adelaide Island. We imagined the excited discussions as a strange dark object on a distant floe resolved itself into a perfectly good car, and who could the madman be driving south over the heaving pack?

I was keen to get down to the southern bases, and as ice conditions were obviously precluding this, the alternative was to fly; but in our vicinity there was nowhere for a plane to land. It was therefore suggested, and decided, that we should seek a suitably large iceberg which could act as an aircraft carrier. The 'choppers' were sent off, and very soon they landed on one to inspect the surface. It proved ideal – about 1,000 yards long, with a smooth uncrevassed surface on which our small Beaver could land. Its position was radioed to Flight Lieutenant Bert Conchie who was to fly up next morning if good weather persisted.

Conditions were fine and clear, and we heard when Conchie was airborne. I had invited the Admiral and the General to come on the trip, and with good-natured banter we had now been dubbed 'the three Antarctic knights'. Everyone found this very funny and there were ironic cheers as we were helicoptered up onto the chosen iceberg, where we stood in our bright orange survival suits while the 'choppers' flew around waiting for the Beaver's arrival.

Soon we spotted it some distance away, Conchie apparently circling to look for us. We thought he was off course, but it transpired that overnight our 'airfield' had drifted five miles northwest. However, he knew he had arrived when he saw 'three large orange penguins standing on a 'berg'. The 'choppers' took station on either side, hovering with their rotors just below the top to leave him a clear run in, and he made a perfect landing using only a third of the available runway.

Within minutes we were all airborne, flying south in brilliant sunshine past Darbel Bay, Hanusse Fjord, The Gullet and Laubeuf Fjord. It was a magnificent spectacle, and for me the first time I had seen the area since we had sledged from Stonington to The Gullet twenty-one years before. Two hours later we landed on the airstrip above the base at Adelaide. It had to be such a quick visit that there was not time to go down to the hut, but Hesbrook and most of his men had come up to meet us and in a long talk a number of their problems were sorted out.

Conchie then flew us sixty miles on to Stonington, where again we were short of time and had to be content to talk to Tony Bushell and the Fids on the airstrip, where they had come to greet us. It was another useful discussion during which many points were clarified, and I was glad to see everyone in good heart.

By evening we were back at our splendid 'berg, and once more the 'choppers' took us back to *Endurance* while Conchie turned south again. It had been a fruitful, as well as an enjoyable excursion which my guests too had greatly appreciated, and I was later at a loss to understand the concern felt in London in case we came to grief – I suspect more on account of the Beaver than for the three old men who flew in it.

In January 1971 I again went south, this time to visit the stations I missed the previous season. In Stanley on the way out I was invited to stay at Government House by the new Governor, Mr E. G. Lewis, who had arrived just three weeks earlier. Although he had hardly settled in, we had useful discussions about the future running down of the Survey's establishments in Stanley.

I then visited South Georgia and Halley Bay, where it was apparent that the station would again have to be rebuilt in two or three years time. Our visit ended with a quick trip 200 miles further south to the old TAE base Shackleton and the Argentines at Belgrano. Before heading back for a final call at Signy, *Bransfield* sailed into Gould Bay, thus achieving a point further south in the Weddell Sea than any previous ship.

1970–3   Stonington had always been a travelling base, and over the years its members had come to feel themselves something of an élite band in the many miles they covered with their teams. The 20,000 miles travelled in 1969/70 led, in turn, to a competitive enthusiasm in following years, successive Base Commanders reporting very high mileages: Tony Bushell 23,000 in 1970/1, Phil Wainwright 22,376 in 1971/2, Mick Pawley 19,241 in 1972/3, and Steve Wormald 18,446 in 1973/4.

These enormous distances were a measure of their keenness and determination, and during these years a very large amount of valuable work was achieved. But it also became apparent that too much time was being spent trying to travel during winter months, when bad weather and little light reduced the actual work which could be done. This was not only wasteful of expensive sledging rations, but it also resulted in the base installations beginning to deteriorate for lack of proper maintenance.

An autumn journey in 1972 made by Pawley, 'Drummy' Small and Paul Finigan for survey and geological purposes, is an example. They travelled via the plateau to Meridian Glacier in fifty-four days of determined but difficult sledging, and achieved an average of only 4.4 miles per day. They were able to work on only two days. At the end of it their report included the comment, 'it would perhaps be more advisable in the future to concentrate on programmes [in the autumn] in the more immediate vicinity of Stonington, rather than far-flung schemes where a large proportion of the time is spent in travelling to and from the work areas'.

This, and also following reports made by visiting headquarters staff, led me to set a limit of twenty-five miles from base as the maximum distance for field work during the winter of 1973. Rather naturally it was not popular at base. The men felt inhibited, and resentful that their dedication could not be exercised throughout the year. Nevertheless, under the new routine the total distance covered by the sledges was only 795 miles less than in the previous year of unlimited travel. It also transpired that the average mileage on the days travelled had risen from 8.6 to 11.45 per day. So perhaps the spoil-sports at home were right after all.

Since 1971 we had been concerned about the health of the dogs, for an epidemic had persisted which was locally known as 'foot lurk'. This resulted in ulcerated pads, loss of hair on feet and legs, and a pink inflammation of the skin. Although infected dogs were isolated and attempts made to treat them – they recovered after a lapse of one to five months – nothing stopped the spread.

The disease appeared to have originated at Stonington, for it occurred simultaneously at Adelaide and the Argentine Islands, both bases to which Stonington dogs had been transferred. Records showed that all the cases occurred in animals which had been employed in hauling seal carcasses off-loaded from *Biscoe*, and this pointed to a probability that seals were the source of infection. In 1971 thirty-six dogs were affected, and treated unsuccessfully with penicillin, streptomycin and intramycetin.

Later the dog handlers tried tetracycline and potassium permanganate foot baths, but to no avail. They never pin-pointed the cause, but thought it must be either a virus or a bacterium. Mike Holmes, the doctor, suggested it might be a mycobacterium. The trouble persisted throughout 1972, though fewer dogs were affected, the cases were milder and recovery was more rapid.

In 1973 a vet, Bob Bostelman, was recruited to spend a year at Stonington investigating the problem. He had already seen specimens sent home after the first outbreak, and analysis had shown that it was not due to a mycobacterium. At base he worked on a number of infected animals, and was able to distinguish between the cases of genuine 'foot lurk' and a number of other sores of superficially similar appearance. He brought home many more specimens, including some fifty fungi cultured from the dogs' coats and the lesions themselves.

He finally discovered that the epidemic had been caused by a trichophyton, which is a form of ringworm fungus, but since there are no records of fungal infection in seals, they seemed to be an unlikely source, especially as it is unlikely that trichophyton could survive in sea water. He therefore concluded that it had remained in its free-living form in the detrital material revealed by the unusual thaw of 1971. Happily it apparently did not infect man, for none of those who attended the dogs suffered.

Despite all this, 1971 was a productive year, particularly in the area east of the Wordie Ice Shelf, to the north of Fleming Glacier and east of the Eternity Range.

But there were serious problems at Fossil Bluff where four men were wintering. Ian Rose and Martin Pearson were glaciologists, Roger O'Donovan was a general assistant and Richard Walker the tractor mechanic. In June, the depth of winter, O'Donovan developed mild jaundice. Three weeks later he suffered nausea accompanied by severe abdominal pain, and soon he was losing weight.

Dr Holmes, wintering at Stonington, supervised his medical treatment over the radio, but as anxiety increased he invoked opinion from Dr Ashmore, Chief Medical Officer in Stanley, while in London we also obtained consultant advice which was passed to the base by teleprinter. Investigation of the patient's Army records revealed that in 1967 he had suffered from hepatitis in India, which at least suggested that the cause of the present attack could be liver damage suffered at that time.

O'Donovan had three dedicated nurses, but while Walker was riding a sledge down a steep slope he fell off and broke his thigh. Pearson and Rose quickly put up a tent over him where he lay, keeping it warm inside with an aircraft heater while they attempted a radio contact with Stonington, once more in urgent need of Holmes' advice.

At the Bluff the only man with a fair knowledge of first aid was the sick O'Donovan, so they brought him out to the tent where he promptly fainted. Hastily he was moved back into the hut, where he recovered consciousness and then insisted on returning to the tent to help Walker. Having suggested what should be done for the casualty, he collapsed once more.

This time he was carried firmly back to bed, and for the next three days he deteriorated, unable to speak, and they feared that he might lapse into a coma. Now there were only two fit men to look after two seriously ill patients, as well as all the base chores to contend with and radio 'scheds' to be kept.

Meanwhile, out in the tent the unfortunate Walker was still in severe pain.

On Holmes' instructions they fitted a Thomas's splint, but without being able to see him it was virtually impossible for the doctor to diagnose the type of fracture suffered, or indeed its precise position. When the splint seemed only to increase the pain, it was changed to a mid-thigh splint, but this too failed to improve matters, and it was in turn replaced by a full leg plaster.

Neither of the 'nurses' had ever watched this done, and it became a long and painful operation. Walker had by then been gingerly moved back into the hut on a sledge. There the two sick men were nursed with true Fid skill, but it was a very stressful situation for this tiny community.

Holmes continued to preside over the medical treatment, always concerned about the limitations and constraints involved in caring for invalids in what was only a very small advance base with minimal facilities. By the end of what must have been a long month for everyone concerned, he asked that both men be evacuated by air.

It was the end of August and neither of our aircraft were yet in the Antarctic. The Argentines keep their planes south through the winter, and I decided to seek their help in our predicament. Their response was warm and immediate. Their Pilatus Porter was made ready, and one week later it arrived at the Bluff carrying a crew of two and Dr Busso, whose mere presence gave them all confidence. But immediately the weather closed down, and now there were three extra people to sleep and feed, which stretched the facilities of the four-man base to the utmost, producing its own problems.

The murk lasted three days. On the fourth the patients were put into the plane and flown to Adelaide, where they landed just as the weather closed down again, but at least there were better facilities for their comfort. Another three days elapsed before the plane could take off, and then they were flown to the Argentine station on Seymour Island, whence a larger aircraft moved them to hospital in Buenos Aires.

In due time they both made good recoveries, and we were once more greatly indebted to our Argentine friends. Perhaps the two most relieved among us were Pearson and Rose who had borne the brunt of a very anxious and stressful situation.

Holmes certainly had his fill of radio-doctoring. During his first tour at Stonington in 1968 he had supervised treatment and supported the nursing team at the Argentine Islands throughout Portwine's serious illness. Now two year's later he had been faced with the responsibility of advising and sustaining the 'nurses' at the Bluff. But there were still more anxieties to come his way.

He was due to come home, and on 1 December 1971 he flew to Adelaide to await *Biscoe*'s arrival as soon as the ice broke up. In the course of the general interchange of men which goes on throughout the summer season, the ship had come as far south as Anvers Island, where a number of Fids had been put ashore and then flown down to Adelaide. Among them was 'Malky' Macrae who had already served as a tractor mechanic at both Halley Bay and Fossil Bluff, and was now posted to Adelaide.

One week after his arrival he was working with a hacksaw when the blade snapped, a small piece flew off puncturing his right eye and releasing all the fluid from the eyeball, which then collapsed. This time the doctor was physically at hand to treat him and the wound healed steadily. After ten days the eye chamber had refilled with fluid and he began to distinguish movement, a hopeful sign that he would recover his sight. Fortunately it was high summer, with ships and aircraft available, and we brought him home for skilled treatment as quickly as possible. In London he made a good recovery, but thereafter wore a contact lens.

There was a corollary to this, for two years later the indomitable Macrae re-engaged once more. In February 1973 I sailed south with him in *Bransfield* and having relieved Halley Bay we paid a brief visit to my old TAE base Shackleton in order to pick up the radio-beacon we had left there and which was now needed at Halley Bay. As the ship secured, Macrae was in the forefront of those volunteering to go ashore to collect useful material from Shackleton. Soon he was happily driving a motor toboggan and towing a sledge on which sat a number of men. As I watched, it veered from side to side alarmingly, then careered straight under the guys holding up one of the fifty-foot radio masts, a manoeuvre impossible in the space available.

The inevitable collision broke one of the guys, which brought the vehicle to a halt and tipped the men off the sledge in a sprawling heap of arms and legs. But my impatience with this apparently careless bit of driving quickly evaporated as I rushed across only to discover that Macrae had lost control of his toboggan when his precious contact lens was dislodged. He had been desperately trying to ensure that it was not irretrievably lost in the snow.

In London, on 2 October 1972, we received a message saying that John Hudson, sledging with Graham Wright in Palmer Land, some three hundred miles from Stonington, had been taken seriously ill with a form of bowel obstruction and was in great pain. It happened that just three days before this Conchie and his air mechanic, Dave Brown, had arrived in Toronto.

With commendable speed, the two of them left next morning despite the fog which enveloped the airfield. They faced sixty hours of flying before they could hope to reach Adelaide. Flying up to twelve hours each day, Conchie was in Punta Arenas by the 8th, but then bad weather grounded them for three days. When at last they set out on the final and most 'dicey' lap,

Conchie could see from the satellite weather pictures that conditions were still only marginal. So it was not surprising that after flying 800 miles across the Drake Passage, the weather again worsened as they approached the Antarctic Peninsula, and he was forced to divert to Palmer Station.

There they found an Argentine Otter also waiting for suitable flying conditions, on the same mercy mission. The two pilots agreed that only one of the planes needed to head for Adelaide, and that it should be Conchie's. When dawn broke with clearer conditions, the Argentine Series 200 Twin-Otter had insufficient power to take off over the deep soft surface to return to its base. Conchie's Series 300, with greater power, got off successfully and headed south.

Arriving at Adelaide the plane was refuelled in fifty minutes while Conchie and Brown had a meal, and then they were off again on the last leg of their mission. Dr Steve Vallance, who was to replace Hudson, flew with them.

During this time those in the field had not been inactive. All these days Hudson had lain in his tent at the head of the Clifford Glacier. Our early acute anxiety about him had been somewhat ameliorated, but he was still in constant pain and it was getting worse. This had at first been controlled by drugs they carried on the sledge, and when Neil McNaughton and Dave Singleton, who were also working in the area, arrived to help Wright with the nursing, their supplies extended the period during which the patient could be kept moderately comfortable.

Meanwhile Pawley was organising a support party from Fossil Bluff to go to their assistance. The first men to leave were Martin Pearson and Graham Whitworth, driving a Muskeg which towed two Skidoo motor toboggans. Only five miles up the Otter Glacier they encountered crevasses and the tracks of the vehicle dropped into one of them. Extracting themselves with care, they cautiously retreated to the foot of the glacier and camped, to await the arrival of Pawley, Ian Rose and Denis McConnell who had left the Bluff twenty-four hours after them with one Skiddoo. Midway across George VI Sound rising wind and drift had iced up their machine to such an extent that they were forced to stop and make camp in sixty knots.

Next day they joined the tractor party. Leaving the Muskeg in camp the five men pushed on up the Otter Glacier with the three Skidoos roped together. Although the sledges they towed broke through a number of crevasse bridges, they reached the head of the glacier. Leaving Rose and McConnell there to act as a rear safety link, Pawley, Pearson and Whitworth set off in poor visibility, and covered fifty-three miles in the day.

The following morning they spoke by radio to the Hudson camp, and learnt that Wright and McNaughton were coming out to meet them and guide them in. Seven hours later the two groups met and that evening they

Stonington huts, 1973. (BAS)

were all back with Hudson, Pawley's party having covered sixty-two miles in the day.

Apart from bringing yet more drugs to relieve the patient's pain, the new arrivals also eased the lot of those who had been nursing him with true Fid dedication twenty-four hours a day in very primitive conditions. By the time Conchie finally landed beside the little tent standing in a wilderness of snow, Hudson's ordeal had lasted thirteen days, and the last batch of drugs brought in from the Bluff was running out.

By nightfall he was in the relative comfort of a bed at Adelaide, and the next day Conchie flew him north to Rio Gallegos in Argentina. From there an Argentine military plane took him to Buenos Aires where he underwent immediate surgery at the British Hospital. He was found to be suffering from a partial blockage of the bowel, resulting from an appendix operation over a year previously. Happily he made a full recovery.

This episode faced us with a difficult situation, for Hudson's appendectomy had been prophylactic. It was something which we had been encouraging among new recruits (the Australians even insisted on it), for statistics showed that we could expect at least one case of appendicitis every second year among the age group and number of men we employed. In fact there had been three cases in the previous two years.

Now the problem was whether to risk cases of appendicitis, or the less likely, but more serious, possibility of a repetition of poor Hudson's experience. We decided to stop offering advice to recruits, who after all had their own doctors to consult on this matter, and remain content to take the natural risks.

Although the advent of aircraft, tractors and Skidoos had so dramatically opened up the most distant work areas, in 1973 dogs were still being used. Though slower, they were more reliable than mechanised transport, and the teams could operate in places where tractors were impracticable. It therefore still seemed most efficient to combine the old methods with the new, by flying dogs the long distances into the field and picking them up again at the end of the season.

Arguments raged between dog-men and tractor drivers, but no one could deny that huskies inspired more love and entertainment in isolated groups of men than could be matched by machines. Nor were they ever felt to be expendible – men would go to any length to save a dog in trouble.

At the end of that year a party had been in the field for many weeks, during which 'Wig' had got herself pregnant. When a plane bringing in supplies picked up Robin ('Twiggy') Walker who was returning to base, he brought her back with him to have her pups. They were landed on the runway above Stonington, and the passengers then came down the Northeast Glacier on Skidoos, which also hauled sledges. Walker sat on one of these nursing Wig in his lap.

Not far from the hut the group stopped among some crevasses to adjust the loads, and while this was going on Wig wriggled free, pulled her head through her collar, and ran off refusing to be caught. The party moved on slowly, confident that she would follow, and from some distance they watched anxiously as she cautiously crossed the wider crevasses one by one. Just as she seemed to be safely over she vanished.

Rushing back to the rescue they found her wedged fifteen feet down a hole, and in imminent danger of drowning in the melt water which had collected at the bottom. The crevasse was so narrow that a man going down normally would have been unable to reach the dog, so Walker tied a rope around his ankles and was carefully lowered head first.

Twice he stuck on the way down, and when at last he reached her Wig was frenzied – she began biting his hands and arms. He finally got a hold on her, but she was too firmly wedged for him to pull her free. With the rope cutting painfully into his legs, and the blood rushing to his head, they brought him up again quite exhausted and staunched his wounds.

Meanwhile Wig was swallowing water and weakening. None of the other men were small enough to go down and get her out, so everyone frantically shovelled snow into the hole until it formed a sufficiently large mound for her head to rest on clear of the water. Then they lowered the rope, hoping to lasso her round the neck, but Wig seized it between her teeth and nothing would persuade her to let go.

As they cautiously exerted increasing pull on the rope, she gripped it the tighter – and quite suddenly her body came free. Hopefully they continued hauling, every moment expecting her to let go and fall back into the crevasse, but she hung on grimly and soon they had her lying shakily on the surface, wet through, shocked and exhausted. But still no one could remove the rope from her mouth.

They brought her into base on a sledge, and placed her on a blanket to dry out in front of the open fire in the hut. Much cherished by everyone, she got up two hours later and walked about, very subdued but apparently unharmed. Within a few days she was once more her eager self, and they all settled down happily to await her confinement.

But however cherished the dogs, the writing was on the wall for the teams: dog pemmican was becoming more and more expensive, and the time necessarily spent on sealing each season to ensure the winter food supplies was beginning to seem disproportionate. In 1974/5 the dogs were phased out, though a small nucleus is still retained, ready to be built up again if required, and meanwhile providing rewarding companionship for the men serving at the bases where they live.

The 1972/3 season saw the last of my visits to the Antarctic stations. Perhaps it was fitting that I arrived at Stonington in the new *John Biscoe* in February, just twenty-five years after I had landed there from the original wooden *John Biscoe*, making her maiden voyage.

The scene had certainly changed. Our old hut had been purposely burnt down, and its charred remains lay awaiting disposal. The new buildings, a two-storey affair capable of housing up to twenty men, was a vast improvement on the one large room in which we had all slept and lived our lives. My sense of nostalgia was somewhat abated by this change, but the surrounding features still carried one back to the old days.

There stood Roman Four and Mount Nemesis, near at hand the sharp top of Neny Island, and away to the south the dark rocks of Little Thumb rising above Red Rock Ridge. But even these old friends were not the same. Their steep gullies, once filled with permanent ice and snow, were now bare rock. Stonington itself, where once we had skied down to the shore, was almost completely free of snow.

On a rock point to the west the crosses marking our final farewell to John Noël and Tom Allan rose starkly against the fiery midnight sun. To the north the now delapidated American buildings lay at the foot of the slope of Northeast Glacier, up which so many generations of Fids had sledged to 'Sodabread' and so on to the plateau itself. Once a snow slope, it was now a steep icy incline, virtually impassable to dog teams and certainly impossible for tractors. It was narrower, too, for the ice cliff over which McClary had fallen into the sea in 1947 had retreated, and so had the cliffs of Back Bay.

Perhaps it would not be many years before the slope would disappear completely, and Stonington would truly become an island. Even as I looked there was a loud report as a huge mass of ice fell into the bay, frightening five crabeater seals onto the ice floes and hastening a lazily cruising whale on its way.

It was time for us to go too. After saying goodbye to Mick Pawley and his wintering party, *Biscoe* sailed for Adelaide. We did not then know that Stonington's days were numbered, but the end was near and on 23 February 1975 this much loved station of many adventures was finally closed.

15

Isolation

'He went away a boy – he's come back a man', was once said to me by the father of a Fid. It was not just a recognition of his son's capability in practical things but also a tribute to his self-sufficiency and the self-confidence resulting from his experiences.

For many Fids it is the first time they have left Britain, for others the first time away from home. Some families do not immediately understand the urge that drives a young man to such an adventure, nor do they imagine that any purpose will be served. But many see their sons being offered an opportunity which never came their way, and are glad for them. In the end almost all find pride in the spirit which leads their young men to volunteer.

To live for two years isolated from the normal amenities of life seems to be beyond the imagination of most people. They nearly all ask the same questions: 'What did you do during the winter night?' 'Didn't you miss girls?' 'How did you get along together without friction – or didn't you?' Perhaps the easy answer is, 'No problems', but in reality it is not so simple.

Much, of course, depends on the successful selection of men, and more on the ability of those selected to be self-disciplined in their personal relationships. At first everything is new, so much to see and wonder at, everything to learn, it is all exciting. But as the first exhilaration wears off, mundane matters come to the fore. Who is going to do the unpopular tasks? How much time should be devoted to a particular activity? Why has the food become so monotonous? Who will go on the next sledging trip? These questions all lead to discussion, quite apart from the normal arguments which develop spontaneously and sometimes end in quite disproportionate difficulties.

Perhaps for a year or more the same faces appear day after day, individual behaviour becomes predictable, the same discussions lead to no acceptable conclusions. Thus life can become increasingly stressful. All this adds up to a parochial outlook where small matters assume undue importance, whether they be problems and difficulties or happy events.

In general both individuals and the group as a whole tend to react in ways which would be regarded as childish in larger communities, where a degree of sophistication helps to control the expression of spontaneous reaction. Whether or not this release from community control is turned to good or bad account depends largely on each person's recognition and judgement of what is happening in the group. This may be a subconscious reaction due to a man's inherent make-up, or it may depend on the conscious effort to maintain equilibrium both for himself and the community.

An important factor is the nature of the leadership displayed by a Base Commander, who by example and that nebulous quality of 'expectation' can usually set the pattern of behaviour to be followed. The standard he achieves, especially if he is really supported by even a few of his companions, will set the scene for the year. Furthermore, when the relief ship arrives, newcomers are likely to adopt the existing mores, which will then continue to be followed by those remaining for their second year.

Experience shows that in this way a base can remain happy, efficient, and with high morale over a number of years. But conversely, lack of morale and low standards can also be passed on, with increasing unhappiness for those concerned. When this happens there is only one ultimate remedy – to replace all the men at one go, and to send in a new and carefully chosen Base Commander. With completely fresh faces the community is given a chance 'to start again'.

This very rare situation is perhaps the only real disadvantage of the two-year tour, which has been unique to Britain among all the nations working in Antarctica. Its advantages have been our ability to pass on to newcomers the experience and techniques necessary for safe and efficient operations by small groups of isolated men. Furthermore, men usually become more effective in their second year, particularly where field work is carried out from their base.

It also enables us to choose the new Base Commanders from among those who already have experience and have shown their capabilities. The annual appointment of six to eight leaders is difficult enough even when a pool of known men is available. The chances of success can be greatly reduced when leaders have to be picked from untried recruits, and those appointed are then in the much weaker position of finding themselves in charge with less experience than their fellows.

It might be thought that a two-year tour would make recruiting doubly difficult, but this has not been the case. Indeed, on occasion men who have been sent out for one year only have been most reluctant to leave at the end of their time. Some have requested extensions for a second year, and a few have even wanted to remain for a third, perhaps with a change of base. With rare exceptions, for very special reasons, this has been refused because we have thought that too long a separation from normal community life is not in a man's best interests. However, a number have re-engaged after a summer at home.

In this technological age men have to be chosen for the particular skills needed, but even so more than half the marks they are awarded at an interview are for their personal qualities. The most gifted and hard-working scientist in the country would still be turned down if the Selection Board felt dubious about his ability to live successfully with his companions.

How can one know for certain who will be right in a particular group? Some countries have resorted to psychological tests. These may weed out totally unsuitable personalities, but it is doubtful whether they achieve a better overall standard. From an administrative point of view the method is convenient, for such tests can be carried out by people without personal Antarctic experience. However, it is unlikely that they can be made year after year by the same examiners, so the great benefit of experienced selectors is lost.

In the Survey, where the permanent staff not only have practical experience of the environment but remain in their posts for many years, we do it differently. Experience in selection grows with the years because the same interviewers are used. Therefore there is a good chance that the men they choose will have at least some common characteristics. This leads to a greater likelihood that in the field the men will get along more easily as a group.

Once a recruit is accepted, his period of training in Britain, the long voyage south, and his weeks or months in the Antarctic before the ships finally withdraw for the winter, are all a part of his 'proving time'. He is always under experienced scrutiny. If any weakness of purpose shows up, or bad personal relationships develop, experience has taught us, sometimes the hard way, that he must not be allowed to winter. Occasionally men who had created doubts on personality grounds, but whose skills were badly needed, have been left at a base. Nearly always this has been a mistake, leading to varying degrees of difficulty later on.

When such a mistake is made, it affects the work and behaviour of the entire community but the man himself suffers most. Whatever characteristic may first make him a misfit, reaction from his fellows compounds the trouble by extending the friction into other fields – all this resulting in an unhappy and less efficient year for the base.

Sometimes the culprit does not even recognise the origin of his problems, blaming everyone else for his difficulties. He may later even volunteer for a second tour. But re-engagements are reserved only for the successful and he has to be told, often to his great surprise, how, and even why he was found deficient. Too much introspection is bad, but an occasional stock-taking of one's personal relationships can be valuable, often showing that the behaviour of others is a reaction to one's own attitudes, and the recognition of this enables more stable relationships to develop.

Despite every care in selection, in the end it is the quality of a man himself which makes him a success or failure as a Fid. They are all ordinary chaps. We do not seek, or find, supermen. To be acceptable a man must behave naturally, without affectations, he must be helpful to others and capable of self-control, and of course it is essential that he is efficient at his particular job. When after two years at Halley Bay Dick Worsfold returned in 1965, he was asked what he was enjoying most about being back. Without hesitation he replied with a grin, 'The freedom to lose my temper if I happen to feel like it!'

Antarctic bases are some of the few places in the world where democracy truly flourishes. Egalitarian cultures in communist countries, while based on the ideal of equality and equal worth, in fact have differing degrees of living standards, and differing intellectual values insidiously develop. Some nations man their Antarctic stations with scientists who do nothing but science and are served by others who take care of their domestic background. This usually produces a division in the community and an elitist outlook.

I believe that the chief reason why Fids bases have been happy places for most of the time is due to two factors – first that the normally fairly calm British temperament is well suited to a hard, outdoor, adventurous life, and secondly that at our stations every man is truly appreciated for the efficiency he shows in his job regardless of what it is. Everyone shares the chores, some of which are very hard work, the Base Commander washes up with the rest, and the cleverest physicist comes to realise the true value of the diesel mechanic who keeps the generators turning and always ensures that power is available for his scientific equipment.

Sometimes there has been a tendency for newly graduated scientists, especially those who have attained high academic success, to suffer and perhaps exhibit a degree of intellectual arrogance on arrival at base. Dudeney was a very bright young man who came to us with a First Class Honours Degree in Physics, and now freely admits to feeling just such a measure of superiority as he sailed south. All his previous experience had been confined to a narrow field of science, and he felt out of place in a group whose very existence depended more on practical skills than scientific erudition. He found his first three months disappointing, discouraging and unhappy as he slowly came to realise that whereas the base would get on just as well without his presence, he would certainly not be able to live or work without the tradesmen who were the real heart of the station. He learnt to change his priorities and to value human qualities which had previously passed him by. Soon he found he was enjoying himself and began to play a full part in base life. In his second year he was appointed Base Commander, and proved himself one of the best we ever had under the most testing circumstances.

Years later Dudeney told me that he was appalled and frightened when told that he had been chosen to take charge of the base. He could not believe that anyone should think him an appropriate choice. Yet having been offered the appointment he was damned if he was going to refuse the chance. It is not always the scientists who make the best leaders. A very large proportion of our most successful Base Commanders have been drawn from the trades, and the scientists have been well content to work under their leadership.

Small isolated groups are apt to develop a unique and remarkable corporate spirit, founded on each man's confidence in the competence and reliability of his companions. Their interests tend to become entirely concerned with local life, stories and jokes begin to form a local lore impossible for an outsider, even from another base, to understand. Words become invested with meanings never hinted at in the dictionary, others are coined in obscure ways which, if explained, baffle the intruder. For instance 'to degomble' means, at Fossil Bluff anyway, to shake the snow from one's outer clothing.

All this leads to idioms and forms of speech which convey nothing to the newcomer, but it is part of the cement which holds the group together. Another example of community play, at Stonington this time, led to the appearance of the term 'grappler'. This referred to anyone who, forgetting his table manners, endeavoured to acquire for himself the largest or best-looking portion of food. After a time it became a competitive game, but soon an anti-grappler movement began. When the desired object of a grappler was identified he was likely to find himself served with a 'grappler's model'. Mike Fielding, who was particularly fond of hot crusty rolls, was once caught with a giant one containing the sole of an old and very sealy boot, whilst McArthur nearly broke a tooth on a sausage roll wrapped around a length of broom handle.

Such odd developments are not confined to Fids. An interesting variation was reported by Phillip Law, lately Director of the Australian National Antarctic Research Expedition. Arriving at one of their stations in the relief ship, he was astonished to find his tough talking, brawny, hard-swearing men speaking to each other in quaint, gentle English, and behaving with a charming old-world courtesy – which was incongruous to say the least. It transpired that their favourite film, shown almost weekly throughout the winter, had been *Pride and Prejudice*. Once they had memorised the dialogue, it was projected with the sound turned off, the audience chanting the words at the tops of their voices. Gradually Jane Austen permeated all their activities, and what had begun as a derogatory jeering session somehow took over their life style.

Quite often, for reasons usually obscure, one man becomes a butt for everyone, suffering their concerted leg-pulling and practical jokes. If he can withstand this good-humoured persecution, he not only contributes greatly to the general morale, but may himself achieve unusual personal popularity. But should he find it a stress hard to bear, the Base Commander must relieve him from his ordeal by suppressing excessive teasing. An interesting aspect of this situation is the way in which newcomers or visitors to the base are prevented from joining in the baiting. The ranks are closed, and the butt suddenly finds himself being angrily protected by his erstwhile tormentors – outsiders may not share the privilege.

Inevitably there are times when self-control is stretched to the limit, but this is not the moment for a grand gesture. The man who sweeps out of the base slamming the door behind him can feel remarkably small when the cold winds quickly drive him in again. On the other hand, the deliberate action of dressing for the weather and then paying a visit to the dog lines has soothed many a ruffled temper. At Stonington Dalgliesh would warn everyone that he was 'going to have a word with 'Caesar'', and the wise among us would then leave him alone for a bit.

The dogs are always delighted to see a visitor, and their vociferously affectionate welcome can charm away the darkest mood. So therapeutic have they been found, that over the years either individual animals or a small team of 'pensioners' have been sent to end their days at static bases. At Fossil Bluff, normally manned by only four men, 'Rudolph' featured in all the monthly newsletters. The base was equipped to work with tractors, but Rudolph went on all their field journeys, helping to pull the sledge if they were man-hauling, or riding on it when he got tired.

There are subconscious stresses too, invidious and often unrecognised. At Hope Bay Hugh Simpson's eosinophil studies (Chapter 8, p. 173) not only showed up stress during journeys but, more surprisingly, demonstrated that it also occurred in those about to start their week of cooking for the base. As the days went by without too many complaints, the eosinophil level gradually fell, until by Saturday night it was back to normal. In the early days before professional cooks were provided, each man took his turn at this rather daunting task. Even if advice was freely offered, complaints tended to be few, for everyone realised that his turn would come, and it was wise to preserve some immunity from retaliatory comment.

Even at home we are all subject daily to a variety of stresses, but these are largely lost or dissipated in our complex social situations. In small communities the cumulative effects are more apparent in the relatively simpler life style. A man may even surprise himself by his own reactions to quite normal situations, and it is then that an ability to exercise self-control will stand him in good stead. Sometimes he may feel the need to unburden himself, and here the doctor has a special role. He is often the chosen confidant, because the status of his profession places him in a special category apart from the others. The doctor, too, has the special ear of the Base Commander and, with tact, can convey to him problems about which he might otherwise be unaware. Indeed, this can work both ways – the doctor finding himself the catalyst which solves many a problem.

Often small well-integrated groups develop a community defence against outside influences. Any critical comment by the home authority, and deficiency – or seeming deficiency – in supply, even failure to receive official agreement to some local proposal can produce strong reaction. Sometimes this is couched in quite unsuitable terms which would never normally be used. This constitutes 'community temperament', resulting from the parochial inward-looking life being led, and those at home who have triggered it must know how to administer the necessary reproof with understanding.

At the same time, a Base Commander should be able to remain sufficiently detached to make his point or his protest in controlled and courteous language. But it is understandable that he, too, is sometimes carried along by the prevailing attitude, and feels that he would be letting down his men if he was not seen to express himself in the forceful terms being used around him. His position is always vulnerable.

It has been interesting to find that when Fids come home and are questioned about some such problem which arose and caused umbrage, they usually deny that it was of importance. Once more back in normal society their perspective has returned, and they see for themselves that the whole affair had got out of proportion.

Since both individual and community behaviour tend to be conditioned by environmental factors, it is difficult to judge the suitability of a man's character before he ever sets out. Nevertheless, the Survey has had a high rate of success. Even when it has become apparent that we at home have made a mistake in selection, it may be only the man's inability to compete with the exceptional environment which caused his personal failure. On the other hand, one who has been a success and enjoyed his Antarctic life is very unlikely to be a personality misfit at home.

Because those who go south are now chosen for some special expertise, they come from every walk of life and from all over Britain. Often their backgrounds have provided little opportunity to gain experience in practical things such as carpentry, mechanics, boats, needle and cloth, electrical problems and the like. At base this kind of practical capability is invaluable, for one cannot call in the plumber or electrician, there is no one to mend your clothes or your boots, even water will not run from the tap unless the tanks are filled with ice, the fuel dug up and carried in, and the heaters working.

Maintenance is an everyday need in which all must play their part, and it is pleasing to see how quickly the newcomers learn from the experienced.

Sometimes there are tragedies, perhaps injury or death in the field, but more often a family loss at home. Then there is usually nothing that can be done to bring the family together, since Antarctic conditions prevent a return to the world outside for many months of the year. The reaction of families in these sad circumstances has been quite remarkable in its generosity and sacrifice.

There was the father of a boy at Halley Bay who knew he had terminal cancer but did not want his son to be told. When he died, the mother now alone insisted that the boy should not be brought home until the end of his normal tour. We watched this kind of unselfishness many times, and it shows a sensitive understanding of a young man's need to succeed.

On the question of withholding bad news, we always gently insisted that this does more harm than good, for to keep back the truth until a man's return would be a breach of trust. He cannot be cocooned from suffering, and he wants to share in family sorrow when it is happening. He wants to know what happened, how it happened, and when to think of the loved one's funeral taking place, even if he cannot be physically present.

When teleprinters revolutionised our communications, they provided the relief of being able to send and receive messages about private tragedies, and it would be wrong to shield the men from the normal emotional outlets of a shared bereavement. On such occasions the London office and our radio station in Stanley became the family link, and everyone tended to find themselves emotionally involved as the unselfish courage being shown at both ends was revealed.

More complicated and fragile are the relationships between the men and their girls, or between newly married couples. At first agreeing to the departure of their men, all too soon a new wife sometimes makes a *cri de coeur* in the hope of calling her husband back, on occasion even before the ship has reached Montevideo or Stanley. It has shown us that it is unwise to accept married men until the marriage has had time to stabilise and the couple know what they are doing. Though I do not subscribe to the suggestion sometimes put forward that married men should automatically be barred from consideration, we have had problems with wives, and sometimes with the men who have left them behind.

However, the story of Chris Brown is a complete vindication. In 1961 he arrived in the office announcing that he had been an RAF pilot during the war, now he was a doctor, and always he had longed to go south. Grey-haired and in his forties, he had a wife and four children – all eager that he should go, he assured us – and if we would pay a locum to run his practice, he would go for nothing.

On paper he was clearly a non-starter from every angle, but rather dubiously we let him talk, and he was very convincing. Since there is virtually no illness in Antarctica, it is correspondingly difficult to recruit doctors, so we finally appointed him to Halley Bay for one year, which entails being away from home for eighteen months.

Six weeks before departure date an injury required the removal and replacement of his kneecap and we mentally wrote him off. But he assured us that he could manage his own plaster cast, and sure enough the whole family turned up at Southampton to see the ship off. Reporters who covered the annual sailing of our relief vessels were always pressing for 'human interest' stories – here was one indeed. A middle-aged man hobbling on crutches, a charming wife and four excited children rushing around telling them proudly where Daddy was going – the next day's pictures were terrific!

Dr Brown was a splendid Fid. Inevitably he became a father figure at Halley Bay, and provided strong support to the Base Leader. But he had not gone just to sit around in case of accidents; he was determined to travel. They assigned him to accompany Edwin Thornton on a dog-sledging trip to reconnoitre a route through a crevasse zone. Unfortunately Brown fell into a crevasse, damaging his back and one ankle. Thornton picketed the dogs, used the sledge to bridge the chasm, and extricated him very ably, later being awarded the Bronze Medal of the Royal Humane Society for life saving. Brown's particular contribution to the situation was some of the best colour pictures we have of a crevasse seen from the bottom.

In due time we all went back to Southampton to welcome the ship home. There again were our friends the reporters and, of course, Mrs Brown with four exhuberant children only too eager to be interviewed about their father's exploits. Brown himself limped rather self-consciously off the ship still in plaster, and the reporters didn't bother to talk to anyone else. Now he is back practising more sedately. One should be chary of making rules over either marriage or old age.

Obviously the best emotional state of mind in which to go south is to be heart-whole and fancy-free, but a large number of young men do leave behind steady girlfriends or fiancées. This can cause great stress, and an absence of eighteen months or two-and-a-half years with such poor communications has often killed the relationship, resulting in a 'Dear John' message going out to the base.

The recipient may then keep the news to himself and brood, but more often release from the emotional stress comes with sharing it. Bases have developed individual methods of bringing comfort. Such messages are frequently just pinned up on the Notice Board, or even the dartboard, perhaps in mute appeal for support. The response is often both jocular and vociferous, leading to an improvised and rowdy 'celebration' the same evening – which lets off a lot of steam. Next morning the sufferer probably has a very bad headache, but everyone is tolerant and considerate until he has had time to readjust his future plans and face up to the new home situation.

However, even girlfriends are not always complications. I once happened to be alone in the teleprinter-room watching the incoming messages being tapped out, and suddenly found myself 'eavesdropping' on a proposal of marriage from a physicist at the Argentine Islands. Feeling out of place, I went into the General Office where I was promptly introduced to a mother and daughter who, being in London for the day, happened to pay us a visit and hear the latest base news. The girl was very attractive, charmingly vivacious and warmed one's heart. For a moment I wondered whether I ought to let the postal system take its anonymous course, but could not resist suggesting that she went next door and read the news coming in on the teleprinter for herself.

None of us will ever forget her astonished and radiant face when she came out, blushing and embarrassed, but very, very happy. I do not know the odds against her just happening to walk in at the precise moment her proposal was being transmitted, and never again have I played Cupid so dramatically.

In recent years young men have tended to form relationships with the opposite sex at a much earlier age than their fathers did, yet many of them still seek their personal adventures, and wish for experiences outside the mundane daily round which they expect to be their lot in later years. This must produce emotional stresses, and usually leads to problems for the girls too. If she prevents a man from doing something on which he has set his heart it may always stand between them. Yet if he goes there is bound to be some heartbreak, and most of this is faced by the woman left behind. Only the two people concerned can decide what their relationship can stand.

Once happily established at a base, some men fail to make full use of the communications with home that are now available. Many mothers have appealed to us for news of sons when the expected monthly messages have failed to arrive. Assuring them that no news must always be good news, for we would always let them know immediately if anything went wrong, we have then to appeal to the Base Commander to exert pressure on the culprit to keep in touch with his home. This seems to be a measure of a man's total involvement with his new way of life, and represents a temporary withdrawal from his old existence which now seems far away and is but dimly perceived. He has not forgotten his family, but the two life styles are so different that he feels unable in a few words to convey a satisfactory picture of his thoughts and activities. It is difficult for families to accept that it is his busy happiness and absorption in what he is doing which causes the default. At the travelling bases dog drivers have become so totally obsessed with their teams that girlfriends at home have frequently complained that their messages 'are never about me – only about the damned dogs'.

Teleprinters have done much to solve the problem of lack of news. Now, apart from the private personal messages, a general monthly 'newsletter' is transmitted from each base. These are collated and typed at home and circulated to all the families. Written by men in turn, they have developed into delightfully racy and light-hearted accounts of daily events, and go a long way towards answering all the questions parents want to ask.

Some nations have arrangements which enable men to telephone home. It might be thought that this is an excellent way of keeping contact, but there are disadvantages too. When it is possible for trivial home problems to be known at base, the effect on a man unable to do anything about them can be disturbing and depressing. There is also a tendency for him to count on these calls, and to be reluctant to go about his business away from base in case he misses one. It all interferes with the even tenor of his life, for he is looking over his shoulder and reducing his whole-hearted involvement with his environment.

Sometimes such communications are arranged through 'ham' radio enthusiasts, but the British Post Office regulations forbid amateur participation of this sort, and the cost of using their official lines are prohibitively expensive. On the whole this is a good thing for local morale, and in any case the time that would be taken up in handling a large number of private calls could seriously interrupt the flow of scientific and adminstrative messages, even involving the employment of additional radio operators.

The British have always shown themselves remarkably adaptable to isolation. They seem to have the ability to sustain morale without the need for frequent contact with home. This has also shown itself in their group behaviour, for at base it is seldom necessary to issue direct orders. The daily chores and the professionl work schedules are understood and performed as a matter of course, without the need to issue orders – a result of inherent self-discipline.

Some years ago, when we were establishing something of a reputation for happy, efficient bases, the prospective leader of another country's expedition asked to make a summer tour round our stations to find out how we did it. He himself appeared to have all the necessary qualities of leadership and was popular amongst us, but subsequently his own party completely failed to integrate. He ascribed this to their national characteristic of 'individualism', which did not allow them to temper their behaviour in the interests of the community.

It is often suggested that the absence of women, and indeed of sex, must be a very real deprivation, but to most of the men it has little importance. They have to put it behind them and are wholly occupied with the life they are leading. It is unusual for the topic to arise, even in conversation.

Perhaps a major reason is the complete lack of stimulation. At some bases it has from time to time become fashionable to cover the walls with pin-ups. This may enable some to enjoy their fantasies, but often the men do not even want this, perhaps recognising it as inappropriate in a barren world. Should it happen one day that women are included as part of the base complement, problems will certainly arise. To add such stresses, with their consequent jealousies and disputes, to the difficulties of adjustment would surely lead to the breakdown of that sense of unity which is so important to the group.

This does not mean that women could not compete with the environment – they certainly could – but it might be wise for them too to form single-sex communities, where they could form the same bonds as their male counterparts. It is no part of scientific exploration to provide for family life in isolated groups, where modern facilities could only be built-in at the expense of the work for which they exist.

Although Antarctic experience benefits a man in many ways, it is a specialised life which might be thought to have little bearing on his future activities. Yet very few, whatever their speciality, have found it difficult to obtain employment on their return. Of the 489 Fids who served during the sample period 1957–65, the subsequent occupations of sixty-eight per cent of them is known to us. They were widely dispersed both at home and overseas. Universities, technical colleges and scientific institutes absorbed eighty-eight. Seventy-seven went into industry, and forty-six became schoolmasters. Thirty-eight returned to, or entered, the armed services, fifteen went into medical practice, and nineteen joined other expeditions or became instructors in climbing or skiing. The remaining fifty-eight accepted posts in national or local government, thirty-one of them at home, twenty-seven overseas. Clearly Antarctic service is no hindrance to later advancement.

It seems that prospective employers recognise that a man who has the energy and enterprise to volunteer for such a life is likely to have the basic qualities they are looking for. In making such a judgement, they have the added advantage that the original selection for Antarctic work has enhanced the chances that such men will be well adjusted, and energetic in their application to whatever they may do later.

Everyone is born with his own basic characteristics and temperament, but these are modified by his environment, and his own willingness to learn and to adjust to situations. The Antarctic demands these qualities, and though it may be a hard school, it develops self-sufficiency, self-control and a determination to succeed – all useful in the world at large.

I hope I have not made the reader feel that Antarctic life presents one long series of personal problems which anyone might be lucky to survive on an even keel. Far from it. Through the years Fids have shown that they not only survive but even want to go back for more. Difficulties fade and blur. It is the achievements, the joyous days of travel and companionship, the knowledge that one's own small community has withstood nature at her worst, which remains in the mind. How good it is to see a gathering of such men recalling their experiences. They feel that they have qualified in a field which it is given to only a few to know – as indeed they have.

Epilogue

Swans sing before they die – 'twere no bad thing
Did certain persons die before they sing.
Coleridge

I am very conscious that Fids who read this story will find many gaps, and feel that I have done less than justice to *their* party. I can only plead that within the confines of one book it has been impossible to cover the adventures of more than 1,250 men over thirty years, and that I could only build with bricks I was given. The modern insistence on nothing but Christian names, even in official papers and reports, is very friendly but not helpful to the researcher. I regret that many a 'John' or 'Bill' or 'Dave' has disappeared into oblivion because it was impossible to identify which one he was.

On the other hand I am greatly indebted to those who sent me anecdotes or allowed me to see their private journals. Even though it has not been possible to use all the material, reading it helped me enormously in trying to create the unique atmosphere of base life, and many of the episodes ascribed to particular parties are also representative of the kind of experience shared by those whose names have necessarily been left out.

V.E.F.

Appendix 1 :

The purpose is science

It is of no purpose to discuss the use of knowledge. Man wants to know, and when he ceases to do so he is no longer Man.
Nansen

Since the early years of FIDS, when the work could be regarded as little more than a scientific reconnaissance, there has been an increasing degree of sophistication both in the studies and the equipment used. The question is often asked, 'How important is it to carry out much of the work being done in the desolate uninhabited continent of Antarctica? Surely it could be done so much more comfortably and cheaply elsewhere?'.

It must be emphasised that the importance lies only in work which cannot be done equally well in more easily accessible places. The Antarctic continent south of latitude 60°S forms about one-sixteenth of the earth's surface, and if we are ever to understand the interplay of natural forces or the behaviour of life in a global context, this large area cannot be ignored. There both animals and plants are competing with extreme conditions which reveal their limitations and adaptive capabilities. From this much can be learned which is applicable to life in more congenial habitats. Furthermore, the relative simplicity of ecological relationships, where the number of species is few but the number of each is great, make interpretations possible which would be beyond us in more complex communities.

In Antarctica oceanography is also important for it is the cold currents originating there which carry nutrients northwards to nourish life in warmer waters.

In the earth sciences there is much to learn regarding the ancient history of the world, the drifting of continents, climatic change throughout the ages and, more practically, what resources may be available to Man to ameliorate the stress of increasing population.

So far no mineral worth exploiting has yet been discovered but are we to believe that so great a landmass is devoid of useful minerals? We know that huge reserves of coal exist, even if they are of little value today. What of oil? Already drilling for scientific purposes in the Ross Sea has revealed the presence of gas in the continental shelf. At present the terms of the Antarctic Treaty preclude any form of national exploitation, but at least it is wise to discover what is available in case future generations find themselves *in extremis*.

Glaciology is not only concerned with the amount of water locked up as ice, its structure and characteristics, but also with its erosional force and the material included within it.

Study of the foreign material it contains can reveal much regarding volcanic episodes, the arrival on earth of cosmic matter, and Man's contamination of the atmosphere in more recent times.

In the atmospheric sciences each discipline needs to be studied in a global context. Air mass movement between pole and equator governs the climate of the southern hemisphere, indeed together with the Arctic it affects the whole world. To understand our environment, its dangers and potential benefits, we must look beyond the surface of the earth, to outer space where radiation, the solar wind, and the magnetosphere affect the envelope inside which we live.

In geophysics it is necessary to test theory at places where the active forces are especially large or simple. In practice such conditions are more frequent, and more extreme, in the Antarctic than in the Arctic, so the scientific possibilities are very exciting. For some of these studies we need recordings made at conjugate points – that is, from stations placed where the same lines of magnetic force reach the surface in the northern and southern hemispheres. Such studies are especially important in the polar regions.

These are some of the reasons why so many scientists, from many different nations, have wanted to work in the Antarctic – they hope to solve problems which cannot be answered anywhere else.

In the early days of the Survey science was spoken of somewhat glibly, for it formed a convenient front for what was being done for quite different reasons. Indeed much of what was accomplished was achieved *despite* the arguments put forward for promoting science, rather than because of them. The first recruits accepted the situation without demur, for they were drawn largely from the Services, accustomed to using their talents to further the national need without delving too deeply into reasons. They were happy to enter a new field where action and adventure followed naturally the pattern set by the war years, but without its accompanying destruction. Now they had only to battle with nature. Those who were scientifically trained saw, too, an opportunity to take up again the interests that had been abandoned for so long.

So the means to promote an Antarctic expedition were provided by the political climate, the men were available and conditioned by war to volunteer. Only an overall scientific plan was lacking. Despite this much was accomplished in the early days, though it was not until the Scientific Bureau was opened in 1950 that analysis and publication of results began. This concided with a short period of recession in field work, but by 1953 the Survey entered on a new and increasingly active phase, which was given a tremendous fillip by the 1957–8 International Geophysical Year.

By 1956 our bases were in a position to play their part. The normal programmes continued, but meteorological work was adjusted to meet the new international requirements, while observatory geophysics was stepped up at the Argentine Islands and Port Lockroy. In addition the Royal Society established its observatory at Halley Bay. The IGY demand for uniform observing practices in all its disciplines, the setting up of World Data Centres, and the rapid expansion of interest in the results, generated a marked improvement in quality. The Survey soon gained a reputation for exceptionally reliable data, which it has maintained ever since.

When Halley Bay became a FIDS base in 1959, geology and topographical survey were added to its programme. Post-IGY analyses of the data showed that our geophysical observatories were strategically placed for critical tests of theory, especially in auroral studies, ionospherics, and magnetism. In particular, collaboration with the Radio Research Station (now the Appleton Laboratory) led to widespread use of the results by theoreticians in many countries. To a lesser degree this had parallels in other disciplines.

At the end of 1973 it was possible to look back with considerable satisfaction over thirty years of steady improvement, achieved despite political, financial and logistic difficulties. By then under the terms of the Antarctic Treaty (1961), the political considerations had been left in abeyance, and freed from this constraint, the Survey's scientific work continued to expand until it finally became organised in three overlapping groups – life sciences, earth sciences, and atmospheric sciences. What follows represents the status of scientific research in 1973, at the end of the thirty years covered by this book. Since then there have been many further advances under the directorship of Dick Laws. In 1979 certain base names were changed – the South Georgia station officially became 'Grytviken', the Argentine Islands are now known as 'Faraday', and Halley Bay (which no longer has a bay) is 'Halley'. Here I have thought it better to retain the old names by which these stations were known during the period described.

Life sciences

From being something of a poor relation, the life sciences expanded until they occupied equal place with atmospheric physics and earth sciences. Early biological research had been directed mostly to observational studies of penguins and seals, demanding little more equipment than a notebook and pencil, a few Kilner jars and a supply of formalin.

Now the Antarctic biologist may be equipped with a variety of electrical meters, telling him the oxygen concentration or the temperature of his study site, he may use motorised drills to cut through the sea ice to sample the bottom with a kind of underwater vacuum cleaner, or he may go to work dressed in a wet-suit with an aqualung on his back, to roam at will over the bottom of the sea or some inland lake. Back at base he can continue his studies in well-equipped laboratories. Of course the notebook and pencil are still a vital part of his equipment, and the need for patient observations, with meticulous recording, still exists, however sophisticated the methodology.

One of the greatest innovations since the inception of the Survey has been the study of the Antarctic seas. The environment of the maritime Antarctic is dominated by the vast Southern Ocean which encircles the continent. Its clearly defined circulation pattern results in a steady recycling of nutrients, and so induces a great amount of primary production in the form of phyto-plankton – minute plant life. The high production in turn supports a high standing crop of zooplankton dominated by shrimp-like 'krill'. This forms the staple diet of many Antarctic animals, from penguins and the astonishingly abundant crabeater seal (the latter believed to represent about two-thirds of the world's seal 'biomass') to the great baleen whales.

It is not only in the open waters but also on the floor of the sea, in the benthic habitat (bottom living communities), that such a high-standing crop occurs. It is on this particular habitat that marine biologists have been concentrating during the last few years. Shallow water in higher southern latitudes has an almost constant but nearly freezing temperature throughout the year. Species which occur in these areas have developed very specialised adaptations to live successfully in temperatures at which temperate species would be only just alive. The marine biological programme has been aimed at finding out where these compensations occur, for although there may be plenty of food for an animal, it must be active enough to capture sufficient to maintain itself (a relatively high-energy cost at low temperature) as well as to grow and reproduce.

Biologists using wet-suits and aqualungs now dive through the ice to observe at first hand the situation on the sea bed, and use specialised apparatus for sampling particular groups – for example, the vacuum cleaner. These quantitive field techniques are complemented by detailed experiments on specific topics in metabolism, using various forms of respirometers or analytical instruments for the determination of carbon, hydrogen, nitrogen and dissolved oxygen. In special cases radio-isotopes may be used to follow one particular substance through the food chain. Although some of the causes limiting the distribution of marine organisms are superficially obvious (for example, the paucity of inter-tidal organisms as a result of ice scour) many species may be limited by a combination of factors which are only revealed by lengthy research.

In addition to direct ecological studies of the distribution and inter-relationship of animals, it has been possible to study certain specialised physiological adaptations. The unique group of 'bloodless fish' which, as the name implies, lack haemoglobin, has been studied both to see how its metabolic rate compares with that of other Antarctic fish, and to find out why this particular adaptation is so successful.

Birds and seals too form part of the marine ecosystem. Early work covered much of the basic biology of penguins and two species of seal, the elephant and the Weddell, whose breeding was easily observed by shore-based workers. More recently bird studies have been concerned with the position occupied in the ecosystem by closely related species pairs, as revealed by their feeding habits. The ease with which many Antarctic birds can be persuaded to vomit their last meal into a plastic bag has greatly faciliated this line of research.

In the nineteenth century the sealers almost exterminated the southern fur seal, and fifty years ago it was believed that only a few hundred remained. As a result of careful conservation the population has made an astonishing recovery, to almost 200,000 in 1973, and the most recent seal studies have been concentrated on this phenomenal expansion which still continues. As recently as the 1950s they were rarely seen away from some isolated islands off the northwest of South Georgia, now they are relatively abundant and are once more beginning to breed in the South Orkney and South Shetland Islands. The course of this population recovery has been documented, and much information collected, about an animal which many eminent naturalists had thought to be on the way to extinction.

On land the variety of the life is more restricted but no less interesting. Apart from the sheathbill (which, although depending directly or indirectly on the sea for its food, is strictly speaking a land bird) the largest terrestrial animals in the Antarctic proper are two small midges which are about three millimetres long. Even these are relatively rare, and the largest common animals are a springtail and a mite which both measure only about two millimetres in length.

Since 1961 research into these and other organisms has revealed that although all are of small size and respresented by relatively few species, those that do occur are often present in very large numbers. The groups include bacteria, fungi, algae, protozoa, rotifers (wheel animalcules), nematodes, tardigrades (bear animalcules) and arthropods. Having established the species composition within these groups and their ecological distribution, the task now is to discover the inter-relationship within some of the relatively simple communities which exist. Two contrasting moss sites have been set up at Signy in order to undertake this ecosystem approach. The micro-climate of the moss is recorded automatically at hourly intervals, and field samples are taken regularly for laboratory examination. Laboratory facilities are good, and it has been possible to carry out sophisticated studies on some of these difficult groups. For instance, measuring the respiration rate of a mite barely visible to the naked eye calls for delicate handling and complex apparatus, but the information yielded by such experiments is vital if we are to have an understanding of the relations between plants and animals in the moss communities.

Intensive botanical research in the maritime Antarctic and at South Georgia has been going on since the early 1960s. At first this consisted mainly of the collection and recording of vascular flowering plants and cryptograms (mosses, liverworts, lichens), but some general ecological work on the plant communities together with detailed investigations into growth and reproductive behaviour, particularly of mosses, laid a sound basis for the development of more recent studies which have concentrated on functional aspects of individual species and of ecosystems.

Certain groups of species associate to form distinct assemblies wherever a particular combination of environmental conditions exist, and the adaptations, requirements and tolerances of the more important of them are being investigated in detail. Plant communities from South Georgia, the South Orkney and South Shetland Islands, and localities on the west side of the Antarctic Peninsula have been examined, and a classification of the communities for the maritime Antarctic as a whole has been drawn up. Plant records totalling over 30,000 entries have been entered in a data bank.

During the years 1967–71 Survey botanists under Dr Stanley Greene participated in a Bi-Polar Botanical Project, for which comparative studies were made in the Arctic and South Georgia. As part of this work experiments were organised using crop plants as indicators to assess yield potential, growth rates and performance in habitats representative of different communities and varying micro-climate. In this connection it is of interest that the Antarctic lichens and mosses themselves, and the grass *Deschampsia*, can withstand a diurnal temperature range of 50°C. Indeed, within a few hours they can change from frozen immobility to active growth, a capability which is not yet understood.

Deep moss banks, which are a unique feature of some maritime regions, are being investigated at Signy where the base of a bank nearly two metres in depth has been radiocarbon-dated at around 2,000 years. The various phases of peat accumulation and erosion have been studied by examining cores extracted from the frozen banks by an ice corer. At South Georgia extensive deposits occur in bogs, and from the indentification and quantitative assessment of pollen grains and spores the history of the island's flora and vegetation development over the past 10,000 years is beginning to emerge.

There too the long-term effects of increasing numbers of reindeer (introduced in the early part of this century) on different plant communities are being studied by comparing the changes in the vegetation within deer-proof enclosures and in unfenced control sites. Parallel work on the deer themselves is revealing the relationships of a group of large herbivores living in the absence of any natural predator.

Another fruitful field of research is connected with freshwater biology, centred on a series of small lakes at Signy. These are covered with one to two metres of ice for eight to twelve months of the year. The depth and duration of ice cover and the overlying snow determine the amount of solar energy entering the lake, and hence the biological production. In spite of long periods of little or no light, algae and even mosses have colonised the lakes. Extremely small forms of algae form a phytoplankton, and it has been found that these plants are adapted to living under very low light levels. In fact the peak of their activity occurs at the end of winter when the lakes are still covered with thick but snow-free ice. Other algae form a mat over rocks and stones. In the shallows the mat is frozen into the ice and is often subject to ice scour. Nevertheless, in many lakes these algal mats appear to be the most active form of plant life.

Mosses are also adapted to low light levels and thrive on the bottom of the deeper areas of clear lakes. In continental Antarctica aquatic plant life may be much more important in terms of biomass than terrestrial plants. The lakes also contain numerous microscopic forms of animal life, which have to survive long periods when food and oxygen are very scarce. They appear to have adapted either their body chemistry or their life style, or both, to this purpose. Some can only live by wintering in the egg form which is resistant to freezing, desiccation and low oxygen levels. In these, development of the embryo is delayed until stimulated by improved conditions. Other animals can apparently survive by changing their diet from fresh algae in summer to plant debris in winter, and by tolerating very low oxygen levels. All species produce their young at the peak of phytoplankton activity.

All this work is revealing the special adaptations of living things in extreme environmental conditions, but the knowledge is also of value in the global context, for it can be used in evaluating survival and behaviour of other forms in other habitats. The field research is supported by studies in the Survey's own laboratories in the United Kingdom and in those of various university departments. Already considerable contributions have been made towards understanding the Antarctic ecosystem, which is one object of the nations participating in the Scientific Committee for Antarctic Research.

Earth sciences

The earth sciences include a wide range of research topics in geology, solid earth geophysics and glaciology. The fundamental purpose of the geological work is to understand the origin, properties and evolution of the earth and its constituents. In recent years the theory of continental drift has become generally accepted, and the concept of plate tectonics (the movement of sections of the earth's crust relative to one another) provides the mechanism by which the continents have come to lie in their present positions. Perhaps the most important problem of southern hemisphere geology is the history of how the once single landmass of Gondwana broke up into the present continents. Many aspects of the Survey's recent geological and geophysical activities are contributing to an understanding of this, and in particular how Antarctica achieved its present position and climate. As there are mineral-rich areas in the other southern continents, the knowledge of how the Antarctic once fitted into the jig-saw could lead to similar discoveries there.

Work in the early 'seventies was concerned with past and recent volcanism, the use of fossils to relate the rocks with those of other continents, and seaborne geophysical studies of the ocean bottom to reveal the crustal movements associated with continental drift; the latter carried out largely by a group from the University of Birmingham in association with the Survey and the ice patrol ships HMS *Protector* and *Endurance*.

The nature of the terrain has made geomagnetic and gravity studies on land difficult and, at best, laborious to achieve. Yet they are of vital importance for the general interpretation of the region, particularly because so much lies beneath the ocean or is deeply buried in ice. With the advent of airborne magnetometry the situation eased, and in the first year (1973) 5,300 miles of magnetic profiles were recorded, largely over areas inaccessible on the surface. This revealed magnetic trends previously unknown, and it is clear that future work will add greatly to the understanding of the structure.

The volcanic studies are revealing the geochemical evolution of volcanism in relation to crustal movements, and local geothermal mineralization associated with the volcanism. The fossiliferous horizons found in Alexander Island, the South Shetlands and the South Orkneys, as well as the Antarctic Peninsula itself, have provided correlations with rocks of other Antarctic areas and with those of the southern continents. From a practical point of view this work may show relationships with the oil-producing regions of Patagonia; on the other hand, the fossil floras in particular are showing us the pre-glacial climatological history.

All branches of the research are dominated by the ice environment. Three-quarters of the earth's total supply of freshwater is in the form of ice and snow, and of this ninety per cent lies in Antarctica. In order that effective use may be made of the world's water resources, international efforts have been made to determine the heat, ice and water balances, together with variation of glaciers in a wide range of environments. Contributions have been made to this programme by establishing at South Georgia and Alexander Island the only observing stations in the Antarctic. The results obtained reveal differences in the response of polar and temperate glaciers to changes in the heat input. In time it should be possible to assess the state of health of a glacier from the prevailing meteorological conditions. Then, by correlation with climatic trends, we may expect to be able to assess regional glacier behaviour.

Another aspect of the great Antarctic ice sheet is that for many thousands of years it has provided an area of accumulating precipitation from the atmosphere. Since the region is almost free from local contamination, the snow contains chronologically stored identifiable airborne contaminants. Thus it is possible to determine not only the past rate of precipitation but also the amount and age of terrestrial and extra-terrestrial material it contains. Studies of such impurities are revealing past levels of these pollutants.

This knowledge is of increasing importance in view of man's expanding industrial contamination of the global atmosphere. The Survey has established base line levels of organochlorines (DDT, etc) in the snow, and similar methods can be applied to other organic pollutants which attain global significance in future. Similarly, heavy metal contaminants of the atmosphere can be assessed, and it is planned to compare present levels with those of the pre-Industrial Revolution period by obtaining deep ice cores.

Experimental radio-echo sounding of the ice depth was begun in 1963. Later, by fitting the equipment into aircraft, it was possible to obtain photographic records of the ice surface and the ice/rock interface over many thousands of miles. It follows that whereas in the past geological work was confined to areas of exposed rock, it is now becoming possible to extend it to areas covered by ice. The sounding is not only important in determining the thickness and volume of ice, but in correcting gravity and magnetometer measurements used to determine the sub-glacial geology and topography.

Atmospheric sciences
Today field work in the atmospheric sciences is concentrated at Halley Bay (Halley), the Argentine Islands (Faraday) and South Georgia (Grytviken), while at home there is a support capability for the Survey as a whole which consists of computing and data handling, together with advisory services. The field work produces synoptic observations in meteorology, magnetism, ozone, radiation and ionospherics. Seismological measurements are also made at the two main geophysical observatories. Although strictly belonging to the earth sciences, this work is handled by the Atmospheric Sciences Division.

The different aspects of meteorology, surface observations, upper air, ozone and radiation, vary in importance and application. Surface meteorology has been carried out since the earliest days, and mainly provides for studies of climatic change which is one of particular interest to glaciologists and biologists. It also assists in short-term weather forecasting for ships and aircraft during the summer season.

Upper air measurements have been made at Halley Bay and the Argentine Islands since the beginning of the IGY. Their main value has been to southern hemisphere meteorology, especially as the wide ocean areas increase the importance of land stations. It is also true that these observations apply directly to other projects, increasing their value. They can be combined with ozone data to evaluate upper air movement, with radiation data to show the influence of cloud temperature on radiation in overcast conditions, and to show the relations between cloud and surface temperatures needed to interpret the $^{16}o/^{18}o$ ratio method of measuring mean surface temperature in snow. They are also valuable for studying anomalous winter changes in the ionosphere associated with stratospheric phenomena.

The ozone measurements at Halley Bay and the Argentine Islands, again since the IGY, have assumed a new importance. This is because atmospheric pollution could possibly reduce the ozone in the upper atmosphere, allowing a dangerous amount of radiation to penetrate to the surface. Ozone can also be used as a tracer to determine atmospheric circulation. In both cases Antarctic observations have a particular importance since the continual production of ozone during the long summer day contrasts with the equally long night when little or none is produced and dispersal by air mass movement is to be expected.

The general purpose of radiation measurements is to establish the local direct heat impact and its long-term variations associated with climatic change. In the Antarctic these have special applications in relation to the albedo of snow-covered ground and cloud cover. Radiation also has special interest as a measure of stratospheric pollution, and therefore atmospheric circulation, besides providing information for certain aspects of biology and glaciology. It seems that the Survey's control of the observations has been at least as effective as that at the international standard laboratories, in some cases perhaps more effective.

In the absence of local pollution, turbidity in Antarctica is a useful monitor of world-wide pollution of the stratosphere. Therefore radiation recordings which directly measure the presence of aerosols and volcanic dust are particularly valuable – major eruptions are readily detectable. Furthermore, they help to interpret the upper parts of the ozone circulation.

In the field of geomagnetism the absolute magnetic observations provide material for studying the long-term changes in the earth's magnetic field in a region where few observations are available, and a check on the continuous observations which give data for linked ionospheric magnetosphere and auroral studies. The high quality and ready availability of these records has resulted in the Argentine Islands and South Georgia being adopted internationally to cooperate in the circumpolar chain of seven stations which together establish the main magnetic activity index *Ks* for the southern hemisphere. Owing to the large difference in magnetic activity in the two hemispheres, and serious universal time distortion of the planetary index *Kp* due to most of the reference stations being in the north, the importance of *Ks*, *Kn* and *Km* is rapidly increasing. One difficulty in producing these indices is that they involve insight into the behaviour of quiet magnetic day variations which is important when choosing very quiet days. As the Argentine Islands and Halley Bay records since the IGY have been evaluated from this point of view, they form reference sets for the whole southern hemisphere. Since these stations lie in the zone where geographic and magnetic latitudes show maximum differences, the observations are particularly valuable, especially in separating the effects of dynamo and magnetospheric current systems.

Medical research

The major medical interest has been to study the effect on man of the polar environment, the low temperature, the pattern of light and darkness, and the isolation. From the research point of view the advantage of working in the Antarctic is that many 'subjects' are available for two years, at bases isolated for the greater part of each year. Apart from examining the effects of the environment on man, it is possible to exploit the opportunities by planning experiments which do not depend on weather, but would be extremely difficult to carry out in this country.

One example of such study was mounted at Halley Bay to test the effect of replacing all the sucrose in the diet with glucose. Previous work in the United Kingdom had shown that in short-term studies such replacement altered the metabolism of the body, not only of carbohydrates but also of fats, and hence might be of importance in considering dietary effects on coronary heart disease. The long-term study at Halley Bay showed that the metabolic changes observed in this country did not persist, and made it necessary to revise the conclusions previously reached.

Nutritional studies have been prominent. The first question asked was, 'How much food does a man require in this unusual environment?' – a simple question which has proved difficult to answer because there is great variation between individuals, and in any one individual in the course of the year. Since energy intake should balance energy output, there have been studies of the energy cost of Antarctic life. These led to a detailed investigation, also carried out at Halley Bay, of the various techniques for measuring intake and expenditure of energy in man. Again, this was an example of using the Antarctic for work which could not have been done in this country, because of the almost insuperable difficulty of recording and measuring events in an individual throughout a year.

Recently other topics have become of interest, particularly microbiology and the study of virus infections. It has been observed for a long time that after the last ship leaves a base, there are no cases of coughs and colds, or rather that these gradually cease during the two weeks following her departure. There is then freedom from upper respiratory tract infection until a relief ship arrives from seven to eleven months later, when the coughs and colds usually start again. Dr David Tyrell, Deputy Director of the Clinical Research Centre, has organised research on this aspect of the common cold, and a number of Survey doctors have done valuable work testing the degree of resistance or immunity amongst members of bases during the Antarctic winter.

An activity which has intrigued medical officers is Antarctic diving, and the very low temperatures to which divers are exposed. The results of this cold tolerance work could be relevant to the problems facing divers in other parts of the world, notably the exploration of North Sea oil fields.

The light/dark pattern in the Antarctic, with the long winter nights and the long summer day, has often been considered to affect men's behaviour, and in particular there have been frequent complaints about the difficulty of regular sleep. Recently an American sleep laboratory was set up at the South Pole, which led to the surprising discovery that electrical changes in the brain associated with deep sleep became progressively less during the time spent there. Furthermore, these alterations in the electroencephalogram persisted on return to the United States. A study was made at Halley Bay which partly confirms the findings at the South Pole – only partly because the changes are less and they do not persist. Further studies are needed at other latitudes on the continent.

It is evident that medical research in the Antarctic is fully justified, and has even greater future possibilities.

From this necessarily brief review of scientific activities we see that the Survey's work has come a very long way since 1944. From being a politico-military expedition, with tentative uncoordinated essays in science, it has become a properly established organisation dedicated to science alone. The broad sweep of reconnaissance work has been replaced by innumerable detailed studies in many fields. The results not only improve our knowledge of Antarctica, but contribute directly to the solution of some world-wide problems.

Through the Antarctic Treaty the continent has become an international laboratory. If exploitation of its natural resources is ever permitted, it is to be hoped that the controls the Treaty has established will prevent man's usual despoliation, and allow it to remain relatively untainted by his presence.

Since the end of this story in 1973, the work of the Survey has gone from strength to strength and its members now participate in the many international scientific projects concerned with the far south. The old stations at the Argentine Islands, Halley Bay, Signy and South Georgia are still occupied, but Adelaide was closed due to crevassing on the runway. It has been replaced by Rothera, on the southeast side of the island. *Biscoe* has been re-engined and adapted for marine research, while *Bransfield* continues to be the main supply vessel.

In 1976 the administration and the science divisions were brought together in new buildings at Cambridge. With the Scott Polar Research Institute already established there, the city has become the main centre for polar research in Britain.

Those wishing for up-to-date information on the Survey's activities or the scientific programmes should consult the *Annual Reports* published by the Natural Environment Research Council, the *BAS Scientific Reports* which appear as programmes are completed, or the *BAS Bulletin* which is published about four times a year.

Appendix 2: List of stations occupied

A	Port Lockroy	64°49′S, 63°31′W	11.2.44–8.4.47 23.1.48–14.2.49 24.1.50–11.2.51 15.12.51–16.1.62
B	Deception Island	62°59′S, 60°34′W	3.2.44–5.12.67 4.12.68–23.2.69
C	Cape Geddes	60°41′S, 44°34′W	18.1.46–17.3.47
D	Hope Bay	63°24′S, 56°59′W	10.2.45–4.2.49 4.2.52–13.2.64
E	Stonington Island	68°11′S, 67°00′W	24.2.46–12.2.50 9.3.58–7.3.59 14.8.60–23.2.75
F	Argentine Islands	65°15′S, 64°16′W	7.1.47 onwards (new site 5.2.54)
G	Admiralty Bay	62°05′S, 58°25′W	25.1.47–23.3.47 18.11.48–19.1.61
H	Signy Island	60°43′S, 45°36′W	18.3.47 onwards
J	Prospect Point	66°00′S, 65°21′W	1.2.57–23.2.59
KG	Fossil Bluff	71°20′S, 68°17′W	20.2.61 Occupied intermittently including 10 winters
M	King Edward Point Grytviken	57°17′S, 36°30′W	1.1.50–1.1.52 13.11.69 onwards
N	Anvers Island	54°46′S, 64°05′W	27.2.55–10.1.58
O	Danco Island	64°44′S, 62°36′W	26.2.56–22.2.59
T	Adelaide Island	67°46′S, 68°55′W	2.2.61–1.3.77
V	View Point	63°32′S, 57°23′W	8.2.53–25.11.63
W	Detaille Island	66°52′S, 66°48′W	21.2.56–1.4.59
Y	Horseshoe Island	67°49′S, 67°18′W	11.3.55–21.8.60
Z	Halley Bay (position has varied with ice movement and rebuilding)	75°31′S, 26°37′W	6.1.56 onwards

Glossary

Antarctic Circle: latitude 66°30′S where, for one 24-hour period each year, the sun remains above the horizon in summer and is totally obscured in winter. Further south these times increase until, at the South Pole, there are six months of continuous daylight in summer and six months of total darkness in winter.

Bergy bit: a floating piece of ice, generally less than 15 feet above sea level and not more than 30 feet across.

Beset: situation of a vessel surrounded by ice and unable to move.

Brash ice: small fragments of broken ice not larger than 6 feet across – the wreckage of other forms of ice.

Cow-catcher: curved fender at the front of a Nansen sledge extending from one side to the other.

Crevasse: fissure formed in a glacier; they are often hidden by snow bridges.

Fast ice: sea ice which remains attached to the coast.

Floe: a piece of floating ice other than fast ice or glacier ice.

Ice cap: an extensive dome-shaped area of ice, usually covering a highland region – considerably smaller than an ice sheet.

Ice piedmont: ice covering a coastal strip of low-lying land backed by mountains.

Ice sheet: a mass of ice and snow of great thickness, and generally greater than 20,000 square miles.

Ice shelf: a floating sheet of ice of considerable thickness attached to the coast; usually of great horizontal extent, having a level or gently undulating surface.

Leads: navigable passages through floating ice.

Man-hauling: hauling a sledge by means of a harness.

Nunatak: rocky crag or small mountain surrounded by a glacier or ice sheet.

Pack ice: any area of sea ice other than fast ice.

Sastrugi: fluted ridges carved by wind on a snow surface. These may be from a few inches to 5 feet high and lie parallel to the prevailing wind.

Snow bridge: a covering formed by drifting snow which may completely obscure a crevasse.

Water sky: dark patches on the underside of clouds which denote the presence of open water or broad leads in the floating ice.

Whiteout: an atmospheric condition in which daylight is diffused by multiple reflection between a snow surface and an overcast sky. Contrasts vanish, there are no shadows, and it becomes impossible to distinguish the horizon or any snow-surface feature, though dark objects can be seen even over long distances.

Nominal Roll of Wintering Personnel

In compiling the following nominal roll certain descriptive difficulties have arisen through changes of nomenclature applied to the various categories. In the early days there were 'wireless operator/mechanics', in later years 'radio operators'; 'carpenters' or 'handymen' became 'General Assistants'. The latter designation was originally a blanket term for men who had no specific tasks of their own, but who might drive dogs or tractors, help put up buildings, or do anything else required at base. Later many General Assistants with special practical skills such as mountaineering experience or qualified divers were recruited. They were then designated as 'GA (mountaineer)' or 'GA (diver)' as appropriate. After 1966 Base Leaders were designated Base Commanders.

Similarly there were qualified scientists, Assistant Scientific Officers and Scientific Experimental Officers, senior meteorologists, observers, and meteorological assistants, qualified surveyors and assistant surveyors. In the following list all these categories are more simply shown under blanket headings which indicate their special tasks at base or in the field.

During OPERATION TABARIN each station had a cook, usually a naval rating, but from 1947 onwards this duty was shared equally, usually for a week at a time, by all base members. After 1959 professional cooks were gradually re-introduced, first only at the larger bases, but they also played a full part in many other activities in a community where everyone was expected to share all the base chores – making and mending, cutting ice blocks for water, digging up fuel drums, dog feeding etc. There were no 'servants' – truly a case of 'All for one and one for all'.

No decorations are listed, though many were held by those who served during and immediately after the war. Polar Medals are also omitted, but it may be of interest that 168 were awarded during the thirty years of this story.

ABBREVIATIONS USED

Comdr FIDS	Overall Commander FIDS
BL	Base Leader
BC	Base Commander
OIC	Officer-in-Charge
Bacterio	Bacteriology
Bio Asst	Biological Assistant
Bot	Botany
Bldr	Builder
Cptr	Carpenter
DEM	Diesel Electric Mechanic
Elect	Electrician
F.Ops	Field Operations
GA	General Assistant
Geol	Geology
Geophys	Geophysics
Geophys (fld)	Field Geophysics
Glacio	Glaciology
Iono	Ionospherics
Mech	Mechanic
MO	Medical Officer
Met	Meteorology
Mntr	mountaineer
Physio	Physiology
Radio Op	Radio Operator
Surv	Survey
Tech	Technician
WOM	Wireless Operator/Mechanic
Zool	Zoology

OPERATION TABARIN

1944

Deception Island
W. R. Flett *BL, Geol*
Sub-Lt G. A. Howkins RNVR *Met*
N. F. Layther *WOM*
J. Matheson *Handyman*
C. Smith *Cook*

Port Lockroy
Lt Comdr J. W. S. Marr RNVR **Comdr FIDS**, *Zool*
L. Ashton *Cptr*
Surg Lt E. H. Back RNVR *MO, Met*
A. T. Berry *Stores*
J. Blyth *Cook*
G. Davies *Handyman*
J. E. B. F. Farrington *WOM*
I. Mackenzie Lamb *Bot*
Capt A. Taylor RCE *Surv*

1945

Deception Island
Sub-Lt A. W. Reece RNVR *BL, Met*
S. Bonner *Handyman*
J. E. B. F. Farrington *WOM*
C. Smith *Cook*

Hope Bay
Capt A. Taylor RCE **Comdr FIDS**, *Surv*
L. Ashton *Cptr*
Surg Lt E. H. Back RNVR *MO, Met*
A. T. Berry *Stores*
J. Blyth *Cook*
G. Davies *Handyman*
T. Donnachie *WOM*
W. R. Flett *Geol*
Lt D. P. James RNVR *Surv*
I. Mackenzie Lamb *Bot*
Capt. N. B. Marshall REME *Zool*
J. Matheson *Handyman*
Capt V. I. Russell RE *Surv*

Port Lockroy
Sub-Lt G. J. Lockley RNVR *BL, Met, Zool*
J. K. Biggs *Handyman*
N. F. Layther *WOM*
F. White *Cook*

FALKLAND ISLANDS DEPENDENCIES SURVEY

1946

Cape Geddes
Lt M. A. Choyce RNVR *BL, Met*
E. T. Cummings *WOM*
D. Nicholson *Handyman*
W. Watson *Handyman*

Deception Island
Sub-Lt J. P. Featherstone RNVR *BL, Met*
D. R. Crutchley *WOM*
S. Newman *Cook*
B. Reive *Handyman*

Hope Bay
Capt V. I. Russell RE *BL, Surv*
J. D. Andrew *MO*
Capt W. N. Croft RE *Geol*
Lt S. J. Francis RE *Surv*
Sub-Lt T. P. O'Sullivan RNVR *Met*
Sub-Lt A. W. Reece RNVR *Met*
Lt S. H. Small RCS *WOM*
W. R. Wallin *Handyman*

Port Lockroy
Lt G. F. M. Hardy RNVR *BL, Met*
K. A. McLeod *Handyman*
G. D. Stock *WOM*
F. White *Cook*

Stonington Island
Surg Comdr E. W. Bingham RN **Comdr FIDS**
Major K. S. Pierce-Butler RCS *WOM*
Lt R. L. Freeman RE *Surv*
Capt J. R. F. Joyce RE *Geol*
Capt D. P. Mason RE *Surv*
Major W. M. Sadler SAS *GA (F.Ops)*
Lt W. de C. Salter RNVR *Met*
Surg Lt R. S. Slessor RNVR *MO*
Major J. E. Tonkin SAS *GA (F.Ops)*
Lt (E) E. W. K. Walton RN *GA (F.Ops)*

1947

Argentine Islands
O. R. Burd *BL, Met*
B. Reive *Handyman*
G. D. Stock *WOM*
W. Watson *Handyman*

Deception Island
Lt J. S. R. Huckle RNVR *BL*
F. J. Buse *Handyman*
E. T. Cummings *WOM*
J. R. Ewer *Met*
A. B. Massey *Met*

Hope Bay
F. K. Elliott *BL*
R. J. Adie *Geol*
Lt M. A. Choyce RNVR *Met*

Lt S. J. Francis RE *Surv*
D. Nicholson *Handyman*
J. M. Roberts *MO*
Lt S. H. Small RCS *WOM*
J. T. Smith *Handyman*
W. R. Wallin *Handyman*

Signy Island
G. de Q. Robin *BL, Met*
J. H. Anderson *Handyman*
P. E. Biggs *Handyman*
W. H. Roberts *WOM*

Stonington Island
Major K. S. Pierce-Butler RCS **Comdr FIDS**
A. R. C. Butson *MO*
Lt R. L. Freeman RE *Surv*
F/Sgt H. D. Jones *Air Fitter*
Capt D. P. Mason RE *Surv*
K. A. McLeod *Handyman*
T. M. Randall *WOM*
B. Stonehouse *Met*
Lt W. H. Thomson RNVR *Pilot*
Major J. E. Tonkin SAS *GA (F.Ops)*
Lt (E) E. W. K. Walton RN *GA (F.Ops)*

1948

Admiralty Bay
E. Platt *BL, Geol*
I. J. Biggs *Handyman*
G. E. Davis *Handyman*
D. G. Farmer *Radio Op*
J. D. Reid *Met*

Argentine Islands
T. M. Nicholl *BL*
F. J. Buse *Handyman*
G. D. Golton *Met*
W. G. Thomas *Radio Op*

Deception Island
A. G. Scadding *BL, Met*
P. E. Biggs *Handyman*
E. C. Gutteridge *GA (met)*
J. W. Knox *Radio Op*

Hope Bay
F. K. Elliott *BL*
O. R. Burd *Met*
M. C. Green *Geol*
B. Jefford *Surv*
S. St C. McNeile *Surv*
J. L. O'Hare *Radio Op*
W. J. L. Sladen *MO*

Port Lockroy
G. P. J. Barry *BL, Radio Op*
J. Blyth *Handyman*
K. Pawson *Met*
W. G. Richards *Handyman*

Signy Island
R. M. Laws *BL, Zool*
R. A. Lenton *Radio Op*
D. H. Maling *Met*

Stonington Island
V. E. Fuchs **Comdr FIDS**, *Geol*
R. J. Adie *Geol*
K. V. Blaiklock *Surv*
C. C. Brown *Surv*
Surg Lt D. G. Dalgliesh RN *MO*
J. S. R. Huckle *GA (F.Ops)*
F/Sgt H. D. Jones *Air Fitter*
T. M. Randall *Radio Op*
R. E. Spivey *GA (F.Ops)*
B. Stonehouse *Met*
P. A. Toynbee *Pilot*

1949

Admiralty Bay
G. F. Hattersley-Smith *BL, Glacio*
J. H. Chaplin *Met*
D. Jardine *Geol*
B. Jefford *Surv*
R. A. Lenton *Radio Op*
K. Pawson *GA (F.Ops)*

Argentine Islands
T. M. Nicholl *BL*
D. G. Farmer *Radio Op*
J. D. Reid *Met*
M. F. Tait *Handyman*

Deception Island
G. D. Stock *BL, Met*
J. W. Knox *Radio Op*
P. Peck *Handyman*
W. G. Richards *Handyman*

Signy Island
R. M. Laws *BL, Zool*
J. A. Kendall *Radio Op*
D. H. Maling *Met*
C. Skilling *Handyman*

Stonington Island
V. E. Fuchs **Comdr FIDS**, *Geol*
R. J. Adie *Geol*
K. V. Blaiklock *Surv*
C. C. Brown *Surv*
Surg Lt D. G. Dalgliesh RN *MO*
J. S. R. Huckle *GA (F.Ops)*
F/Sgt H. D. Jones RAF *Air Fitter*
T. M. Randall *Radio Op*
R. E. Spivey *GA (F.Ops)*
B. Stonehouse *Met, Zool*
P. A. Toynbee *Pilot*

1950

Admiralty Bay
J. A. Kendall *BL, Radio Op*
A. G. Burton *Met*

R. W. Crampton *GA (met)*
J. Gallacher *Handyman*

Argentine Islands
H. G. Heywood *BL*
N. R. Broadbear *Met*
P. D. Starling *Radio Op*
M. F. Tait *Handyman*

Deception Island
J. R. Green *BL*
W. Calder *Radio Op*
A. W. R. Hewat *Met*
A. N. Walton *Met*

Port Lockroy
J. H. Chaplin *BL, Met*
T. Burgess *Radio Op*
K. R. Gooden *GA (surv)*
W. A. Walker *GA (met)*

Signy Island
W. J. L. Sladen *BL, MO, Zool*
J. J. Cheal *GA (met)*
D. B. E. Duke *Radio Op*
E. M. P. Salmon *Met*
R. F. Worswick *Met*

South Georgia
D. Borland *BL, Met Forecaster*
I. J. Biggs *Met*
J. D. Lankester *Met*
P. Peck *Cook*
G. D. Stock *Radio Op*

1951

Admiralty Bay
K. R. Gooden *BL*
T. Burgess *Radio Op*
A. G. Burton *Met*
P. W. Mander *Met*
R. A. Todd-White *Met*

Argentine Islands
J. R. Green *BL*
N. R. Broadbear *Met*
A. F. Lewis *Met*
P. D. Starling *Radio Op*
W. A. Walker *GA*

Deception Island
R. A. Lenton *BL*
W. Calder *Radio Op*
E. M. P. Salmon *Met*
A. N. Walton *Met*

Signy Island
J. J. Cheal *BL, Met*
J. A. Brown *Radio Op*
N. H. Thyer *Met*
A. J. Vernum *Met*
R. F. Worswick *Met*

South Georgia
R. M. Laws *BL, Zool*
I. J. Biggs *Met*
A. W. Mansfield *Met*
A. I. Macarthur *Met*
J. C. Newing *Radio Op, Met*
*Between 1952 and 1969 the base was
a government meteorological station*

1952

Admiralty Bay
W. J. Meehan *BL, Radio Op*
F. Burns *Met*
R. S. Edwards *DEM*
A. F. Lewis *Met*
A. J. Vernum *Met*

Argentine Islands
N. S. W. Petts *BL, DEM*
W. T. Kelley *Radio Op*
A. I. Macarthur *Met*
N. H. Thyer *Met*

Deception Island
Capt E. D. Stroud RM *BL, Met*
R. A. Berry *Met*
A. F. Christie *Radio Op*
B. G. Ellis *Met*
A. H. Farrant *DEM*
R. A. Todd-White *Met*

Hope Bay
G. W. Marsh *BL, MO*
K. V. Blaiklock *Surv*
J. A. Coley *Met*
E. W. B. Hill *DEM*
B. D. Hunt *Met*
B. Kemp *Met*
P. W. King *Radio Op*
R. Stoneley *Geol*
D. G. Stratton *Surv*
M. F. Tait *Met*
M. J. Unwin *Met*

Port Lockroy
R. A. Lenton *BL, GA (radio, bldr)*
D. A. Barratt *Met*
C. G. Collop *Radio Op*
W. A. Etheridge *Iono*
H. J. Robinson *DEM*

Signy Island
A. W. Mansfield *BL, Met, Zool*
F. L. Johnson *Met*
P. W. Mander *Met*
J. L. O'Hare *DEM*
L. A. Wilson *Radio Op*

1953

Admiralty Bay
R. F. Worswick *BL, Met*
R. J. Banks *Met*
B. L. Golborne *DEM*
G. E. Hemmen *Met*
J. Turnbull *Radio Op*

Argentine Islands
D. A. Barrett *BL, Met*
D. A. Clarke *DEM*
F. L. Johnson *Met*
W. T. Kelley *Radio Op*
H. Smith *Met*

Deception Island
I. W. N. Clarke *BL, Met*
A. H. Farrant *DEM*
D. J. George *Met*
F. A. Hall *Met*
B. Taylor *Radio Op*

Hope Bay
G. W. Marsh *BL, MO*
K. V. Blaiklock *Surv*
G. H. Brookfield *Met*
J. A. Coley *Met*
B. Kemp *Met*
P. W. King *Radio Op*
K. E. C. Powell *DEM*
A. J. Standring *Geol*
D. G. Stratton *Surv*
M. F. Tait *Met*

Signy Island
A. G. Tritton *BL, Met*
R. A. Berry *Met*
T. G. Owen *Radio Op*
D. Parsons *Met*
R. J. Tanton *DEM*

1954

Admiralty Bay
D. J. George *BL, Met*
B. L. Golborne *DEM*
R. H. W. Nalder *Radio Op*
G. C. Rumsey *Met*
R. L. Tapp *Met*

Argentine Islands
R. A. Lenton *BL, GA (bldr, radio)*
R. J. Banks *Met*
H. J. Buckman *Radio Op*
F. D. Byrne *Met*
A. N. Graham *Met*
J. E. Raymond *GA (cptr)*
E. M. P. Salmon *Met*
I. H. Simpson *Met*
R. J. Tanton *DEM*
A. B. N. Widgery *Met*

Deception Island
G. E. Hemmen *BL, Met*
D. C. G. Mumford *Radio Op*
D. Parsons *Met*
L. J. Shirtcliffe *Met*
J. E. Smith *DEM*

Hope Bay
W. Turner *BL, MO*
J. A. Barber *Radio Op*
G. H. Brookfield *Met*
I. W. N. Clarke *Met*
R. R. Kenney *Surv*
N. A. G. Leppard *Surv*
A. F. Lewis *Met*
R. C. Mottershead *Met*
K. E. C. Powell *DEM*
A. Precious *Met*
A. J. Standring *Geol*
R. J. F. Taylor *Dog Physio*

Port Lockroy
F. G. Bird *BL, Iono*
M. J. Faulkner *Iono*
A. M. Swain *Radio Op*
R. H. Watton *DEM*
B. Weeks *Iono*

Signy Island
H. Smith *BL, Met*
P. A. Cordall *Met*
G. B. Davis *Radio Op*
J. B. Pearce *DEM*
A. A. Smith *Met*

1955

Admiralty Bay
J. R. Noble *BL, Met*
G. B. Davis *Radio Op*
N. A. Hedderley *Met*
J. B. Pearce *DEM*
G. C. Rumsey *Met*

Anvers Island
P. R. Hooper *BL, Geol*
J. Canty *Radio Op*
W. J. Hindson *Surv*
D. B. Litchfield *GA (mntr)*
A. J. Rennie *Surv*
A. L. Shewry *GA (cptr)*

Argentine Islands
R. V. Hesketh *BL, Met*
R. A. Berry *Met*
H. J. Buckman *Radio Op*
F. D. Byrne *Met*
L. Catherall *Met*
G. C. Cumming *GA (bldr)*
R. N. Ogley *DEM*
A. B. N. Widgery *Met*
J. H. Winstone *Met*

Deception Island
C. H. Palmer *BL, Radio Op*
R. P. K. Clark *Met*
R. E. Cooper *DEM*
B. Gilpin *Met*
W. McDowell *Met*
P. Phipps *Met*

Hope Bay
W. E. Anderson *BL, Met*
D. A. Clarke *DEM*
R. R. Kenney *Surv*
N. A. G. Leppard *Surv*
A. F. Lewis *Met*
P. W. Mander *Met*
P. M. O. Massey *MO*
A. Precious *Met*
M. F. Tait *Met*
R. J. F. Taylor *Dog Physio*
D. R. Willis *Radio Op*
R. F. Worswick *Met*

Horseshoe Island
K. M. Gaul *BL, GA*
D. Atkinson *DEM*
J. A. Exley *Geol*
G. A. Farquhar *Radio Op*
B. Kemp *Met*
D. J. H. Searle *Surv*
R. D. Taylor *Met*
G. T. Vine-Lott *Met*

Port Lockroy
A. M. Carroll *BL, Iono*
J. E. Smith *DEM*
B. Taylor *Radio Op*
R. J. Whittock *Iono*

Signy Island
H. Dollman *BL, GA*
G. J. Bull *DEM*
P. A. Cordall *Met*
R. G. Napier *GA*
L. J. Shirtcliffe *Met*
W. L. N. Tickell *Met*
L. C. Tyson *Radio Op*

1956

Admiralty Bay
C. C. Clement *BL, DEM*
G. E. Broome *Met*
D. K. Brown *Met*
M. J. Royle *Radio Op*
A. L. Shewry *GA (cptr)*
R. W. Tufft *Met*

Anvers Island
P. R. Hooper *BL, Geol*
G. J. Bull *DEM*
L. V. Harlow *GA (mntr)*
D. Kershaw *Surv*
J. W. Thompson *GA (mntr)*
J. P. Wylie *Surv*

Argentine Islands
N. A. Hedderley *BL, Met*
O. S. Connochie *Radio Op*
G. T. Cutland *GA (cook)*
G. R. Ibbotson *Met*
H. A. Imray *MO*
D. McNab *Met*
D. Skilling *DEM*
R. L. Tapp *Met*
R. A. Todd-White *Met*

Danco Island (Paradise Harbour)
R. A. Foster *BL, GA*
M. B. Bayly *Geol*
L. Harris *GA (cptr)*
J. Ketley *Surv*
C. H. Palmer *Radio Op*
F. E. Wooden *Surv*

Deception Island
P. Guyver *BL, DEM*
J. W. Fellows *Met*
J. Hill *Radio Op*
C. Johnstone *Met*
L. Maloney *Met*
J. P. Smith *Met*

Detaille Island (Loubet Coast)
T. L. Murphy *BL, Surv*
R. E. Cooper *DEM*
R. Miller *GA (mntr)*
D. P. Moore *Radio Op*
M. J. H. Orford *Surv*
E. M. P. Salmon *Met*
J. Thorne *Met*
H. G. Wright *Geol*

Hope Bay
R. F. Worswick *BL, Met*
L. Catherall *Met*
D. A. Clarke *DEM*
W. W. Herbert *Surv*
K. V. Hill *Radio Op*
G. M. Larmour *Met*
J. S. Madell *Surv*
W. A. G. Nicholls *GA (mntr)*
J. R. Noble *Met*
H. W. Simpson *MO, Physio*
P. B. Thompson *Met*
R. I. Walcott *Met*

Horseshoe Island
D. J. H. Searle *BL, Surv*
D. Atkinson *DEM*
D. Chalmers *Met*
G. C. Cumming *GA*
A. K. Donnelly *Radio Op*
M. Evans *MO*
J. A. Exley *Geol*
F. B. Ryan *Met*
C. D. Scotland *Met*
G. T. Vine-Lott *Met*

Port Lockroy
A. M. Carroll *BL, Iono*
P. J. Bunch *Radio Op*
D. R. H. Davis *Iono*
L. J. Fox *Iono*
B. L. Golborne *DEM*

Signy Island
W. L. N. Tickell *BL, Met*
F. G. Axtell *Met*
J. F. D. Bridger *Surv*
A. Grant *DEM*
A. B. Hall *Met*
P. W. Mander *Met*
D. H. Matthews *Geol*
S. M. Ward *Radio Op*

1957

Admiralty Bay
A. Precious *BL, Met*
P. J. Bunch *Radio Op*
G. J. Davey *Surv*
R. H. Hillson *Met*
G. Monk *Radio Op*
H. M. Noble *Glacio*
D. R. K. Stephens *Met*
A. Wensley-Walker *DEM*

Anvers Island
J. W. Thompson *BL, GA (mntr)*
B. L. H. Foote *Radio Op*
J. Ketley *Surv*
G. K. McLeod *GA (mntr)*
J. P. Wylie *Surv*

Argentine Islands
D. Emerson *BL, MO*
G. T. Cutland *GA (cook)*
J. C. Farman *Geophys*
E. R. Hughes *Met*
G. R. Ibbotson *Met*
J. M. Nantes *Met*
W. A. G. Nicholls *GA (met)*
M. J. Royle *Radio Op*
G. C. Rumsey *DEM*
D. A. Simmons *Geophys*
R. L. Tapp *Met*

Danco Island (Paradise Harbour)
R. A. Foster *BL, GA*
D. G. Evans *Surv*
G. J. Hobbs *Geol*
D. Kershaw *Surv*
E. R. McGowan *GA (radio)*
V. M. O'Neill *Radio Op*

Deception Island
J. Paisley *BL, Met*
R. D. Clements *DEM*
J. E. Dagless *Met*
C. Johnson *Radio Op*
P. O. White *Met*
J. Witcombe *Met*

Detaille Islnd (Loubet Coast)
Lt A. B. Erskine RN *BL, Surv*
O. S. Connochie *Radio Op*
D. C. Goldring *Geol*
J. S. Madell *Surv*
W. McDowell *Met*
F. Oliver *DEM*
J. M. Scarffe *GA (mntr)*
J. P. Smith *Met*
J. Thorne *Met*
H. T. Wyatt *MO, Physio*

Hope Bay
L. Rice *BL, Surv*
S. C. B. Blake *Radio Op*
D. K. Brown *Met*
H. J. Dangerfield *Radio Op*
W. W. Herbert *Surv*
C. Johnstone *Met*
M. J. F. Reuby *Met*
H. W. Simpson *MO, Physio*
P. B. Thompson *Met*
R. W. Tufft *Met*
R. I. Walcott *Met*
J. S. Walsh *DEM*

Horseshoe Island
P. Guyver *BL, DEM*
J. W. Fellows *Met*
P. McC. Gibbs *Surv*
H. A. Imray *MO*
G. M. Larmour *Met*
L. Maloney *Met*
N. A. A. Procter *Geol*
B. R. Roberts *Radio Op.*
J. M. Rothera *Surv*

Port Lockroy
C. C. Clement *BL, DEM*
L. J. Fox *Iono*
G. A. Farquhar *Radio Op*
P. R. Gale *GA (DEM)*
J. M. Smith *Iono*
J. Tinbergen *Iono*

Prospect Point (Graham Coast)
R. Miller *BL, GA*
D. Chalmers *Met*
R. Curtis *Geol*
B. Holmes *Surv*
A. R. Rumbelow *Radio Op*
F. E. Wooden *Surv*

Signy Island
C. D. Scotland *BL, Met*
S. E. Black *Met*
J. F. D. Bridger *Surv*
A. K. Donnelly *Radio Op*
D. W. McDowell *Met*
R. L. Sherman *Surv*
D. Skilling *DEM*
D. Statham *Met*

1958

Admiralty Bay
D. R. K. Stephens *BL, Met*
D. R. Bell *Met*
G. J. Davey *Surv*
J. L. Franks *Met*
A. Gill *Met*
G. Monk *Radio Op*
C. D. Souter *DEM*

Argentine Islands
J. C. Farman *BL, Geophys*
K. R. Bell *DEM*
E. C. J. Clapp *Radio Op*
B. D. Giles *Met*
J. M. Hunt *Met*
D. P. McN. Jones *MO*
C. W. Pearson *GA (cook)*
G. J. Roe *Met*
J. B. Shaw *Met*
D. A. Simmons *Geophys*
C. M. Smith *Met*

Danco Island (Paradise Harbour)
G. D. Boston *BL, GA (mntr)*
D. G. Evans *Surv*
G. J. Hobbs *Geol*
E. B. Jones *Radio Op*
J. F. Malden *DEM*

Deception Island
J. E. Dagless *BL, Met*
R. D. Clements *DEM*
K. V. Gibson *Met*
P. J. Hodkinson *Met*
V. M. O'Neill *Radio Op*
P. R. Rowe *Radio Op*
J. Witcombe *Met*

Detaille Island (Loubet Coast)
B. L. H. Foote *BL, Surv*
D. C. Goldring *Geol*
J. G. Graham *MO*
C. Johnson *Radio Op*
F. Oliver *DEM*
R. M. Perry *Met*
J. M. Rothera *Surv*
P. O. White *Met*
J. W. Young *Met*

Hope Bay
D. McCalman *BL, Surv*
T. N. K. Allan *MO*
J. S. Bibby *Geol*
S. C. B. Blake *Radio Op*
H. J. Dangerfield *Radio Op*
R. M. Koerner *Met*
M. J. F. Reuby *Met*
M. D. Rhodes *Met*
L. Rice *Surv*
T. H. H. Richardson *Met*
R. W. Tufft *Met*
J. S. Walsh *DEM*
J. D. J. Wildridge *Met*
P. L. Woodall *Met*

Horseshoe Island
J. Paisley *BL, Met*
S. E. Black *Met*
R. H. Hillson *Met*
A. K. Hoskins *Geol*
D. W. McDowell *Met*
E. R. McGowan *Radio Op*
D. Statham *Met*
G. Stride *DEM*

Port Lockroy
J. M. Smith *BL, Iono*
H. A. D. Cameron *Iono*
M. A. Crockford *Radio Op*
D. M. Price *DEM*
J. Tinbergen *Iono*

Prospect Point (Graham Coast)
G. K. McLeod *BL, GA (mntr)*
P. Catlow *Radio Op*
T. A. Hanson *Surv*
K. Kenyon *GA*
J. F. S. Martin *Surv*

Signy Island
P. A. Richards *BL, Met*
B. Beck *Met*
G. D. Mallinson *Radio Op*
A. Sharman *Met*
J. W. Stammers *Met*
G. F. C. White *DEM*

Stonington Island
P. McC. Gibbs *BL, Surv*
P. D. Forster *Surv*
A. K. Hoskins *Geol*
N. A. A. Procter *Geol*
B. R. Roberts *Radio Op*
H. T. Wyatt *MO, Physio*

1959

Admiralty Bay
M. J. Stansbury *BL, Glacio*
C. M. Barton *Geol*
D. R. Bell *Met*
K. V. Gibson *Met*
J. C. A. Stokes *Surv*
R. D. Thompson *Met*
E. Watson *DEM*
B. C. Williamson *Radio Op*
J. M. Wilson *DEM*

Argentine Islands
K. R. Bell *BL, DEM*
H. E. Agger *Geophys*
A. Cumming *MO*
B. D. Giles *Met*
C. N. Horton *Geophys*
J. M. Nantes *Met*

G. J. Roe *Met*
C. W. Pearson *Cook*
A. Piggott *Radio Op*
J. B. Shaw *Met*
C. M. Smith *Met*

Deception Island
P. J. Hodkinson *BL, Met*
I. T. Jackson *Met*
E. B. Jones *Radio Op*
M. D. Kershaw *DEM*
P. R. Rowe *Radio Op*
P. L. Woodall *Met*

Halley Bay
G. R. Lush *BL*
G. M. Artz *Met*
M. J. Blackwell *Geophys*
J. Bothma *Met*
N. A. Hedderley *Met*
D. W. S. Limbert *Met*
C. J. Mace *Cook*
J. N. Norman *MO*
D. R. Savins *Radio Op*
M. A. Sheret *Geophys*
J. A. Smith *Met*
W. Whitehall *DEM*

Hope Bay
D. McCalman *BL Surv*
K. Allen *GA (mntr)*
J. Ashley *Geophys*
J. S. Bibby *Geol*
C. G. Brading *Surv*
J. E. Cheek *Radio Op*
E. C. J. Clapp *Radio Op*
A. Gill *Met*
I. F. G. Hampton *Physio*
T. A. Hanson *Surv*
R. M. Koerner *Met*
L. Maloney *Met*
C. A. Murray *Surv*
N. W. M. Orr *MO*
M. D. Rhodes *Met*
T. H. H. Richardson *Met*
C. D. Souter *DEM*
R.Tindal *GA (mntr)*
J. D. J. Wildridge *Met*

Horseshoe Island
R. M. Perry *BL, Met*
J. L. Franks *Met*
A. K. Hoskins *Geol*
J. M. Hunt *Met*
J. F. Malden *DEM*
G. D. Mallinson *Radio Op*

Port Lockroy
H. A. D. Cameron *BL, Iono*
M. A. Crockford *Radio Op*
P. H. Leek *Iono*
A. G. Lewis *Iono*
D. M. Price *DEM*

Signy Island
J. W. Stammers *BL, Met*
R. B. Harrison *Met*
K. Kenyon *GA*
C. F. Le Feuvre *Radio Op*
W. Mitchell *DEM*
F. A. O'Gorman *Zool*
R. Pinder *Radio Op*
G. F. C. White *DEM*
J. W. Young *Met*

1960

Admiralty Bay
M. D. Kershaw *BL, DEM*
C. M. Barton *Geol*
N. Y. Downham *Met*
J. Elliot *Radio Op*
J. E. Ferrar *Met*
N. V. Jones *Met*
J. M. Wilson *DEM*
R. G. Wright *Met*

Argentine Islands
C. A. Murray *BL, Surv*
H. E. Agger *Geophys*
A. W. Gallagher *Met*
R. S. M. Harkness *DEM*
P. J. A. Haynes *Cook*
D. R. Jehan *Met*
A. Piggott *Radio Op*
I. Preece *Geophys*
J. A. Quinn *Radio Op*
F. P. Smith *Met*
B. R. Sparke *MO*
M. R. Sumner *Met*
R. H. Thomas *Met*
J. B. Wigglesworth *Met Forecaster*

Wordie House
E. C. J. Clapp *BL, Radio Op*
A. Crouch *Met*
A. G. Fraser *Geol*
H. C. G. McCallum *GA (mntr)*
F. Preston *Surv*
J. C. A. Stokes *Surv*

Deception Island
I. T. Jackson *BL, Met*
P. C. Bates *Air Fitter*
Flt Lt D. P. English *Pilot*
G. F. Fitton *Radio Op*
Flt Lt R. A. Lord *Pilot*
R. P. Matthews *Met*
C. J. Pearce *Met*
T. R. Sumner *Air Fitter*
M. H. Tween *DEM*
B. P. Westlake *Met*
F. A. Whyte *Radio Op*

Halley Bay
N. A. Hedderley *BL, Met*
D. A. Ardus *Glacio*
J. R. Blackie *Geophys*

M. F. Brittain *Radar Tech*
C. H. Dean *Geophys*
C. R. Forrest *MO*
C. N. Horton *Geophys*
C. Johnson *Radio Op*
A. G. Lewis *Iono*
J. E. MacDonald *Iono*
A. Millar *Met*
G. Moore *Cook*
G. H. Talmage *DEM*
M. H. Taplin *Met*
M. H. Thurston *Zool*
W. H. Townsend *Met*

Hope Bay
N. W. M. Orr *BL, MO*
N. Aitkenhead *Geol*
A. Allen *Geophys*
K. Allen *GA (mntr)*
D. S. Baron *Met*
C. G. Brading *Surv*
J. E. Cheek *Radio Op*
I. L. Fothergill *Met*
I. F. G. Hampton *Physio*
R. A. E. Harbour *Surv*
R. Miller *GA (mntr)*
W. Mitchell *DEM*
P. H. H. Nelson *Geol*
J. M. Smith *Met*
R. Tindal *GA (mntr)*
W. O. Tracy *Met*
J. Winham *Met*

Horseshoe Island
P. D. Forster *BL, Surv*
A. G. Davies *MO*
P. H. Grimley *Geol*
C. F. Le Feuvre *Radio Op*

Port Lockroy
J. C. Cunningham *BL*
K. Austen *Iono*
P. J. Leek *Iono*
E. Watson *DEM*
B. C. Williamson *Radio Op*

Signy Island
R. B. Harrison *BL, Met*
D. A. Clarke *DEM*
R. Filer *Met*
P. W. Mander *Met*
R. Pinder *Radio Op*
P. O. White *Met*

1961

Adelaide Island
F. Preston *BL, Surv*
A. Crouch *Met*
G. J. A. Dewar *Geol*
G. F. Fitton *Radio Op*
H. C. G. McCallum *GA (mntr)*
A. F. Wright *Surv*

Argentine Islands
R. S. M. Harkness *BL, DEM*
A. W. Gallagher *Met*
P. J. A. Haynes *Cook*
J. W. P. O'Kirwan *Geophys*
A. Piggot *Radio Op*
F. B. Potts *Met*
I. Preece *Geophys*
F. P. Smith *Met*
L. J. Shirtcliffe *Bldr*
R. H. Thomas *Met*
G. B. Thompson *GA (electronics)*
W. H. Townsend *Bldr*
F. A. Whyte *Radio Op*

Deception Island
J. B. Killingbeck *BL*
D. S. Baron *Met*
Flt Lt P. R. Bond *Pilot*
R. Brand *Air Fitter*
J. E. Ferrar *Met*
B. Hodges *GA*
G. F. C. Kyte *Met*
C. Lehen *Radio Op*
Flt Lt R. Lord *Pilot*
T. R. Sumner *Air Fitter*
D. Tegerdine *DEM*

Fossil Bluff
C. J. Pearce *Met*
J. P. Smith *Met*
B. J. Taylor *Geol*

Halley Bay
C. Johnson *BL, Radio Op*
D. A. Ardus *Glacio*
M. Bethell *Iono*
G. Blundell *Geophys*
M. J. Brittain *Radar Tech*
C. H. Dean *Geophys*
E. H. Docchar *Bldr*
D. L. Easty *MO*
D. Edwards *Bldr*
G. M. Jarman *Geophys*
D. R. Jehan *Met*
E. B. Jones *Radio Op*
R. G. Lee *GA (tractors)*
J. S. Marsden *Geophys*
G. Moore *Cook*
P. J. Noble *Radar Tech*
B. J. Peters *Iono*
A Precious *Met*
J. Skilling *Bldr*
M. R. Sumner *Met*
G. H. Talmage *DEM*
M. H. Taplin *Met*
A. C. Thorne-Middleton *Cook*
E. Thornton *Met*
M. H. Thurston *Zool*

Hope Bay
I. L. Fothergill *BL, Met*
N. Aitkenhead *Geol*

A. Allen *Geophys*
R. H. C. Catty *MO*
J. E. Cheek *Radio Op*
O. J. Collings *Bldr*
N. Y. Downham *GA*
K. A. Edwards *Surv*
R. A. E. Harbour *Surv*
P. H. H. Nelson *Geol*
J. M. Smith *GA*
G. F. C. White *DEM*
J. Winham *Met*
R. G. Wright *Met*

Port Lockroy
J. B. Nixon *BL*
K. Austen *Iono*
M. A. Crockford *Radio Op*
E. W. Grimshaw *Iono*
D. J. Hounsell *DEM*

Signy Island
R. D. Thompson *BL, Met*
D. A. Clarke *DEM*
N. V. Jones *Met*
R. Pinder *Radio Op*
B. P. Westlake *Met*

Stonington Island
J. C. Cunningham *BL*
B. A. Bowler *GA (tractors)*
H. E. Chapman *Surv*
A. G. Fraser *Geol*
R. P. Matthews *Met*
R. J. Metcalfe *Surv*
J. A. Quinn *Radio Op*
B. R. Sparke *MO*
W. O. Tracy *GA*
M. H. Tween *DEM*
J. B. Wigglesworth *Met*

1962

Adelaide Island
J. G. Dewar *BL, Geol*
R. B. Bryan *Met*
F. J. Gibbs *GA*
D. J. Hounsell *DEM*
J. B. Killingbeck *GA*
R. H. Leckie *Met*
D. F. Nash *Surv*
J. B. Nixon *GA*
E. W. Smith *Radio Op*
W. S. L. Woolley *Met*
A. F. Wright *Surv*

Argentine Islands
E. W. Grimshaw *BL, Iono*
C. P. Kimber *Met*
R. E. J. Lewis *Geophys*
A. J. R. Mack *Met*
J. W. P. O'Kirwan *Geophys*
B. Porter *DEM*
F. B. Potts *Met*

T. A. Reece *Cptr*
A. J. Schärer *Met*
G. Straughan *Radar Tech*
A. C. Thorne-Middleton *Cook*
W. I. Vickerstaff *Iono*
C. Wade *Radio Op*

Deception Island
E. J. Chinn *BL*
Flt Lt P. R. Bond *Pilot*
K. G. S. Boulter *Air Fitter*
R. T. Brand *Air Fitter*
D. M. Bridgen *Radio Op*
M. J. Byrne *Cptr*
M. J. Cousins *Met*
G. F. C. Kyte *Met*
R. F. Lewis *Radio Op*
Flt Lt W. D. Lincoln *Pilot*
B. Lynch *Met*
J. H. Sutherland *Cptr*
T. H. Tallis *DEM*

Fossil Bluff
L. J. Shirtcliff *OIC, GA*
S. C. B. Blake *Radio Op*
B. J. Taylor *Geol*
R. J. Walker *Met*

Halley Bay
G. M. Jarman *BL*
F. Bent *Met*
M. Bethell *Iono*
P. R. Blakeley *Met*
G. Blundell *Geophys*
C. T. Brown *MO*
R. E. Dean *Cook*
D. M. Finlayson *Geophys*
J. C. Griffiths *Met*
J. Hill *Radio Op*
J. P. Holt *Cook*
K. L. Lambert *DEM*
R. G. Lee *GA*
J. S. Marsden *Geophys*
B. J. Peters *Iono*
D. A. Robinson *Radar Tech*
C. H. Ruffell *Cptr*
C. L. Spaans *Cptr*
E. Thornton *Met*
P. I. Whiteman *Met*
M. J. Winterton *GA*

Hope Bay
I. L. Fothergill *BL*
M. J. G. Cox *Geophys (fld)*
K. A. Edwards *Surv*
D. H. Elliot *Geol*
M. Fleet *Geol*
J. L. Franks *GA (mntr)*
G. K. McLeod *GA (mntr)*
R. C. Robson *Radio Op*
R. M. Wilkinson *GA (mntr)*

Signy Island
P. J. Tilbrook *BL, Zool*
P. S. Cawson *Cptr*
M. J. G. Chambers *Met*
R. B. Heywood *Zool*
P. A. F. Hobbs *Radio Op*
T. Mason *Met*
T. Rodger *DEM*
F. W. Topliffe *Met*

Stonington Island
J. C. Cunningham *BL*
B. A. Bowler *GA (tractors)*
J. J. O. Clennell *GA (mntr)*
W. Gilchrist *Radio Op*
R. V. Gill *GA (tractors)*
B. Hodges *GA*
I. McMorrin *GA*
R. J. Metcalfe *Surv*
I. P. Morgan *Surv*
J. M. Wilson *DEM*

1963

Adelaide Island
R. H. Leckie *BL, Met*
R. B. Bryan *Met*
M. J. Cousins *Met*
W. Geddes *Radio Op*
F. J. Gibbs *GA*
R. V. Gill *GA (tractors)*
K. L. Lambert *DEM*
I. P. Morgan *Surv*
D. F. Nash *Surv*
R. G. Palmer *GA (tractors)*
J. L. Shirtcliffe *GA (bldr)*
W. S. L. Woolley *Met*

Argentine Islands
E. J. Chinn *BL*
F. Bent *Met*
P. R. Blakeley *Met*
C. C. Davies *Geophys*
R. E. Dean *Cook*
C. P. Kimber *Met*
R. E. J. Lewis *Geophys*
A. J. R. Mack *Met*
A. J. Schärer *Met*
F. C. Slater *Iono*
G. Straughen *Radar Tech*
T. H. Tallis *DEM*
W. I. Vickerstaff *Iono*
C. Wade *Radio Op*

Deception Island
B. Lynch *BL, Met*
H. D. Ashworth *Met*
G. C. Barrett *Air Fitter*
Flt Lt D. A. Blair *Pilot*
A. Bottomley *Met*
W. Gilchrist *Radio Op*
R. F. Lewis *Radio Op*
W. L. Pennock *Air Fitter*
F/Off G. W. Stutt *Pilot*
J. E. Tait *DEM*

Halley Bay
M. R. Sumner *BL*
G. T. Bowra *MO*
N. Brind *Radar Tech*
I. L. Buckler *Met*
A. J. Champness *Cook*
D. Egerton *Met*
W. A. Etchells *GA (tractors)*
D. M. Finlayson *Geophys*
J. C. Griffiths *Met*
D. Hollas *Met*
J. P. Holt *Cook*
C. J. S. Jefferies *Iono*
D. R. Jehan *GA (tractors)*
B. J. Kraehenbuehl *DEM*
G. D. Mallinson *Radio Op*
N. S. Mann *Surv*
H. M. O'Gorman *Radio Op*
D. L. Petrie *Iono*
M. M. Samuel *Surv*
M. E. R. Walford *Geophys*
J. V. B. Westwood *Geophys*
P. I. Whiteman *Met*
M. J. Winterton *GA*
R. J. Worsfold *Geol*

Hope Bay
N. Y. Downham *BL*
C. F. Le Feuvre *GA (radio)*
J. Mansfield *Geophys (fld)*
R. C. Robson *Radio Op*
J. M. Smith *GA*
R. J. Walker *Met*
R. M. Wilkinson *GA (mntr), DEM*

Signy Island
P. J. Tilbrook *BL, Zool*
A. Amphlett *DEM*
A. D. Bailey *Bot*
M. J. G. Chambers *Met*
R. B. Heywood *Zool*
P. A. F. Hobbs *Radio Op*
F. W. Topliffe *Met*
W. Townsend *Met*

Stonington Island
J. J. O. Clennel *BL*
A. D. G. Beynon *Dentist*
S. C. B. Blake *Radio Op*
M. Fleet *Geol*
B. Hodges *GA*
R. R. Horne *Geol*
P. Kennett *Geophys (fld)*
A. F. Marsh *Geol*
G. K. McLeod *GA (mntr)*
I. McMorrin *GA*
R. Tindal *GA*

1964

Adelaide Island
J. C. Cunningham *BL*
E. B. Armstrong *Surv*

H. D. Ashworth *Met*
M. E. Ayling *Geol*
E. K. P. Back *Met*
A. Bottomley *Met*
J. H. Common *GA (stores)*
K. Darnell *Cook*
J. L. Gardner *GA*
W. Geddes *Radio Op*
R. R. Horne *Geol*
R. E. Owen *Met*
J. F. Pagella *Geol*
R. G. Palmer *GA (tractors)*
M. H. C. Rice *MO*
A. H. Rider *Surv*
B. P. Smith *Met*
W. Smith *GA*
J. E. Tait *DEM*
M. R. A. Thomson *Geol*
D. T. Todd *GA*

Argentine Islands
R. W. M. Corner *BL, MO, Physio*
N. Brind *Radar Tech*
C. C. Davies *Geophys*
D. Egerton *Met*
D. S. Evans *Met*
M. C. Galletly *Cook*
P. J. Hope *Met*
T. P. Jones *Geophys*
A. A. Lovejoy *Met*
B. Murton *Iono*
H. M. O'Gorman *Radio Op*
F. C. Slater *Iono*
F. Stacey *Geophys*
N. Sutton *DEM*
R. J. Tidey *Met*

Deception Island
L. U. Mole *BL, Met*
G. C. Barrett *Air Fitter*
C. A. Howie *Met*
J. D. S. Leigh *Radio Op*
J. McDermott *Air Fitter*
Flt Lt W. J. Mills *Pilot*
D. S. Parnell *Radio Op*
Flt Lt E. J. Skinner *Pilot*
M. E. Warr *Met*
J. M. Wilson *DEM*

Halley Bay
D. R. Jehan *BL*
A. Baker *Cptr*
W. H. Bellchambers *Iono*
G. T. Bowra *MO, Physio*
I. L. Buckler *Met*
A. J. Champness *Cook*
J. P. D. Cotton *Surv*
L. W. Dicken *Iono*
W. A. Etchells *GA (tractors)*
R. A. Fewster *Radar Tech*
D. B. George *Geophys*
P. C. Goodwin *Met*

D. Hollas *Met*
L. M. Juckes *Geol*
B. J. Kraehenbuehl *DEM*
G. D. Mallison *Radio Op*
C. J. R. Miller *Met*
D. L. Petrie *Iono*
H. B. Rogers *Cook*
S. G. Russell *Radio Op*
M. M. Samuel *Surv*
D. M. Shipstone *Geophys (fld)*
W. M. Sievwright *Geophys*
B. P. Smith *Geophys*
G. A. Thomson *GA (tractors)*
M. W. Turner *Met*
J. V. B. Westwood *Geophys*
D. P. Wild *Surv*
R. J. Worsfold *Geol*
J. C. Wright *Iono*

Signy Island
A. D. Bailey *BL, Bot*
R. W. Burton *Met*
W. M. Dawson *DEM*
B. J. A. Goodman *Met*
J. P. B. Noble *Cook*
M. J. Northover *Met*
P. S. Pilkington *Radio Op*
P. Redfearn *Zool*
R. F. Stocks *GA (bldr)*
J. H. Sutherland *Cptr*
A. J. M. Walker *Zool*

Stonington Island
N. Y. Downham *BL*
J. E. Cheek *Radio Op*
G. Grikurov *Geol*
A. F. Marsh *Geol*
A. L. Muir *MO*
R. G. B. Renner *Geophys (fld)*
A. J. Schärer *GA*
J. S. Steen *GA*
G. M. Stubbs *Geol*
E. Thornton *GA*
D. N. Vaughan *GA (tractors)*

1965

Adelaide Island
L. U. Mole *BL, Met*
E. K. P. Back *Met*
J. H. Common *GA (stores)*
T. W. Davies *MO, Physio*
G. M. Green *DEM, GA (tractors)*
T. H. Miller *Cook*
J. F. Noël *Radio Op*
R. E. Owen *Met*
M. E. Warr *Met*

Argentine Islands
R. J. Tidey *BL, Met*
A. N. Bushell *Met*
K. Darnell *Cook*

P. J. Hope *Met*
D. L. Hughes *Met*
T. P. Jones *Geophys*
R. I. H. Macnee *Radar Tech*
C. J. Moretti *Iono*
B. Murton *Iono*
I. Sadler *Geophys*
F. Stacey *Geophys*
T. H. Tallis *DEM*
J. A. Thoday *Met*
M. T. Whitbread *Radio Op*

Deception Island
C. D. Walter *BL, Met*
P. G. Bird *Met*
Flt Lt J. Brett *Pilot*
B. M. Chappel *Met*
H. A. Field *Air Fitter*
W. Geddes *Radio Op*
G. L. Hodson *DEM*
J. McDermott *Air Fitter*

Halley Bay
J. P. D. Cotton *BL*
A. Amphlett *Elect*
B. M. F. Armstrong *Geophys*
J. T. Bailey *Geophys (fld)*
A. Baker *Cptr*
B. J. G. Barnes *Met*
G. D. Beebe *GA (tractors)*
W. H. Bellchambers *Iono*
L. W. Dicken *Iono*
J. L. Duff *Met*
R. W. Fewster *Radar Tech*
P. C. Goodwin *Met*
P. J. A. Haynes *Cook*
W. T. Izatt *Geophys*
L. M. Juckes *Geol*
G. W. Lovegrove *Surv*
C. J. R. Miller *Met*
S. W. Noble *Iono*
B. Porter *DEM*
R. Reid *DEM*
R. D. Rhys Jones *Surv*
H. B. Rogers *Cook*
J. Ross *Geol*
S. G. Russell *Radio Op*
D. M. Shipstone *Geophys*
W. M. Sievwright *Geophys*
J. R. Stokes *Met*
H. Strafford *Radar Tech*
A. B. Weeks *Radio Op*
D. P. Wild *Surv*
J. K. Wilson *MO, Physio*
J. C. Wright *Iono*

Signy Island
M. J. Northover *BL, Met*
N. C. Bacon *Cook*
R. W. Burton *Met*
W. M. Dawson *DEM*
I. Everson *Zool*
B. J. A. Goodman *Met*

C. F. Herbert *Zool*
C. A. Howie *Met*
P. S. Pilkington *Radio Op*
M. G. Purbrick *Cptr*
A. J. M. Walker *Zool*

Stonington Island
M. J. Cousins *BL*
J. L. Gardner *GA*
K. D. Holmes *Geol*
N. Marsden *Surv*
D. W. Matthews *Geol*
D. S. Parnell *Radio Op*
A. H. Rider *Surv*
J. W. Steen *GA*
J. E. Tait *GA*
M. R. A. Thomson *Geol*
E. Thornton *GA*
D. T. Todd *GA*
D. N. Vaughan *DEM*

1966

Adelaide Island
G. M. Green *BL, GA (tractors)*
P. G. Bird *Met*
B. M. Chappel *Met*
P. R. Hay *Met*
N. O. S. McLaren *Radio Op*
T. H. Miller *Cook*
F. W. A. Wilkinson *Met*

Argentine Islands
D. L. Hughes *BL, Met.*
B. J. G. Barnes *Met*
D-J. Biggadike *Cook*
G. Blanshard *DEM*
A. N. Bushell *Met.*
R. R. Diamond *Radio Op*
J. L. Duff *Met*
C. J. Leigh-Breese *Iono*
P. C. Mitchell *Geophys*
C. J. Moretti *Iono*
P. D. Morgan *Geophys*
J. A. Thoday *Met*
B. H. A. Walker *Radar Tech*

Deception Island
C. D. Walter *BL, Met*
J. Barlow *Met*
R. T. Brand *Air Fitter*
Flt Lt R. W. Burgess *Pilot*
A. B. Coggles *Air Fitter*
G. M. Jones *DEM*
P. G. H. Myers *Met*
M. G. Purbrick *Cptr*
M. T. Whitbread *Radio Op*

Halley Bay
P. I. Whiteman *BL*
B. M. F. Armstrong *Geophys*
G. D. Beebe *GA (tractors)*
P. R. Blakeley *GA (tractors)*

D. C. Blossom *Cook*
D. Brook *Geol*
P. J. Cotterill *Met*
R. D. Cuthbertson *DEM*
C. J. Gostick *Radio Op*
P. J. A. Haynes *GA*
W. T. Izatt *Geophys*
A. Johnston *Surv*
R. C. Keyte *Radio Op*
R. M. Lloyd *MO, Physio*
G. W. Lovegrove *Surv*
D. K. McKerrow *Cook*
G. McWilliam *Geophys*
S. W. Noble *Iono*
C. M. Read *Met*
M. M. Samuel *Surv*
M. J. Shaw *Geophys*
J. E. Skipworth *Elect*
J. R. Stokes *Met*
B. Swift *Radar Tech*
R. H. Thomas *Glacio*
A. R. Williams *Met*
A. B. Wilson *Iono*
C. M. Wornham *Met*

Signy Island
J. R. Brotherhood *BL, MO, Physio*
N. C. Bacon *Cook*
J. H. Baker *Bot, Met*
J. R. Beck *Zool*
M Burgin *GA (physio)*
I. Everson *Zool*
D. C. Lindsay *Bot, Met*
S. A. O'Shanohun *Radio Op*
D. F. Salter *Met*
R. I. L. Smith *Bot*
E. A. Thornley *DEM*
M. G. White *Zool, Met*

Stonington Island
T. H. Tallis *BL*
T. J. Allan *GA (tractors)*
A. Bottomley *DEM*
R. A. Boulding *Surv*
K. C. Doyle *GA*
K. D. Holmes *Geol*
D. Horley *GA*
N. Marsden *Surv*
D. W. Matthews *Geol*
J. R. B. Noble *GA*
J. R. Noël *Radio Op*
J. Ross *Geol*

1967

Adelaide Island
A. Bottomley *BC*
J. Barlow *Met*
J. D. G. Beard *GA (tractors)*
D. Bowen *Bldr*
D. W. Darroch *Radio Op*
B. Gibson *Cook*
R. B. Ledingham *Met*

F. G. Meeds *DEM, GA (tractors)*
D. F. Salter *Met*
F. W. A Wilkinson *Met*

Argentine Islands
B. Swift *BC, Radar Tech*
D-J. Biggadike *Cook*
P. J. Cotterill *Met*
R. R. Diamond *Radio Op*
J. R. Dudeney *Iono*
R. S. Hesbrook *Met*
C. J. S. Jeffries *Iono*
G. M. Jones *DEM*
P. C. Mitchell *Geophys*
P. D. Morgan *Geophys*
I. S. Tyson *Met*

Deception Island
P. G. H. Myers *BC, Met*
Flt Lt J. R. Ayers *Pilot*
N. O. S. McLaren *Radio Op*
D. J. McLoughlin *Air Fitter*
S. M. Norman *Met*
R. V. M. Perren *Air Fitter*
G. D. Seear *DEM*
F/Off R. P. Vere *Pilot*

Halley Bay
E. J. Chinn *BC*
A. Baker *Cptr*
M. A. Baring-Gould *DEM*
D. C. Blossom *Cook*
D. Brook *Geol*
J. R. Brotherhood *MO, Physio*
M. Burgin *GA (physio)*
J. F. Carter *DEM*
P. H. Coslett *Glacio*
R. H. Docchar *Bldr*
M. J. Durrant *Met*
W. A. Etchells *GA (tractors)*
N. J. Fothergill *Cook*
K. J. Gainey *Radar Tech*
J. M. Gallsworthy *Cptr*
C. J. Gostick *Radio Op*
K. W. Halliday *Radio Op*
D. J. Hill *Cptr*
J. H. Jamieson *Geophys*
A. Johnston *Surv*
W. R. Laidlaw *Geophys*
N. Mathys *GA*
D. K. McKerrow *Cook*
G. McWilliam *Geophys*
P. H. Noble *GA (mntr)*
J. F. Porter *GA (mntr)*
C. M. Read *Met*
M. M. Samuel *Surv*
L. J. Shirtcliffe *Bldr*
M. J. Skidmore *Geol*
A. Smith *Bldr*
G. Smith *Elect*
C. C. R. Sykes *GA (tractors)*
R. H. Thomas *Glacio*
P. Wharton *Elect*

A. R. Williams *Met*
A. B. Wilson *Iono*
C. M. Wornham *Met, GA*

Signy Island
E. R. Hillier *BC, MO, Physio*
J. H. Baker *Bot, Met*
D. G. Bone *Bio Asst*
D. N. Bravington *DEM*
D. W. Brown *Met*
L. U. Mole *Met*
S. A. O'Shanohun *Radio Op*
G. Pearce *GA (diver)*
R. N. Smith *Zool*
D. A. Spencer *Cook*
M. G. White *Zool, Met*

Stonington Island
A. H. McArthur *BC*
R. A. Boulding *Surv*
O. J. Collings *Cptr*
W. M. Dawson *DEM*
R. England *GA*
D. Horley *GA*
E. C. Madders *Radio Op*
G. K. McLeod *GA (mntr)*
J. R. B. Noble *GA*
D. Postlethwaite *Surv*
L. E. Willey *Geol*
R. A. Williams *MO, Bacterio*

1968

Adelaide Island
D. S. Parnell *BC, Radio Op*
D. Bowen *Bldr*
O. J. Collings *Cptr*
M. H. Elliott *Geol*
B. Gibson *Cook*
A. D. McKeith *GA*
F. G. Meeds *DEM*
D. J. D. Y. Rinning *GA (tractors)*
E. B. Sheldon *Met*
I. M. Willey *Met*

Argentine Islands
J. R. Dudeney *BC, Iono*
D. N. Bravington *DEM*
P. R. S. Burns *Radar Tech*
R. W. Davidson *Radio Op*
A. Feenan *Radio Op*
B. G. Gardiner *Geophys*
B. D. Gilbert *Geophys*
R. S. Hesbrook *Met*
R. I. Kressman *Iono*
L. N. Philp *Met*
K. J. Portwine *Cook*
I. S. Tyson *Met*

Fossil Bluff
R. B. Ledingham *OIC, Met*
Flt Lt J. R. Ayers *Pilot*
M. J. Bramwell *Met*
C. G. Smith *Geol*
J. C. Walsh *Air Fitter*

Halley Bay
C. C. R. Sykes *BC*
J. F. Carter *DEM*
J. A. Chalmers *Geophys*
P. D. Clarkson *Geol*
P. H. Coslett *Glacio*
M. J. Durrant *Met*
W. A. Etchells *GA (tractors)*
D. E. French *Met*
A. J. Fry *Physio*
K. J. Gainey *Radar Tech*
J. M. Gallsworthy *Cptr*
D. C. Groom *Iono*
K. W. Halliday *Radio Op*
C. M. Hodson *Radio Op*
J. H. Jamieson *Geophys*
C. L. Jones *Cook*
W. R. Laidlaw *Geophys*
D. S. MacLennan *Cook*
A. S. MacQuarrie *GA (tractors)*
N. Mathys *GA*
P. S. Mountford *Met*
P. H. Noble *GA (mntr)*
P. T. Pitts *Iono*
F. C. E. Platt *Met*
N. W. Riley *GA*
A. M. Roberts *MO, Physio*
M. J. Skidmore *Geol*
G. Smith *Elect*
A. C. Wager *Glacio*
T. H. Wiggans *GA*

Signy Island
D. W. Brown *BC, Met*
J. A. Ball *MO, Physio*
D. G. Bone *Bio Asst*
P. K. Bregazzi *Zool*
J. W. H. Conroy *Zool*
S. P. Finigan *Met*
L. A. Graves *Met*
R. E. Liddall *DEM*
A. Losh *GA (diver)*
P. J. Rowe *Geol*
V. W. Spaull *Zool*
D. A. Spencer *Cook*
H. Taylor *Radio Op*
W. Taylor *Met*

Stonington Island
A. H. McArthur *BC*
J. T. Donaldson *GA*
K. C. Doyle *GA (explosives)*
H. M. Fielding *Surv*
M. J. Holmes *MO, Physio*
W. A. Keith *DEM*
E. C. Madders *Radio Op*
S. M. Norman *GA*
D. Postlethwaite *Surv*
I. F. Smith *Geophys (fld)*
I. A. Sykes *GA*
P. Wainwright *Surv*
L. E. Willey *Geol*

1969

Adelaide Island
I. M. Willey *BC, Met*
T. R. Allen *MO, Physio*
R. J. Bird *Cook*
H. J. Blakley *Bldr*
M. J. Bramwell *Met*
I. Curphey *GA*
R. W. Davidson *Radio Op*
D. J. Hill *Bldr*
J. Newman *GA (tractors)*
R. C. Pashley *GA*
B. D. Snell *Radio Op*
W. Taylor *Met*
B. Whittaker *DEM*
S. Wormald *Met*

Argentine Islands
D. F. Salter *BC*
R. M. Chambers *Met*
B. G. Gardiner *Geophys*
B. D. Gilbert *Geophys*
R. W. Harris *Iono*
R. I. Kressman *Iono*
P. S. Mountford *Met*
L. N. Philp *Met*
D. N. Rumble *DEM*
C. R. Walker *Radio Op*
A. J. Wearden *Cook*
A. R. Woods *Geophys*

Fossil Bluff
A. C. Wager *OIC, Glacio*
C. M. Bell *Geol*
M. H. Elliott *Geol*
G. W. F. Kistruck *Glacio*

Halley Bay
P. D. Clarkson *BC, Geol*
J. F. Carter *DEM*
J. A. Chalmers *Geophys*
R. K. Chappell *Iono*
C. A. Clayton *Surv*
D. E. French *Met*
C. J. Gostick *Radio Op*
D. C. Groom *Iono*
M. J. Guyatt *GA*
D. J. Hoy *DEM*
R. V. James *Bldr*
C. L. Jones *Cook*
D. S. MacLennan *Cook*
M. D. Macrae *GA (tractors)*
R. G. Palmer *GA (tractors)*
F. C. E. Platt *Met*
N. W. Riley *GA*
D. J. Sealey *Radar Tech*
G. Smith *Elect*
I. D. Smith *Geophys*
G. J. Soar *Met*
R. M. Tiffin *Met*
A. True *Surv*
C. J. Wells *Radio Op*
R. J. Wells *Geophys*

T. H. Wiggans *GA*
D. C. Wilkins *MO, Physio*
G. K. Wright *GA*

Signy Island
V. W. Spaull *BC, Zool*
O. H. S. Darling *Bio Asst*
J. A. Edwards *Bot*
S. P. Finigan *Met*
L. A. Graves *Met*
P. Hardy *Zool*
J. Howarth *Radio Op*
A. Losh *GA (diver)*
E. J. Mickleburgh *Met*
M. J. Pinder *Cook*
D. J. D. Y. Rinning *GA (tractors)*
E. L. Twelves *Zool*
E. P. Wright *Bot*

Stonington Island
S. M. Norman *BC*
P. I. Bentley *Surv*
F. M. Burns *Geophys (fld)*
A. N. Bushell *GA*
J. T. Donaldson *GA*
A. Feenan *Radio Op*
H. M. Fielding *Surv*
B. Gargate *GA*
W. A. Keith *DEM*
M. R. Pawley *GA*
P. J. Rowe *Geol*
E. B. Sheldon *GA*
A. C. Skinner *Geol*
I. F. Smith *Geophys (fld)*
I. A. Sykes *GA*

1970

Adelaide Island
R. S. Hesbrook *BC*
E. K. P. Back *Met*
C. M. Bell *Geol*
R. J. Bird *Cook*
R. M. Chambers *Met*
E. J. Mickleburgh *Met*
A. H. Milne *MO, Physio*
R. C. Pashley *GA*
R. C. Scoffom *Met*
C. R. Walker *Radio Op*
R. S. Walker *DEM*

Argentine Islands
A. R. Woods *BC, Geophys*
A. L. Apps *Met*
M. W. Atkins *DEM*
J. C. Davies *Geophys*
H. J. Hall *Radar Tech*
R. W. Harris *Iono*
M. H. Hinchliffe *Radio Op*
P. K. Kinnear *Met*
N. J. MacPherson *Met*
R. M. Tiffin *Met*
A. J. Wearden *Cook*
J. P. J. Zerfahs *Iono*

Fossil Bluff
G. W. F. Kistruck *OIC, Glacio*
P. W. Gurling *Surv*
B. T Hill *GA*
M. D. Macrae *GA (tractors)*

Halley Bay
C. A. Clayton *BC, Surv*
S. P. Bean *DEM*
P. Burton *Bldr*
R. K. Chappell *Iono*
D. L. Clark *Cook*
B. Cornock *Geophys*
D. W. Devitt *Radio Op*
A. E. Gannon *Met*
J. P. Gauntlett *Met*
R. V. Gill *GA (tractors)*
M. J. Guyatt *GA*
D. J. Hoy *GA (tractors)*
B. A. Jarvis *Radar Tech*
H. J. Jones *Met*
I. M. Leith *MO, Physio*
J. E. I. Nockels *Iono*
D. A. Peel *Glacio*
M. J. Pinder *Cook*
I. D. Smith *Geophys*
G. J. Soar *Met*
M. Taylor *Elect*
M. Vallance *GA*
M. A. Warden *GA*
C. J. Wells *Radio Op*
R. J. Wells *Geophys*
G. K. Wright *GA*

Signy Island
E. L. Twelves *BC, Zool*
R. J. Cook *Cook*
O. H. S. Darling *Bio Asst*
A. Feenan *Radio Op*
A. H. Gilmour *DEM*
P. Hardy *Zool*
J. J. Light *Zool*
I. W. Rabarts *Zool*
H. G. Smith *Zool*
R. Townley-Malyon *GA (diver)*

South Georgia
E. J. Chinn *BC*
J. T. Chamberlain *Iono*
S. P. Chellingsworth *Iono*
W. A. Etchells *DEM*
J. M. Gallsworthy *Bldr*
D. J. Hill *Bldr*
C. Stephenson *Bot*
B. Summers *Radio Op*
O. Summers *Met*
D. W. H. Walton *Bot*

Stonington Island
A. N. Bushell *BC*
P. I. Bentley *Surv*
H. J. Blakley *GA*
F. M. Burns *Geophys*
P. F. Butler *Geophys*
T. J. C. Christie *Surv*

T. G. Davies *Geol*
A. Linn *Geol*
N. R. D. MacAllister *GA*
J. Newman *DEM*
M. R. Pawley *GA*
A. C. Skinner *Geol*
R. P. Smith *Radio Op*
J. I. Woodhouse *GA*
S. Wormald *GA*

1971

Adelaide Island
R. C. Scoffom *BC, Met*
A. L. Apps *Met*
E. K. P. Back *Met*
P. Burton *Bldr*
R. J. Cook *Cook*
R. P. Smith *Radio Op*
D. Williams *DEM*

Argentine Islands
N. J. MacPherson *BC, Met*
D. A. Binney *Iono*
D. L. Clark *Cook*
J. C. Davies *Geophys*
J. T. Gauntlett *Met*
R. V. Gill *DEM*
R. O. Hall *Geophys*
A. Hankins *Radar Tech*
M. H. Hinchliffe *Radio Op*
P. K. Kinnear *Met*
C. M. Kynaston *Met*
J. P. J. Zerfahs *Iono*

Fossil Bluff
R. S. Walker *OIC, GA (tractors)*
R. J. O'Donovan *GA*
M. R. Pearson *Glacio*
I. H. Rose *Glacio*

Halley Bay
M. Vallance *BC*
S. P. Bean *GA (tractors)*
B. Blackwell *DEM*
P. G. Brangham *Bldr*
I. T. Bury *Cook*
B. Cornock *Geophys*
J. G. Devine *Met*
N. J. Eddleston *Geophys*
J. J. Flick *Radio Op*
A. E. Gannon *Met*
H. J. Jones *Met*
P. A. Jones *Geophys*
R. Lee *Radio Op*
R. S. B. Loan *Met*
J. E. I. Nockels *Iono*
R. A. H. Patterson *MO, Physio*
J. J. V. Rushby *Radar Tech*
A. J. Smith *Geophys*
K. S. Stewardson *Cook*
H. G. Stoneham *DEM*
M. Taylor *Elect*
T. W. Thomas *Iono*
M. A. Warden *GA*

Signy Island
J. J. Light *BC, Zool*
B. E. Grantham *Bio Asst*
J. R. Hyde-Clarke *DEM*
P. G. Jennings *Zool*
M. J. Langford *Cook*
M. McManmon *Bot*
I. W. Rabarts *Zool*
M. G. Richardson *Zool*
P. A. Skilling *GA (diver)*
H. Taylor *Radio Op*
R. Webb *Bot*

South Georgia
B. Jones *BC, Bldr*
A. C. Clarke *Zool*
D. W. Devitt *Radio Op*
G. H. Firmin *Iono*
A. R. Hart *Bldr*
J. H. Jamieson *Geophys*
A. Keeley *Met*
R. I. Kressman *Iono*
F. E. Lines *DEM*
A. J. McManus *Cook*
J. M. Merson *Met*
J. R. B. Tallowin *Bot*
G. Whitworth *GA*

Stonington Island
P. Wainwright *BC*
T. J. C. Christie *Surv*
R. J. Collister *GA*
N. G. Culshaw *Geol*
T. G. Davies *Geol*
S. P. Finnigan *GA*
P. W. Gurling *Surv*
B. T. Hill *GA*
M. J. Holmes *MO, Physio*
W. A. Keith *DEM*
N. R. D. MacAllister *GA*
M. McArthur *Geophys (fld)*
N. Meades *Radio Op*
M. V. Mosley *GA*
D. B. Small *GA*
J. I. Woodhouse *GA*
R. B. Wyeth *Geol*

1972

Adelaide Island
F. E. Lines *BC, DEM*
R. V. James *Bldr*
M. Jozefiak *Radio Op*
C. M. Kynaston *Met*
J. M. Merson *Met*
S. Vallance *MO, Physio*
A. J. Wearden *Cook*
R. W. H. Wilkins *Met*

Argentine Islands
A. Keeley *BC, Met*
P. Barton *Met*
D. A. Binney *Iono*

M. R. Butterfield *Met*
P. H. Fitzgerald *Iono*
R. O. Hall *Geophys*
K. W. Hughson *Met*
A. J. McManus *Cook*
D. J. Orchard *Met*
S. A. F. Urquhart *DEM*
R. W. Wade *Radio Op*
K. L. Webber *Geophys*

Fossil Bluff
M. R. Pearson *OIC, Glacio*
I. H. Rose *Glacio*
A. C. Wager *Glacio*
G. Whitworth *GA*

Halley Bay
A. J. Smith *BC, Geophys*
K. J. Acheson *Physio*
B. Blackwell *DEM*
T. D. Boyt *Met*
P. G. Brangham *Bldr*
I. T. Bury *Cook*
I. T. Campbell *MO, Physio*
R. Daynes *Met*
J. G. Devine *Met*
J. T. Donaldson *GA*
N. J. Eddleston *Geophys*
D. D. W. Fletcher *GA*
J. J. Flick *Radio Op*
D. F. C. Habgood *Geophys*
A. L. Jackson *Elect*
D. B. Jenkins *Iono*
P. A. Jones *Geophys*
R. S. B. Loan *Met*
G. H. P. Ramage *GA (tractors)*
K. S. Stewardson *Cook*
H. G. Stoneham *GA (tractors)*
T. W. Thomas *Iono*

Signy Island
M. G. Richardson *BC, Zool*
S. C. Amos *Bio Asst*
P. A. Broady *Zool*
I. B. Collinge *Bio Asst*
D. G. Goddard *Zool*
J. N. Hoogesteger *Bio Asst*
T. N. Hooker *Bot*
J. R. Hyde-Clarke *DEM*
P. G. Jennings *Zool*
B. W. Kellett *Zool*
C. J. Palfrey *Cook*
J. J. V. Rushby *Radio Op*
P. A. Skilling *GA (diver)*
D. J. Tomlinson *Elect*
D. L. M. Weller *Zool*
T. M. Whitaker *Zool*

South Georgia
J. R. B. Tallowin *BC, Bot*
K. F. Avery *Met*
R. C. Barker *Cook*

J. C. Burke *Radio Op*
A. C. Clarke *Zool*
A. S. Ferguson *Iono*
G. H. Firmin *Iono*
B. E. Grantham *Bio Asst*
R. J. C. Hayward *Glacio*
I. G. G. Hogg *Glacio*
D. G. Hughes *MO, Physio*
A. W. Jamieson *Glacio*
J. H. Kilroy *Geophys, Met*
M. J. Langford *Cook*
E. G. Lawther *GA*
J. G. H. Maxwell *Zool*
M. R. Payne *Zool*
P. A. Prince *Bio Asst*
T. Pye *GA*
D. N. Rumble *DEM*
G. Smith *Elect*
R. L. Waller *Met*

Stonington Island
M. R. Pawley *BC*
S. P. Finigan *GA*
P. W. Gurling *Surv*
B. D. Hudson *DEM*
J. M. Hudson *Geol*
B. Jones *GA*
M. McArthur *Geophys*
D. J. McConnell *GA, Dentist*
N. C. McNaughton *Geophys (fld)*
N. Meades *Radio Op*
M. V. Mosley *GA*
D. G. Singleton *Geol*
D. B. Small *GA*
A. A. Thomson *Bldr*
G. K. Wright *GA*
R. B. Wyeth *Geol*
J. Yates *Surv*

1973

Adelaide Island
K. J. Roberts *BC*
C. J. H. Andrews *MO, Physio*
K. F. Avery *Met*
R. C. Barker *Cook*
M. Jozefiak *Radio Op*
G. H. P. Ramage *GA (tractors)*
I. G. Taylor *Met*
R. W. Wilkins *Met*

Argentine Islands
K. W. Hughson *BC, Met*
P. Barton *Met*
M. R. Butterfield *Met*
P. J. Fisher *Met*
P. H. Fitzgerald *Iono*
K. J. Hunt *Cook*
A. S. Rodger *Iono*
A. G. Scott *Met*
B. Summers *Radio Op*
S. Wellington *DEM*
K. White *Geophys*

Fossil Bluff
A. W. Jamieson *OIC, Glacio*
J. F. Bishop *Glacio*
S. A. Hobbs *GA*
R. C. Tindley *GA*

Halley Bay
R. Daynes *BC, Met*
C. H. Bienkowski *Geophys*
T. D. Boyt *Met*
J. C. Burke *Radio Op*
C. Cuthbert *Met*
J. Dawson *MO, Physio*
P. Ellis *Met*
G. A. Gay *Bldr*
D. F. C. Habgood *Geophys*
C. Holder *Bldr*
A. L. Jackson *Elect*
D. B. Jenkins *Iono*
D. I. Jones *Iono*
I. MacInnes *DEM*
D. C. Mackay *Bldr*
C. Palfrey *Cook*
K. J. Stevenson *Geophys*
A. J. Turner *Bldr*
R. S. Walker *DEM*
R. L. Waller *Bldr*
A. Wincott *Bldr*

Signy Island
D. D. W. Fletcher *BC*
S. C. Amos *Bio Asst*
P. H. Bissell *GA (diver)*
P. A. Broady *Zool*
I. B. Collinge *Bio Asst*
A. Cooper *Cook*
P. Fuller *Bldr*
D. G. Goddard *Zool*
R. M. Hastings *Zool*
M. H. Hinchliffe *Radio Op*
J. N. Hoogesteger *Bio Asst*
T. N. Hooker *Bot*
B. W. Kellett *Zool*
P. Vane *DEM*
D. L. M. Weller *Zool*
T. M. Whitaker *Zool*

South Georgia
A. S. Ferguson *BC, Iono*
J. P. Barker *Radio Op*
R. L. Berry *Bio Asst*
J. F. Carter *DEM*
R. Clunas *Bldr*
P. Crossland *Cook*
T. C. Gunn *Bot*
P. R. D. Harmar *Iono*
R. J. C. Hayward *Glacio*
I. G. G. Hogg *Glacio*
J. A. Keville *Met*
J. G. H. Maxwell *Zool*
D. J. Orchard *Met*
M. R. Payne *Zool*
H. M. Platt *Zool*

P. A. Prince *Bio Asst*
N. A. J. Sheppard *Glacio*
P. W. Small *Iono*
G. Smith *Elect*
C. Stephens *Zool*
N. C. Tappin *Bio Asst*
R. Whitfield *Cook*

Stonington Island
S. Wormald *BC*
A. A. J. Almond *Geophys (fld)*
J. F. Anckorn *Geol*
R. W. Bostelmann *Vet Offr*
D. M. Burkitt *GA*
P. F. Butler *Geophys (fld)*
C. W. Edwards *Geol*
A. E. Gannon *Bldr*
E. G. Lawther *GA*
N. R. D. MacAllister *GA*
M. D. Macrae *DEM*
J. Newman *DEM*
R. J. Scott *Surv*
D. G. Singleton *Geol*
C. R. Walker *Radio Op*
J. Yates *Surv*

List of illustrations

Colour illustrations

1 RRS *John Biscoe* at old Grytviken whaling station, summer.
2 Millerand Island seen from Stonington Island.
3 Recovering men who fell with collapse of ice cliff – no wet feet!
4 Break-up of sea ice at Signy Island with a Great Skua in foreground.
5 Mount Edgell, Palmer Land (left), with Alexander Island in far distance.
6 Shackleton's Cross at King Edward Point, South Georgia.
7 and 8 'Krill' (Euphorbia superba) the food of whales, seals and birds; a potential source of protein for man.
9 Emperor penguin and chick, Halley Bay.
10 King penguins, Royal Bay, South Georgia.
11 Emperor penguin rookery, Halley Bay.
12 Heavy tractor in crevasse, 1969.
13 Recovering tractor, 1973.
14 Tractor winching itself up a 45° slope.
15 Descent into crevasse.
16 View over Alexander Island.
17 Eureka Glacier, northern Palmer Land.
18 Argentine Islands and Lemaire Channel.
19 Twin Otter flying over southern Marguerite Bay: Alexander Island in distance.
20 Fossil Bluff field station.
21 HMS *Endurance*.
22 RRS *Bransfield*.
23 Sunshine Glacier, Coronation Island.
24 RRS *John Biscoe* and MV *Kista Dan* at the Argentine Islands 1960.

List of maps

A and B (endpapers). Antarctica in relation to the southern continents, with key to sketch maps.

All bases are shown by a bold dot

Index

*Figures in bold type refer to page numbers
of illustrations*